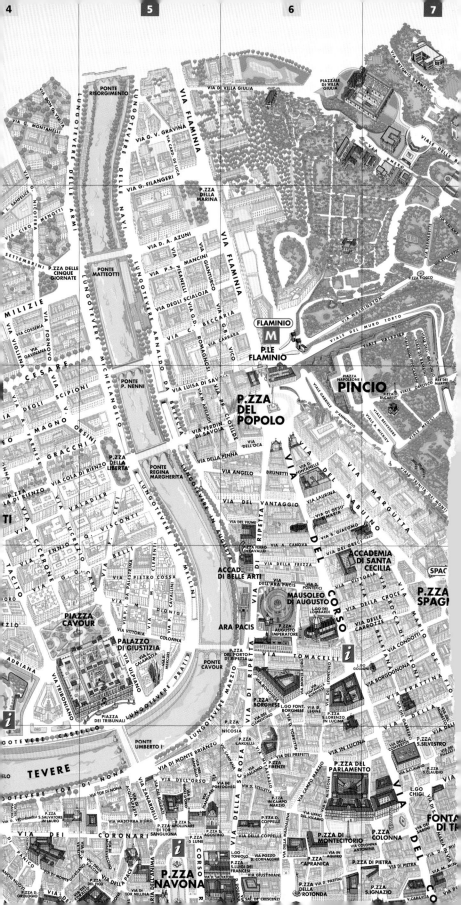

Key to
ROME

Key to
ROME

Frederick and Vanessa Vreeland

The J. Paul Getty Museum
Los Angeles

Original edition © 2000 Fratelli Palombi Editori, Via Timavo, 12, Rome, Italy

Fratelli Palombi Editori, *Original Editing and Coordination*

Paolo Bernacca, *Original Art Direction*
Roberto "Steve" Gobesso, *Original Design and Layout*

© 2006 The J. Paul Getty Trust

First published in the United States of America in 2006 by
Getty Publications
1200 Getty Center Drive, Suite 500
Los Angeles, California 90049-1682
www.getty.edu

Christopher Hudson, *Publisher*
Mark Greenberg, *Editor in Chief*

Dinah Berland, *Editor*
Jim Drobka, *Design Coordinator*
Pamela Heath, *Production Coordinator*
Hespenheide Design, *Graphic Design and Typesetting*

Printed in Hong Kong by South Sea International Press Ltd.

The publisher and the authors have made a great effort to find the copyright holders for all the illustrations. We would be pleased to insert corrections in subsequent editions of this book.

We wish to express appreciation to the following institutions, photographers and publishers who have authorized the reproduction of their illustrations: Archivio fotografico Fratelli Palombi, Archivio fotografico Ghirotti & Gobesso, Danièle Ohnheiser, Dino Audino Editore, Editalia, Fabbrica di San Pietro, Giunti Editore, Granada Publishing Limited, Luca Sorrentino, Mondadori Editore, Monumenti Musei e Gallerie Pontificie, Oxford University Press, Soprintendenza Archeologica per l'Etruria Meridionale, Soprintendenza Archeologica di Roma, Soprintendenza Galleria Nazionale d'Arte Moderna, Soprintendenza ai Beni Culturali del Comune di Roma, TECLA e Roberto Lucifero, Umberto Allemandi & C., and Vanessa Somers. CHARTA ROMA – *The official City-Map* © Fratelli Palombi Editori e A & C, Rome.

Library of Congress Control Number: 2005930842
ISBN-13: 978-0-89236-802-0
ISBN-10: 0-89236-802-0

Every effort has been made to ensure that the information in this book is up-to-date. However, details such as opening hours, telephone numbers and bus numbers are subject to change.

CONTENTS

The triple-KEY icon 🔑 *on these pages, and within each section, indicates a "must-see" monument. Single-KEY icons* 🔑 *throughout the book highlight our personal favorites.*

Introduction

The key to enjoying Rome is seeing it through its four layers of cultural history, which remain vivid even today. Come with us as we lead you through the gates of the "eternal city" from ancient times to the early Christian era, to the Renaissance and Baroque, to the Grand Tour—and then let's go shopping!

ANCIENT
Legendary Romulus, who founded Rome in 753 BC, protected his flock of itinerant shepherds and farmers from the flooding Tiber River by leading them into the nearby hills. On the seven hills, and at the adjoining Forum, Romulus's heirs later established the Roman Republic with its parliamentary rule of law, and finally the emperors multiplied their public buildings and staged their military triumphs. This was the center of civilization from the early days of western European history to the fall of the empire in the 5th century AD – about a millennium. It's exciting to realize that more monuments of Western civilization can be found in Rome today than any place else in the world.

pages 8-71

CHRISTIAN
Christianity came to Rome with St. Peter, who was crucified here in AD 64. It was declared the state religion of the Roman Empire in AD 379 and precipitated another building spree. For a thousand years the two centers of Christianity were St. Peter's Basilica on Vatican Hill and the Cathedral of St. John of Lateran on Celian Hill. Christian Rome is dated from the 5th through the 14th century, or roughly from the fall of the Roman Empire to the eruption of the Renaissance. For those thousand years the popes ruled the burgeoning city and the yearning hearts of western Europeans.

pages 72-143

RENAISSANCE and BAROQUE
The Renaissance literally meant the *rebirth* of the classical arts of ancient Greece and Rome. Suddenly those great edifices, used widely to support simple dwellings and lean-tos – after being reviled as pagan and pillaged for a millennium – were the inspiration and springboard for an exuberant age. Between the ruins of ancient Rome and the religious buildings of Christian Rome the newly rich papal families built luxurious palaces and ever-more-imposing churches. The Renaissance in Rome was from 1450 to 1600. After the Reformation came the Counter-Reformation, when, from 1600 to 1750, Rome revived itself with the Baroque, which has left its indelible mark on this multilayered city.

pages 144-99

SHOPPING and THE GRAND TOUR
The Grand Tour refers to the 18th-century tradition of aristocratic English youths traveling for months to complete their education by experiencing the glories of Italy, and particularly Rome. These first "tourists" gave Rome a new impetus. When they arrived in droves in their horse-drawn carriages, splendid hotels and fancy shops sprang up to welcome them. The intention of the Grand Tour was cultural, but the tourists went home laden with souvenirs and Roman luxury goods. Whereas the pilgrims had come for Christian Rome, these travelers came for memories of the ancient capital and its reflection in Renaissance and Baroque Rome. The tradition of the Grand Tour continues today as you, gentle reader, seek out and discover each of the four cultural-historical epochs of the eternal city.

pages 200-253

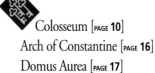

ANCIENT

Colosseum

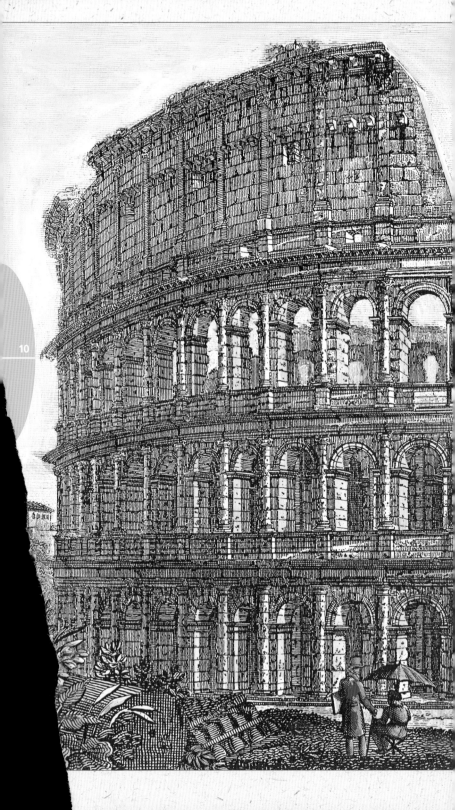

[G/H 9]
Piazza del Colosseo.
Tel. 0639967700.

Getting there
Bus 60, 75, 85, 87, 175,
186, 204, 810, 850,
Tram 3 or
B Metro
Colosseo stop.

Fee
Open 9 am-6:15 pm
(entry up to one
hour before closing).
Closed January 1,
May 1 and
December 25.

Ironically, this sublimely beautiful arena was built for people to enjoy the ugliest spectacle of all: death to man and beast. Other amphitheaters are in France, Italy, Spain, North Africa – many still in use for shows, bullfights, operas.

At its inception in the first century AD, this gigantic ellipse was called the Flavian Amphitheater, *Flavius* being the family name of Emperor Vespasian, who started it. He took the lake from the inordinately large garden of Nero's nearby Golden House, filled it in, and here built the largest amphitheater in the world, to "amuse" the populace with fantastic spectacles of gladiators in bloody combat with wild animals – and other men. Entry was free, part of the emperors' policy of keeping Romans contented with "bread and circuses"; many emperors also gave away flour for the people's daily bread.

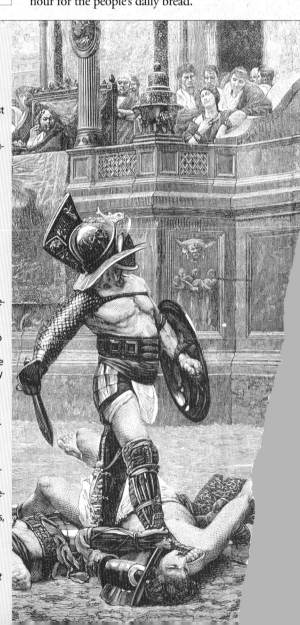

History AD

• **72** Emperor **Vespasian**, to obliterate Nero's memory and amuse the crowds, started building the ancient world's largest and finest stadium.

• **80** Vespasian's son Emperor **Titus** inaugurated the amphitheater with a festival lasting 100 days and the slaughter was fearsome: 5,000 beasts, mostly from North Africa, were killed along with hundreds of men.

• **407** Gladiatorial combats were outlawed.

• **5c** The arena was being used for imperial ceremonies and celebrations, according to inscriptions on some large blocks of marble deciphered in 1997 by archaeologist Silvia Orlandi.

• **523** Killing wild beasts was forbidden.

• **673** The Venerable Bede, an English monk, visited Rome and is said to have uttered the famous adage, "If the Colosseum falls, then Rome falls, and if Rome falls, so will the world" *(Quandiu stat Colysaeus stat et Roma, quando cadet Colysaeus cadet*

The name Colosseum was originally used for the **Colossus of Nero**, a huge nude statue the emperor had originally placed at the entrance to his **Golden House** and which was subsequently moved to the front of the Flavian Amphitheater. The arena acquired its present name from the statue, which later was, happily, pulled down.

The Colosseum rises four stories high, a perfect oval of brick, faced with white travertine. The first story has Doric pilasters, the second Ionic, the third and fourth Corinthian. It covers 18.5 hectares (7.5 acres) and has a circumference of about 494 m (540 yards).

The large holes in the facade – making the building look as if it had been shelled – are where the stone blocks were originally held together by bronze clamps, which were stolen during the Middle Ages.

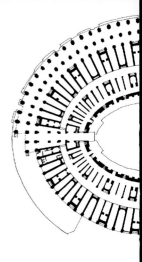

ARENA

As long as the Colosseum stands so will Rome,
but when the Colosseum falls Rome will fall,
and so will the world! The Venerable Bede

...es and banners. All
...stone were literally
...rld's largest quarry

...tors could be seated
...l large corridors for
...uite had their own
...diators, the Gate of
...d didn't finish until
...vel as the emperor,
...women still higher,
...he topmost section.
...ep the sun and rain
...e a doughnut, leaving the arena in the center open to the
...sailors pulling the ropes to the beat of a kettledrum. The
...m nautical precision, chanted to keep themselves in time.
...ously dressed, solemnly parading around the arena – which
...covered by sand (*sand* in Latin is *arena*). The sand, by the
...the blood. They would then shout the ritual *Ave Caesar*
...Hail to the emperor, those about to die salute thee). Dozens
...manned by slaves working pulleys could bring up 1,000
...the same time, 10 men per lift – or else hundreds of lions,
...1. Christians were sometimes hurled to hungry lions. During
...inauguration in AD 80 the arena was allegedly flooded for a
mock naval battle.

Gladiator School. Little remains of the ancient three-story *Ludus Magnus*, school and barracks for gladiators.
Its courtyard was a tiny replica of the Colosseum's arena.
Domitian built three other gyms for gladiators nearby.
They often used real weapons during training sessions.
Gladiator fights evolved from their Etruscan origins into
gigantic spectacles which sometimes lasted 100 days
and involved as many as
5,000 pairs of gladiators
fighting each other. The
more famous had their own
fan clubs and enjoyed
special privileges, but few
lamented them when they
died.

et Roma, quando
cadet et Roma cadet
et mundus).
• **13c** The Frangipani
family made the Colos-
seum a fortified castle.
• **15c** This was the
worst epoch for steal-
ing materials from
the Colosseum and
it was only when
the Catholic Church
made a chapel inside
that the pillaging
stopped.

*Corner of Via San
Giovanni in Laterano
and Via Labicana,
immediately west of
the Colosseum.*

Our favorite
Every Good Friday,
the pope walks
around the Colosseum
carrying a cross in a
long procession of the
stations of the cross.

0   60 RF

0   20 METERS

Also, there used to be brackets supporting paraffin torc
the metal (estimated at 300 tons) and a great deal of the
ripped off the building, making the Colosseum also the w
for building materials.

Superb engineering went into the building; 50,000 specta
within 10 minutes through the 80 numbered entrances an
easy access for the raucous throngs. The emperor and his
entrance. The Gate of Life was the exit for pardoned gla
Death for those killed. The spectacles started at dawn, an
dusk. High officials, nobles and senators sat at the same l
rich merchants in the section above, freedmen above them,
and slaves and the sailors responsible for the *Velarium* in t
The *Velarium* was an enormous circular tenting, used to ke
off the spectators. This giant awning was a hollow disc li
skies. Hauling it up was a Herculean task, with squads of
sailors, whose experience raising ships' sails had taught the
The show started with the gladiators, gorge
was surfaced with wooden planks
way, was there to soak up
morituri te salutant
of elevators r
warriors a
or bot
the

VELARIUM

POOR,
WOMEN
AND SLAVES

PLEBIANS

KNIGHTS

SENATORS

Arch of Constantine, AD 315

This is the largest and most magnificent of the triumphal arches, giant gates through which victorious generals would lead their vanquished enemies, with chains clanking satisfactorily behind.

[H 9]

Getting there
Bus 60, 75, 84, 85, 87, 117, 175, 186, 204, 810, 850 or
B Metro Colosseo stop.

History AD
• **312** Constantine defeated his coruler Maxentius at the Battle of Saxa Rubra.
• **315** This triumphal arch was erected to commemorate the victory.
• **Middle Ages** The arch was incorporated into a fortress by the Frangipani family, who ruled this part of Rome with an iron hand.
• **1808** The medieval buildings were torn down and the arch restored.

The quality of carving in the 4c had fallen to a new low. Among the few relief carvings of the same epoch as the arch is one of Emperor Constantine addressing a sycophantic crowd. Most of the rest were simply stolen or copied from other monuments!

Description of the relief sculptures

NORTH SIDE *Facing the Colosseum.* Upper part: The four statues are from Trajan's wars (AD 98-117) against Dacia – roughly corresponding with today's Romania. The four low-relief carvings are from Marcus Aurelius's time (AD 2c). But the emperor's head has been knocked off, a favorite pastime in Roman days, and substituted with Constantine's. The four circular medallions are from Hadrian's time (AD 117-138).

SOUTH SIDE *Facing away from the Colosseum.* Reliefs at the top are from Trajan's victories. Reliefs lower down are of mythical gods and goddesses – rather shocking for a much-advertised convert to Christianity. This all seems to have been done with undue haste, probably to please Constantine, who, by conquering Maxentius, was now emperor of the East and the West.

Below: North side, closest to the Colosseum.

Arch of Constantine

Meta Sudans

Arch of Titus

Fountain of Meta Sudans, AD 1C

This used to be a large mound covered with porous stone which *sweated* water in a permanent stream from an underground spring. Today one can see some of that stone covered with moss – though a few years ago it was hidden under a busy roadway.

Then cars, trucks and buses were trundling past here in all their polluting glory. Now traffic has been banned as the vibrations were making the giant marble blocks of the Colosseum shimmy apart (there are no more metal grips to hold them in place – stolen in the Dark Ages to make cannonballs).

History AD
• **1c** In Augustus's time it was a public meeting place, a bucolic area in the valley with a stream running through it.
• **2c** Gladiators came to refresh themselves before combat in the nearby Colosseum.

17

Colossal statue of Nero – disappeared

Nero was determined to have himself remembered as the most glorious of all the Caesars. What better way than with a statue of oneself? He modeled this gigantic erection after one of the seven wonders of the ancient world: the Colossus of Rhodes (3c BC), which stood 32 m (105 ft.) high. So Nero had his nude statue go up to 34 m (112 ft.); it originally stood on higher ground near the Via Sacra at the vestibule gate of Nero's gargantuan Golden House. Emperor **Hadrian** had the statue in all its gilded glory moved by 40 elephants to a spot near the Meta Sudans fountain. It stood here for centuries, known as the Colossus, and it lent its name to the later Flavian Amphitheater, which by the year 1000 was called the *Colosseum*. Of course, heads have rolled here, as many an emperor knocked down whichever head was up there to replace it with his own!

Domus Aurea

Nero's Golden House, AD 64

Even the 30 rooms now open to the public, out of the original 250, give a clear idea of what a gigantic and outrageous mansion Emperor Nero built on an estate covering a third of Rome.

[**G 10**] *Via Domus Aurea off Via Labicana, 136. Tel. 0640802147.*
Getting there
Bus 85, 87, 186, 204 or **B Metro** Colosseo stop.

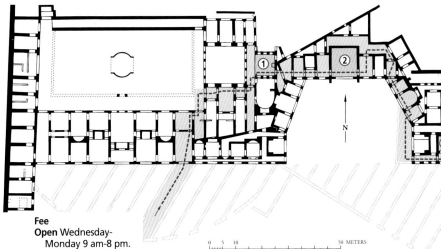

Fee
Open Wednesday-
   Monday 9 am-8 pm.
   Reservation required.
   Visit limited to 25
   people every 15
   minutes. One-hour
   tour.

History AD

- **54** Nero took power with the help of his mother and later his presumed lover (there were telltale stains on his toga after their frequent rides in a closed litter) **Agrippina**, who killed her second husband, Emperor **Claudius**, to put Nero on the throne. In the course of his reign, Nero had her killed, along with two of his three wives and countless other victims, especially senators. His sex life was publicly debauched and depraved.
- **64** A great fire destroyed much of Rome, while **Nero** fiddled. He then confiscated about 200 acres of central Rome from the victims of the fire for his personal estate and was fiercely detested for it. As a reaction, Nero blamed the Christians and had hundreds of them put to death, including Saints Peter and Paul.
- **64-68** Domus Aurea built by architect **Severus** and engineer **Celer**. The era's great-

The entire house, including the 356 m (400 yard) facade, was buried 19 centuries ago by his successors to efface the shame of Nero's infamous reign. Virtually everything the mad emperor did was inappropriate, except perhaps his artistic endeavors. And this house, sparkling with gold and precious objects, was his masterpiece.

For Nero's estate, nothing was too much. Wild beasts roamed. Gardens and vineyards stretched over three hills. On the Celian Hill, using the platform intended for a temple, Nero built a giant fountain fed by a new aqueduct spur, a huge water tank providing pressure for gushing water. The spill-off flowed down to Nero's artificial lake, where the Colosseum was later built; this was the occasional scene of frolicsome banquets while well-born maidens were forced to await Nero's pleasure in brothels built around the water's edge.

The guided tour highlights

❶ **Ninfeo.** High barrel-vaulted cave originally had a waterfall. In the world's first figurative vault mosaic, **Ulysses** offers a cup to giant **Polyphemus**.

❷ **Hall of the Gilded Vault.** Fresco of **Mars** embracing **Venus**, **Cupid** driving a panther-drawn chariot, and **Satyrs** chasing **Nymphs**. The entablatures of plaster and gilt were much copied in the Renaissance and imitated by **Robert Adam** in the 18c.

❸ **Cryptoportici.** These long inner corridors have floral, animal and nymph paintings copied by **Raphael** and others for such commissions as the Vatican Loggia and Villa Farnesina.

❹ **Hall of Achilles at Skyros.** Giant shell motif in the niche has inspired generations of decorators.

❺ **Octagonal Hall.** The center of the mansion is this banqueting rotunda, centrally lit like the later Pantheon, which opens out into five other dining halls. The great dome lacks decoration, but we have this record from contemporary chronicler **Suetonius**: "Dining rooms had

est painter, **Fabullus**, was kept here while he covered the walls with frescoed decorations and mythological scenes.
• **68** Condemned to death by the Senate, crowds calling for his blood, Nero got a servant to help him cut his own throat.
• **79-81** Nero's baths, spewing both sulfurous and salty water, were remodeled for public use as Emperor **Titus's Baths**.
• **104-109** Emperor **Trajan** obliterated all traces of the mansion, building his public baths on top. For the building foundations, Nero's exquisite rooms were filled up with rubble, after the gorgeous mosaics, marbles and artworks had been pillaged.
• **1494** A worker, digging among the ruins of Trajan's Bath, saw some paintings through a hole in the pavement. **Raphael** and other artists were lowered by rope to copy, by candlelight, what they assumed were decorations in a grotto (hence their copies were called "grotesques"). This discovery influenced the course of architecture (including Michelangelo's), painting and decoration during and after the Renaissance.
• **1506** Among Nero's sculptures, the famous **Laocoön** was found here (see page 88).
• **1983-99** The house was closed to the public because of falling masonry and calcium covering the frescoed walls from the buildup of humidity inside. Archaeologists working under Professor Adriano La Regina have restored parts of one wing as well as the Octagonal Hall.

Fabullus's frescoes, above, were copied by Raphael in his loggia at the Vatican, below.

ceilings of ivory with sliding panels, from which flowers and perfumes showered on the guests. The main dining room ceiling was circular, revolving day and night, like the heavens" – with Nero seated in the middle, lit from above and slowly revolving for all to admire.

❻ Hall of Hector and Andromache. Frescoes illustrating Homer's *Iliad*: Paris with Helen, and Thetis bringing Achilles his shield.

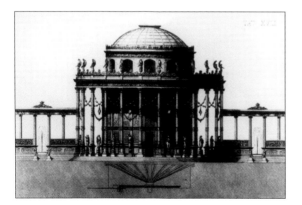

Fanciful reconstruction of the revolving Octagonal Hall, showing the oculus opening in the roof.

Roman Forum (Foro Romano)

A Walk through the History of Ancient Rome

[G 8] **Entrances at** *Via dei Fori Imperiali, Via San Teodoro, the Campidoglio and Arch of Titus* Tel. 066990110.

Getting there
Bus 11, 27, 85, 87, 175, 186 or
B Metro Colosseo stop.

No fee
Open Daily 9 am-6 pm (until 7 pm in summer).

If you look down at the Roman Forum from the steps behind the Campidoglio, especially at night, the magic is inescapable: you are at the center of the ancient Western world. From here we derive our finest traditions, including representative government, rule of law, market economy and, later, religious tolerance.

Yet ancient Rome also featured colonialism, exploitation, pollution and man's inhumanity to man and beast. Rome either invented or reinvented nearly everything for the Western world, and always in excess. Fountains, statues, temples, basilicas, columns, paving stones are here piled

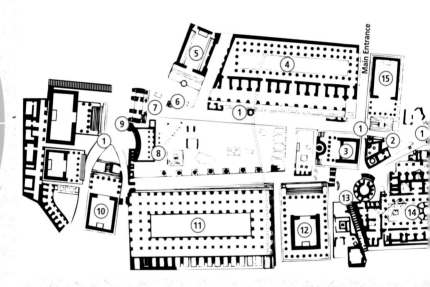

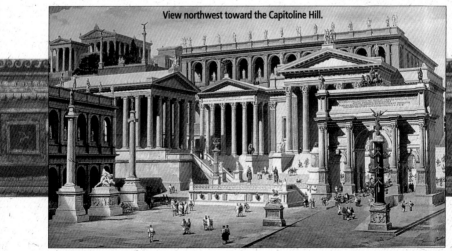

View northwest toward the Capitoline Hill.

one upon another in apparent disorder. But make no mistake; order is what the hub of the empire was about. Go down into the Forum and try to imagine ancient Rome . . . AS IT WAS.

This walk begins at the Forum's entrance from the Via dei Fori Imperiali.

❶ **Via Sacra.** When you reach the bottom of the entrance ramp, to your left and to your right stretch the original paving stones of what was once the most important street in the world: literally the Sacred Way. Along this road victorious generals paraded through the cheering Roman population to receive the accolade of the city when they were accorded a triumphus – precursor of the parades for the Fourth of July and Bastille Day. So, imagine yourself standing right here two thousand years ago, toga-ed out in your holiday best, applauding the passing military heroes. They would have entered the Forum from the Colosseum end, passed under the Arch of Titus (18), trooping in front of you from left to right, proceeding through Septimius Severus's Arch (7) on your right, and then up to the top of the Capitoline Hill for a religious ceremony. You would have seen – and heard – not only the returning Roman legionnaires but also creaking carts carrying captured booty and, in clattering chains, the enemies taken prisoner to become Roman slaves. When

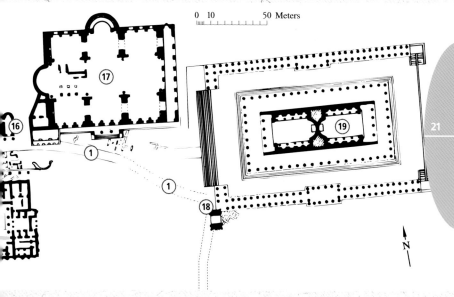

View southeast toward the Palatine Hill.

the honored general passed before you in a sumptuous chariot you might have heard a slave standing right behind today's hero whispering in his ear, "Remember, thou art only a man" – the Romans' way of making sure the crowd's cheering would not turn the victorious general's head.

❷ **Regia** (8c BC). The small triangular area covered with dark-colored stones that you see on the other side of the Via Sacra just to your left was the Forum's earliest, and once most revered, official site: the residence of King Numa, who succeeded Romulus as Rome's leader around 715 BC. During the Republic, 6c to 1c BC, it was the headquarters of the high priest, or Pontifex Maximus, and at the end of this period Julius Caesar used it when he bought that title for himself. The glorious title, though not the paltry site, was used by successive emperors, and until today by the pope, who can be referred to as "pontiff" (the word originated from the Latin *pons* and *fecit*, meaning "bridge"/"make"; bridge building was a responsibility of pre-Christian pontiffs, but not of the modern ones). You will be struck by the minuteness of this tiny plot and realize that the successors to this humble Roman king became megalomaniacs, taking entire hills for their palaces.

❸ **Temple of Julius Caesar** (29 BC). This raised stone platform was once a soaring temple marking the spot where Caesar was cremated. It was built by his young grandnephew Octavian 15 years after Brutus and his coconspirators assassinated Caesar. The intervening period was a time of civil strife as the factions for and against Caesar maneuvered, and murdered, in their drive for power. The Forum literally ran with blood, and if you had lived in those times your only objective would have been self-preservation. Finally in 27 BC it was Octavian who destroyed all competitors and took supreme control, becoming Caesar Augustus, Rome's first emperor, two years after dedicating this temple.

❹ **Basilica Aemilia** (2c BC, rebuilt early AD 1c). Built during Rome's republic and sponsored by the Aemilia family (which explains its name), this was one of the earliest of Rome's basilicas, vast hangarlike structures that covered the outdoor markets, sheltering shoppers from rain and sun. This one was large enough so that on the long row of steps leading up to it, and on the second-story balconies, almost 1,000 citizens and slaves could stand watching those triumphus parades that passed in front down the Via Sacra. During the years

Sit for a while on the Senate steps and gaze around at thousands of years of glory. Using the map on pages 20-21 you can spot the half dozen most important monuments. All of them date from the golden years between 8c BC and AD 4c, except for the **Column of Phocus (Foca)**. That is the single column opposite the Senate, which was erected in AD 608 in honor of Phocus, emperor of the Eastern Empire who gave the Pantheon to Pope Boniface IV, thus saving it from the destruction visited on Rome's pagan temples. This column was the last honorary monument built in the Roman Forum.

Stone found under the Lapis Niger.

of the empire, law courts were installed on the premises to settle commercial disputes, and meeting halls were also added, so that these buildings became neighborhood centers much like today's shopping malls. They were probably noisier, and inside this basilica you can imagine the lawyers haranguing each other during their amicable and endless debates.

The basic basilica structure – one long, high central nave with a narrow and low aisle on either side – was copied by Emperor Constantine in the 4c when he built large Christian churches in Rome's suburbs. Thus, today the Vatican uses the term *basilica* as an honorific title for the most distinguished Catholic churches throughout the world, regardless of their shape.

❺ **Curia, the Roman Senate** (1C BC, reconstructed AD 3C). The best-preserved building in the Forum, where you can go inside and relive the bitter political debates, especially of the late-Republican era. It was then that Julius Caesar, just before his death, ordered the construction of this well-proportioned Senate building to curry favor with the aristocratic senators, whom he fiercely opposed but could not afford to displease. Although a senator himself, ambitious Caesar supported the aspirations of the common people against the greedy actions of the senators, who were all from powerful and wealthy families. Since Caesar had decided to pack the Senate with his own men, he made room here for over 600 of them – twice the previous number – seated in three tiers on either side of the president's low podium. During Rome's republic, the fate of the then-known world was decided by the senators, who moved back and forth across the aisle to signify their yes or no votes. But with the establishment of the empire the previously decisive role of the senators became largely ceremonial.

❻ **Lapis Niger.** As its Latin name indicates, this *black stone* slab in front of the Curia marks a venerated burial place of great antiquity, the legendary tomb of Romulus (8c BC).

❼ **Arch of Septimius Severus** (AD 203). The reality of political power under the emperors gives us reason to question the inscription along the top, which says the Senate and the Roman people offered this heavily sculpted symbolic gateway to celebrate the 10th year of Emperor Septimius Severus's 18-year reign. He had made Rome's eastern frontiers safe by defeating the Syrians (he married one), the Assyrians (of present-day Iraq)

SPQR =
Senatus Populusque Romanus =
The Senate and the People of Rome

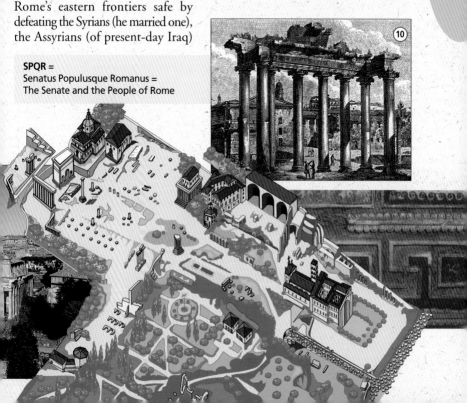

and the Persians of Parthia. The inscription said it was also in honor of Septimius's two sons, Geta and Caracalla. But when Caracalla, on his way to succeeding his father as emperor, murdered his brother, Geta's name was scratched out.

Throughout the ages triumphal arches all over our world copied this pleasing form of a large central opening and smaller ones on either side, often topped with a monumental bronze chariot.

❽ Rostra. Try to conjure up Rome's great orators arguing eloquently from this wide podium and changing the course of humanity. It was here that Marc Antony, speaking (according to Shakespeare) to "friends, Romans and countrymen," praised

(13)

Julius Caesar right after his assassination and successfully whipped up the emotions of the crowd against the conspirators Cassius and Brutus. During the ensuing civil upheaval Rome's great orator Cicero was executed and his hands and head were displayed here, where he had so often harangued the crowds (and where Fulvia, first wife of Marc Antony, had allegedly stabbed the great orator's tongue with her hairpin). Oratory here was largely for the benefit of the plebians, or "plebs," the nonaristocrats, who were not represented in the Senate and met nearby in a kind of theater-in-the-round called the Comitium. During the 500 years of Rome's republic, the Senate and Comitium resembled the upper and lower legislative houses in today's representative government (except that their unwritten constitution kept final decisions for the Senate).

Rostra means "beaks," referring to the bronze rammers on the prows of ships used to ram the enemy fleet in wartime. The ancient Romans mounted the prows of defeated ships here to impress the populace.

❾ Umbilicus Urbis. Literally the "navel of the city," this circular brick base near the Rostra once marked the center of Rome – and therefore of the universe.

❿ Temple of Saturn (497 BC, restored in 42 BC). Those eight glorious Ionic columns once ennobled the front porch of a temple that became ancient Rome's Treasury. Julius Caesar broke in and made off with about 15,000 bars of gold and twice as many of silver to finance his ambitious plans for Rome and for himself. The temple was dedicated to the god Saturn, in whose honor the Romans celebrated the "Saturnalia" at the end of December with banquets, candles and exchanges of gifts. Early

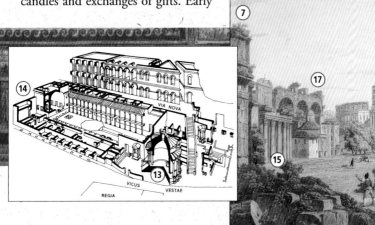

Christians, who assimilated many of Rome's traditions, emulated the timing and the spirit of the Saturnalia for celebrating the birthday of Jesus in what came to be called "Christ-mass." They did not, however, perpetuate the ancient tradition that during this festival Roman slaves and household servants were waited on by their masters.

⓫ Basilica Julia (1C BC). Shortly before he was stabbed to death in 44 BC Julius Caesar launched a plan to modernize and beautify the Forum, including this long covered hall across from, and even larger than, the Basilica Aemilia (see page 22). All his spending for public works was to buy popular support. Civil law cases, especially inheritance suits, were heard here. Caesar's grandnephew Octavius dedicated the basilica for the glorification of their family, the Julians, after he became, in 27 BC, the first emperor, Caesar Augustus. And on the roof above, Caligula (AD 12-41), the third and maddest emperor, would stand and throw coins down to the underprivileged plebs.

⓬ Temple of Castor and Pollux. These three striking marble Corinthian columns, almost 13 m (40 ft.) high, formed part of the Forum's most architecturally perfect temple, which became ancient Rome's Office of Weights and Measures. It was dedicated to the mythological brothers Castor and Pollux, called the "Dioscuri," horse-riding demigods who helped the Romans defeat the Latins in a 5C BC battle at Lake Regillus. Castor was born mortal, Pollux immortal. Magically, right after the battle, their horses came to drink near here at the **Fountain of Juturna**.

⓭ Temple of Vesta (AD 2C). The graceful feminine curves of this house of worship were inspired by the mythic, round, thatched huts of Rome's founders. The temple was dedicated to Vesta, Goddess of the Hearth. The "sacred fire" burned here, symbolizing the hearth of every home – family shrines being very important in ancient Rome. That flame, like those in today's tombs of the unknown soldiers, was extinguished and relit on ceremonial occasions, but otherwise had to be kept burning permanently. To assure this continuity was the task of the vestal virgins, six upper-class girls, recruited at puberty who served 30 years: the first 10 devoted to learning, the next 10 to performing the rites, and the final 10 to teaching the new girls. The relighting of the sacred flame was entrusted to the Pontifex Maximus, who would come over from his nearby Regia on March 1, which they chose for New Year's Day because it was the beginning of spring.

⓮ House of the Vestal Virgins (AD 2C). A multistory building surrounding this open area housed the six vestals as well as the secret and sacred documents entrusted to their care. Catch a glimpse today of their large garden, and imagine the virgins pacing around them in their white sleeveless gowns, their hair pulled back in striking linen wreaths. Once they had served their 30 years they could marry --but they would be a bit old, since most Roman maidens

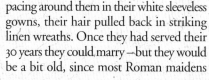

were married off in their early teens. The chief vestal was venerated and, in order of precedence, came right after the empress herself. All six of them had honored places at the circus, theater and games, and just by passing a criminal in the street they could stay his execution. But if one of them lost her virginity she was buried alive, and her seducer was whipped to death!

⑮ Temple of Antoninus and Faustina (AD 141). Highlights of this gracious 2c temple are the remains of a staircase leading up, past an outdoor altar, to the 10-columned façade and the beautiful frieze running along the two sides with

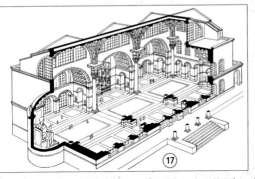

griffins and candelabra. Higher up, on the architrave, are two separate dedicatory inscriptions since Emperor Antoninus's name was added when he died, some 20 years after he had built the temple to honor his wife Faustina – despite the general knowledge that she had been serially unfaithful. The interior of the temple is now a church, San Lorenzo in Miranda, whose door is on the side, in a lane off Via dei Fori Imperiali.

⑯ Temple of Romulus (late AD 3c). This domed circular building was dedicated by the grieving Emperor Maxentius to the memory of his son Romulus, who died young. (See also Romulus's tomb on the Via Appia, page 67.) During the Middle Ages its beautifully preserved bronze doors were the entrance to the church behind (see Santi Cosma e Damiano, page 140). The concave niches on either side of the façade seem precursors of later Rome's sinuous Baroque style.

In a cellar just opposite this holy temple were the Lupanaria, seedy state-run houses of ill repute, where the Hetaerae were recognizable by their yellow gowns. They plied the oldest profession in stuffy little cubicles at or below ground level.

⑰ Basilica of Maxentius (AD 306). This has been called the climax of Roman architecture, being based on mammoth baths, such as Caracalla's and Diocletian's. Sheer size was everything for imperial Rome. Emperor Maxentius began this giant courthouse, but before its completion he was killed and succeeded in AD 312 by his brother-in-law Constantine, who then renamed it after himself. Constantine's giant statue presided in the apse, overlooking the three vast vaults with their still-visible deeply coffered ceilings; impressive limbs, veins and all, from that statue can be seen in the courtyard of Palazzo dei Conservatori Museum on the Campidoglio (see page 161).

⑱ Arch of Titus (AD 81). Emperor Domitian built this single-span triumphal arch in honor of his older brother, Titus. It was to celebrate Titus's reconquest and rampant destruction of Jerusalem in AD 70, when the Jewish uprising against Roman rule was suppressed mercilessly. Inside the arch is a bas-relief showing Roman soldiers carrying the great candelabrum (menorah), pillaged by the Romans during their devastation of the Temple of Solomon. The ancient candleholder has disappeared from Rome's storerooms, but the sculpture has survived, and so have bitter memories of Roman brutality in foreign wars.

⑲ Temple of Venus and Rome (AD 2c, reconstructed AD 310). This largest and grandest of the temples in the Forum consisted of two vast compartments under one enormous roof. The one with its façade toward the Colosseum was dedicated to the goddess Venus, and the one at the other end to deified Rome. Its builder, Emperor Hadrian, took credit for drawing the plans and proudly sent them to Apollodorus of Damascus. Tradition has it that the great Syrian architect was so scathing in his criticism that Hadrian, who had already exiled Apollodorus, ordered him killed. This is far from the treatment Apollodorus had received from Hadrian's predecessor, Trajan, who had commissioned him to design Trajan's Forum and Market (page 31), which are works of genius. Imperial megalomania again?

All the palaces in the world are named after this hill – because here the emperors built their stupendous homes. Neither before nor since the Roman Empire did the world see such, yes, *palatial* houses.

Palatine Hill

[I 8/9] *Piazza Santa Maria Nova, 53 (near Arch of Titus), and Via di San Gregorio, 30.* Tel. 0639967700.

Getting there
Bus 75, 81, 85, 87, 115, 175, 186, 204, 810, 850,
Tram 3 or
B Metro Colosseo or Circo Massimo stop.

Fee (admission includes museum).
Open Monday to Saturday 9 am-7 pm in summer, 9 am-3 pm in winter; Sunday 9 am-1 pm.

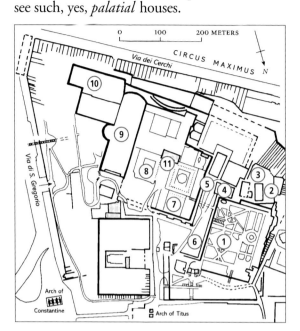

Starting with Octavian Augustus, most of the emperors lived and ruled from atop this hill that Romans considered holy as it was the original site Romulus and Remus settled. The massive ruins only hint at past magnificence. Walk south up the *Clivus Palatinus* from Titus's Arch in the dusty Roman Forum and you find yourself on glorious tree-shaded lawns. Walk on the grass, but keep it clean. Here it is even harder than in the Forum to imagine the magnificent buildings of this cradle of Rome's history – and the 30,000 slaves who worked in this city!

Start your walk by turning right at the top of the Clivus; follow the signs to
❶ **Orti Farnesiani** (Farnese Gardens). Don't miss the box-hedge maze or the views over the Roman Forum. When Renaissance architect Vignola planned what was the first botanical garden in the world, it started at the

History BC
• **753** Rome was founded by a tribe of wandering shepherds, whose traditional leader **Romulus**, having dispatched his brother, **Remus**, after a plowing contest around this hill, decided they should build a hamlet of thatched huts here not far from the Tiber.
• **27** Octavian, **Julius Caesar**'s adopted son, was proclaimed **Augustus** (emperor) by the Senate. Born on this holy hill, he strengthened his claim of supreme power by moving to a house near "Romulus's Hut," building a temple to his favorite god, Apollo, within his home, and placing there the sacred Sibylline books from the Temple of Jupiter.

History AD
• **14-68** Augustus's successors **Tiberius**, **Caligula** and **Claudius** built ever-grander additions. The fifth emperor, **Nero**, included the Palatine in his vast *Domus Aurea*.

The main gate to the Palatine, Via di San Gregorio, 30, with the now-destroyed buildings of the Orti Farnesiani in the background.

- **68-96 Vespasian, Titus** and **Domitian,** the emperors of the Flavian family who succeeded the hated Nero, outdid each other in covering the Palatine with their monumental residences.
- **193-211** Emperor **Septimius Severus,** finding his predecessors' vast compound constricting, added palaces, cantilevering over the edge when the hill was all covered.
- **476** Odoacer lived here as first barbarian king of Italy after destroying the empire of the West by forcing Romulus Augustulus to abdicate as the last of the Roman emperors.
- **12c** Christian churches built here, including a Greek monastery. The **Frangipani** family fortified the hill in their struggle against the popes. Imperial palaces were pillaged and allowed to fall into ruin.
- **1535** Alexander **Farnese,** grandson of Pope Paul III, had Vignola build him a villa here with extensive gardens.
- **19c** Charles **Mills,** English eccentric, built a Gothic villa, but by the end of the century archaeologists had ordered it and virtually all nonimperial buildings torn down.

level of the Forum (which was then half hidden by landslides from this hill) and ascended in terraces like the Hanging Gardens of Babylon. Very little of the Domus Tiberiana (Tiberius's House) below the gardens has been excavated. Caligula, whose palace was at the edge closest to the Forum, had an aerial walk, **Pons Caligulae,** built over to the Capitol to save time when going to official functions at the Temple of Jupiter!

From the side of the gardens furthest from the Forum, walk down to the ruins of

❷ **Temple of Cybele** (204-191 BC). This goddess, also known as *Magna Mater* (big mamma), was brought from Phrygia to Rome in the form of a black stone when things looked bleak during the Second Punic War, against Carthage. Since the tide of battle immediately turned, the appreciative Romans built a temple here for Cybele's statue – which is about all you can see today; it has been placed nearby under an arch of Tiberius's Palace.

Two antique cisterns (6c BC) are here. The best preserved is round, with a beehive vault. Romans from the very beginning showed a healthy concern for having water available. One thousand years would pass before the invading Goths cut off their clean water.

At the rear of Cybele's temple are excavations of

❸ **Romulus's Hut Village.** Although many were skeptical,

17c reconstruction of imperial palaces on the Palatine Hill.

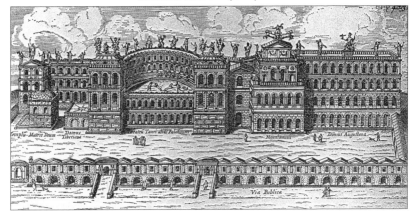

mythology held this to be the site of the founding of Rome, where the twins Romulus and Remus had been nursed by the she-wolf in the nearby *Lupercal,* or wolf's cave. They had a contest to decide who would be leader, but when Romulus plowed the area he proposed for the city, Remus mocked him by jumping over the furrow – so Romulus killed his brother in the first of what would be a long history of sibling rivalry and dynastic murder in the Eternal City. In 1907 archaeologists were surprised to find the postholes for three huts that they dated to approximately the 8c BC, partially vindicating the myth.

Walking toward the center of the Palatine, you reach

❹ **Livia's House.** So called because of lead pipes you can see here engraved IULIAE AV (Julia Augusta), which is interpreted as meaning "Emperor Augustus's wife." Since Augustus probably moved into his wife Livia's first husband's house, this seemed logical, but current experts think this was actually where Augustus himself lived. (Augustus, after divorcing his first wife, Scribonia, was besotted with, and married, Livia when she was pregnant by her divorced husband. Later Augustus became a prude and passed laws against sexual libertinism when he became emperor.) Delicately frescoed walls have been maintained here and give a good idea of the sophisticated taste that epitomized the *Golden Age of Augustus*. (The same delicately woodsy dining-room frescoes were in her Villa of Livia at Prima Porta on the outskirts of Rome, and are now on view in the Palazzo Massimo Museum; see page 256.) Don't miss the griffins and false marble in these paintings, which date to the time of the finest houses in Pompeii.

Adjoining are the sparse remains of

❺ **Temple of Apollo** and **Augustus's House.** Emperor Augustus built this private temple as an act of thanksgiving to the god who helped him defeat his brother-in-law and last rival, Marc Antony (who scandalized the family by running off with Cleopatra). It was also a smart career move to show the Romans that he was a "favorite of the gods." Rome's great biographer Suetonius (2c AD) wrote, "Augustus found the city of Rome brick, and left it marble . . . lived in an unpretentious house . . . slept in the same bedroom for over 40 years."

Extending from the corner of Livia's House closest to the Forum is

❻ **Cryptoporticus.** A Greek-sounding name for a network of passages under a large Roman palace, permitting slaves to scurry unseen between houses. This one runs 130 m (400 ft.) along the side of the Farnese Gardens. You can see the openings for light and air as well as copies of the finely stuccoed vaults.

❼ **Domus Flavia** (AD 81-92, Rabirius). These ruins are part of the "golden ghetto" that Emperors Vespasian, Titus and especially Domitian built for themselves. Flavia is not a woman, but the name of their family dynasty. This part, being closest to the Forum, was for official business and ceremonies. The first four of the six state rooms are *Basilica,* where the emperor met with his councilors and meted out justice from a niche perched above the others; *Aula Regia*, the Throne Room, which impressed visitors with its huge size, almost as large as the Pantheon, and its gigantic statuary; *Lararium*, nominally the emperor's private chapel (graffiti

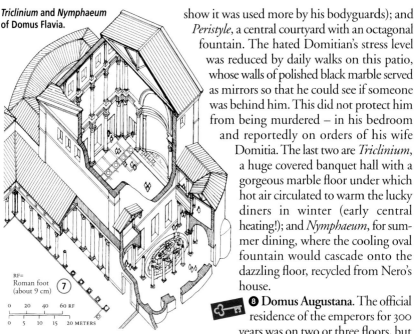

Triclinium and *Nymphaeum* of Domus Flavia.

RF=
Roman foot
(about 9 cm) **7**

0   20   40   60 RF
0   5   10   15   20 METERS

show it was used more by his bodyguards); and *Peristyle*, a central courtyard with an octagonal fountain. The hated Domitian's stress level was reduced by daily walks on this patio, whose walls of polished black marble served as mirrors so that he could see if someone was behind him. This did not protect him from being murdered – in his bedroom and reportedly on orders of his wife Domitia. The last two are *Triclinium*, a huge covered banquet hall with a gorgeous marble floor under which hot air circulated to warm the lucky diners in winter (early central heating!); and *Nymphaeum*, for summer dining, where the cooling oval fountain would cascade onto the dazzling floor, recycled from Nero's house.

❽ **Domus Augustana.** The official residence of the emperors for 300 years was on two or three floors, but all you see today are two peristyles (courtyards) and immense ruined walls. There may have been a thousand rooms. The peristyle to the north had a pool with a small temple reached by a soaring bridge. Look down at the southern peristyle on the lower floor, with symmetrical tracery in the central fountain, surrounded by sumptuous apartments that were complete with toilet facilities. From there the imperial family had direct access to its private box for watching races in the **Circus Maximus** far below (from which you get a good view up at the engineering feat these palaces represent).

❾ **Stadium.** Look down at Domitian's private Hippodrome, about the size of a football field, where imperial guests could view the races from all sides. The oval ruin down at the far end was a riding school built by the gentle Ostrogothic king Theodoric, who ruled between here and his main seat in Ravenna from AD 493 until Byzantium became all-powerful in 526.

❿ **Domus Severiana** (House of Septimius Severus, AD 193-211). As virtually the whole of the Palatine Hill had been covered with imperial p alaces, this African-born emperor built his beyond Domitian's palace on a terrace supported by enormous brick arches. Adjoining the *Stadium* he added gorgeous *Baths* connected to the Aqua Claudia springs by the aqueduct you can see at the west end of the Palatine. At the very end, in sight of both the Circus Maximus and the Colosseum, but torn down in the 16c, was his *Septizonium,* a multistory fountain to dazzle all those arriving in Rome from the south.

⓫ **Museo del Palatino.** The tiny jewel of all Rome's ancient art museums is that white building at the top of the Capitoline. Sculpture, sarcophagi, frescoes, artifacts – but only the best of all that was found here at the emperors' palace. Personally selected and arranged by the top expert, Professor Adriano La Regina, former State Superintendent of Roman Archaeology (a title that dates back to Raphael).

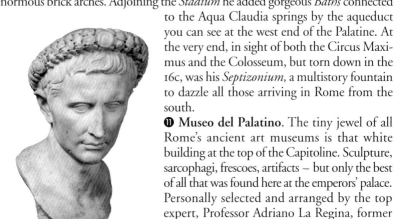

Emperor Augustus.

Via dei Fori Imperiali

Benito Mussolini, dictator and urban planner, in 1933 wanted to see the Colosseum from his office in Palazzo Venezia, and impress Hitler during his future visit to Rome. So he had this wide boulevard rammed through the ancient heart of Rome, straddling the Forum of Peace, imperial forums and the Forum of Trajan. He leveled Renaissance churches, palaces, medieval housing and even a small hill, raising an enormous hue and cry.

Imperial Forums

[**F/G 8**] *Forum of Trajan, Via dei Fori Imperiali.* Tel. 066790048.

Getting there
Bus 44, 46, 60, 62, 64, 75, 81, 85, 87, 95, 160, 170,175, 186, 628, 716.

Fee
Open Tuesday to Sunday 9 am-7 pm in summer; 9 am-5 pm in winter.
Closed Monday.

Trajan's Market **Main entrance** *Via IV Novembre, 94. Also Piazza Madonna di Loreto.* Tel. 0636004399.

Start from Piazza Venezia (toward Colosseum). Left side:

Forum of Trajan (inaugurated AD 113, Apollodorus of Damascus). Part of the vast complex this genius sculptor-architect designed: Trajan's Column, Trajan's Forum, the Basilica Ulpia, and Trajan's Market.

❶ **Trajan's Column**. With extraordinarily deeply sculpted bas reliefs (very unusual), and the *seamless* way in which the sculpting continues up the column, it must be one of the greatest masterpieces to come down to us intact from ancient Rome, showing Trajan's victories in eastern Europe (he coveted those metal mines in Dacia). Archaeologists feel the drums were sculpted in situ, as they have suffered little damage.

History AD
• **312** When Constantine, formerly emperor of the eastern Mediterranean, came to Rome after defeating Maxentius, the freshly victorious emperor of the Roman world visited Trajan's Forum and spluttered: "I will never be able to construct anything to compare with that."

The 26,000 figures were originally painted in bright colors. The bronze statue of the emperor on the top was replaced with one of St. Peter in 1587.

There is a persistent rumor that Emperor Trajan's ashes reposed at the base, although normally no bodies could be buried within the "Pomerania," the inner circle of Rome. This law could have been circumvented by cremation of the emperor. The column, in Luni (lunar = moon white) marble, is 40 m (131 ft.) high; 18 drums of marble, each 1.5 m (4 ft.) high and 3.5 m (11 ft.) in diameter – with a spiral staircase curling up the center. (Behind the column, where there is now a church dedicated to *Nome di Maria*, was the Temple of Trajan, built by Hadrian, as one could not build a temple to oneself – how modest! Nothing is left of this temple, unless it's lurking inside the church's walls.)

❷ **Center of the Forum.** Not much of the ancient elegance is left in this enormous meeting place where lawyers pleaded their clients' cases and a cross section of Rome business was conducted. The original area was double the present size, continuing across the road, with another semicircle stretching to where the "Wedding Cake" Vittoriano now is. A gilded statue of Trajan graced the center of the square and brilliant marbles were on floor and wall. At the back were two libraries, Greek and Latin – of course all the "books" were scrolls. The Roman library on the Campidoglio side of the column still shows the brick and mortar of the cupboards housing the scrolls. This masonry was needed to absorb humidity, since marble – which was used everywhere else in the complex – is not as porous.

❸ **Basilica Ulpia** (adjacent to and part of the Forum). Ulpia was Trajan's family name. This is the largest and latest building of the complex and most of it is underground. Its marbles were pillaged in the Middle Ages as building material for houses and churches which were built on top.

❹ Trajan's Market. For us this is the most satisfying building of the complex, combining symmetry, beauty, space and supple lines. It rises six floors in a semicircle on the hill overlooking the Forum; 150 booths distributed free grain in the hall on the entrance level, while wine, oils, fruit and vegetables and a myriad of other commodities were sold on the other levels. Via Biberatica (3rd floor) had taverns believed to have faced each other, so that senators and other important people in the Forum below could not hear the joyous noises emanating from here! It is still covered with its original floors. 4th floor: exotic spices and pepper; 5th floor: offices of Public Assistance (ancient Roman Social Security); 6th floor: ponds with live fish, one fed by an aqueduct with fresh water, the other with sea water from Ostia. (Some scholars say it was all government offices with no shops.)

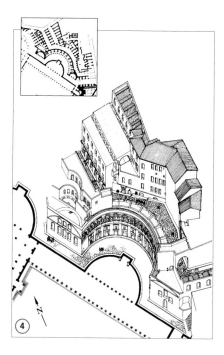

The other **imperial forums** (1C BC–AD 2C). Four huge meeting places with temples are scattered to the left and right of Mussolini's avenue, Via dei Fori Imperiali, which runs on top of them, more or less down the middle. In the summer these forums can often be visited by night with a guide. You pass from one side of the main road to the other by means of a 15c drain the height of a man. On the right side of the road is a new type of archaeological dig in which all of the strata are exposed. Lowest level: the giant Etruscan drain, the Cloaca Maxima; above that, a Roman mosaic floor of perhaps a servant's room; above that, a medieval house with loggia (large balcony). On the other side of a small footpath was the abattoir; animal bones embedded in the pavement show that they were slaughtered here.

Over the centuries, the area was filled in with sand, making a still-life floor with bones.

❺ Forum Julium (50 BC). Caesar's forum is the very first example of a privately financed forum. On the right side looking at the Colosseum is a large, well-proportioned rectangle. At the end of it, the Temple of Venus Genetrix rests atop a soaring flight of stairs, reaching for the gods. At its base is the pedestal for a **quadriga** statue (four horses galloping with the dictator standing in a chariot behind). On the edge of Caesar's Forum is the large public lavatory which could accommodate 50 people. Trajan built these into the first floor of Caesar's shopping mall facing Via Subura 150 years later.

Only the seating area was covered, comfortable even in the rain. Fresh running water was piped in under the seats and in the urine channel in front. And what did they use for paper? Sponges! In imperial times the rich used the feathers on the tummies of live birds. Next to Trajan's Forum on the left, is the

❻ Forum of Augustus (2 BC). Augustus had to buy many private houses – an expense in those days too – in the "suburbs" to make room for *his* forum, which was peopled by giant statues, the one of himself 17 m (50 ft.) high!

A DAY IN THE LIFE OF ANCIENT ROME

Roman life was as complex and so-phisticated as ours today. Romans had most of the machinery we have, but it was operated by *human* force and the laws of physics – and not by electric or other power. Their acqueducts would be a marvel in any age. Their furniture was more complex than ours, and beautifully

tooled with bronze and gold sculptural overlays. They knew and used elevators, winches, cranes, weight-balances and archimedial water pumps. They used false perspective to enhance the grandeur of their buildings. They had advanced agriculture; fish husbandry was common (such as moray eel breeding). They had dormouse hatcheries, with nests of clay tunnels inside amphoras – all for delectable culinary delights.

Doctors were highly specialized in surgery on gladiators and soldiers, performing miracles routinely, and the Romans had cures for many common diseases. Glass making (with quartz and limestone), glass cameos and glass window panes were widespread, as were astronomy and surveying, land measurement with sophisticated instruments.

Julius Caesar outlawed delivery carts clogging the streets during the day – so nights were noisy. Everybody but the super rich got up at dawn, threw cold water over their hands and face, and slipped a longer tunic over their nightshirt (or more in winter). On top of these was draped the toga, a long crescent of white wool that was difficult to keep elegant, as it would flop to one side and needed constant adjustment. In imperial times men adopted the short-sleeved tunic top with a short pleated skirt, so their legs and arms were often cold (they despised barbarians who wore trousers and leggings), and donned a Greek cloak

Only part of a crooked finger and the back of his hand (bigger than a man's arm) is left. It stood against the fire wall he had built between the populace's housing and his forum complex. The wall rose to 35 m (110 ft.) high and was meant to keep the Augustan space safe from the rampages of fire that swept through the mud-brick and wooden crowdedness outside. A statue of Augustus on a chariot showed how much he must have admired Caesar's similar statue of himself. (Copying is the highest form of flattery.) All the covered spaces were beautified with expensive marbles, *giallo antico* (bright veined yellow) and purple being the favored colors. The pavement outside was made of whiter-than-white Luni marble. It must have blinded the eye on a sunny day without the

In *The Decline and Fall of the Roman Empire* Edward Gibbon (1737-1794) quoted the emperor's title as **Your Sincerity, Your Gravity, Your Excellency, Your Eminence, Your Sublime and Wonderful Magnitude, Your Illustrious and Magnificent Highness**

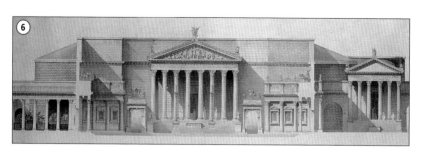

cut on the square. Slaves were allowed to use gloves in winter. After a quick glass of water, the men went to get shaved or have their beards trimmed – a painful business, as steel had not been invented, and razors were of iron (not very sharp). No one shaved himself, slaves included! In BC times haircutting was "short back and sides," but later barbers became prima donnas, inventing hairstyles, putting in curls with hot irons, and hiding men's pimples with opaque creams. They dressed senators' and consuls' hair with oil, curling it fetchingly around their laurel wreaths. Women's ablutions were sparse until it came to beauty. Their hair was dressed, sometimes up to three tiers. Madame could dye her hair blonde and use barbarians' blonde hairpieces to add height. Face masks, astringents, perfumes, creams and colored powders, eye shadow and eye liner, and lipstick were de rigueur. But don't forget toothpaste first (pumice powder and mastic or perhaps powdered horn). Her dress went over her night-shift, perhaps in cotton with gold braid, and a supple silk overgarment was a luxury any self-respecting lady had to have. A shawl covered her shoulders if it was cold. A superb tiara crowned her hair or she wore a hair band across her forehead, with earrings, necklaces, bracelets and rings.

Patrician and pleb lived side by side in crowded streets – some apartment blocks rose a dozen stories, with shops on the ground floor – except up on the

Palatine, the *palace* hill. A great man would have a formal garden, with private hot baths and a lavatory complex in his house. But apart from these, public lavatories in every neighborhood were communal affairs, with multiple marble toilet seats where people would sit and chat all together. Each house had a shrine to a household god, which was venerated daily. Their walls were rich with superb frescoes depicting mythology and local heroes. These served to decorate but also to inspire emulation. Constantly passing in front of noble lessons made the owners strive to improve, to do better in their daily lives.

Life was ordered and Romans lived by the clock. After breakfast of a crust of bread and cheese around 9 am, children would go off to school with leftovers from the night before in a handkerchief

benefit of sunglasses. The giant temple in the middle is dedicated to Mars the avenger, god of war. Vast fluted columns held up a triangular pediment, with images on either side of Mars, Venus, Aeneas and Romulus. The sculptural remnants around the friezes are very fine and detailed. There is one of a rolling wave which is almost modern in its beauty (right side).

Going toward Via Cavour the next oblong was

❼ **Nerva's Forum** (AD 98). All that remains today are two lofty columns with lovely sculpting, a statue of Minerva and a deep frieze showing women at work.

❽ **Temple of Peace** (Vespasian's Forum, AD 75). Joined by a colonnade to Nerva's Forum, this public park was where Nerva put ancient Greek statues that Nero had stolen from Athens 15 years earlier.

Main entrance
Via Clivo Argentario, 1.
Tel. 066792902.

No fee, offering expected.
Open 9 am-noon, 2-6 pm.

Mamertine Prison (formerly Tullianum). Below the Chiesa of San Giuseppe dei Falegnami (1598).

In *Etruscan* times (pre-5c BC) this was probably a cistern for collecting water. It does seem to connect with the great Etruscan hydraulic miracle, the Cloaca Maxima, the drain that got rid of the water in the Forum. In *Roman* times (late BC-early AD) it was a dungeon and prison for enemies of the state, although very small in size. Its most illustrious occupant, vanquished King Vercingetorix of Gaul, was led from here in AD 49 to be killed. There is a small spring in what is said to be

Shrine to the Lares and Penates household gods.

(the rest would be finished off by their parents at lunch).

They were careful to beware of chamber pot liquids, which were often chucked out of the window from the upper stories of the housing apartments. Although Trajan's Market (see page 33) offered every conceivable fruit, vegetable, meat and fish, Madame left food shopping to the household slaves. She did go in the afternoon for silks and satins, or special items such as Arabian spices or oysters from Colchester (which took only four days to arrive from England by relay runners – the DHL of those times).

Every man was a patron or a client. Every morning the poor man went to his patron for handouts – the businessman to his lawyer, the artist or artisan to his benefactor (in whose palace he might be working). The rich man went to see *his* patron in a litter (carried by slaves). All had to pay court and wait their turn to give greetings. The laborer and slave were last on the totem pole. The whole fabric of society, from ropemaker and pastry cook to bureaucrat and senator, revolved around this patron-client phenomenon. Everybody had a patron higher then himself, even the richest man. The

emperor was the sole exception. Commerce took place in the Roman Forum, then later in those of Caesar, Augustus, Trajan, etc. Romans were supreme merchants and lawyers, and filled the basilicas with their haranguing, magistrates presiding to settle differences.

The workday finished about noon. A trip to the baths (see page 59) was de rigueur, visiting hours changing under different emperors, who ruled by a policy of *panem et circenses* (bread and circuses): flour was often distributed free, a gift of the emperor, and rulers sometimes declared as many holidays as workdays. These were filled with circuses, plays and chariot races. Theater began to lose its charm by AD 1c as blood sports took over.

Gladiators slaughtered hundreds of animals or each other, to packed houses. Temperatures ran high, and one famous riot in Pompeii, when fans from opposing gladiatorial teams went for each other's throats, resulted in fines and the closing of the amphitheater for 10 years. To compete with the Colosseum, theaters put on tableaux plays in which convicts, acting the victims, were killed – live onstage.

The main meal of the day was dinner, taken in midafternoon. It could last a couple of hours or all night, could be frugal or lavish (lark's tongue paté or dormouse brochette).

At banquets there were jugglers or dancers between courses. Guests removed

the cell of its most famous Christian prisoner: St. Peter. Tourists throw in coins and we noticed visitors fishing them out and keeping them for luck.

On the right side of Via dei Fori Imperiali, between the main entrance to the Roman Forum and the Colosseum, are the extremely interesting marble wall maps of imperial Rome through the ages. Study how Rome grew from a small town to become leader of the world (*caput mundi*). Brass plaques from these maps were stolen by an American G.I. during the liberation of Rome in 1944; they recently surfaced in a farmhouse in the American Midwest and were returned to Rome.

Roman living room, AD 2c.

their shoes at the entrance, where their feet were washed, and proceeded barefoot. Reclining on couches, propped up on their left elbow, everybody ate with the right hand. By imperial times, women had graduated from stools to couches. Children and slaves ate sitting on stools. Guests' hands would be washed with perfumed water between the seven courses. At a nouveau riche's house a feather down the throat made room for yet more courses. Serious uninhibited dallying with slaves, guests or prostitutes provided yet more entertainment. Many Romans prided themselves on eating frugally and behaving morally. *Garum*, an anchovy marinade, was the taste enhancer (like Vietnamese *nuoc mam*). Honey was used as a sweetener since sugar was unknown. Wine was cut with water, often laced with honey – and flowed plentifully. The happy revelers would drop into their beds in the wee hours of the morning, just as the hardworking citizens, who went to bed with the sun, would be facing the new day.

Readings: Lindsey Davis's detective novels, set in imperial Rome, give the flavor of how that life differed from, and resembled, today's.

ROMAN NUMERALS

You most likely learned this numbering system at school but here's a summary:
M = 1,000, **D** = 500, **C** = 100, **L** = 50, **X** = 10, **V** = 5, **I** = 1
1-10 = **I, II, III, IV, V, VI, VII, VIII, IX, X**
First Jubilee year: 1300 = **MCCC**. Sack of Rome: 1527 = **MDXXVII**. 1800 = **MDCCC**. 1900 = either **MCM** or **MDCCCC**.
First World War: 1914 = **MDCCCCXIV**.
But don't get caught by **MDXC** = 1590.
The date on the Palazzo Cancelleria is **MCCCCLXXXXV** = 1495.
On the facade of the Museo Barracco *(Corso Vittorio Emanuele, 168)* is a Latin inscription saying "Perfectly restored in the year . . . ." You find it and figure it out! 1999 = **MCMXCIX** or **MDCCCCXCIX** – which is right?
The last Jubilee year was **MM**.

Pantheon, AD 2C

[E/F 6]

Piazza della Rotonda.

Getting there
Bus 60, 62, 64, 70, 116, 492.

Open Monday to Saturday 9 am-6 pm in summer, 9 am-4:30 pm in winter; Sunday 9 am-1 pm.

History BC
• **27** Consul Marcus Agrippa, son-in-law of Emperor Augustus, built a small Greek-style temple, dedicated to "all gods" (*Pantheon*). Its entrance was to the south, facing his complex of baths, basilica and gardens.

History AD
• **118-125** Emperor Hadrian incorporated Agrippa's temple into the portico of the temple you see today, and turned the entrance around to the north.
• **608** Phocas, emperor of Byzantium, presented this temple to

The best preserved of all ancient Roman buildings, and one of the world's architectural masterpieces. The simplicity of the Pantheon is breathtaking: a circular rotunda with a rectangular porch, each of perfect proportions and joined together without decoration. It was built in AD 2c by Emperor Hadrian, who also designed his beautiful country house – see 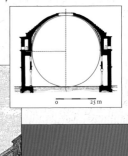 Tivoli, page 241.

Standing in front, look up at the inscription on the Pantheon's huge triangular pediment: **M.AGRIPPA L:F: COS TERTIVM FECIT**, meaning "Marcus Agrippa, son of Lucius, in his third consulate, made it" (L:F:COS = Luci filius Consul). Hard to tell if Hadrian was being selfless or self-serving in attributing his temple to the much-loved Agrippa, ancient Rome's most popular founding father. Take in the majesty of those 16 soaring columns in front; each is a solid shaft of granite. The massive bronze doors may well be the original ones; they can still swing effortlessly on their hinges. Hadrian's greatest engineering feat was designing this enormous dome with a large hole in the top – the **oculus**. His solution was to divide the construction into a series of rings, one on top of the other, all made of different building materials and of different thicknesses, which get lighter and thinner as they rise up. The massive base is of solid travertine; the lowest ring is a 6.1 m (20 ft.) thick drum of mixed travertine and volcanic tufa; the next is a thinner drum of tufa and brick; then just brick; then brick and pumice stone; finally the rim of the oculus, only 1.5 m (4.5 ft.) thick, contains hollow earthenware pots supported by pumice stone. The dome's

43 m (142 ft.) span is even greater than that of St. Peter's. As for perfection of proportions, the interior height from floor to oculus is the same as the diameter, meaning that a ball with that diameter would fit snugly inside the Pantheon's rotunda. Hadrian synthesized the old with the new: Greece's old temple form – an open group of tall columns topped by a triangular pediment – with Rome's new hemispherical dome. It sounds simple, but nobody has equaled it. Now go inside and experience the shock of that oculus, the only source of light for the whole building. About 8 m (9 yards) across, it lets in a dazzling amount of light and symbolizes the sun, the source of life. We've never had the opportunity, but have heard that on nights with a full moon the view of that great orb through the oculus is an unforgettable experience. The great Renaissance painter Raphael chose to be buried here, as did the first two kings of Italy.

Piazza della Rotonda. Giacomo della Porta's 16c fountain was topped with an ancient Egyptian obelisk in the 18c. The cafés that surround it are busy all day and far into the night as this, along with Piazza Navona, is one of Rome's major destinations for kids of all ages who come to stroll and stare.

Ruins of the Baths of Agrippa (25 BC). Earliest of the great bathing establishments, built by Agrippa as part of a complex including his original Pantheon and a lake. At his death he left it to the Roman people for their free use. The baths, supplied with hot air and water, were adorned with frescoes and tiles. The entire complex, including a club, library and restaurant, burned down in AD 80 and only a few remnants survived. The cavelike hollow at the back of the Pantheon was part of Agrippa's Baths, as were the circular brick excrescences in nearby Via dell'Arco della Ciambella, showing the proportions of what was originally a bath for one man.

Pope Boniface IV, who consecrated it as the Church of Mary and All Martyrs. So, unlike most ancient buildings, it wasn't vandalized – with two notable exceptions:
• **655** One of Phocas's successors, Constant II, took away the fine bronze tiles covering the cupola for his capital in Constantinople, but they were hijacked by Arabs, ending up in Egypt. Served him right!
• **1623-44** Pope Urban VIII Barberini stole the bronze beams from the portico and had them melted down to make Bernini's baldacchino in St. Peter's and some cannonballs for Castel Sant'Angelo. This provoked the talking statue of Pasquino to say "What the barbarians didn't do, the Barberinis did" *(quod non fecerunt barbari, fecerunt Barberini).*

Our favorite
Try to visit the Pantheon when there is a storm; rain pouring down in a perfect circle on the marble floor is astounding. And if you also get thunder and lightning, you will count that visit among your most precious memories of any time, any place.

[F 6]
Piazza della Minerva.

Getting there
Bus 46, 60, 62,
64, 70, 81, 87,
115, 116, 186,
492, 628, 810 or
Tram 8.

History AD

- **1c** Under Emperor Domitian, a charming circular temple was built near here to Minerva, goddess of wisdom.
- **8c** Christian church built.
- **1280** Dominican monks built this church, taking the name of the nearby temple to call it "St. Mary above Minerva." This was the headquarters of the Dominican order, leaders in the **Inquisition**.
- **1347-80** St. Catherine of Siena, patron saint of Italy, lived, died and is buried here. "Holy Anorexia" (she was severely anorexic, living on herbs, bread and water, as did many holy women in those times) joined the Dominican order, but after a diet such as this she wasted away and died at 33. Her greatest miracle was getting the popes to return from Avignon to Rome.
- **1455** Dominican monk Fra Angelico, the great 15c painter, is buried here (under the floor of the first chapel, left of the altar).
- **1555-1642** Paul IV Carafa (r. 1555-59), the most virulent of the Inquisition popes, is buried here (Carafa chapel), as is Galileo (1564-1642), the most famous of the sages tried for heresy. Heretics were tried here.

Chiesa di Santa Maria Sopra Minerva, 1280

Though known as Rome's only Gothic church, the Church of St. Mary above Minerva is a showplace for some of the Renaissance's greatest names: Fra Angelico, Michelangelo, Filippino Lippi and the two Medici popes.

The bland facade with its rose window is from 1453. A 19c Gothic restyling can be seen inside, with the gray marble wrapping of the columns in the nave. It belittles Bernini's High Baroque tomb (1653) of Sister Maria Raggi,

alone and lost in ecstasy. But over the centuries the interior has become an amazing museum of art treasures. Michelangelo and his pupils created the statue of Christ holding his cross (1514), but the modest gold cloth is definitely not the master's and the sandal is to protect the foot from being kissed away (left of high altar).

Antoniazzo Romano painted the gilded Annunciation (1485, fifth chapel on right). The high point is the **Carafa** chapel (at the end of the transept). Its Renaissance entrance was created by Mino da Fiesole, Verrocchio and Giuliano da Maiano. And Filippino Lippi painted the ◄—⏪ masterpiece frescoes (1489), now restored to their original beauty (main wall and over the altar).

Minerva Obelisk (1667). **Bernini** designed this most charming of Rome's myriad monuments: an Egyptian obelisk from the 6c BC atop an enchanting elephant. It honors Pope Alexander VII, who, on the Baroque base, explained that the monument's significance is that only a robust intelligence can uphold solid wisdom.

40

Pagan/Jewish/Christian Walk

Forum Boarium/Ghetto/Tiber Island

Remains of pagan Rome, the Jewish Ghetto and the Christian churches are all intertwined in the usual Roman layers of history. We suggest enjoying the day in this area, with a welcome break at one of the fine Jewish/Roman eateries in the Ghetto. (There are many restaurants in this area; see page 297.)

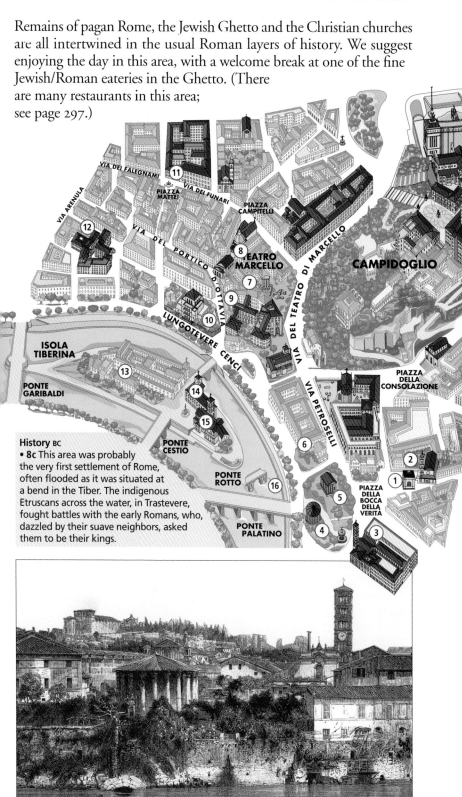

VIA DEI FALEGNAMI

VIA ARENULA

PIAZZA MATTEI

VIA DEI FUNARI

PIAZZA CAMPITELLI

VIA DEL PORTICO D'OTTAVIA

TEATRO MARCELLO

VIA DEL TEATRO DI MARCELLO

CAMPIDOGLIO

LUNGOTEVERE CENCI

ISOLA TIBERINA

PONTE GARIBALDI

PIAZZA DELLA CONSOLAZIONE

VIA PETROSELLI

PONTE CESTIO

PONTE ROTTO

PIAZZA DELLA BOCCA DELLA VERITÀ

PONTE PALATINO

History BC

• 8c This area was probably the very first settlement of Rome, often flooded as it was situated at a bend in the Tiber. The indigenous Etruscans across the water, in Trastevere, fought battles with the early Romans, who, dazzled by their suave neighbors, asked them to be their kings.

❶ Arch of Janus (Arco di Giano, AD 4c). A double-facing arch for a two-faced god who protected travelers at crossroads. This late-empire monument was neither a triumphal nor a memorial arch; it marked the intersection of two important streets, running north-south and east-west. This area of ancient Rome was the Forum Boarium, literally the cattle market. Nearby stood the most fanciful of all Etruscan temples, with giant buffalo-horn excrescences on the roof, segments of which can be seen at the Centrale Montemartini Museum (see page 261). *Via del Velabro.*

❷ Arch of the Money Changers (Arco degli Argentarii, AD 204). Where there's a market, there's money. The Guild of the Money Changers erected this in honor of Emperor Septimius Severus and his family, whose portraits are sculpted on the arch, though two are defaced. In AD 212 Caracalla lured his brother Geta to their mother's apartments and had him killed cowering in his mother's arms. Soon after this, Caracalla became sole emperor and both his brother's and his wife's portraits were effaced from this arch (she too was murdered).

Chiesa di San Giorgio al Velabro. Attached to the Arch of the Money Changers, it dates from 683. A century later Pope Zachary brought St. George's head here from Jerusalem, where he was decapitated during the persecutions of Emperor Diocletian (284-305). A Christian officer of the Roman army, his fame rests on the legendary dragon slaying to save a maiden – making him England's patron saint in 1348. In Pietro Cavallini's glorious fresco (1295) over the altar, George carries his red-crossed white banner on the far left next to the Madonna; Christ and Saints Peter and Sebastian stand by. The portico high-water mark shows where the 1870 flood reached – 1.2 m (1.3 yards) – and photos inside show reconstruction after the 1993 anarchist bombing. Faith is mightier than affliction.

Via del Velabro, 19.
Tel. 066920451.

Open 10 am-12:30 pm and 4:30-6:30 pm.

Our favorite
The brilliant and intricate 12c mosaic decoration on the edges of the altar and the reliquary (for the saint's cranium, spear and banner) directly under the altar's delicate baldacchino.

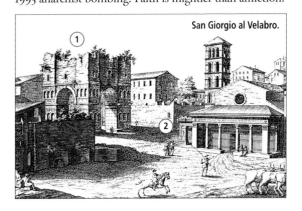

San Giorgio al Velabro.

❸ Basilica di Santa Maria in Cosmedin. One of our favorite churches: medieval (6c) and very austere. Le Corbusier in *Towards a New Architecture* (1923) wrote "a church for poor people, set in the midst of noisy and luxurious Rome, proclaims the noble pomp of mathematics, the unassailable power of proportion, the sovereign eloquence of relationship."

[**H 7**] *Piazza della Bocca della Verità, 18. Tel. 066781419.*

Open 10 am-7 pm in summer; 10-12 am and 3-5 pm in winter.

History BC
• **Legend** Aeneas, arriving from Troy, is said to have settled here.
• **495** On these marshlands stood a massive Roman altar and temple to Hercules.

History AD
• **69-81** Columned hall built for inspectors of the nearby grain-fruit-vegetable market (Forum Boarium). They watched out for cheating. Next door was a stable of purebred horses for chariot racing at Circus Maximus. Also a temple to Mithras, where charioteers popped in for a prayer before a race.
• **200** A tiny chapel underground (now the crypt) was built for Christians, who risked death worshiping.
• **6c** A small church erected by and for Rome's Greek population.
• **782** Pope Hadrian I enhanced the building for refugees from Constantinople's iconoclast persecutions (when the Byzantine church forbade image worship).
• **1223** Restored again, including the floor, which is perhaps the first **Cosmati** work.

The bell tower. A fine example of medieval brick work: seven stories of windows with tiny columns, and plates or porphyry discs stuck into the facade.

Interior. Unchanged in character since the 12c. All the columns and capitals date from Roman times. In the Dark Ages there was a gallery upstairs where women worshiped away from the men's gaze. "In Cosmedin" means "cosmetics," therefore beautiful, in Greek. In the 12c the revolutionary use of broken Roman artifacts to make beautiful floors became the height of fashion.

The **Cosmati** family (did their name come from the church?) had a lucrative business for 200 years.

The rood screens of the same work between the

KIDS **Bocca della Verità** *(Mouth of Truth).* About 100 BC. Ancient giant marble disc sculpted into a human face, formerly a drain (how nice for functional drains to be beautiful and funny). Tradition has it that if you tell a lie while putting your hand into the mouth, it will bite your hand off. A priest hid behind the marble face to whack the wrists of known liars. A favorite for mothers with unruly children, and wives with unfaithful husbands.

43

altar and public area are particularly fine. The altar is a porphyry bath from Roman times. On the sacristy wall is an 8c mosaic on gold ground, originally in the old St. Peter's.

❹ **The round Temple of Hercules Victor** (formally known as Vesta's Temple, 2c BC). This round temple, modeled on a hut of wattles and thatched roof, is the oldest marble building in Rome and is represented on ancient coins. It became a medieval church, St. Peter of the Carts, named for its proximity to the markets.

❺ **Temple of Portunus** (better known as Fortuna Virilis, 2c BC). A square temple. Both temples were covered with stucco and painting. They were next to the ancient port of Rome, right opposite the southern tip of the Tiber Island, where the river could periodically be forded. This building survived by being turned into a church from the 9c until the 19c.

Piazza della Bocca della Verità.

Via Petroselli, corner of Via Ponte Rotto.

Up the street at *Via del Foro Olitorio* is another example of an ancient temple being swallowed into a later building.

Cloaca Maxima (509 BC, King Tarquinius Superbus). The Etruscan genius for draining water by constructing deep channels is epitomized here. The sewage pipes are as tall as a man and can sometimes be visited with special permission. The whole Forum area, between four of the seven hills, was dried up in this way and became the focal point of the world for a thousand years. The mouth of this brilliant engineering feat is visible on the east bank just below the Ponte Palatino.

❻ **Casa dei Crescenzi** (AD 1100). One of Rome's most powerful families built this stronghold incorporating ancient friezes and immortalizing themselves with dedicatory inscriptions. This tower guarded the now-broken Aemilius Bridge (Ponte Rotto).

❼ **Teatro di Marcello** (11 BC). Julius Caesar started this impressive construction to rival the nearby Theater of Pompey (see page 55). Augustus finished it, naming it after his heir apparent, who died too young at age 19 in 23 BC. He was the son of Augustus's favorite sister, Octavia (see page 52).

[G 7]
Via del Teatro di Marcello.

This impressive auditorium had 41 arches in two tiers, topped by a flat surface containing the bleachers. Greek-style dramas were presented on festivals and religious holidays. Fourteen thousand spectators could fill the 137 m (150 yard) semicircular seating area – about one

third of which is visible today from the Via Teatro di Marcello. The stage was on the river side.

In the 12c it was incorporated into a fortress of the Fabi family. In the 16c, Baldassarre Peruzzi tranformed it into a palace for the Savelli. Today some very lucky people have opulent apartments in this ancient construction, now the Palazzo Orsini, whose entrance, on the other side, overlooks the Tiber.

[G 6] JEWISH LUNCH BREAK

From Teatro di Marcello a narrow walkway, Via della Tribuna di Campitelli, leads to Portico d'Ottavia in the Ghetto.

Ghetto. This area has been home to a Jewish community for over 1,000 years. When enclosed in the 16c, the Ghetto was a tiny area bounded by Via del Progresso, Via del Portico d'Ottavia and Lungotevere Cenci.

❽ **Portico d'Ottavia** (27 BC) and **Chiesa Sant'Angelo in Pecheria.** The superb triangular pediment with soaring columns was recently excavated down to its original level. Built by Emperor Augustus to honor his sister, Octavia (whose husband, Marc Antony, was repudiated for his love of Cleopatra), this covered walkway with Greek statues and 300 columns leads from the Theater of Marcellus to Crypta Balbi (see page 258). In the early Middle Ages a church nestled behind this gateway, soon replaced by

COUNTER-REFORMATION

Part of the reason for the ghettoization of Rome's Jews stemmed from Martin Luther's disgust at both the Church's opulence – the lifestyle of the cardinals – and its sale of indulgences, which forgave sins. In 1517 he nailed his famous 95 "Theses" on the Wittenberg church door. The Protestant – in protest – movement was born! The Catholic Church responded with the Counter-Reformation and oppressed the Jews in Rome because Church dogma blamed them for killing Christ.

Saint Angelo in Pecharia (the Fish Market). Fish was sold in the archway, where it was decreed that the front end of fish over a certain size be given to the city authorities. Here, centuries later, under piles of rotting fish, the **Uffizi Venus** sculpture (now in Florence) was discovered.

❾ **Chiesa di San Gregorio della Divina Pietà.** The tiny Church of St. Gregory of Heavenly Mercy is across from the Great Synagogue of Rome, at the entrance to the Ghetto. Over the door the inscription from Isaiah in the Old Testament says it all: *I spread out my hands all the day unto a rebellious people which walketh in a way that was not good after their own thoughts.*

This finger-slapping rebuke to the Jews inscribed in Latin *and* Hebrew seems out of step with our times, when both Pope John XXIII and Pope John Paul II

History BC

- **In ancient times**, Rome's Jews were just another ethnic minority attracted to the big city. All non-Romans were obliged to reside in Trastevere, but could circulate freely doing their business during the day.
- **220** The Circus Flaminius (in part of the present Ghetto) was inaugurated to amuse the populace with racing and other sports. Being near the river, it was often flooded for games, as in 2 BC when 36 crocodiles were butchered here.
- **162** A delegation of Maccabees (Jews) came to Rome asking for help to repel the Syrians.

History AD

- **In Christ's time** Israel was a handful of Hebrew Roman provinces (Canaan, Philistia, Judah, Israel, etc.).
- **50** In Nero's court the most famous actor was Jewish, and Empress Poppea showered the actor's co-religionists with her intimate favors.
- **66** Following the great Jewish rebellion against Rome, Judea was conquered.
- **70** While Vespasian was emperor, his son Titus attacked Jerusalem, destroyed the Temple of Solomon and slaughtered or enslaved many of the Jews. A large number of the survivors fled, starting the Diaspora. He carried back to Rome the famous golden 7-branched candelabra (see Arch of Titus, page 26). Judaism was recognized as a legitimate religion by Rome.
- **13c** Many Jews moved across the river from Trastevere to this area.
- **1555-59** Pope Paul IV Carafa forbade Jews to live outside the Ghetto and built a wall to enclose them. The gates opened at dawn and closed at dusk. There were humiliating and stringent limits to what trades they could practice (sale of old furniture and used clothing) and even how many rings they could wear. The area was absurdly small for so many people. After Pope Paul IV's death the rules were eased, but Jews still had to run on foot in the annual horse races down Via del Corso.
- **1808** Napoleon rescinded the Ghetto laws during the French invasion of Rome. Then they were reinstated.
- **1848** The Ghetto was abolished, temporarily.
- **1888** Its walls were demolished.
- **1904** The Great Synagogue of Rome was built.
- **1938** Mussolini, who had been tolerant of Jews, passed racial laws against them (though 200 had participated in his march on Rome in 1922).
- **1943** 2,091 Romans (about 1,000 Jews) were sent to concentration camps. Only 16 returned.

- **1944** 335 civilians, including 100 Jews, were executed by the German occupiers at the **Fosse Ardeatine** (see page 69).
- **1986** Pope John Paul II Wojtyla treated the rift between the Church and the Jews by removing that part of the Church's ritual that blamed the Jews for killing Christ. His visit to the Rome synagogue was the first time ever for a pontiff.
- **Today** the Ghetto is a picturesque quarter of Rome where Jew and Gentile live happily together as in ancient times. Italy's Jewish population is the same today as it was in the city of Rome under Emperor Nero.

GHETTO *CUCINA*

There are many fine Roman-Jewish restaurants in this area, and of course lots of other ones as well. "Roman-Jewish" food is really medieval cuisine with Jewish overtones (but usually not kosher). Each pope came from a different part of Italy or Europe, so food at the Vatican court was never from Rome but from Molise, Savoia, Venice, Burgundy, etc. The closest you can get to the taste treats of the Dark Ages is to try the Jewish restaurants. Particularly fabulous is the *carciofi alla giudia*, crispy fried whole artichoke, and *fritto misto vegetale* (deep fried pieces of zucchini, artichokes, apple, mozzarella cheese, cauliflower) and a host of other surprising dishes.

Lungotevere Cenci.
Tel. 066840061.

Open Monday-Thursday
9 am-5 pm; Friday
9:30 am-2 pm; Sunday 9 am-12:30 pm.
Closed Saturday.

Cenci story
The palace's owner, Francesco Cenci, had already bought off the courts when tried for sodomy. He was a terror to his 12 children and violently raped his daughter Beatrice. After a fierce argument, he took his wife and Beatrice to a castle outside Rome. Beatrice found solace with the castle keep and they hatched the plot to kill her father with the connivance of her stepmother and two brothers. They bludgeoned him to death as he slept. First imprisoned, Beatrice and her stepmother were then beheaded on Piazza di Ponte Sant'Angelo, while brother Giacomo was tortured with hot pincers, bashed with a mace, and drawn and quartered. The younger brother fared better, let out for good behavior after just one year in prison. The pope confiscated all their properties and the Cenci family fell into oblivion. This served to frighten the powerful families, warning them to end their bloody feuds.

made gestures to end the enmity between the Catholic Church and the Jews. While Rome's Jews were forced to live in the Ghetto they were herded into this church every Thursday in an attempt to convert them to Christianity. The cozy interior has a single nave with charming frescoes on ceiling and walls, and a Baroque sun- and cloudburst behind the altar framing a Virgin and Child.

Via Portico d'Ottavia.

⑩ Main synagogue (1904, Armanni and Costa). This aluminum-domed temple is a choice example of Assyrian-Babylonian style, built after the Ghetto walls were destroyed. In addition to being a place of worship, it houses the **Jewish Community Museum** (see Museums, page 262). A major development in interreligious relations was **Pope John Paul II**'s attendance at a special service in April 1986.

⑪ Fontana delle Tartarughe (Turtle Fountain, 1585, Taddeo Landini). A block away from the Ghetto, a *must see* is this charming fountain. A Florentine sculptor, following the drawings of Giacomo della Porta, has created playful young boys pushing turtles into the basin while stepping on pet dolphins squirting water.

Piazza Mattei.

⑫ Palazzo Cenci (late 15c). (Technically just outside the Ghetto.) This vast palace straddles a small hill of rubble from the ancient theater of Balbi. The flight of stairs at the entrance leads to an antique statue. This elegance belies the grisly doings of the 16c.

Vicolo dei Cenci.

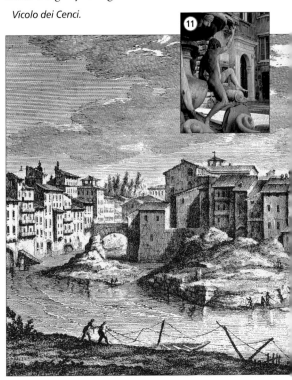

[G 6/H 7] BEGIN AFTERNOON CHRISTIAN WALK

Isola Tiberina (Tiber Island). Reputedly the world's smallest inhabited island, Isola Tiberina measures only 242 by 73 m (300 by 80 yards). The two bridges spanning the divided river both date from ancient Roman times.
Pons Fabricius (62 BC). The oldest continuously used bridge in Rome. Its bronze rail was replaced by the more homogeneous marble parapet in 1679 (Pope Innocent XI Odescalchi).
Pons Cestius (46 BC). The other superb stone bridge links the island to Trastevere. The river's only island (until the Middle Ages there was one other) is boat shaped and was clad in travertine in ancient times to disguise it as a ship. Its travertine stern downstream is still visible today. The picturesque central square is dominated by a hospital that enjoys a good medical reputation.
⓭ Fatebenefratelli Hospital. This attractive medical institution, created in 1548 for the religious order of the Do-good Brothers(!), is known for its user-friendly emergency ward. **Chiesa di San Giovanni Calibita** is part of the hospital.

History BC
• **293** During a plague, the Roman Senate sent envoys to consult the medical god Asclepius in Greece. They returned with a miracle-dispensing snake which slipped overboard at this spot in the river. A temple was built there, serving as a hospital for centuries.

History AD
• **12c** Rahere, court jester to King Henry II of England, recovered from malaria here. He returned to London, where he founded what is still known as St. Bart's Hospital.
• **19c** Until the river was tamed at the end of the 19c by isolating it from the city with high banks, there were flour mills here floating on pontoons.

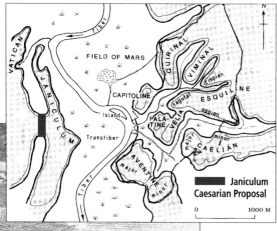

Janiculum
Caesarian Proposal

0   1000 M

Caesar wanted to channel the Tiber behind the Janiculum Hill.

These small buildings, using the river's current to grind wheat for Rome's daily bread, were often washed away.

⓮ Caetani Tower. Built before the year 1000 by the Pierleoni family, of Jewish origin, which produced Anacletus II, a powerful 12c antipope.

Pierleoni-Caetani Castle. Another medieval tower which served in 1087 as a refuge for the papal champion **Countess Matilda of Tuscany**; and for several fugitive popes who fled from their enemies to be protected here by the impregnable Pierleoni family, and later by the equally powerful Caetani.

⓯ Chiesa di San Bartolomeo all'Isola. Exterior 1624. The Baroque facade masks the 10c church built by Holy Roman Emperor Otto III. Fancying himself as successor to the Caesars, Otto personally installed two popes, Gregory V, the first German pontiff, and Silvester II, the first French one. His palace was on the Aventine Hill, over the ruins of the 3c BC Temple of Asclepius. The beautifully carved altar steps (12c) show that there used to be an ancient spring of sacred water.

⓰ Ponte Rotto. Originally Pons Aemilius, 2c BC. Rebuilt by Pope Gregory XIII in 1575, it self-destructed again a few years later. The death knell came in the 19c when it was accidentally blown up during construction of the present-day metal bridge, Ponte Palatino.

Ara Pacis Augustae
Augustus's Altar of Heavenly Peace, 13-9 BC

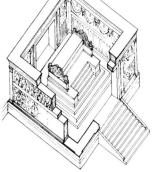

[D 6]
*Lungotevere in Augusta, corner of Via Ripetta.
Tel. 0636010385.*

0   15 RF

0   5 METERS

RF=
Roman foot (about 9 cm)

Getting there
Bus 81, 115, 119, 590, 628, 913, 926 or
A Metro to Flaminio.

Open Tuesday to Saturday 10 am-1 pm, 4 -7:30 pm.

The sculpture on this ancient monument is considered to be of the highest quality that relief carving has ever attained. The American architect Richard Meier has enveloped it in a modern building with a conference hall.

At some point in the Dark Ages this great monument disintegrated and was lost. Some of its broken friezes were buried under Rome's rubble, others scattered far and wide. Scholars had read about the fabled altar in ancient scrolls, but many suspected that it was only a myth. Truth is stranger than fiction: miraculously, after

History BC
• **4** Consecrated July 13. A solemn dedication to peace, celebrating Rome's role as the sole superpower in a tumultuous world, coinciding with its transition from republic to empire. It is an amazing portrait gallery with likenesses of the most important people who participated in the actual consecration ceremony and with an altar for praying and making sacrifices to Pax, goddess of peace. Pax was fundamental to the Roman Empire system, often called *Pax Romana.*

AUGUSTUS   AGRIPPA

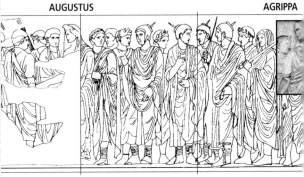

CHIEF PRIESTS

two millennia, all the pieces are finally together again.

Description of the relief sculptures

ON THE LOWER SECTIONS The acanthus scrolls, intertwined with swans, are similar on all four sides.

MAIN ENTRANCE The legendary origins of Rome. *Right panel.* Aeneas, with serious mien, is preparing to sacrifice a fat pig on a small altar. *Left panel* (now destroyed). Romulus and Remus's cave, the Lupercal (Lupe = wolf).

BACK ENTRANCE *Left.* Tellus (Italy), a buxom earth goddess with two babes. Also deities of air (on a swan) and water (on a sea monster). *Right.* Goddess Rome (very damaged).

EXTERNAL SIDE PANELS These depict the great parade of 13 BC. Augustus and the senators had something to celebrate. He had been magnificently victorious against Spain and Gaul (France) on the fringes of the Roman world.

Side away from the river. Though this long panel is damaged, it is a faithful rendition of the emperor with his family and followers. *Lictors* (honor guards) lead, holding *fasces* (bundles of sticks symbolizing authority – origin of the word *fascism*). Then comes the emperor; though part of his body is missing and the break goes through his face, one can see enough to make out a tall, handsome young man. Next to him is future emperor Tiberius, touching his arm. Then the Flamens in their head-hugging caps; they were responsible for the ceremonial fires. After an old man carrying the sacred imperial ax comes Agrippa, the emperor's best friend and son-in-law, with Augustus's wife Livia and her daughter

History AD
• **1525** Some large pagan marble reliefs came into the hands of Cardinal Andrea della Valle, leading art connoisseur. The provenance of these beautiful pieces was a mystery, but they were thought to be from Domitian's triumphal arch. These went to Villa Medici, Rome.
• **1545** Cardinal Ricci of Montepulciano (see Villa Medici, page 206) bought some other panels being excavated from Via in Lucina, Rome. These were so large he had them sawed into three pieces. They went to the Uffizi Gallery, Florence. The nascent art world was excited by these panels, showing people in a procession in exquisite high relief with natural drapery and expressive body movements. Other panels were scattered across Europe: the Louvre, the Vatican, Vienna.
• **1840s** More slabs were found during the reinforcement of an old palace in Rome (although the excavators didn't know it, it was the same area as in 1545).
• **1898** The leaders of the new Italian state were casting about for former grandeur. Scholars mooted the idea that maybe these different sculptural panels were from the famous, perhaps mythical, Altar of Augustan Peace. Excavations were started again under the palace at Via in Lucina – at great risk as the building was in danger of collapsing if one dug too far. Soon they had to give up, and the last great slabs were left behind because it was too perilous to continue. Some weighed more than 10 tons!

IMPERIAL FAMILY

- **1937** Under Mussolini's fascism, with revolutionary technology they *froze* the ground and very gently dislodged the last marble panels, which had become part of this palace's foundations.
- **1938** Italy then tried to get back all those other panels. How often do foreign countries return works of art? Almost never. But this time, they did.

Julia. The children are a delight of natural movement. One is tugging at his father's toga for attention. Many of the men are wearing the laurel wreath of victory, marking VIP status.

On the river side. Continuing the procession come other VIPs, priests, magistrates, senators. The high priest, Pontifex Maximus, crowned by a laurel wreath, has his toga over his head since this is a religious ceremony.

INNER ALTAR WALLS Though the ceremonial inner altar is lost, some beautiful scroll and leaf work is visible. The priests leading luckless animals to be sacrificed on the day of consecration are the finest carvings of ancient Rome – even better than those on Trajan's Column.

Mausoleum of Augustus, 23 BC

[**D 6**] *Piazza Augusto Imperatore.*

Getting there
Bus 32, 70, 81, 186, 204, 628, 913, 926.

To visit *call the City Office of Fine Arts, Tel. 0667103819.*

The great tomb of Octavian Julius Claudius, who became Caesar Augustus, first emperor of Rome. When King Mausolus in Asia Minor died in 353 BC, Queen Artemisia built him the most fantastic tomb, one of the seven wonders of the ancient world.

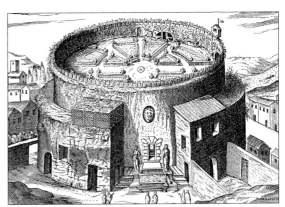

History BC
- **1c** This plain was low lying and frequently flooded. Temples to foreign gods were tolerated. Called Campus Martius (War Field), it was here the troops exercised. **Julius Caesar**, with his engineers, wanted to drain the plain forever by partially diverting the river Tiber behind the Janiculum (Gianicolo) Hill. He was murdered too soon.
- **28** A year before becoming emperor, **Octavian** ordered a superb family tomb, outside the residential area. His favorite nephew, heir apparent Marcellus, was the first to be buried here. Poisoned – but by whom? Maybe Livia, Octavian's second wife, to help her son Tiberius. Fifteen family members followed in quick succession, many

Envy, greed and all those good things made other rulers desirous of copying that great burial chamber. In so doing the word *mausoleum* became part of our vocabulary, signifying a magnificent tomb. This one was the most magnificent of all.

Covering over two acres, this circular tomb was originally garnished with white marble. Above this rose a little hill – as in Etruscan tombs – planted with thin

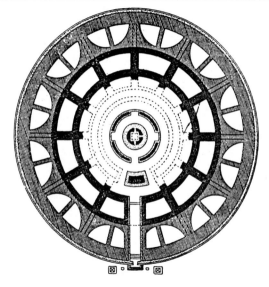

cypresses and topped with a statue of the emperor.

There were two obelisks at the entrance (Roman copies), now at Piazza dell' Esquilino and Piazza del Quirinale.

The central room, where the most important urn reposed, was surrounded by a ring of niches for other family members.

The emperors' ghosts lie quietly, undisturbed by the twentieth-century would-be emperor, Mussolini, who never made it.

dying before their time – presumably poisoned. Soon temples dotted the plain, and the city grew in this direction.
• **7** Greek geographer **Strabo** described it as a "great Tumulus on a high foundation of white stone thickly covered with trees" (according to **Amanda Claridge's** superb book).

History AD
• **14** Augustus died, and his ashes were interred in the central core. Tombs were used for holding parties honoring the dead. Feasts were held on birthdays and death-days, wine quaffed, speeches given.
• **10c Colonna** family made this a fortified castle with moat.
• **1354** Patriot **Cola di Rienzo** tried to revive the Roman Republic (popes had been hijacked to Avignon). A Colonna servant stabbed him in mid-speech and his army was butchered.
• **16c** The tomb became an ornamental garden.
• **17c** A wooden amphitheater was built, making it a bullring for intimate corridas.
• **19c** It was turned into a circus.
• **19c to late 1920s** The top section was converted into a concert hall.
• **1930s** Mussolini re-excavated the building down to its roots – dreaming up a fitting tomb for himself. He built the square of fascist-style buildings around it.
• **1945** Mussolini ended up at the wrong end of a partisan's gun, as did his mistress Clara Petacci, considered traitors. Half-naked, his body was hung upside down from butchers' hooks in central Milan.

Area Sacra di Largo Argentina

Ruins of four Roman temples, 6c–2c BC

Mussolini saved this *area sacra*, or "sacred area," from real estate developers as part of his policy of assimilating his regime with the Roman Empire. Actually, the temples date from before the empire, when Rome was a (more-or-less democratic) republic.

Little is known of these buildings, so they are referred to by the letters *A* to *D*. They are now well below street level because – as with all the remains of ancient Rome – in subsequent centuries, especially during the Dark Ages, the accumulated dirt and neglect elevated the ground about one meter (or yard) every 500 years.

[F 6]
Largo di Torre Argentina.

Getting there
Bus 46, 60, 62, 64, 70, 81, 87, 186, 492, 628, 810
or
Tram 8.

Closed except with permit from Rome City Archaeological Office.

History BC
• **71** Gnaeus Pompeius, 35, elected consul for military victories in Spain and crushing Spartacus's slave insurrection.
• **61** Pompey (as he was known) given a magnificent triumph celebration, as conqueror of Spain, North Africa and the Near East.
• **60** Pompey formed the First Triumvirate with Julius Caesar – to whose daughter Julia he was married – and Crassus.

54

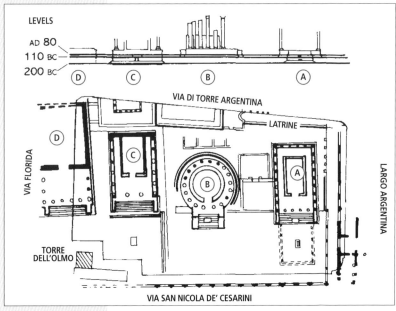

If you stand looking down on the archaeological area from Via San Nicola de' Cesarini, you have a good view of each temple, starting at the Largo Argentina end on the right and moving toward Via Florida on the left: **Temple A** (1c BC). In its present form this is the most recent, and also best preserved, thanks to a 12c church that was built into it – leaving those round shapes that have nothing to do with the original temple.

Temple B (101 BC). The only originally round structure, it has a handsome mosaic pavement. Probably dedicated to *Fortuna Huiusce Diei* (Good Fortune of the Day).

Temple C (3c BC). The oldest of the temples still has its podium of tufa blocks.

Temple D (2c BC). The largest of the four is unfortunately three-quarters covered by Via Florida.

All four of these temples had their levels gradually lifted over the years of their use. Behind Temple A, don't miss the **public latrine**, an impressive 18 m (20 yard) long convenience made of marble, with seats facing the garden and portico behind the **Theater of Pompey**, of which it was part.

Theater of Pompey (55 BC, now disappeared). Though only traces remain today, this was once the world's most important stage – the first permanent theater built in Rome, since it was made of masonry when only wooden ones were legal. Pompey, anxious to add popularity to his military successes, evaded this rule by topping the balcony with a temple. The drama between Pompey and Julius Caesar was acted out on this stage.

Rome invented its own form for theaters, since the Greeks had built theirs into the sides of hills with no attempt to isolate the stage from the surrounding countryside. Pompey's theater was the first in the world to have a monumental *scaenae frons*, an elaborately decorated back wall of the stage that rose to the same height as the top of the auditorium so that the audience and actors were enclosed on all sides. Accounts differ on whether it held 10,000 or 40,000 spectators; it was big. Pompey extended it behind the stage with a giant square portico featuring sculpture gardens and taverns for the leisure-loving Romans. The complex included a convention hall with a statue of Pompey (which can be seen in Palazzo Spada). Caesar was rebuilding the Senate House, or Curia, in the Forum; it was here in Pompey's theater on the fateful fifteenth of March (*the Ides of Mars*) that Caesar met the same end as Pompey, only four years after he thought he had rid himself of all danger from his ancient rival. He died clutching Pompey's statue.

To get an idea of the monumentality of Pompey's theater, walk from Largo Argentina up Via dei Giubbonari to Campo de' Fiori following the side of Pompey's ancient portico. Once in Campo de' Fiori, look up at the buildings on your right, behind the movie theater; notice that they are curved, for they follow the rounded rear perimeter of Pompey's theater. Now, following Via del Biscione, slip through the passageway (closed at night) into Via di Grottapinta. This semicircular street with its curved building fronts follows the edge of the former *orchestra* area in front of the giant stage. There is even a tiny theater, *Teatro Dei Satiri*. As in ancient times, there are many places to eat in and around Piazza del Biscione, and you can still see parts of Pompey's theater in the restaurants Costanza and Grotte del Teatro di Pompeo (page 296).

- **55** Theater of Pompey dedicated. Elaborate games and the slaughter of 500 lions and 18 elephants. In the next two years Crassus and Julia died.
- **48** Caesar defeated Pompey, who was killed by his own centurion in Egypt.
- **44** Caesar was killed in the portico attached to Pompey's theater, stabbed by a group of fellow senators, including Brutus, his adopted (perhaps natural) son. Caesar was entering the temporary Senate, where many expected he would be made king, when they fell upon him. Gasping *Et tu Brute* ("You too, Brutus") and pulling his toga over his head, he expired near the grandiose statue of his rival and son-in-law Pompey.

Column of Marcus Aurelius, Campus Martius and Piazza Colonna

Campus Martius (field of the god of war), the plain within the Tiber's large curve, was where the Roman legions drilled. Monuments which have disappeared include a giant sundial laid out in bronze on a huge travertine circle that covered most of Piazza Parlamento and the block beyond it. It was centered on an Egyptian obelisk which has since been moved to Piazza Montecitorio.

[**E 7**]
Piazza Colonna.

Getting there
Bus 52, 53 , 56, 58, 61, 62, 71, 95, 116, 492.

History AD
• **176** Inspired by Trajan's Column, **Marcus Aurelius's** family erected this one, commemorating his wars and victories – recorded on a spiraling band, like a comic strip. The emperor was 54 and, having served a lifetime at the front, was exhausted. Yet his likenesses on the column glow with stature and statesmanship. The facial expressions of the vanquished run the gamut from fear to gratefulness at being spared. The victories brought peace for 200 years.
• **180** The emperor, philosopher-warrior, who was adored by the populace, died.
• **1589** The statue of the emperor was taken off the top and **Pope Sixtus V** Peretti replaced it with **St. Paul.**

56

❶ Column of Marcus Aurelius (AD 176-193). In olden times Rome was full of columns erected to glorify wars won, grandiose personages and military triumphs. They were mostly for self-glorification, and this is no exception.

Like Trajan's, this column is exactly 100 Roman feet high, made of 27 superimposed marble drums. But it tapers less than Trajan's and therefore seems more massive. The sculptured spiral band turns on itself 21 times. The whole thing is 42 m (126 ft.) high, including the statue on top; ground level was 4 m (12 ft.) lower in those days (remember all that rubbish everybody was throwing out with impunity in the Dark Millennium). Within the column are 203 stairs corkscrewing up to the statue. Special permission is needed to visit inside.

❷ Palazzo Chigi (1580, Carlo Maderno). Originally built by a cardinal, nephew of Pope Clement VIII Aldobrandini, it was bought in 1659 by Pope Alexander VII Chigi, who had his architect, Felice della Greca, add the facade overlooking Marcus Aurelius's column. Maderno's hand can be seen in the entrance (unused) on Via del Corso. It housed the Italian Foreign Ministry until they got their own modern pile, the Palazzo Farnesina near the Foro Italico, and is now the prime minister's office.

❸ Palazzo di Montecitorio (1650, Gian Lorenzo Bernini). Like the Italian Parliament it houses, this vast Baroque building is a product of countless compromises. Democracy Italian style is certainly Baroque, partly genius and partly pragmatism, and very much a show – which is what Italians enjoy. Two dramatic touches of Gian Lorenzo Bernini: the facade is not straight, but has two side pieces sloping back like a stage set, and the base is made of huge rough-hewn travertine blocks making it seem to emerge from natural rock – the appropriate scenery for politicians.

(1)

History AD
• **1650 Pope Innocent X** Pamphilj had Bernini build this palace as a present for the family of the late **Pope Gregory XV** Ludovisi.
• **1694** Carlo Fontana imposed his design for a papal law court.
• **1871** The new government of united Italy remodeled it as the Chamber of Deputies.

(3)

Circus Maximus

Today an enormous quiet field (six football fields in length), yesterday reverberating to the roar of the madding crowds, exhorting the horses they wagered on, and the screams of the charioteers urging their steeds ahead. The movie *Ben Hur* illustrates exactly how these chariot races functioned.

[H 7/8 - I 8]
Via del Circo Massimo.

Getting there
Bus 81, 160, 628 or
B Metro Circo Massimo
stop.

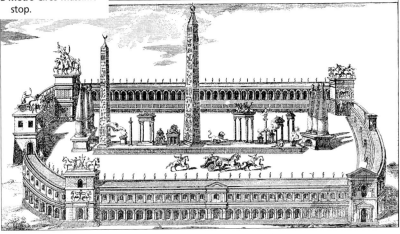

Below the Palatine's ruins the Circus Maximus became a vegetable garden.

History BC
• **8c** Rome's first recorded games were horse races organized here by city founder Romulus. He took advantage of this event to stage the **Rape of the Sabine Women**, when the lonely Roman men invited their neighbors from the Sabine hills, but killed the male visitors and married most of their women.
• **42** Julius Caesar's murder interrupted his plan to modernize this stadium, which was completed in its permanent form by Emperor Augustus.

History AD
• **64** The stands being of wood, this was where the great fire of Nero broke out. Subsequent emperors beautified it into a marble marvel.

A capacity crowd was 250,000 people, plus the emperor's private stand, which was an extension of his own mansion on the Palatine Hill. Magistrates ruled the races at either end, and the central *spina* (spine) was crowned with obelisks and markers to show how many laps the chariots had run. The horses were famous all over the Roman world and betting was fierce. Each team had its own colors. At the Tiber River end, just behind the present Church of Santa Maria in Cosmedin, were the stables which housed not only these million-dollar horses but also the temple of the pagan god Mithras, where the charioteers went to pray before a big race.

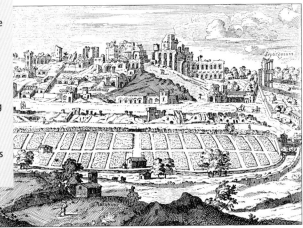

For Romans, "bathing" was a way of life. Everybody, even slaves, made a daily visit to their local baths or to one of the imperial baths, with room for up to 3,000 bathers.

The Baths
Caracalla and Diocletian

Hot baths (some with private cubicles), tepid baths, cold baths, perfumed baths, medicinal baths and torrid invalid baths. Floors and walls were heated by the fires below with hot air piped through hypercausts, ingenious hollow bricks of precise measurement (invented in the first century BC by C. Sergius Orata). Used water and aqueduct overflows were piped off to clean out Rome's many public lavatories.

The noise was excruciating. Philosopher Seneca (4 BC-AD 65), who lived above a small bathing establishment, said, "The hubbub makes one long to be deaf." The worst cries were from epilators, who drowned out the screams of their victims as they extracted beard and chest hairs. Thieves marauded through the changing rooms substituting old togas for new. Sexual favors were also on sale. The large baths had *palestrae*, or gyms, where ball games and wrestling took place. The nude wrestlers would then be rubbed down with essential oils and scraped off with a curved implement called a *strigil*. For ball games both men and women wore tunics and leggings. There were an infinite number of games, with

History BC
• **33** Rome already had 170 small public baths serving different parts of the city.

History AD
• **212** Caracalla started this building, employing an average of 9,000 workers per day for five years and using

more than 20 million pieces of brick. It had 250 columns (16 of which weighed 90 tons).
• **217** Baths were opened to the public (but Caracalla, himself responsible for thousands of murders, was assassinated in faraway Mesopotamia by the head of his Praetorian Guard – who seized the reins of power).
• **6c** Invading Goths cut the aqueducts, effectively stopping all water sports.
16-17c Of the great artworks found buried under the ruins, the Farnese Hercules and Flora are in the Naples Museum, and the finest mosaics of athletes are at the Vatican Museums. Two huge marble bathtubs are in Piazza Farnese.

balls stuffed with sand or feathers, blown full of air: handball, scrimmage ball and bladder ball – even early types of tennis, soccer and basketball. Large balls were filled with flour for pummeling. These sports were followed by a plunge in the unheated swimming pool and a vigorous massage. Snack and drink vendors roamed. Two libraries, Greek and Latin, where you could study books written on scrolls (books as we know them were invented in the Renaissance) of papyrus parchment or goat skin (*pergamon*). You could stroll in the gardens or sit under a tree and review the world (or discuss who gave the best party last night). All the arts were on parade: theater, sculpture, painting, music and particularly mosaic (of which some examples are still to be seen here).

Hours, under most emperors, were compartmentalized: men in the mornings, women in the afternoons, and slaves between 4 and 6 pm. Caracalla's was the first bath that remained open, with fires blazing and water pouring in from an aqueduct, day and night! Under Emperor Nero (scandal, scandal) there was mixed bathing.

The place itself was so beautiful one felt rejuvenated and refreshed with all that self-indulgence.

There was a minimal admission fee, though an emperor or philanthropist would occasionally finance

AQUEDUCTS

Ancient Rome had 7 hills, but 11 aqueducts. Rome's greatness expanded as the volume of water brought into the city grew, and when the aqueducts were cut by the barbarians, Rome fell.

There are still places in the city where you can see spans of these antique engineering masterpieces, notably in Via di San Gregorio, and at Porta Maggiore. Rome's grandeur is also demonstrated by monumental remains of aqueducts on the vast plains southeast of Rome at Parco degli Acquedotti near Cinecittà (3 km of winding waterways on Via Lemonia, a 10-minute walk from **Metro A** stop Giulio Agricola) – and of course in France, Spain, Great Britain and North Africa (see map, page 245). Aqueducts were channels, lined with waterproof cement and covered with stone lids, leading the water collected from mountain springs or lakes down a shallow grade (one in 1,000) to the big city. At the water's source Romans constructed large reservoirs not only to assure a continual flow but also to increase the pressure of the water at the start of its multimile trip to Rome. The watercourse often started through an underground chan-

History BC
• **8c-4c** The early Romans, finding the Tiber River polluted, drew their water from various springs and wells dotted around the city.
• **312** The Senate decided that overpopulation had exhausted the local supply

and entrusted the job of bringing in water from the outside to Appius Claudius Caecus, builder of the Appian Way. This first aqueduct, **Aqua Appia**, was almost entirely underground.
• **144 Aqua Marcia**, the first and longest elevated

aqueduct, led to the Capitoline Hill.
• **33 Marcus Agrippa** in a year repaired all 4 existing aqueducts and built another, **Aqua Julia**, as well as 500 fountains and 700 public basins and pools. Twenty years later he built the first grand

free bathing. At the end of the day their obsession with cleanliness made the ancient Romans different from other peoples. Whether or not this sybaritic life caused the Roman Empire's decline, it certainly disappeared when the empire fell.

Terme di Caracalla (212-217 AD). Emperor Caracalla built this enormous compound (10 hectares/25 acres, larger than the entire complex of London's Houses of Parliament) to curry favor with the Romans. And for three centuries it was at the center of Roman life, until it fell into disuse and then literally fell into the still glorious ruins you see today. When Mussolini started the performances of grand opera here in the 1930s on warm summer nights, the baths lived again. He would be driven via underground passages to a point below

[OFF MAP]
Viale delle Terme di Caracalla, 52.
Tel. 0639967700.

Getting there
Bus 160, 628, 760 or
B Metro Circo
    Massimo stop.

Fee

Open Tuesday to
    Saturday 9 am-5 pm
    in winter; Tuesday
    to Saturday 9 am-
    7 pm in summer;
    Monday and
    holidays 9 am-2 pm.

his box, and would appear magically in his seat at the start of the show, for under these baths, as in many Roman ruins, there is a vast infrastructure of *cryptoporticii*, subterranean passages. In those caves enormous quantities of wood were

nel, but to cross ravines, rivers and valleys the aqueduct was lifted on lengthy aerial bridges, sometimes two or three tiers high, of stone, brick or concrete. On arrival in downtown Rome, the water was fed through pipes of lead, sometimes terracotta or wood, to public fountains and public buildings, notably baths. An appreciable part of Rome's budget was spent on the never-ending repairs needed to keep fresh, clean water streaming into the city.

At its height, ancient Rome was a city flowing with water, which effectively slaked the citizens' thirst, cleansed their bodies and carried away their sewage. During the barbarians' various sieges, more and more of this water was chopped off, until civilization, as the Romans knew it, literally dried up. That is one aqua theory of history; another is that daily consumption of water from lead pipes, as well as eating from lead-based vessels, over the years gave the Roman race lead poisoning until it could no longer stand up to its enemies.

The third theory is that the Romans' pampered way of life, exemplified by the overabundance of domestic water and baths, made them so soft and overconfident that the Goths and Visigoths could just blow them away. We subscribe to all three.

For almost a millennium Romans were again reduced to using the polluted Tiber. Health and cleanliness suffered. The Dark Millennium was also the dirty millennium. Finally, the Renaissance popes started rebuilding the aqueducts and Romans started washing and having sanitation again. Today, three ancient watercourses supply part of the fresh, clear water that runs plentifully through the city, thanks also to some modern aqueducts. The waters are never mixed, so you will still see Romans drawing water from one of the thousands of street fountains – indicating that either their taps have run dry at home or they prefer this particular aqua, perhaps for what they consider spiritual attributes.

imperial bath (see Pantheon) for which he constructed another watercourse, **Aqua Virgo** (see Trevi Fountain).

History AD
• **410** When the Goths first sacked Rome, the 11 aqueducts were supplying 1,212

public fountains and 937 public baths, including the 11 grand imperial thermae. Roman society was spoiled rotten and very vulnerable.
• **537** Aqueducts cut by Vitges the Goth. Roman general **Belisarius** had them filled in to prevent Goths

from creeping through the giant ducts.
• **1453** Finally, after 900 years, **Pope Nicholas V** had the great Florentine architect **Alberti** restore Aqua Virgo, calling it Acqua Vergine. Repairing the other acqueducts followed rapidly.

stocked for the fires to heat the water coming in continually through the aqueducts. Sadly, in the last few years these musical evenings have stopped. No longer can you see the famous super productions of *Aida* with elephants and dromedaries enlivening the stage. When the sopranos hit high C, archaeologists shuddered as they felt the walls, like glass, were being shattered by the sound waves. But summer music is returning to the baths, so stay tuned.

Description of the interior. Enter at room ❶. Next is room ❷, the *Palestra* (open exercise room for ball games and gymnastics); this and its circular niche had glass mosaics on the ceiling, and black and white marble mosaics on the floor. The door at the far corner leads to room ❸, the *Apodyterium* (changing room), and then room ❹, originally an ornate entrance. It leads directly to room ❺, the *Natatio* (open-air swimming pool; in meters: 1 deep, 50 long, 30 wide), situated on the building's center axis, against the outer wall. The pool could also be reached from room ❻, the *Frigidarium* (the cold hall), at the middle of the building, about as large as the pool, but with a vaulted roof 34 m (111½ ft.) high. Moving further along the center axis, next is room ❼, a smallish *Tepidarium* (tepid room), which leads to room ❽, the great round *Caldarium* (hot room), almost the size of the Pantheon, the inner surface of its soaring dome shiny with gilded brass. The other rooms on either side of the Caldarium provided dry heat, its floor-to-ceiling windows adding solar warmth; it was all shiny with glass mosaics. The building was perfectly symmetrical, rooms on the left of the center axis repeating those on the right.

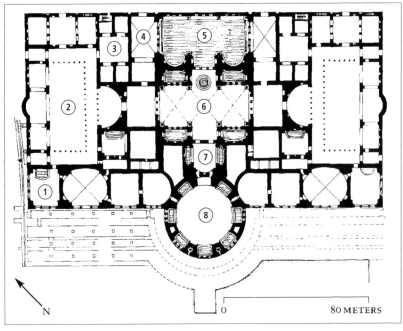

N   0   80 METERS

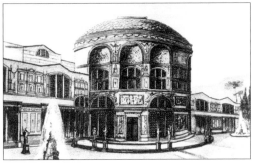

Terme di Diocleziano (AD 305). A century after Caracalla's gargantuan baths, Diocletian, who only once visited Rome, outshone his predecessor with the largest and most gorgeous *Terme* the world had ever seen. Seating 3,000 bathers, it could hold over twice that, vastly more than Caracalla's, and had the full panoply of changing rooms, gymnasiums, libraries, meeting rooms, theaters, concert halls, sculpture gardens, vast basins for hot, lukewarm and cold plunges, as well as mosaic floors and marble facades. Today's luxurious spas and health resorts are but pale copies of the Baths of Diocletian.

This complex was built on a gigantic manmade platform of 12 hectares (30 acres). The underground reservoirs covered much of the area between here and the Termini train station.

Fragments of the baths' core were incorporated into the Renaissance Church of Santa Maria degli Angeli. But half of the ancient bathing complex has fallen down. The curved colonnade of Piazza della Repubblica follows the outer wall of the former great exedra. A few blocks away in either direction are two graceful rotundas marking the corners of the gardens, one of which is now the Baroque (1600) Church of San Bernardo alle Terme (Via Torino off Largo Santa Susanna).

The baths were built of brick that was faced on the inside with marble and on the outside with white stucco, imitating blocks of white marble, like the Baths of Caracalla. The enormous central hall, 280 by 160 m (919 by 524 ft.), is an engineering wonder that was the model for the Basilica of Maxentius in the Roman Forum (AD 306-312).

When the Medici pope called in his chosen architect, Michelangelo, both of these aging Renaissance men wanted to honor the architectural wonders of the past by converting a monument of pagan hedonism into a religious masterpiece, Santa Maria degli Angeli (see page 175).

[E 10] *Piazza della Repubblica.*

History AD
- **298** Emperor Maximian, on his return from Africa, began constructing a vast bathing establishment, acting on behalf of his co-emperor, Diocletian, who was reigning in Asia Minor.
- **300-305** Diocletian is considered responsible for the forced labor of 10,000 Christians in the back-breaking task of construction. At about the time of completion, AD 305, both emperors had to abdicate.
- **538** The Goths cut off Rome's water by demolishing the aqueducts, rendering Rome's 900 baths increasingly useless.
- **1561** Pope Pius IV Medici commissioned the 86-year-old **Michelangelo** to build a church honoring the angels and the Christian martyrs who died in the baths' construction. The ruins had inspired Michelangelo's designs for St. Peter's.
- **1749** Luigi Vanvitelli reconstructed the basilica.

63

Pyramid of Cestius,

18-12 BC

Although a few pyramids once dotted the Roman landscape, two millennia later this is the only survivor.

[OFF MAP]
Piazzale Ostiense.

Getting there
Bus 23, 75, 716 or
B Metro Ostiense stop.

*Via Caio Cestio, 6.
Tel. 065641900.*

Open Monday-
Saturday 9 am-
4:30 pm.
Closed Sunday.

History BC
• **12 Gaius Cestius Epulo** died. The ancient Romans had conquered Egypt, and Epulo got a pyramid for a tomb, which was the height of fashion.

History AD
• **3c** It was incorporated into the Aurelian walls of Rome.
• **1663** Restored under **Pope Alexander VII** Chigi, who marked it "MDCLXIII."

Via di Monte Testaccio and Via Galvani.

Getting there
Bus 23, 75, 716 or
B Metro Ostiense stop.

Inscriptions identify Cestius as "son of Lucius, of the plebs." His tomb has frescoes inside, but is closed.
Ostia Gate (AD 271-275). Part of the Aurelian walls, this massive gate was enlarged in 401 by Emperor **Honorius**. When the doors clanged shut at night, nobody could enter or exit until dawn.
Via Ostiensis joined Rome with its seaport, Ostia.
Protestant cemetery. The *Acattolico*, or *Poets and Artists Cemetery.* In the 17c a visiting nobleman asked the pope to be buried in Rome. The pope gave this land; the foreigner died and was the first corpse. Keats, Shelley and his son William, and

Pyramid, Ostia Gate.

Goethe's son are here. Keats's epitaph: "Here lies one whose name was writ in water." Four thousand people repose here.
Monte Testaccio. This manmade mountain of broken amphoras – terracotta vessels to carry merchandise to the greedy capital of the world – was started around AD 144 and used for a century. A 1991 dig revealed that it was built in flat terraces, each terrace filled with **oil** amphoras, from either Spain or North Africa (Romans thought oil ones could only be used once). Donkeys brought four amphoras to the terrace at a time; they were broken on the spot and small pieces were used to fill gaps. This 46 m (50 yard) high hill has grottoes excavated later around the bottom, now filled with nightclubs and restaurants. (See pages 271, 302.)

TOMB OF EURYSACES (THE BAKER) IN PORTA MAGGIORE

Marcus Vergilius Eurysaces was a contract baker who made good. Very good. He lived in the last years of the first century BC, at the end of the republic, and having made a mint he chose to commemorate himself and his wife, Atistia, with a strange monumental tomb. (The equally pretentious pyramid-shaped tomb of Gaius Cestius was built just a few years later.) The Tomb of the Baker consists of a core of brick and cement faced with travertine. Its many tubes and holes seem to replicate the appearance of granaries and oven mouths, and the frieze around the top depicts scenes of baking: if you look closely at the north side you will recognize, from the right, men milling grain, kneading dough, and a domed oven. Other scenes include sorting grain, weighing and delivering bread. Eurysaces himself, wearing a toga, and Atistia, swathed in drapery, were depicted in high-relief statues, and inscriptions reveal that the tomb also contained the remains of their friend Ogolnius, a pastry cook.

Piazza Porta Maggiore.

Getting there
Bus 71, 105 or
Tram 5.

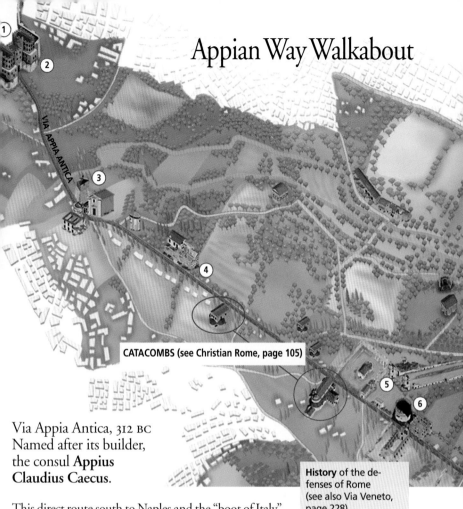

Appian Way Walkabout

CATACOMBS (see Christian Rome, page 105)

Via Appia Antica, 312 BC
Named after its builder,
the consul **Appius
Claudius Caecus**.

This direct route south to Naples and the "boot of Italy"
eventually reached Brindisi, 330 miles to the southeast.
From that port on the Adriatic, Rome's legions, after a
two-week march from the capital, sailed off to conquer
the eastern part of the empire.
Ancient Roman generals were
great engineers. Their fabulous
consular roads radiated out
from the *Urbs* like the spokes
of a wheel – hence "all roads lead to Rome." The roads
had to be wide enough for five Roman soldiers to march
abreast, or two carriages to pass each other.

Getting there
For transportation by
Archeobus, see page
278.

Via Appia *Regina Viarum* (Queen of Roads) was
surprisingly straight and superbly surfaced with massive
blocks of volcanic stone. You can still find patches of
these paving blocks that were originally flat, but now
have grooves worn into them by carriage wheels. Near
the GRA (the beltway that circles Rome) you feel you
have stepped back 2,000 years, although the ancient
tombs that grew like mushrooms on either side of the
road have fallen on hard times.

Most of the Appia Antica is a pedestrian park on
weekends, with police keeping out (most) unauthorized
vehicles. Some parts are permanently closed.

History of the defenses of Rome
(see also Via Veneto, page 228).

History AD
• **408** Alaric the Goth
marched his army to
the walls of Rome and
began a tight blockade. Soon the Senate
sent out ambassadors,
hoping to terrify him
with threats of what
military routs he
should expect from
Rome's invincible
armies. Alaric gave
his famous reply, "The
thicker the hay, the
more easily mowed,"
and demanded a ruinous ransom of gold,

silver, silk and 3,000 pounds of pepper. When the envoys asked what would be left for themselves and their fellow Romans, Alaric answered smoothly, "Your lives!" Rome paid.

• **409** Alaric again blockaded Rome and again the Senate compromised.

• **410** Arriving unexpectedly, Alaric and his Goths burst through the walls at the Salarian Gate and occupied Rome with minimum damage. This was the first **Sack of Rome** since 390 BC, when it had fallen to a surprise attack by the Celts of Gaul. That was at the end of Rome's beginning, but this was the beginning of Rome's end.

• **411 Emperor Honorius** built the fortified gate of Porta San Sebastiano to replace the old Porta Appia.

• **6c** General Belisarius strengthened it, adding towers for protection against attack.

❶ **House of Cardinal Bessarione.** Wonderful early-Renaissance (15c) country house where the cardinal, humanist and theologian, entertained the intelligensia of the day. The loggia and frescoes are well preserved.

[**OFF MAP**] *Via di Porta San Sebastiano, 8. Tel. 0677201599.*
Getting there - Bus 714.
Guided tours only
Open Saturday and Sunday 10-11 am and 12-1 pm.

❷ **Museum of the Walls of Rome.** Just inside the Porta San Sebastiano is this largely neglected museum where you can march along the Aurelian Walls, just the way the imperial legionnaires did when on guard duty (see also Porta Pinciana, page 228).

Via di Porta San Sebastiano, 18. Tel. 0670475284.
Fee - Open 9 am-7 pm. **Closed** Monday.

In the museum, models and pictures illustrate the millennial history of these beautiful walls and gates. The Porta San Sebastiano (named after the basilica and catacombs that were frequently the destination of pilgrims passing through) is an early medieval fortress four stories high, with battlements on the twin towers and a portcullis in the center that could be lowered to protect Rome against invaders. Just inside the gate is the early 3c monumental "Arch of Drusus," part of an aqueduct built by Emperor **Caracalla** for his eponymous **Baths**.

Arch of Drusus.

❸ Domine Quo Vadis Church (1637). Built on the site where Jesus Christ appeared to St. Peter, who was running away from Emperor Nero's persecution of Christians in Rome. Peter, amazed by this miraculous vision, asked, *Domine Quo Vadis?* (Lord, wither goest Thou?). Jesus answered, *I'm going to Rome to be crucified again*, and disappeared. Peter, understanding the message as a rebuke, returned to Rome and martyrdom. In the nearby Church of San Sebastiano you can see the paving stone with the supposed imprint that Christ's feet left when he shamed St. Peter.

Via Appia Antica. Tel. 065120441.
Open daily 7 am-12:30 pm and 3-7:30 pm.

❹ Columbarium. This is not a dovecote but an ancient repository for urns that contained the ashes of dead slaves who had been set free by their masters. Today it houses an attractive restaurant, **Hosteria Antica Roma**. The burial hall, with its myriad niches lining the walls, is open to the skies, and provides a beautiful and cozy atmosphere for savoring traditional Italian cuisine. The indoor tables are in the adjoining medieval building, where there is an 18c engraving by Giambattista Piranesi showing it hasn't changed much.

Via Appia Antica, 87. Tel. 065132888.
Closed Monday.

❺ Maxentius's Circus and Romulus's Tomb (309). Set in its magnificent brick-wall perimeter, the round tomb of Emperor Maxentius's beloved son Romulus is partially hidden by a medieval farmhouse. Next to it is Maxentius's private circus for chariot racing. The public entrance to this complex is 91 m (100 yards) further. Unfortunately nothing remains of **Maxentius's Villa**, considered extraordinary by his contemporaries. The Circus is nearly as big – 475 m (520 yards) long and

Our favorite
We can see here how the ancient Roman builders lightened the weight of the masonry canopy arching behind and above the spectators' seats by inserting hollow pots in the cement (similar to those at the top of the Pantheon dome).

Via Appia Antica, 153.

Getting there - Bus 118, 218.

Fee - Open Tuesday to Sunday
9 am-7 pm in winter; 9 am-5 pm in summer.
Closed Monday; December 25, January 1, May 1.

• **2c** This was the site of a villa owned by rich aristocrat Herod Atticus, tutor of two emperors: Marcus Aurelius and Lucius Verus.
• **306-312** Maxentius ruled over the Roman Empire at its height.
• **309** Maxentius's son Romulus drowned in the Tiber River.
• **312** Maxentius drowned in the Tiber during his defeat by Constantine the Great.

Via Appia Antica, 161. Tel. 067806832 or 067811895.

Getting there
Bus 218.

Fee
Open Monday to Friday 9 am-6 pm in summer, 9 am-4 pm in winter; Saturday, Sunday and holidays 9 am-1 pm.
Closed Monday.

84 m (92 yards) wide – as the Circus Maximus, and worth taking time to visit since far more of the grandstand is visible than at the Circus Maximus. Although most of the tiers of seats have collapsed, the supporting structure is plainly apparent. Here 18,000 spectators once cheered the charioteers – or at least their favorite, in hopes he would win the seven-lap race and they would go home rich. The long brick *spina* (center line) divided the race track, dominated by the **Obelisk of Diocletian**, now in Piazza Navona.

Romulus's Tomb has the same form as the Pantheon: a square porch in front of a drum, now hidden by the medieval farmhouse. Immense, it stood in a large square surrounded by the walls you now see on three sides – but they were lined with a covered walk or portico. Visit the tomb's underground areas.

❻ **Tomb of Cecilia Metella** (IC BC). Built for the daughter-in-law of Crassus, the richest man in Rome. Crassus's eldest son served Caesar as a general, inherited vast wealth and married Cecilia Metella, the daughter of Creticus, another consul. British poet Lord Byron in *Childe Harold* mused about her while describing this "Stern round tower of other days." It is the finest surviving Roman monument on the Appian Way. Note the almost perfect marble facing and the elegant frieze topped by garlands

and ox heads. The crenallations were added in the Middle Ages when it became a roadside fort which in 1302 Pope Boniface VIII Caetani gave to his family so that they could collect tolls on the heavy traffic between Rome and the independent state of Naples.

Small museum with a few interesting displays (see Museums, page 260).

Relief from the tomb of Ilario Fusco.

Off the map: Villa of the Quintilius Brothers (see Museums, page 259).

Story of Crassus BC
• **115-53** Marcus Licinius Crassus acquired his wealth from silver mines, real estate and slave trading. As a general he put down the Spartacus rebellion.
• **70** Elected consul with Pompey, he entertained the Roman populace at a banquet of 10,000 tables and distributed enough corn to last each family three months.
• **60** Befriended by Julius Caesar, with Pompey they formed the **First Triumvirate**, effectively ending democracy in Rome.
• **55** Again consul with Pompey, he accepted control of the province of Syria in expectation of inexhaustible wealth.
• **53** The Parthian leader captured Crassus and killed him by pouring molten gold down his throat. (Moral: live by the gold, die by the gold.)

69

We mustn't forget **Fosse Ardeatine** (Ardeatine Graves). Mausoleum and **Museum of the Resistance** on the spot where on March 24, 1944, Rome's Nazi occupiers executed 335 civilians in reprisal for a bomb planted by the Italian resistance movement that killed 32 German soldiers. The victims, unrelated to the bombers, included priests, officials, about 100 Jewish adults and a boy of 14. The Teutonic grimness of the mausoleum, with its walls like a thicket of thorns, seems appropriate to the deed.

Via Ardeatina, 174. Tel. 065136742.

Getting there
Bus 218.

Open daily 8:30 am-
    5 pm.

Villa Giulia

Etruscan Museum, 1553

A perfect setting for the Etruscans since they were as partial to partying as was the pope who built this palace. The most important collection of artifacts from the precursors of the Romans.

[**A 6**] *Piazzale di Villa Giulia, 9.* Tel. 063201951.

Getting there
Bus 52, 95, 490, 495 or Tram 19.

Fee - Open Tuesday to Sunday 8:30 am-7:30 pm.
Closed Monday.

Snack bar One can get refreshments and, thus reconstituted, continue.

On summer evenings there are occasional concerts in the garden.

The Etruscans were a mysterious people, whose language is still not widely understood (though Etruscologists hope to crack it with the discovery of a bronze tablet found near Cortona in 1994 and exhibited here). Their way of life is well documented in their tomb paintings and we have gleaned some information from what was buried with them. From 9c to 4c BC they lived in an area between Florence and Rome – but did they originally come from further north? Or elsewhere?

It was their engineering skills which drained the swamps in the Roman Forum. They perfected the arch by inserting the "keystone" in the center. They were also more sophisticated than the early Romans, who were so dazzled by the Etruscans that they chose them as their kings for 200 years.

Things went badly, however, in 509 BC when the Etruscan monarch Tarquinius Superbus (his own title for himself) killed a Roman senator by kicking him down the Curia steps. Rome rose against Superbus, who asked his Etruscan cousins to help. There ensued a war which the Romans won – King Superbus wasn't superb anymore, and was kicked out.

The museum also has a few artifacts from the Iron Age, some three to four millennia ago when the Etruscans' precursors, called Villanovans, lived in the Italian peninsula. By 10c BC they had domesticated cats, lived in huts with central fires, wore jewelry and shaved with iron razors.

The Etruscan Museum

Totally remodeled, it's glorious. The 16c ceiling frescoes in the ground-floor corridor have been cleaned, and chubby cherubs scamper over green trellises, probably getting into trouble.

The museum is organized by place and not time; individual artists are honored. Extraordinary, larger-than-life-size clay

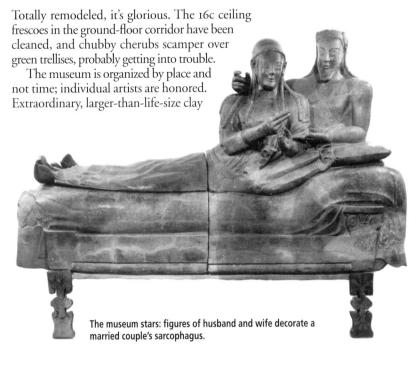

The museum stars: figures of husband and wife decorate a married couple's sarcophagus.

statues and some large jars all show that the Etruscans were probably the greatest artists in terracotta. How they fired these big pieces is a mystery even today.

GROUND FLOOR Bronze models of the round huts the Etruscans lived in during their early period were used as containers for ashes of the dead. These show how simply their startling culture began.

In their tombs all their favorite utensils were buried for use in their next life. Very soon you come upon the stars of the museum, even more sensational than the jewelry and the specialized instruments (doctors' scalpels, cooking tools, massaging utensils). These are the lifelike and almost life-size **Husband and Wife**. Made of terracotta once highly painted, they are reclining happily on their own coffin, as if they were at a dinner party. They seem so in love, so young and beautiful. Was it life they were celebrating, or death? Were women equal with men, as they seem to be in sculptures like this, or were they deemed inferior?

Further on, don't miss the sculptures of **Hercules** and **Apollo**. They too are wonderfully expressive, and have that peculiar Etruscan look about the eyes.

There is a plethora of black vases with terracotta figures (leaving out the bodies and painting in the black background first), and terracotta vases with "blackface" design (when the figures are painted black and the background is left clay colored). Most are from Greece and at that time were so highly regarded by the Etruscans that they learned to make copies. Then their own *Bucchero* pottery is extremely thin, black and shiny.

Sports were important in Etruria, and there are many objects celebrating this. The sheer plethora of wonderful artifacts can make one too lazy to visit the upper floor.

In the garden, apart from Pope Julius's nymphaeum, is a reconstructed Etruscan temple: the end tiles, that stand up like a frightened fringe, are a handsome device to finish a roof, and at the corners are the high priestesses, peering out disapprovingly.

History AD
• **1553** When **Pope Julius III** Ciocci del Monte (a compromise choice when the English cardinal Reginald Pole lost by one vote!) had Vignola and Ammannati build this splendid palace, it was bucolic and far from town. The existing house was small, but the pope, a Renaissance man, interested in art, architecture and classical statuary, consulted the great artists of his time, including Michelangelo, on how to transform it. His tastes were lavish, so it cost him a pretty packet. He would go by boat up the Tiber with friends to a little landing stage, take a carriage, and be at his country villa in time for lunch. The formal garden behind had a cool *nymphaeum* (grotto) for alfresco dining. There they would while away the afternoons and evenings in pleasant company. Sometimes very pleasant.

Attic Hydria
with black figures.

Etruscan
decorative
roof tile.

St. Peter's Basilica [PAGE 74]   Piazza San Pietro [PAGE 82]

Sistine Chapel and Vatican Museums [PAGE 85]

Castel Sant'Angelo [PAGE 91]

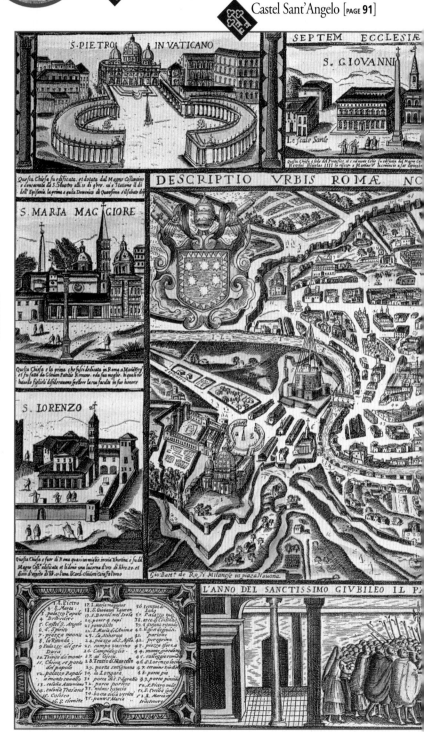

Getting there
- **Bus 64** - This line runs from the main train station (Stazione Termini) to St. Peter's. It is probably the most frequent and most crowded bus line in Rome as well as being the favorite bus line for pickpockets (and girl gropers). Beware!

- **Bus 62** takes you from Piazza Bologna through the center to the Vatican area. Again, watch your purse, wallet and companion!

- **Buses** 23, 32, 49, 81, 492 and 991 all have their last stop in Piazza del Risorgimento, a five-minute walk from St. Peter's.

- **Subway** Take the **A train** (follow the orange signs) and get off at the Ottaviano/San Pietro stop. Look for the dome!

History AD
- **64** The first pope, Peter the Fisherman, is said to have been crucified by order of Emperor Nero at the edge of the nearby Circus of Caligula and Nero (the obelisk that stood at the center of that ancient arena was moved to St. Peter's square in 1586).
- **315** A large basilica was built on this spot, where, according to tradition, Peter was buried, on orders of Constantine, first Roman emperor converted to Christianity.
- **15c** The building was falling apart.
- **1506** Pope Julius II della Rovere laid the cornerstone of a new church. As first of the chief architects he appointed **Bramante** (1444-1514), who spent the rest of his

The largest and most beautiful church in the world is built over St. Peter's tomb. It took 22 popes a century and a half to finish the curren basilica with the help of 10 of the world's great artists and architects. This is the stuff that leger are made of.

"It doesn't seem very large" is a typical reaction wh you get inside St. Peter's Basilica – even though it is t length of two football fields (about 236 m, or 200 yard The reason this church *feels* small is that all its proportio are harmonious. Michelangelo's plan gives unity to th church since each part was designed in exactly the same scale as the rest; he championed the concept of making the size of artworks larger than life; and since each part is in perfect proportion to the rest, the totality does not seem overwhelming (also note: his gigantic figures in the Sistine Chapel seem to be of normal size).

There are so many wonders both inside and outside St. Peter's that we will limit ourselves to the following highlights: ❶ **Portico** (1608, Carlo Maderno). This long, covered entrance was finished by Bernini, who designed the pavement, the relief sculpture of sheep over the central door, the statue of Constantine on the far right and the adjoining ❷ **Scala Regia**. You will be prevented from mounting this grandiose staircase by the Swiss Guards in their colorful uniforms (couture by Raphael). There are five doors into the basilica: the central bronze gate,

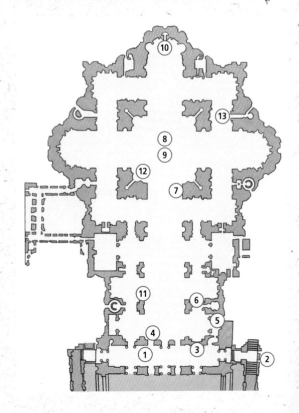

life tearing down the old basilica – earning the nickname *Mr. Destroyer* (church services continued without interruption). Bramante's dream was to superimpose a Pantheon-like cupola over a central-plan church (a Greek cross of equal segments), similar to his tiny but perfectly proportioned **Tempietto** (see San Pietro in Montorio, page 124), the other spot where rumor had Peter buried. Subsequent popes consulted

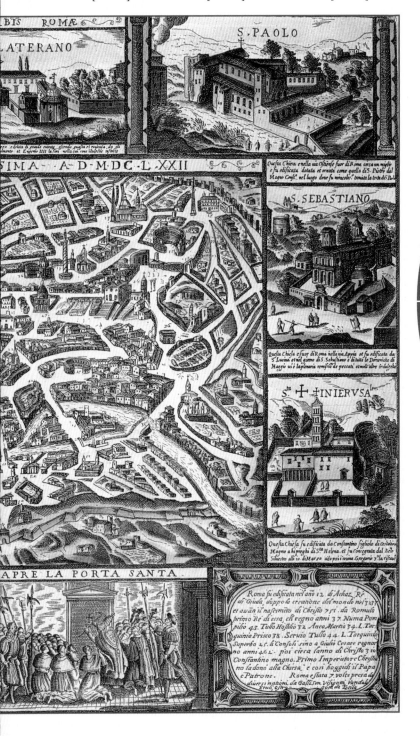

73

Jesus said to a fisherman,
"You are Peter and on this rock
I shall build my Church."

Gospel of Matthew

the adoption of Raphael's Latin cross plan, Michelangelo and Bramante's dream of a central-plan church was sacrificed – and so was any chance of your seeing the magnificent dome from the basilica steps.

• **1626** Pope Urban VIII Barberini (who allowed his old friend Galileo to be arrested and condemned for "vehemently suspected heresy" by the Inquisition) consecrated this basilica on the 1,300th anniversary of the first basilica.

• **1656** Bernini, who designed much of the dramatic interior decoration, was commissioned by the great literary pope Alexander VII Chigi to frame the basilica with the monumental Piazza San Pietro, **St. Peter's Square.**

sculpture. The curling columns, 29 m (66 ft.) tall (higher than the Tower of Pisa), are of bronze stolen from the crossbeams of the Pantheon's entrance. Pope Urban VIII Barberini, who permitted this vandalism, is aptly represented by swarms of bees, his heraldic sign.

Borromini collaborated in the heavenly sculptural top layer. Under it is the vast altar used only by the pope. In front and below is the **❾** *confessio*, a balustrade and stairs, groaning with golden lamps, leading down to the crypt and St. Peter's tomb.

❿ St. Peter's Throne (1665). Bernini's other imaginative masterpiece, at the very end of the apse, contains the Episcopal chair presumably used by the first pope. Its gilded cherubs seem to have flown over from the baldacchino, giving unity to the church's enormous interior. Light streaming through the sunburst, with the dove of the Holy Spirit, makes this late work of Bernini unforgettable.

⓫ Roof. Take an elevator up for a splendid view of Bernini's piazza.

Top of the dome. Then climb 537 stairs (not for the fainthearted) for a breathless but deathless view over the city and the world.

Our favorite
⓬ If you are in Rome long enough, do not miss the **Tomb of St. Peter**, the apostle's presumed burial place. For 16 centuries it lay undiscovered, buried deep under the massive foundations of the churches built on top of it. Thanks to recent excavations, you can stroll along the ancient Roman street and visit the unadorned tomb of the first pope.

Vatican Gardens and Mosaic Studio (guided tour only). **L'Arco della Campana** (Arch of the Bell) is Swiss guarded, and though their halberds have been changed to rifles, they are still in their colorful and elegant 16c costumes. Through the big square and under the first arch of the sacristy of St. Peter's you will see a black-and-white stone design on the ground, showing where the obelisk was before its removal to the center of St. Peter's Square. This was the center of the *spina* (see Circus Maximus, page 58) of the **Circus** of **Caligula and Nero**, where many Christians, some say including Peter, were martyred. Other unfortunates who died: prisoners of war, criminals, people who had fallen into disfavor with the emperor or his thugs.

Vatican Studio of Mosaics (Studio del Mosaico della Fabbrica di San Pietro in Vaticano) is the best-known surviving center for this art form; the studio repairs existing mosaics and creates new ones with religious or lay subjects. From 1935 until his death in 1985, the late Professor **Odoardo Anselmi** was the finest artist the Vatican had. Today, decorative themes can be ordered as well as religious ones.

Gardens. Magnificently laid out, but filling up with too many buildings. Stretching up the hill, they are peppered with gifts to popes: fountains, statues, etc. The loveliest part is the intimate **Casina** of **Pope Pio IV** (1558). Pirro Ligorio, with Sallustio Peruzzi's help, built twin pleasure pavillions, richly decorated in plaster with columns, niches, statues – and cherubs climbing all over the central fountain. An elliptical court lies between them, with seats running the length of its walls.

⓭ The earliest mosaic made of a new type of glass (see History AD sidebar) is just to the left in the right transept, representing "St. Peter on Lake Tiberius." It took six years for the mosaicist Cristofari to create this masterpiece from the original painting by Ricciolini.

History AD
• **1731** A new type of glass mosaic was invented with a non-reflective, oily finish. The Vatican bought this patent and stopped buying shiny glass mosaic pieces from Venice. Today, all the pictures in St. Peter's are really mosaics, except one (for many of the original paintings see Santa Maria degli Angeli, page 175).

81

The mosaic (top) is a faithful rendition of the painting (above right) by Francesco Trevisano (1700).

St. Peter's hours
7 am-6 pm in fall and winter, 7 am-7 pm in spring and summer, except that on Wednesday if there is a papal audience at 11 am, the basilica is closed until noon. The pope usually blesses the crowds at noon on Sundays from a window in his library overlooking St. Peter's Square.

Dress code
There are elegant gentlemen with badges at the entrance of the basilica monitoring the way you dress, so a word to the wise: NO SHORTS FOR MEN OR WOMEN. Shoulders must be covered, meaning no spaghetti-strap T-shirts or low-cut anything and no minis.

Vatican post office
The Italian mails are not known for efficiency, whereas the Vatican post is reputedly faster. It issues its own, prettier, stamps. There is a post office to the right of St. Peter's Square as you face the basilica, just behind the colonnade. Open longer hours than Italian post offices.

Piazza San Pietro

St. Peter's Square, 1656

Papal audiences
Held on Wednesday
when the pope is in
Rome. If you haven't
received tickets
through your local
parish before leaving
home, you can call
the Vatican and ask
for information.
Once you arrive in St.
Peter's Square you
must ask for the
Portone di Bronze,
which leads you to
**Prefettura della Casa
Pontificia,** which
issues the free tickets.
Open daily 9 am–
1 pm. You can ask
your hotel concierge
to get the tickets for
you. But don't wait
until the last
moment!

Harmonious elliptical square built to enhance and magnify the entrance of the mother of all churches. The deeply spiritual Pope **Alexander VII Chigi** commissioned this work as a symbol of Christianity gathering in the masses with open arms – a Counter-Reformation theme.

The piazza is **Bernini**'s finest sculpture, and his largest: 240 m (262 yards) wide, with 284 Doric columns, each 19 m (21 yards) high, set in four serried rows.

The approach to this piazza was once through crowded alleys and then – surprise! – this large space suddenly dazzled the eye. The sprawling medieval buildings were torn down in the 1930s to push through that spacious Via della Conciliazione (to commemorate the reconciliation between Italy and the Vatican). What a pity, no more surprise.

Here in 1981 Turkish extremist Mehmet Ali Agca shot and wounded Pope John Paul II, who was on a ride-about, saluting his flock in an open popemobile.

Apostolic Palace. The pope's residence is on the right, behind and above the colonnade. At noon Sunday he usually comes to his library window on the top floor and blesses the crowd in many languages.

Obelisk (AD 37). **Caligula** (the first mad emperor)

brought it from Egypt to decorate a circus for chariot races. Nero (also crazy) finished this circus maximus, the size of two football fields in length, situated on the left of St. Peter's Square. In 1586, when, under Pope Sixtus V's personal supervision, the architect Fontana moved the obelisk some 274 m (300 yards), it took five months! Quite a feat! To bring the obelisk safely to the center of the square took 900 men and 140 horses rolling it on wooden logs. But as they were pulling it upright a sailor realized that the ropes would snap if they didn't wet them immediately. So, defying a papal order that anyone who spoke during the operation would be killed (they even erected a gallows in the square), the man screamed "the ropes!" – and saved the day. The good pope saved his

Vatican phone numbers have always started with 69 (giving rise to the canard that Vat 69 Whiskey was named after its major consumer).

Switchboard 066982

Information
0669881662,
fax 0669881664.

Ufficio Scavi
(Tomb visits)
0669885318,
fax 0669885518.

Papal audience info
call switchboard.

Vatican Museums
0669883333,
fax 0669885061.

Our favorite
Stand on one of the two stone markers in the pavement near the fountains, where an optical illusion has the columns all lined up so that only the front ones are visible; the other three rows all disappear!

life. Legend has it the golden ball may contain the ashes of Julius Caesar and the iron cross maybe has wooden chips off the true cross.

Fountains (1613). Towering 14 m (46 ft.) high, Carlo **Maderno**'s is on the right hand, Carlo **Fontana**'s the left.

Did you know?
• St. Peter's (first built in AD 315) has been in use for almost 1,000 years and during its various transformations never missed a service, so it has been functioning continuously for 1,690 years!
• With only 43 hectares (107 acres), the Vatican (officially, "The Holy See") is the smallest and legendarily richest state in the world.
• No book could even begin to list the treasures it holds.

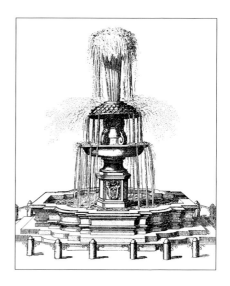

RECENT POPES

1922-39 Pius XI Ratti. When anti-Jewish atrocities became flagrant, he had an American priest, John Lafarge, draft a papal encyclical condemning Nazi cruelty, which at his death remained on his desk unsigned.
1939-58 Pius XII Pacelli was the highly controversial pontiff during World War II. He remained neutral, but is often accused of being lenient toward fascism. His proponents claim that his "impartiality" provided cover for the Church to help save many who were condemned under racial laws.
1958-63 John XXIII Roncalli, "The People's Pope" (child of peasant farmers) who made the Catholic Church more modern and more open to the young. He opened a dialogue with the world irrespective of creed.
1963-78 Paul VI Montini, likened to Hamlet by his predecessor.
1978 John Paul I Luciani, died mysteriously 33 days after being elected. The first pope of working-class origin, called "God's candidate" by the electing cardinals.
1978-2005 John Paul II Wojtyla. Polish, the first non-Italian pope since the Dutchman Hadrian VI (1522-23) and by far the most widely traveled. Highly conservative on religious and social matters. On May 13, 1981, he was shot and badly wounded during a public audience in St. Peter's Square by Mehmet Ali Agca, a Turkish extremist. No direct evidence of Soviet involvement was found, but many were convinced that the Kremlin wanted the pope dead for encouraging freedom in its Eastern bloc. He played a determinant role in the fall of the Iron Curtain and is considered by many to have been, along with John XXIII, one of the most influential popes of the 20c.
2005-present Benedict XVI Ratzinger. German, elected the 265th pope on April 19, 2005, following the death of John Paul II.

Women in Papal Rome *From the Middle Ages to 1870*
Women didn't have much scope for advancement unless born into rich families. They could be nuns, nurses or . . . prostitutes. If you were a foundling baby girl, abandoned by your mother at one of the "revolving windows" at a convent, the pope gave you a small dowry at your coming of age, in the hope that you could snag a husband.

The Papal States were like a kingdom, except that the "monarch" was from another province, often chosen when he was already elderly and infirm, so he reigned only briefly. Whereas in real monarchies women in royal families had certain power (they were chosen for political reasons, not for love), in Rome the priestly hierarchy had no official positions for women. However, women who had more ambition than morals could have influence with popes and with leading cardinals, slipping easily from one regime to another. Meanwhile, in some convents nuns could be co-opted to put on theatrical productions for cardinals!

The three things you MUST see in the Vatican Museums are the **Sistine Chapel**, the **Raphael Rooms** (gigantic frescoes in four large rooms), the **Laocoön** sculpture in the Belvedere Courtyard (to be visited in the opposite order). But as you swish down the long galleries on your way to the Sistine Chapel, don't miss the fabulous tapestries and the frescoes of city maps.

Sistine Chapel and Vatican Museums

[D 1] *Viale Vaticano.*
Tel. 0669884947.

Getting there
Bus 23, 49, 64, 81, 492, 907, 982, 991,
Tram 19 or
A Metro Cipro-Musei Vaticani stop.

Fee
Open Monday to Friday 8:45 am-3:20 pm; Saturday 8:45 am-12:20 pm.
Entry up to 1 hour before closing.
Closed Sunday except last Sunday of month.

The **Sistine Chapel** is at the end of the vast complex of galleries called, in the plural, **Musei Vaticani**, Vatican Museums (described on pages 88-90). The sole entrance to the museums, on Viale Vaticano, is a 15-minute walk around the Vatican wall from St. Peter's. St. Peters' Basilica is among the few Rome churches that do not close at noon; it remains open until 6 pm in summer and 7 pm in winter, so it is advisable to visit the museums first, then return to the church. In fact, your last stop in the museums is likely to be the Sistine Chapel, from which stairs descend directly to the entrance of St. Peter's. As soon as you go into the entrance of the museums, take an elevator up. You will have to select one of the color-coded itineraries since you cannot hope to see everything. As your "Musts" include the ❼ Raphael Rooms and the ❽ Sistine Chapel, which are half an hour's walk from the entrance, save your energy for them. In any case, give yourself a couple of hours for this tour, and there is plenty to keep you enthralled for a long morning. Two or three days would permit you to survey all 7 km (4½ miles) of galleries.

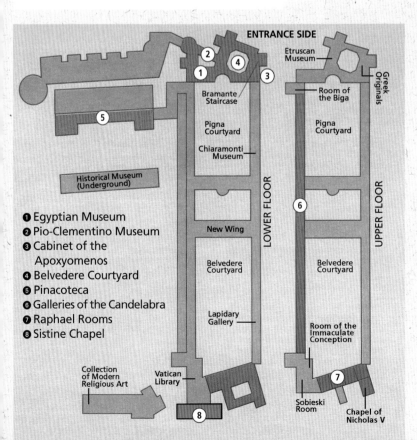

ENTRANCE SIDE

❶ Egyptian Museum
❷ Pio-Clementino Museum
❸ Cabinet of the Apoxyomenos
❹ Belvedere Courtyard
❺ Pinacoteca
❻ Galleries of the Candelabra
❼ Raphael Rooms
❽ Sistine Chapel

Etruscan Museum

Greek Originals

Bramante Staircase

Room of the Biga

Pigna Courtyard

Pigna Courtyard

Chiaramonti Museum

Historical Museum (Underground)

LOWER FLOOR

UPPER FLOOR

New Wing

Belvedere Courtyard

Belvedere Courtyard

Lapidary Gallery

Room of the Immaculate Conception

Collection of Modern Religious Art

Vatican Library

Sobieski Room

Chapel of Nicholas V

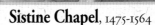

Sistine Chapel, 1475-1564

The masterpieces of Michelangelo on the ceiling and the altar wall have recently been returned to their original vibrant colors. Five centuries of mildew and candle black were swabbed away, square inch by square inch, by a team of world-class art restorers using non-intrusive materials such as distilled water and Q-tips. The colors may look too electric to you, but Michelangelo ground up his own coloring pigments and wanted this fresco to look as bright as you see it today.

The two large central panels on the ceiling represent ❶ *The Creation of Adam*, and ❷ *The Fall of Man*. In the first, a youthful naked figure languidly reaches out his finger to receive the gift of life from an elderly all-powerful God – a paradigm of Michelangelo's relationship with his patron, the dominating pope. In the second, Adam and Eve are expelled from the Garden of Eden. The other large panels are *The Creation of the Heavens* and *The Flood*, flanked by other events from the book of Genesis. Along with *The Mona Lisa* (at the Louvre in Paris) by his contemporary

History AD

• **1477-80** Pope Sixtus IV della Rovere had this chapel built with the exact dimensions attributed to Solomon's Temple in the Bible. Converting the Vatican from a medieval to a Renaissance palace, he commissioned great artists of the day, including Ghirlandaio, Perugino and Botticelli, to fresco the side walls. Raphael later created tapestries (now in the Pinacoteca) that are sometimes hung on these walls.

• **1508-12** Pope Julius II della Rovere, Sixtus's nephew and a gutsy giant of his day (waging war in full armor to win back papal domains other popes had lost), used military threats against Florence to force Michelangelo to come to Rome and paint the Sistine ceiling. It took only four years for Michelangelo, often working alone and famously lying on

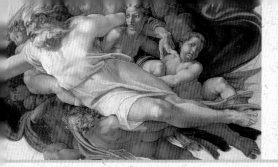

Leonardo da Vinci (1452-1519), this ceiling is considered the world's greatest visual masterpiece. Michelangelo was young and optimistic when he painted this glorious ceiling. He was breaking new ground in both fresco style and iconography; his love-hate relationship with the bullying pope was an inspiration for his enthusiasm.

The Last Judgment (below left, at end of room), painted on the altar wall 25 years after his self-confident ceiling, reflects Michelangelo's dark, melancholy reaction to contemporary developments. In his view the 1527 Sack of Rome at the hands of the Holy Roman Emperor was God's punishment for human sinfulness. He mirrored that pessimism in this surprising scene, in which an implacably judgmental Christ summons the dead from their tombs and assigns them to either heaven or an eternally horrific hell.

Michelangelo's exalted vision is overpowering, but the chapel has other fine frescoes by his Renaissance precursors Pinturicchio, Perugino, Ghirlandaio and Botticelli.

his back, to cover the ceiling with 300 bright-colored figures.
• **1534-41** Pope Clement VII Medici, 22 years later, got Michelangelo to fresco the end wall with *The Last Judgment*, to which the aging painter devoted seven years. It shows 250 figures, most of which were originally nude; panties were added later by prudish popes.
• **Now** the site of papal elections, when voting cardinals (those under 80) are strictly confined to quarters. Cardinals sit along the walls on canopied thrones while two votes are held daily, until a two-thirds vote leads to the senior cardinal's famous cry *Habemus Papam* (We have a pope!). Ballots are burned after each round, with the addition of wet straw producing black smoke after inconclusive votes and dry straw for white smoke announcing the election.

Michelangelo's vigorous characterizations inspired fellow artists through the centuries:
❸ *God* (mosaic) by Paola Frascarelli, 1999, Rome
❹ *Adam and Eva* by Marcantonio Raimondi, 1512
Left side *Delphic Sibyl* by
❺ Serafino Speranza, 1890
❻ Domenico Anderson
❼ Giovanni Bigatti, 1805

Laocoön story
• **1506 Michelangelo**, learning that these – then separated – figures had been discovered at Nero's *Domus Aurea*, rushed there and immediately realized he was looking at what Pliny in AD 1c had rated "above all painted and sculpted works." Michelangelo used the father as a model for such works as his wrathful **Moses**. Pope **Julius II** della Rovere, a godfather of the Renaissance, paid a fortune for the figures and had them reassembled here, in his private courtyard.
• **1515** The victorious king of France, **François I** (who later lured Leonardo to his court), demanded this sculpture as a spoil of war. But Pope **Leo X** Medici, unwilling to part with it, secretly had it copied. In fact, it did not leave until **Napoleon** brought it to Paris, from which it returned after his defeat in 1812.
• **1905** Archaeologist Ludwig Pollack found an arm he recognized as being a missing part of **Laocoön** in a Rome antique shop. This totally changed the sculpture that had for four centuries been incorrectly assembled. Don't miss the nearby photo of the previous reconstruction. You choose.

Vatican Museums (see plan, page 85).

There are recorded cassette guides in half a dozen languages that take you on different circuits, but we suggest the following:

❶ **Egyptian Museum** (Museo Gregoriano Egizio). In 1839 Pope Gregory XVI Cappellari founded this museum, including many of these sculptures of queens, pharaohs, gods and goddesses taken from Tivoli, where Hadrian had filled his villa grounds with statues reminding him of his lost love, **Antinous**. Most famous are the mummies, the black granite throne of **Rhamses II** (13c BC) and the gigantic statue of his mother, **Queen Tuia**. ❷ **Pio-Clementino Museum** (Graeco-Roman sculpture). ❸ **Cabinet of the Apoxyomenos**. Named after the fabulous sculpture of a tired athlete scraping his body with a *strigil* after exercising (AD 1c Roman copy of 4c BC original; see page 123). This suite housed **Leonardo da Vinci** from 1513 to 1516, as guest of Pope Leo X Medici, who expected the great artist/scientist to discover how to transform metal into gold. Leonardo, secretly pursuing his anatomical studies, was evicted by the irate pontiff for bringing prostitutes here – for gynecological drawings.

❹ **Belvedere Courtyard**. Two world masterpieces: **Laocoön** (1c BC, Greek – school of Rhodes). This father and two sons show the most realistic agony possible in their heroic battle against giant snakes. It marks the transition from "idealized" sculpture typical of Greek art to the "realistic" style associated with Roman art.

Apollo Belvedere. Roman copy of a Greek statue of 4c BC. An ideal of masculine beauty as well as realism in

rendering the drapery. Renaissance sculptors considered this the perfection for which they should strive.

❺ Pinacoteca. This superb art collection is largely neglected because of the fame of the Sistine Chapel and the Raphael Rooms. Here the first seven rooms present the first flowering of the Renaissance in different regions of Italy. **ROOM VIII** has world-class **Raphael** works, including the *Coronation of the Virgin* (1505), *The Madonna of Foligno* (1512) and his last work, *Transfiguration* (1520), as well as his tapestries for the Sistine Chapel. **ROOM IX** includes the only **Leonardo** painting in Rome, his unfinished *St. Jerome,* and also a fine *Pietà* by the Venetian master **Giovanni Bellini.**

❻ Galleries of the Candelabra, Tapestries and Maps. Go up the staircase to this long corridor lined with windows that was originally an open walkway between Vatican palaces. Between 2,000-year-old candlesticks you have a view down on the central **Pigna Courtyard** with its giant AD 1C pinecone. On the other side is a rare view of the **Vatican Gardens** with their soaring trees, peaceful pavilion and rolling lawns.

In the central gallery of this corridor are tapestries representing the life of Christ (1524-31, school of Raphael, made in Brussels). Note the elephants and camels, based on examples in the pope's private zoo. Be sure to see the *Supper in Emmaus*, with the mouthwatering wine cooler at lower right. Note how Christ's eyes follow you as you move past this scene.

Map Gallery. The maps frescoed on the walls of this gallery by Ignazio Danti (1580-83) show the pope's gorgeous properties as well as the city of Venice. Unforgettable.

❼ Raphael Rooms (1508-17). Raphael was 25 and unknown outside Umbria and Tuscany when Pope Julius II della Rovere commissioned him to decorate his new apartments. Julius represented the new humanism, a Renaissance man steeped in the classics who welcomed an expression of the Church's links to the past.

ROOM 1 Hall of Constantine (1517-24). Frescoes by Raphael's assistants, based on his sketches, show Emperor Constantine's awakening to Christianity and his victory over Maxentius at Ponte Milvio in 312.

Miniature Mosaics (*mosaici minuti*). The artist heats a few tesserae of glass of different colors. When they melt, the artist pulls them into a long thread (or *filato*) of glass. The mosaic pieces are cut with a file into infinitely small sections of this long thread and assembled cross-section side up into the special glue.

Marble Mosaics The best are the Asaroton mosaics (AD 2c) in the Gregorian **Profane Museum.** This type of mosaic, representing part of an unswept dining room floor, is a whimsical Greek genre the Romans copied.

Our favorite
"After the Meal," a trompe l'oeil mosaic of food scraps littering the floor. Don't miss the mouse!

Our favorite
Chapel of Nicholas V, through the door in the adjoining Room of the Chiaroscuri. This little gem has frescoes (1447-51) by **Fra Angelico** – the vanguard of Florence's Renaissance, imported to Rome 60 years before Raphael – with scenes of Saints Stephen and Lawrence. MUST SEE the trompe l'oeil brocade that the exuberant friar painted at the base of the walls.

ROOM 2 Room of Heliodorus (1508-14). Frescoes by Raphael placing the pope in a historical potpourri, emphasizing spiritual continuity, not chronology.

The Miracle of Bolsena. Consecrated bread, its blood oozing onto an altar cloth, appeared to a pilgrim-priest to resolve his doubts, here witnessed by Pope Julius II.

Attila the Hun, on a black horse, being chased from Rome by Pope Leo I assisted by Saints Peter and Paul. Note the Colosseum and aqueduct. Of course, Attila, though called "the scourge of God," never got near Rome; but Raphael is dealing with philosophical ideas, not historical fact. The key figure of Leo I was originally a portrait of Julius II. After that pontiff's death Raphael painted in his successor, Leo X Medici – but left an earlier likeness of this Medici prelate (with the red hat in the left foreground), making this a double portrait of his new patron.

The Expulsion of Heliodorus. Julius II on a portable throne dominates this dramatic expulsion of the heathen from Jerusalem's Temple.

The Liberation of St. Peter (surrounding a door). Sensational effects of lighting, with the heavenly glow of the angel on the right reflected in the armor of the guard (left); Peter sleeps soundly in his black-grated cage.

ROOM 3 Room of the Signature (1508-11). Truth, Beauty and Goodness are portrayed as guiding principles that unify Christianity and paganism.

The School of Athens. This marvel of Renaissance painting shows a philosophical colloquy starring Plato, who gestures to the heavens, and Aristotle, who points down to earth, as well as Heraclitus, philosopher of fire. Plato has the features of Leonardo, Heraclitus is Michelangelo, and Raphael is on the far right in a cameo appearance.

Dispute over the Holy Sacrament. The apotheosis of Christianity, with martyrs and saints worshipping the host. The first fresco painted in Rome by Raphael.

ROOM 4 Room of the Fire (1514-17). The only fresco Raphael did in this room is *Fire in the Borgo*, showing Pope Leo IV extinguishing the devastating fire of AD 847 by making the sign of the cross. Raphael demonstrates his liberation from convention, highlighting minor personages.

Castel Sant'Angelo is a microcosm of Rome: layer upon layer, building upon building – a palimpsest. This most magnificent of all the Roman imperial tombs became a fortress in the Middle Ages and a papal pleasure dome in the Renaissance. Perhaps the most universal monument in Rome.

Castel Sant'Angelo

[D/E 4]
Lungotevere Castello, 50.
Tel. 066819111.

Getting there
Bus 23, 46, 64, 87, 280, 492, 926.

KIDS

Fee
Open 9 am-7 pm daily except Monday.
Entry up to 1 hour before closing.
Sandwich bar, where you can sit inside or out and have a coffee, tea or beer.

The original AD 2c tomb was six stories high, like a gargantuan birthday cake, sheathed in marble and topped by a manmade hill dotted with cypresses and sculptures – the largest of which was Emperor Hadrian in a chariot driving four prancing horses.

Because of the unplanned way it evolved, you will have difficulty finding your way around the castle. At the ticket booth, take a good look in the hall nearby at the marvelous scale model of Emperor Hadrian's grandiose 2c tomb. Another model shows the building as a medieval fort.

❶ The entrance is down a flight of stairs. Once inside, you wind up through the center of the building, on ❷ a giant corkscrew ramp of Roman bricks, leading to the ❸ tombs of the emperors. Their ashes were kept in this large vaulted area. Don't miss the wooden planks at the beginning and end of the causeway that passes over this room: they were devised as drawbridges that could be removed in the event of an attack – making it impossible for the enemy to get to the upper part of the fort. You emerge into the sunlight at the ❹ Courtyard of the Cannonballs. On the wall are numerous plaques engraved with the number of balls and their size, so that under siege the soldiers could quickly bring the right size to the right cannon. Visit the exhibit of medieval and Renaissance weapons in the low halls on your right.

❺ On your left are Pope Paul III's apartments, usually housing a temporary exhibit.

Various popes occupied the elegantly appointed apartments on the next two floors over a period spanning the Middle Ages and the Renaissance. In the great hall

History AD
• **135** Emperor **Hadrian** began this family vault, unfinished when he died three years later.
• **139** Emperor Antoninus Pius completed it and for almost three quarters of a century, from Hadrian to Septimius Severus (below),

91

it was the repository for emperors' ashes.

• **590** During a procession to stop the plague, **Pope Gregory the Great** saw a shimmering vision of Archangel Michael above the mausoleum sheathing his sword. The pope vowed to put the angel's effigy atop the castle if God stopped the plague. The plague ceased and Gregory kept his word.

• **Middle Ages** For a thousand years the popes used this structure as Rome's citadel and dungeon in their continuous struggle against feudal barons and Holy Roman emperors. They raised defensive fortifications and added watchtowers named after the Evangelists at the corners.

• **Renaissance** Successive popes embellished the castle with a chapel by Michelangelo, loggias by **Bramante** and **Antonello da Sangallo**, paintings from the school of **Raphael**, a theater-court and a papal hot tub. The richest and most sensually explicit of these rooms were frescoed for **Pope Alexander VI Borgia**, who was no prude. He was, however, responsible for the 1494 Treaty of Tordesillas, which divided the undiscovered world between Spain and Portugal at a line of longitude, resulting in the separation of Portuguese Brazil from the rest of Spanish South America.

• **1752** On top, the late-Baroque sculpture of St. Michael the Archangel by Flemish artist Peter Verschaffelt replaced the Renaissance marble angel, now in the Courtyard of the Cannonballs.

❻ Sala Paolina, the trompe l'oeil painting of a cavalier in the doorway is marvelous. Go through to the right to see the small audience chamber, and in the last room in this area the papal bedroom; rather sparse, but imagine the walls groaning with tapestries. Then proceed along the narrow highly frescoed corridor to the next rooms, replete with frescoes on the ceiling. Go next to view the ❼ papal treasure chamber, with an inordinately large metal trunk; imagine it filled with gold, precious jewels and sculpted silver spilling out over the top.

Now proceed up the stairs to see ❽ the view over all of Rome from the very top deck, next to the sculpted Archangel Michael – unforgettable. It is the setting for the finale of Puccini's opera *Tosca*, when the heroine leaps to her death from the parapet.

From the castle's rear bastion to the Vatican runs **Il Passetto** (850, the Leonine wall passageway). Originally part of a defensive wall, a corridor near the top of this

Our favorite
Pope Clement VII installed a heated bathtub in a tiny upper room exquisitely decorated by followers of Raphael but for which you will have to ask directions because it is agonizingly difficult to find. This bath signaled the reintroduction of personal cleanliness, which had gone out of style since the great Roman baths of Caracalla and Diocletian were shut down in the 6c when barbarians cut off the aqueducts.

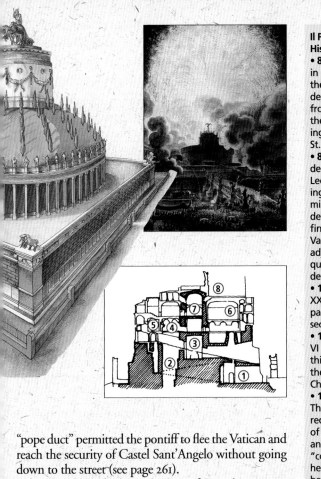

Il Passetto
History AD

• **846** Saracens landed in Ostia, stormed up the Tiber and plundered the treasure from basilicas outside the city walls, including unprotected St. Peter's.

• **852** Pope St. Leo IV dedicated the new Leonine city, protecting it with 3 km (2 miles) of walls and 46 defensive turrets, finally putting the Vatican and the adjacent Borgo quarter within Rome's defensive system.

• **1410** Antipope John XXIII added a covered passage through this section of the wall.

• **1494** Pope Alexander VI Borgia escaped via this passage during the invasion by King Charles VIII of France.

• **1500** Jubilee Year. The Borgia pope rededicated this part of the Leonine wall and completed his "corridor" so that he could move unseen between his apartments in the Vatican and those he built in Castel Sant'Angelo.

• **1527 The Sack of Rome** Pope Clement VII Medici, illegitimate and insecure, changed sides so many times in the wars between King François I of France and Holy Roman Emperor Charles V that the latter finally unleashed his troops against the pope. Hapless Clement hitched up his cassock and dashed the length of this overhead "Corridor of Alexander VI" to the safety of Castel Sant'Angelo. Besieged, he surrendered and crowned Charles as emperor three years later.

• **1999** After renovations, finally open to the public and then quickly closed.

"pope duct" permitted the pontiff to flee the Vatican and reach the security of Castel Sant'Angelo without going down to the street (see page 261).

Ponte Sant'Angelo (AD 133). One of Rome's most ancient bridges and certainly the most beautiful. Its Baroque statuary is from Bernini's studio, but the three central spans are attributed to Emperor **Hadrian**.

Ponte Sant'Angelo – History AD

• **134** Hadrian built a stone bridge called Pons Aelius (the emperor's family name) leading from the main part of Rome over the river to his mausoleum.

• **1450** Pope Nicholas V, toward the end of this Holy Year, exhibited St. Veronica's veil at the Vatican. Thousands of pilgrims were returning to the city center on what was then the only bridge in this area, when horses took fright at the far end of the bridge. Though passage was blocked, the faithful continued to crowd onto the bridge, and 170 people died.

• **1530** Pope Clement VII Medici, for the visit of Emperor Charles V, adorned the bridge with statues of Saints Peter and Paul by Laurenzetto and Paolo Romano.

• **1599** Beatrice Cenci, only 25 years old, and her stepmother were beheaded on the far side of the bridge. Her older brother was drawn and quartered, the younger only imprisoned for a year (see page 48).

• **1667** Pope Clement IX commissioned **Bernini** to sculpt eight angels carrying the symbols of Christ's Passion. They were executed by the Baroque master's assistants.

• **1892** During the construction of the riverside embankments, the bridge received its present form.

ARCHITECTURE
Early Christian, Romanesque and Gothic

Rome gave its name to what architecture historians call "Romanesque" – derived from ancient Roman vaults and rounded arches – but the city has few pure examples of that specific style. As for Gothic – pointed arches, groin vaults and stained-glass windows – there is only one such church in Rome. From the 11c to the 14c those fancy styles flourished throughout the north and also to the south, but Rome was then too poor and too politically unstable to rival the stone marvels of Italy's great city-states. On the other hand, Rome had seen a flurry of fine churches in the 4c and 5c, and some in the 8c and 9c, which represent the cream of early Christian architecture. Emperor Constantine launched that movement, legalizing Christianity in 313 and providing vast edifices for Romans to worship Christ, just outside the imperial city (*fuori le mura*). They took the name *basilica* from the great public halls and meeting places that the emperor and his predecessors had built to glorify Rome's center. And these churches imitated the grandiose but simple basilica form: a long central area under a high roof **(nave)**, with at one end a semicircular bay **(apse)**, while at the other end the entrance gates were covered with a porch **(portico)**. The larger churches also had one or two **aisles** paralleling the nave on either side of it and a **transept** running crosswise between the nave and the apse to form a cross. The other form Rome's early churches followed was the imperial mausoleum, resulting in round churches and baptisteries. Fine churches were built in the 12c and 13c during a revival of building in Rome, but they tended to follow the basilica model rather than the Lombard or Romanesque style as it was practiced elsewhere.

Basilicas (The Vatican maintains a list of churches worldwide with this title of honor.)
San Giovanni in Laterano, cathedral for Rome's bishop; San Pietro, over the tomb
    of St. Peter; San Paolo fuori le Mura, over the place of Paul's martyrdom
    (all three started by **Constantine**, 4c).
Santa Maria Maggiore, first Christian basilica erected inside Rome's walls
    (5c, well preserved). These four, plus San Lorenzo fuori le Mura, are called
    "Patriarchal basilicas."
Santa Sabina all'Aventino, authentic early Christian
    church, with Byzantine touches (5c).
Sant'Agnese fuori le Mura: best preserved of early
    Christian basilicas (7c).

Round churches
Mausoleo di Santa Costanza (built by Constantine, 4c).
Santo Stefano Rotondo (5c).
San Teodoro (4c, rebuilt 6c).
Baptistery of San Giovanni in Laterano (5c).

Romanesque
Cloister of San Lorenzo fuori le Mura (12c).
Santa Maria in Aracoeli (13c).
Gallery (right) of Santi Giovanni e Paolo (12-13c).

Gothic
Santa Maria Sopra Minerva (interior, 13c).

Basilica di San Giovanni in Laterano

St. John Lateran is the Cathedral of Rome and officially "Mother and Head of all the churches in the city and the world." For Catholics, this, after St. Peter's, is the second most important MUST-VISIT basilica. Founded by Emperor Constantine, it was the residence of popes for over 1,000 years. Only the 4c-5c baptistery and 12c cloister give hints of its pre-Baroque beauty.

Facade (1691-1736, A. Galilei). The 15 Baroque statues of Christ and the saints above the main entrance are larger than life, beacons visible from far away, showing the might and strength of the Church. Contemporary wags said they would crush the facade and church.

The central bronze doors (1c BC), faded green beauties with stars, are the originals from the ancient Senate building (Curia) in the Roman Forum.

The little doors on the far right with a bronze cross closing them are only opened in Holy Years and Jubilees.

Portico. Colossal marble statue of Constantine (AD 4c) used to adorn the Imperial Baths on the Quirinal Hill.

Nave. **Gigantic statues of the apostles** (17c). Followers of Bernini. They dwarf the rest of the decoration. First pillar on right: fragments of Giotto's fresco depicting Boniface VIII heralding the first Jubilee Year: 1300.

Ceiling. Original design by students of Michelangelo. Ornate and colorful, it shows the coat of arms of Pius IV (1562).

Floor. Superb 13c mosaic floor originally laid by Vassalletto and his son, cleaned and relaid in the 16c.

[H/I 11] *Piazza di Porta San Giovanni in Laterano. Tel. 0669886433.*

Getting there
Bus 16, 81, 85, 87, 186, 650, 850 or
A Metro San Giovanni stop.

Church and cloister **open** daily 7 am-7 pm.
Museum **open** Monday to Friday 9 am-1 pm and 3-5 pm.

History AD
• **Circa 60** Nero expropriated this vast property from the Laterani family.
• **161** Emperor Marcus Aurelius built a palace on the other side of the square, under part of the present-day hospital.
• **Circa 226** Emperor Septimius Severus returned the land to the Laterani.
• **305-312** Emperor Maxentius's elite bodyguards were housed here, under the present basilica.
• **312 Constantine**, one of the two emperors of a then-divided

empire, married to Fausta, sister of co-emperor Maxentius, destroyed his armies and killed him.
• **313** Fausta turned over her house on this property to Pope Melchiades.

- **324** Constantine ordered construction of the first Christian basilica here, dedicated to the Holy Savior. About this time he had Fausta killed.
- **5c** Barbarian invasions damaged the Lateran complex.
- **896** An earthquake damaged the buildings. Maybe God was punishing Pope Stephen VI for the macabre trial in which he accused his predecessor's corpse, dressed in vestments, of making a treaty with the barbarian king. Found guilty, the corpse was thrown in the Tiber. Pope Stephen was soon imprisoned and strangled. Bloody deeds indeed.
- **12c, 13c** and **16c** Councils of Lateran were held – high churchmen made important ecclesiastical decisions (even excommunicating kings).
- **1309-77** Papacy sequestered in Avignon. When **Pope Urban V** returned the seat of the papacy to Rome he found the Lateran so scarred by the 1360 fire that he switched the official residence to the Vatican and ordered the rebuilding of this basilica.
- **1929** The last Council of Lateran defined the Church's territorial possessions, largely confined to Vatican City, which became the **Holy See**. Mussolini signed the **Lateran Treaty** with the Church, ending a state of war that had existed since the reunification of Italy (for half a century the popes had lived as self-imposed prisoners of the Vatican).

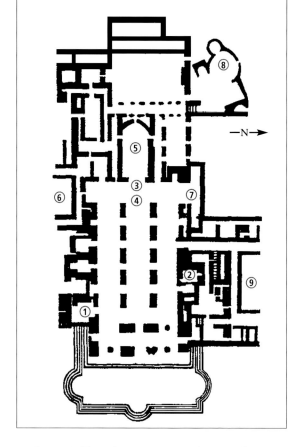

❶ **Corsini Chapel**. Ornate wrought-iron doors are usually closed, but inside is a red porphyry tomb of Clement XII, from the Pantheon.

❷ **Massimo Chapel**. A reproduction of Pope John Paul II's favorite painting, the black Virgin of Czestochowa, was installed the year of his election, 1978.

❸ **Baldacchino altar** (14c). The pope is the only prelate who can officiate at this altar. Visible on its top level are reliquaries of two superb sculpted heads. Inside them are the skulls of St. Peter and St. Paul. Under the altar table are bits of wooden planks: fragments of the first altar of the popes (4c).

❹ **Confessio** (9c). Looking down an open crypt one sees the tomb of Pope Martin V (1417-31). Donatello's brother carved the statue about 1440.

❺ **Apse**. This is part of Constantine's Basilica. The papal throne looks rather small and insignificant, with gold mosaics glittering behind it, and on the wall high above are mosaics from the 5c and 13c (Jacopo Torriti), reworked in the 18c.

❻ **Cloister** (13c) and **Museum**. Vassalletto and his son were busy here too, but so many of the miniature mosaics which should have given sparkle and luster to the curly columns have been picked out and destroyed (armies of soldiers or tourists?) that the columns now are just a lesson in how they were made, rather than a pleasure for the eyes. Not to be missed for the salacious history buff, the supposed *Chaise Percée* or **Sedia Stercoidale**, from beneath which (according to the custodian) it was determined whether the aspirant pope was really a man. We doubt that this tiny hole was used for such purposes (see Pope Joan, page 112).

❼ **Porch on north** (Piazza di San Giovanni). A giant Henri IV of France, in bronze, dressed in Roman gear and swashing around with a sword. He had presented many gifts to the Lateran.

❽ **Baptistery** (4c). Built by **Constantine**, this octagonal hall is where *everybody* was baptized in the 4c and served as the model for all baptistery buildings. Rebuilt in the 5c by Pope Sixtus III, who added the beautiful salami (porphyry) columns around the total-immersion baptismal font. Mosaics of 5c and 7c. Frescoes were added by Pope Urban VIII in 1637. The chapels of St. John the Baptist and St. John the Evangelist were built by Pope Hillary (461-468). The ancient door is a mix of silver, gold and bronze. The Chapel of St. Venantius is 7c, and that of Saints Rufina and Secunda is 12c, but here the apse has 5c mosaics.

❾ **Lateran Palace** (1586). Domenico Fontana built a magnificent home for Pope Sixtus V, now used as offices for Rome's City Vicariate. **Obelisk** in Piazza San Giovanni in Laterano, 15c BC, Egyptian, tallest and oldest in Rome. **Scala Santa** (1585-90). **Sixtus V** tore down the remnants of the enormous old palace, but kept the stairs – ostensibly from Pontius Pilate's palace in Jerusalem. The devout climb up on their knees since Christ is said to have walked up these steps to face judgment. If you wish to walk, use the sides. The little chapel at the top, *Sancta Sanctorum* (Holy of Holies), is the pope's chapel, always closed – yet one can get a glimpse of the lovely Cosmatesque floors through a massive grill. Precious relics from Jerusalem are protected by the Passionist fathers.

Triclinium of Leo III. Next to the Scala Santa. The Roman-style dining room of the medieval pope has been reconstructed. The mosaic, extensively repaired in the 18c, emphasizes the importance of this great builder-pope (795-816) who maintained optimum relations with the Holy Roman Empire – in this case its creator, Charlemagne.

Obelisk
History BC
• **15c** This pink granite obelisk (below) stood in front of a temple in Thebes, southern Egypt.
History AD
• **357** The Romans stole it and placed it on the central *spina* of Circus Maximus.
• **1588** Discovered buried and broken; erected here by Pope Sixtus V's architect Domenico Fontana.

Piazza di San Giovanni in Laterano, 14. Tel. 067726641.

Open 6:30am-noon and 3:30-6:30 pm.

Basilica di Santa Maria Maggiore

[F 11] *Via Liberiana, 27.*
Tel. 06483195.

Getting there
Bus 16, 70, 71,
75, 714 or
B Metro Cavour stop or
A Metro Vittorio
Emanuele stop.

Open 7 am-6:45 pm
(Loggia mosaics
7 am-5:45 pm).

History AD
• **352** Pope Liberius's
dream of a snowstorm
in August came true;
he fulfilled his vow
to build this church at
that very place he had
dreamt of and called it
Santa Maria ad Nives
(*nives* = snow).
• **432 New church** built
by **Pope Sixtus III**.
• **14c** Campanile
added.
• **1740** Baroque facade
by Ferdinando Fuga,
with upper loggia
over a portico.

St. Mary Major is Rome's third most important church and one of the seven basilicas that pilgrims MUST VISIT.

Marble column (AD 4c), located in Piazza Santa Maria Maggiore (from the Basilica of Maxentius/Constantine in the Roman Forum), was topped with Virgin and Child in 1613.

Facade loggia. The **13c mosaics** on the upper story are by painter/mosaicist Filippo Rusuti (his works are in many churches). They were covered in the 18c (more's the pity) by Fuga, with grandiose winged statues and Roman portico. This church's real treats are inside.

Interior. Many of the earliest Christian mosaics. The **nave**, above the arches, is redolent with stories from the Old Testament.

❶ **Chancel arch** (behind baldacchino altar). These **5c mosaics** are divided into four horizontal bands: at the top is the Virgin as a Byzantine queen, then court scenes with baby Jesus on a jewel-studded throne and two cities, Bethlehem and Jerusalem. This mosaic style is *Byzantine* (dark lines outline the figures, like those in Ravenna).

❷ **Apse vault**. More **5c mosaics** of birds in the trees, cunningly woven together by Jacopo Torriti (1295) with his own glowing work, the Crowning of the Virgin surrounded by angels.

Floors (12c). **Cosmatesque** style, ancient deep red salami porphyry disks, with green serpentine marble. Over-restored, by Fuga – and he struck again with his baldacchino over the altar (it hides part of the superb 5c mosaics).

The back of the church has a grand staircase (leading nowhere) and two domes built in 1673.

Ceiling. Started under Pope Callisto III Borja (1455-58), uncle of Pope Alexander VI Borgia, who started his nephew's rise to power by appointing him cardinal-archbishop of Valencia when he was only 25. Five popes later, **Alexander VI** (1492-1503) finished the coffered gilded ceiling with the first Peruvian gold to come from the new continent, a gift from the Spanish monarchs Ferdinando and Isabella – who had chased the Moors from Spain and set Columbus up for his discovery of the New World.

❸ **Tomb** of Cardinal Rodriguez (13c; right aisle facing altar). Typically Gothic with angels guarding the figure in an arched ensemble.

❹ **Cappella Sistina** (right cupola facing altar). The great Vatican administrator and bandit exterminator, **Pope Sixtus V Peretti** (1585-90), ardent redecorator of old buildings and constructor of new, asked Domenico Fontana to design this chapel as his tomb. Set in one of the twin cupolas, it is a miniature church, with frescoed ceiling, and gold and marble everywhere.

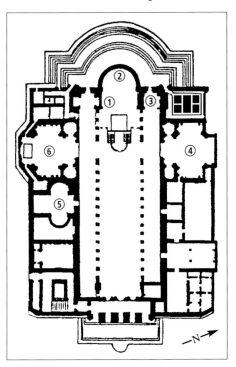

❺ **Cappella Sforza (1539-1602)** (left aisle facing altar). Giacomo della Porta from Michelangelo's drawings.

❻ **Cappella Paolina (1611)** (left cupola facing altar). Also called the Borghese Chapel. Identical in shape to its twin in the other cupola: 17c Baroque was creeping in, and ornate decoration was getting out of hand.

In Piazza dell'Esquilino is an ancient Egyptian obelisk placed by Pope Sixtus V in AD 1587.

Basilica di San Paolo fuori le Mura

Via Ostiense, 186.
Tel. 065410341.

Getting there
Bus 23, 170, 223, 673 or
B Metro San Paolo stop.

Open daily
7:30 am–6:30 pm.

St. Paul Outside the Walls, another of the seven basilicas that pilgrims MUST VISIT in a Holy Year, was inaugurated by **Emperor Constantine** to mark the legendary site of St. Paul's beheading and burial. That venerable 4c basilica went up in flames in 1823, after which it was rebuilt with even more magnificence. The forest of columns inside, though a bit cold, is impressive.

What survived the fire:
❶ **Chancel arch** (5c) with mosaic of Christ, two angels and 24 elders. The inscription (recomposed after the fire) is to Galla Placidia, sister of Emperor Honorius (AD 395); she lavishly ruled the declining Western Empire from Ravenna, but died in Rome.

❷ **Paschal candlestick** (12c) by Nicolò di Angelo and Pietro Vassalletto. Marble sculpture, twice the height of a man, with gorgeous snarling monsters at the base.

❸ **Gothic baldacchino canopy** (1286) by Arnolfo di Cambio. Beneath the angels and fine carving is the main altar. Below the altar is a plaque saying St. Paul is buried here.

**Our favorite
Cloister** (13c). This rose garden surrounded by magnificent arcades is a place to stop and linger, with its myriad columns in all shapes and sizes. Protecting the ancient tombs, moved here after the 1823 fire, are gorgeous spiral columns encrusted with mosaics and sprinkled with gold.

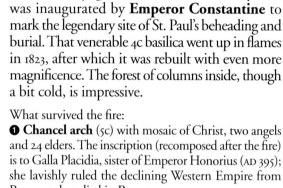

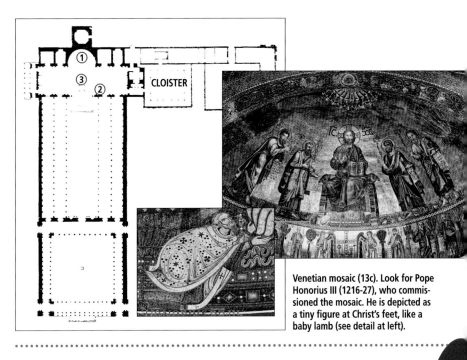

Venetian mosaic (13c). Look for Pope Honorius III (1216-27), who commissioned the mosaic. He is depicted as a tiny figure at Christ's feet, like a baby lamb (see detail at left).

Basilica di San Lorenzo fuori le Mura

One of the seven MUST-VISIT pilgrimage churches, St. Lawrence Outside the Walls, also called San Lorenzo in Verano, referring to the huge **Campo Verano** cemetery stretching behind it.

Piazzale del Verano, 3. Tel. 06491511.

Getting there
Bus 71, 204, 492.

The burial place of St. Lawrence, whose body was taken by Matron (and later Saint) Cyriaca from his place of martyrdom and buried in tufa rock under her field. This became the small catacomb you can still visit.

History AD

- **258** Lawrence, deacon of Pope Sixtus III, was martyred by being roasted on a gridiron during the persecution by Emperor **Valerian**.
- **330** Emperor **Constantine** built a small church over St. Lawrence's tomb on Via Tiburtina.
- **432-440** Pope Sixtus III built the Church of the Madonna next door.
- **845** After being pillaged by the Saracens a fort was added to the church and monastery.
- **1216** Pope Honorius III joined the two churches, demolishing their apses.
- **1943** The only Rome church to suffer war damage, in a direct hit by Allied aircraft. Restoration work started immediately, with a view to preserving its 13c appearance.

Our favorite
The 12c Cosmatesque floors (see Cosmati, page 118) and tombs sunk into the floor.

Our favorite nearby
En route to San Lorenzo fuori le Mura, at *Via Tiburtina, 207* (left side), look up and be amazed by the life-size terracotta sculpture showing a medieval family leaning out of their window and smiling down at you.

The basilica is a pastiche of different churches and epochs, from the 4c original to post-WW II restructuring on the upper walls and roof. Founded by **Constantine**, it is listed by the Vatican as one of the five patriarchal basilicas.

Campanile (12c). There is also a small tower dating to Emperor Constantine, 4c.

❶ Portico (restored). Ancient columns and a series of handsome 13c frescoes of the lives of St. Lawrence and St. Stephen. The 1954 monument of leading postwar politician Alcide de Gasperi is by **Manzù**.

Interior. Built haphazardly on three levels. You enter into the 5c Madonna church, redecorated in the 12c with one of Rome's first Cosmati floors.

At the end of the aisle are flights of steps, going up and down, which mark the beginning of Constantine's 4c church. The stairs at the far sides go down to the level of that ancient church, while those at the center lead up to the choir, remodeled by Honorius in the 13c. Springing from the lower level are the 12 massive fluted columns of the 4c, which seem strangely truncated by the Honorius level with its altar and choir. The tombs of Saints Lawrence, Stephen and Justin are in a 4c crypt down the center stairs.

❷ Mosaics on the chancel arch, which divides the two churches, are 6c.

❸ The **baldacchino**'s porphyry columns are 12c. Both pulpits are 13c, as are the Episcopal throne and paschal candlestick.

❹ The **12c cloister**, to the right through the sacristy, is wonderfully peopled with variegated columns, fragments and pagan sarcophagi. Mighty cypresses tower above the double arcades.

Catacombs of St. Cyriaca
Open Wednesday and Friday 9:30 am-noon.

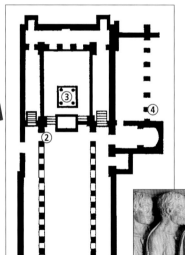

Basilica di Santa Croce in Gerusalemme

The late-Baroque Holy Cross Basilica (1743, Domenico Gregorini and Pietro Passalacqua), another MUST-VISIT pilgrimage church, is noteworthy for its holy relics in their jewel-like reliquaries. On the left of the vestibule is a monastic herbal shop with remedies and perfumes.

Piazza Santa Croce in Gerusalemme, 12. Tel. 067014769.

Getting there
Bus 16, 81 or
A Metro San Giovanni stop.

The heavenly blue frescoes above the main altar set off the golden cherubs and curlicues of the 17c baldacchino.

❶ Go down the shallow steps on the right of the altar to visit St. Helena's Chapel with Melozzo da Forlì's 15c **mosaic of Christ** with saints, including St. Sylvester, who dropped dead while saying mass here. The mosaic was restored a century later by Peruzzi and Zucchi.

❷ Up the stairs through the door on the left is an elegant 1930s chapel housing presumed precious relics, including pieces of the **true cross**, one of its nails, two thorns from Jesus' crown of thorns, and a shriveled finger said to be the one Doubting Thomas the apostle poked into Christ's wound.

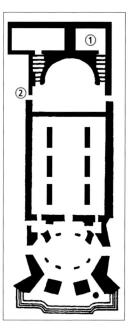

History AD
• **2c** An ancient imperial palace stood here.
• **218-235** Emperors Heliogabalus and Alexander Severus built the Circus Varianus and Amphitheater Castrense on the grounds of this palace.
• **320** While living here St. Helena, Emperor Constantine's mother, added a chapel to house parts of the true cross which she had brought back from a pilgrimage to Jerusalem.
• **1144** The bell tower was added during one of the church's many reconstructions.
• **1741-44** Scholarly and witty **Benedict XIV**, widely admired as a "nephew-less pope," added the facade, oval vestibule and Rococo decorations inside.

Basilica di San Sebastiano

One of the seven MUST-VISIT pilgrimage churches of Rome, with St. Sebastian's remains among its holy relics.

Via Appia Antica, 136.
Tel. 067887035
and 067808847.

Getting there
Bus 218 and Archeobus.

Fee
Open 8:30 am-noon
and 2:30-7 pm.
Closed Sunday.

History AD
• **1c** Three cemeteries built for burying first pagan, then Christian, dead.
• **258-298** Due to Emperor Valerian's persecutions, St. Peter's and St. Paul's corpses were kept here for 40 years.
• **288** Sebastian, a Roman officer, was condemned to death for preaching Christianity to the troops. He survived being riddled with arrows by an execution squad. While recovering, he confronted Emperor Diocletian, who had him beaten to death.
• **4c** Emperor Constantine, "Defender of the Faith," built a basilica over the earlier tombs.
• **1609-12** Cardinal Scipio Borghese had Flaminio Ponzi construct the present church on top of the basilica.

❶ In the first chapel to the left in the Baroque church is a smooth white-marble sculpture of **St. Sebastian** lying down full of arrow holes, after a design by **Bernini**, carried out by Antonio Giorgetti. Adjacent steps lead down to a crypt with the urn containing the saint's relics.
❷ Other holy relics, visited by pilgrims for centuries, are in the right absidal chapel, including what is believed to be the stone with Christ's footprints, left when he met St. Peter fleeing Rome. There are also arrows which pierced St. Sebastian and the column to which he was bound, as well as the hands of St. Calixtus and St. Andrew. The **catacombs**, four levels deep, are similar to those of San Callisto (see page 105). There are fascinating early paintings, graffiti, stuccowork and fine mosaics.

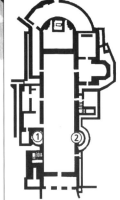

There are 69 catacombs on the outskirts of Rome and thousands of tombs. Under ancient Roman law, no one could be buried inside the city, for sanitary reasons, hence these extraordinary subterranean labyrinths.

All the **consular roads** were lined with the handsome tombs of patricians, most of whom were cremated and their ashes preserved in urns. Because they had to

be ready for resurrection, the early Christian dead were buried, uncremated, in underground caves hollowed out of soft tufa stone. It is now generally accepted that these "catacombs" were not where the early Christian community hid from persecution, but where they gathered to honor their dead, particularly martyrs and popes – usually by staging banquets. The word *catacomb*, now used for any subterranean burial place, presumably comes from the Greek word for "hollow," the name of the area of stone quarries located around the San Sebastiano catacombs. Only five of the catacombs are open to the public. There were also many **Jewish catacombs**, four of which have disappeared; the others, including one at Via Appia Antica, 119A, are closed.

Catacombs of San Callisto. Here are over 17 km (12 miles) of underground galleries, arranged on four and sometimes five levels, reaching deep down into the earth. They are lined with hollowed-out niches (*loculi*), frequently two or three high, in which the dead were wrapped in double layers of cloth interspersed with lye to protect the living.

Via Appia Antica, 126.
Tel. 065130151.

Getting there
Bus 218.

Fee
Open 8:30 am-noon and 2:30-5:30 pm.
Closed Wednesday.

The amazing story of St. Calixtus
• AD **1c** Poor Roman families, pagan and Christian, formed cooperatives to bury the dead in these tufa-stone quarries.
• **180-192** Emperor **Commodus**, soft on Christianity, gave in to his mistress Marcia, and freed her fellow Christians condemned to hard labor in the mines. With them Calixtus, a slave convicted for fraud and brawling in a synagogue, escaped.
• **199** Pope Zephyrinus installed Calixtus as church deacon and keeper of this cemetery, the first to become legal property of the Church.
• **217** Calixtus, always enterprising, became pope. He died five years later and, on dubious evidence

of martyrdom, became a saint.
• **366-384** Pope Damasus I got Emperor Theodosius I to make Christianity the state religion and restored the catacombs, to prove that Rome's real glory was not pagan.

Via delle Sette Chiese, 282. Tel. 065110342.

Getting there
Bus 218.

Fee
Open 8:30 am-noon and 2:30-5:30 pm.
Closed Tuesday and January.

The **Papal Crypt** and the **Crypt of St. Cecilia** are of religious and historical interest. In the former repose at least five martyred and sanctified popes who reigned between 230 and 283. Note the marble plaques with the Greek letters *MTP* for **MarTyR**. Elegant 4c decorations were added by Pope Damasus I.

In these subterranean tunnels watch for the 2c-3c wall paintings in the **Sacraments Crypt** and **Lucina's Precinct.**

Catacombs of Santa Domitilla. St. Domitilla, related to Emperors Domitian and Vespasian and a member of the distinguished Flavian family, was martyred in AD 95. These catacombs, including Christian and non-Christian tombs, were named after her because the entrance was on her property. The decorations of her own burial place were unfortunately defaced by 18c tomb robbers. There is a particularly lovely tomb with 4c frescoes of Saints Peter and Paul on either side of the dead woman's ghostly black square

WHEN THE SAINTS GO MARCHING IN
Martyrology

Legends and other sources of varying authenticity were utilized by the medieval and Renaissance Church so that the largely illiterate congregations could instantly recognize the saintly men and women who had died for their beliefs. Painters of frescoes and wood altarpieces used these vivid symbols to crystallize the saints' *personages* as visual emblems.

Partial list of the worst atrocities, and most important saints and their symbols.
AD • **During the reign of Nero, 54-68**
St. Peter crucified. Shown holding a key.
St. Paul beheaded. Shown with a sword.
St. Luke, apostle. Portrayed with an ox.
St. Matthew, apostle. Portrayed with book and pen.
St. Mark, apostle. Portrayed with a lion.
St. Thecla tossed by a bull. Shown standing on a bull.
St. Faustus. Clothed in animal skins and torn to pieces by dogs.
• **During the reign of Domitian, 81-96**
St. John, apostle, boiled in oil. Shown with an eagle and a book.
St. Domitilla roasted alive. Shown standing on a fire.
• **During the reign of Trajan, 98-117**
St. Ignatius, bishop of Antioch, eaten by lions in the Colosseum.
St. Clement, pope, tied to an anchor and thrown into the sea. Shown with an anchor.
St. Eustace, captain of the emperor's guard. He and his family put in a brass bull and cooked alive over a fire. Shown on horseback with a stag.
St. Simon, bishop of Jerusalem, sawed in half. Shown with a saw.
• **During the reigns of Antoninus Pius & Marcus Aurelius, 138-180**
St. Margaret stretched on a rack and torn to pieces with iron forks. Shown with a rack.
St. Attalus roasted on a red-hot chair.
• **During the reigns of Septimius Severus and Caracalla, 197-217**
St. Alexandrina covered with boiling pitch.
Saints Perpetua and Felicitas torn to pieces by lions.
• **During the reign of Alexander Severus, 222-235**
St. Calixtus, pope, thrown into a well with a stone around his neck. (See History, page 105.)
St. Calepodius, dragged through Rome by wild horses, thrown into the Tiber.
St. Cecilia, patron of music. Survived suffocation, then stabbed in the neck and left to die. Shown with neck wounds while playing a musical instrument.
Saints Cosmos and Damian beheaded. Shown together holding surgical instruments.

St. Cecilia, by Francesco Vanni.

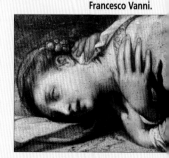

icon. Under the arch of this tomb, visible only if you kneel, is a Last Supper – a thousand years before Leonardo. Most of the corpses were slotted into shallow slits cut in the stone. Many of them were tiny children; rich people had larger tombs with decorated arches and sometimes separate family vaults.

You can only visit two of the four levels of this largest and perhaps earliest of the catacombs. It is a bit off the beaten catacomb path, but worth visiting because it is less crowded than those on Via Appia Antica.

Our favorite
At the intersection of Via Appia and Via Ardeatina, the short road from the gate to the San Callisto catacombs is a moment of bucolic calm and beauty before you descend into the awesome underground passages.

Other catacombs not in the Via Appia area:
Catacombs of Sant'Agnese (see page 136). *Via Nomentana, 349. Tel. 068610840.*
Catacombs of Santa Ciriaca (see San Lorenzo fuori le Mura, page 101). *Piazzale del Verano, 3. Tel. 06491511.*
Catacombs of Priscilla. As old as those of San Callisto and Sant'Agnese (AD 2c). Considered the most remarkable for its early frescoes, an AD 210 Madonna with Child, as well as 3c Old and New Testament scenes. *Via Salaria, 430. Tel. 0686206272.*

• **During the reigns of Valerianus and Gallienus, 253-268**
St. Agatha, breasts cut off. Shown with breasts on a plate.
Saints Fabien and Cornelius, popes, beheaded.
St. Stephen, pope, burnt in his Episcopal chair.
St. Lawrence, a deacon, roasted slowly on an iron bed as he smiled bravely.
• **During the reign of Claudius II, 268-270**
300 Christians burned in a furnace.
St. Marius hung, with a huge weight tied to his feet.
St. Valentine killed by the sword.
• **During the reigns of Aurelian and Numerianus, 275-284**
St. Agapitus, age 15, hung head down over a pan of burning charcoal.
St. Lucy stabbed in the neck. Shown with eyes on a plate.
St. Christopher beheaded by the sword. Shown carrying Jesus across a river.
St. Margaret executed. Shown standing on a dragon.
St. Catherine, gospel preacher of Alexandria, broken on the wheel.
    Shown with a wheel.
• **During the reigns of Diocletian and Maximianus, 285-314**
St. Agnes bound to a stake, then beheaded. Shown with a lamb.
St. Erasmus, patron of sailors, laid in a coffin into which boiling lead was poured.
St. Blaise bound to a column and stoned to death. Shown as an old man with an iron comb.
St. Anastasia thrown from a rock.
St. Lucia shut up in a well full of serpents.
St. Sebastian shot with arrows (which he survived). Shown punctured with arrows.
St. Barbara beheaded by her own father. Shown holding a tower.
• **During the reign of Maxentius, 306-312**
St. Marcellus, pope, died worn out by persecution.
St. Simon and 1,600 citizens cut into fragments.
• **During the reign of Julian the Apostate, 361-363**
St. John beheaded.
St. Artemius crushed between two stones.
St. Nicholas loved children. Shown as a bishop (later as Father Christmas).
• **6c** St. Benedict founded the Benedictine order. Shown with many different things
    (broken glass, ladder, etc.); best known with a black bird – temptation by the devil.
• **11c** St. Elizabeth, princess of Hungary, fed the poor. Shown with an apron full of roses.
• **13c** St. Anthony of Padua. Patron saint of lost things. Shown with a lily and a book.
St. Dominic founded the Dominican order. Shown holding a rosary.
St. Francis of Assisi received stigmata. Shown with animals and birds.
• **16c** St. Ignatius Loyola founded the Society of Jesus (Jesuits).

If you want to see some gory frescoes of the way the saints were killed, visit the horrid 16c frescoes by Pomarancio and Tempesta in the Chiesa di Santo Stefano Rotondo; see page 142.

Medieval Walk

[**F 3**] *Via della Lungara.*

Getting there
Bus 23, 280, 870.

Trastevere is the closest thing in Rome to a medieval town, where building shapes have changed relatively little for over a thousand years.

Trastevere means "across the Tiber." When Rome was founded 27 centuries ago this area was an Etruscan encampment with Etruria spreading from here to the north (see Villa Giulia, page 70). It became the foreigners' quarter since they were mostly forbidden to live in Rome proper. Foreigners, Jews, tanners, potters, cabinetmakers and gardeners – as well as ladies of easy virtue and thieves – all lived here *on the edge*, plying their various trades; a difference, an exoticism, endured during the Middle Ages. Even today the *Trasteverini* celebrate their uniqueness in their midsummer festival called *Noantri* (dialect for "We Others"); they read their poets in Trastevere dialect.

— Via della Lungara. In the Middle Ages a winding lane led from the Vatican through the ancient orchard of the Caesars to the part of Trastevere within the walls. Pope Julius II della Rovere (1503-13) straightened this road to assist pilgrims who, after visiting St. Peter's, walked to St. Paul Outside the Walls via Santa Maria in Trastevere. The river side of this *long* street (hence *Lungara*) had buildings and gardens stretching down to the water, which disappeared when the embankments were built at the end of the 19c.

❶ Borgia House. Now the shop of a kind carpenter. From 1492 to 1503 Pope Alexander VI Borgia reigned. His bullying son Cesare killed and pillaged, attempting to prolong the Borgia dynastic power. Nearby are supposedly two secret tunnels, one to the river, the other to the Vatican. Cesare would lure his victims, kill them and throw them in the river. If things went badly he could escape through the other tunnel to safe haven in the Vatican.

Via della Lungara, 46.

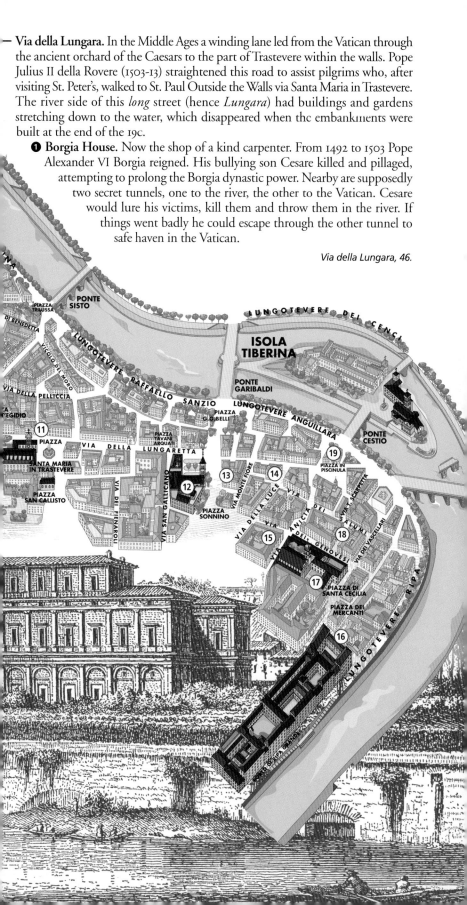

❷ Carcere di Regina Coeli (*Queen of Heaven* Jail). Swindlers await trial in this undistinguished structure. Recently it has seen some of Italy's top dogs. On the back streets, laments waft out on the night air: "Ci vuole una donna!" (I want a woman!), or the more heartrending "Voglio la mamma!" (I want my mamma!).

Via della Lungara, 29.

❸ Casa Internazionale delle Donne inside the **Convento del Buon Pastore** (1615, Order of the Barefoot Dominicans). Founded for "Repentant Women, Sinners and the Condemned" and later unwed mothers and their babies. Today feminist groups have interesting cultural activities here. The building has a bookstore, rooms for ladies only, and a restaurant open exclusively to women at dinner, and to both men and women at lunch.

Via della Lungara, 19.
Tel. 06684017.
Open Monday to Friday
9:30 am-12:30 pm
and 3:30-6:30 pm.

❹ Villa Farnesina (1511, Baldassarre Peruzzi). An exquisite Renaissance villa built on what were once Julius Caesar's orchards and vineyards. Here Caesar reportedly lodged Cleopatra in his Water Palace (44 BC), technically circumventing the Roman rule forbidding foreigners to live inside (or to visit) the capital and saving his wife, Calpurnia, from embarrassment. From here Cleopatra and her illegitimate son by Caesar, Cesarean, escaped by boat a month after Caesar's murder (the cesarean section was performed by Egyptian doctors, and named for Caesar and Cleopatra's son).

Via della Lungara, 230.
Tel. 066802768.
Fee - Open Monday to
Saturday 9 am-1 pm.

Cleopatra's cure for Caesar's baldness (contemporary busts show Julius had only wisps around the edges): 1 part domestic mouse, 1 part vine rag, 1 part horses' teeth, all toasted; 1 part bear's grease, 1 part deer's marrow, 1 part reed bark. Pound and mix all ingredients with honey and continue spreading on bald patch until hair begins to sprout.

This Renaissance villa was built by Agostino Chigi, millionaire banker from Siena, and good friend of **Pope Leo X Medici**. Chigi spared no expense in decorating this lovely place – and offering fabulous banquets. These feasts finished with the precious gold and silver plates being thrown into the river (to be fished out later from the invisible net hidden in the water). One banquet was held in Chigi's stables, to show the Riario family, when they were building their palazzo on the other side of the road, that dinner in the Chigi stables was more luxurious than it could ever be at Riario's palace. **Raphael** (1483-1520) painted the frescoes on and off from 1512 to 1518. Chigi, a great art patron, allowed Raphael's mistress (la Fornarina; see Palazzo Barberini, page 181) to live here

---

THE DARK MILLENNIUM
From AD 400 to 1400

• **404 Rome abandoned** by **Honorius**, perhaps the feeblest of all the emperors, who presided over the Western Empire's dismemberment for 18 years while hiding out in Ravenna. He was one of the two sons of the great **Theodosius I**, last to rule (378-395) over a united Roman Empire, after whose death the empire was divided between his two sons, Arcadius getting the Eastern Empire with its capital at Constantinople. Theodosius, a Christian emperor who made war as far away as Britain and the Balkans, had been for Rome what Franz Joseph was for the Austro-Hungarian Empire: the end. After the capital moved to Ravenna, Rome continued to have its Senate, but the popes, the bishops of Rome, began their ascendancy.

• **409 Britain** declared itself independent, and Honorius agreed.
• **410 Alaric sacked Rome**.
• **431 Council of Ephesus** recognized the cult of the Virgin, Mother of Christ.
• **439 Vandals seized Roman Africa**.
• **452 Attila stopped**. Pope Leo the Great dissuaded Attila the Hun, face-to-face at the gates of Mantua, from invading central Italy.
• **455 Pope Leo** then dissuaded Gaiseric the Vandal, face-to-face at the gates of Rome, from burning Rome and torturing its population, but the city was looted.
• **476 Fall of the Roman Empire**. Odoacer the barbarian became king of Italy and forced Romulus Augustulus to abdicate as the last emperor of the Western Roman Empire. This left Constantinople as the sole capital of the Roman Empire – thereafter called Byzantium. The position of the popes was strengthened.

in order to get the Maestro to do more work, but the painter died at the age of 37. **Giorgio Vasari**, painter and biographer, wrote that Raphael was killed by overexertion, as "he continued his amorous pleasures to an inordinate degree." Others claim it was because la Fornarina was taken away.

Loggia. Once Villa Farnesina's entrance, now the back veranda. A delicious deep leafy glen painted by Raphael and Giulio Romano with their students, bringing the garden into the house. The theme is **Cupid and Psyche,** to celebrate Chigi's marriage to his mistress Francesca. Weddings were the usual excuse for bawdy celebrations in those times. Above Mercury's hand is an erotic symbol, if you can find it! A trompe l'oeil tapestry of the Council of the Godo (above) was painted by Giovanni da Udine (1487-1564).

Room of Galatea: Raphael alone painted the scene of **Galatea** on the half shell being pulled by complaisant, frisky dolphins; his brush strokes shine out with perfect mastery. Michelangelo is said to have passed by one day and painted in the large head on the left wall to show his disapproval of the overly small scale of Raphael's frescoes.

Upstairs: Chigi's bedroom has frescoes painted by Sodoma, said to be his best. Also here is the **Sala delle Prospettive,** where Peruzzi painted a dazzling trompe l'oeil fresco showing the views that one would have if this were an open loggia.

Chigi's descendants cut such a swath through his great fortune that in 1590 the villa was sold to the Farnese family – who hoped to have Michelangelo throw a bridge across the Tiber to join their two palaces. They never made it.

• **535-553 Rome reached its lowest ebb**, conquered by the Eastern Roman emperor **Justinian**. Gothic invasions under Theodoric inflicted repeated sieges and massacres. Starvation and rampant plague reduced Rome to a ghost town for a few months. The whole civic structure collapsed, leaving only the Church.
• **568 Lombards invaded**. After a few years of peace the Lombards, a German tribe, conquered and settled in northern Italy. They got to the gates of Rome. Then the countryside was decimated as malaria took its toll; the waterways were neglected, and swamps and mosquitoes returned.
• **590 England became Catholic. Pope Gregory the Great** brought England into the Catholic fold. Lombards laid siege to Rome but the pope dissuaded them. Papal power was growing and Gregory bolstered papal control over its vast estates, "the patrimony of Peter," not only in Italy and Sicily but also in Dalmatia, Gaul and North Africa.
• **7c** Malaria forced the Romans onto their seven hills and the great city degenerated into clusters of dwellings, the largest cluster being on the Lateran Hill. Roman edifices lay forlornly in the swampy mire. Popes then became the real temporal heads of the city. Popes vs. antipopes, Church vs. aristocracy, emperors vs. the papacy, all jostling for power in a context of anarchy, with the Normans, Lombards, French and Hungarians trying to gain territories. In Rome successive popes strove to protect the independence of the Church: its elections, dogma and possessions. The Venerable Bede (AD 672-735), English sage, historian and saint, is said to have visited Rome and affirmed the city's essential importance in the larger scheme of things (see page 12).

History AD

- **1474 Pope Sixtus IV** della Rovere, though strict in his own life, was lavish with his family. His sister married a Riario who bought a vineyard here. Then Cardinal Domenico Riario built a large house; he had been married to the beauteous Caterina Sforza.
- **1626-1689 Queen Christina of Sweden**, who abdicated to become a Catholic, lived here in grandeur with her mysterious cardinal. She died in the upstairs room with the two wooden columns.
- **December 28, 1797** Joseph Bonaparte, in Rome as ambassador of his brother Napoleon's regime, was caught in a scuffle outside this palace near the Porta Settimiana. Though Joseph escaped death, his companion General Duphot did not. Napoleon's forces promptly occupied Rome and confined **Pope Pius VI Braschi** to the Quirinal Palace (see page 169).

When the embankment roadways were built (1879) Caesar's Water Palace was destroyed, but many of the frescoes and mosaics are now on display at the Palazzo Massimo Museum (see page 256).

❺ **Palazzo Corsini** (begun 1475; facade 1736, Ferdinando Fuga). Cardinal Riario (whose cousin won such a huge sum in a game of dice that he built the Cancelleria Palace) was given this land by his uncle, Pope Sixtus IV della Rovere. Inside the palazzo:

The **Corsini Library** still has its books in the same order as when it was assembled three centuries ago by Monsignore Lorenzo Corsini.

The **National Art Gallery** (or Corsini Gallery) contains 16c and 17c paintings. Guido Reni (1575-1642) painted an

Via della Lungara, 10.
Tel. 0668802323.

Fee
Open Tuesday to Friday 9 am-7 pm, Saturday 9 am- 2 pm, Sunday and holidays 9 am-1 pm.

- **8c Byzantine iconoclasm**. The emperor in Constantinople ordered the destruction of all sacred images of Christ and saints. This official iconoclasm lasted 726-787 and 815-843. The papacy in Rome refused. Many Greek churchmen fled to Rome with their icons and were given churches.
- **754 Charlemagne's father saved the pope.** Pope Stephen II asked the Franks (another German tribe) to save him. Their King Pepin I, father of Charlemagne, defeated the Lombards, creating the Papal States independent of the Byzantine Empire. These states eventually encompassed two thirds of Italy.
- **800 Charlemagne crowned**. In Rome, Pope Leo III crowned Charlemagne the first Holy Roman Emperor to consolidate the unity of the Church. But the 1,000-year history of the Holy Roman Empire was dominated by conflict between popes and emperors. A number of powerful women commanded the towers of Rome and even imposed their will on the popes.
- **849 Arabs repelled**. Pope Leo IV defended Rome from the invasion of Muslim Saracens who had conquered Sicily and were moving rapidly north.
- **855** The infamous and presumably mythical "Pope Joan" elected unanimously as John VIII. English, she studied in north Germany, cross-dressing to gain entrance to the monastic university. She traveled with her professor-lover, settling in Rome, where she taught so brilliantly that she had no rivals for the papal throne when Leo IV died. While riding in a procession between San Giovanni in Laterano and St. Peter's she gave birth to a child! Upon discovering she was a woman, the prelates fell on her and the people stoned her to death, or so the legend goes. A small shrine at the corner of Via dei Santi Quattro

Salomé with John the Baptist's Head, by Guido Reni.

Devils and black magic. The Catholic Church in the Middle Ages believed in witchcraft, spells and the real presence of the devil. Medieval Romans were particularly careful on nights without a moon since black magic and devils were believed to be lurking in the Colosseum and the Campo Marzio. Despite these ever-present dangers, Romans were convinced that in the end Christ would always save them since Rome was head of the Church. Doubts and skepticism about black magic only began to arise in the Church with the advent of the Humanists, whose great pope, Pius II Piccolomini (1458-64), said, "witchcraft is a stupid thing; we can't believe any of this." In the 16c the Inquisition severely persecuted witchcraft as part of the Church's effort to counter the rise of Protestantism. The Catholic Church today still believes in exorcism.

idealized portrait of Caterina Sforza. Cesare Borgia, cruel son of Pope Alexander VI, defeated Caterina's armies at Forlì, but was so impressed by her bravery he sent her to Rome in golden chains. He imprisoned her in Castel Sant'Angelo, from which she was released through French intervention. Also by Reni is a presumed *Salomé with John the Baptist's Head*. Here also are works by Caravaggio, Murillo, Rubens and Van Dyck.

Coronati and Via dei Querceti has recently been identified with Pope Joan. At any rate, the *Chaise Percée* ritual (looking or touching under the future pope's skirts, through a hole in the chair, to determine that the aspirant was really a man) became part of the process of choosing a pope.
• **875 Louis II**, Charlemagne's great-grandson, died and with him all hopes for uniting Italy for another 1,000 years. **End of 9c to end of 10c: anarchy.** Fabulous misdeeds, very little holiness: Roman nobles gave the papal throne to sons and lovers.
• **931 Women ruled Rome.** A young ne'er-do-well, son of Pope Sergius III, became Pope John XI. His mother was Dame Marozia, one of the famous women of Rome, so powerful that she ruled from Castel Sant'Angelo. Later, Countess Matilda of Tuscany (1046-1115) also ruled from her own fortified towers

near Florence. All over northern Italy women asserted themselves.
• **955 Hungarian invasion.** Saxon king Otto ventured south to take the Holy Roman Emperor title for himself, dispatching the Hungarians on the way. Another unsavory youth, Pope John XII, who, his enemies said, "made the Lateran into a brothel," was the son of the last prince of Rome and illegally became pope and prince. **Pope John crowned Otto Holy Roman Emperor.** Although subsequently deposed, Otto reconsolidated the Holy Roman Empire. Saracens continued their incursions.
• **1015 Norman invasion of south.** The Norman conquest of southern Italy and Sicily chased the Saracens back to North Africa. (*Norsemen*, from Scandinavia, the Normans first settled in the Seine valley in France.) These pirates acted as mercenaries among the squabbling Greeks, Saracens and Lombards, but

Largo Cristina di Svezia, 24. Tel. 0672594342.

Fee
Open 9 am-5:30 pm.
Closed Sunday.

Beyond a 400-year-old tree, *Magnolia grandiflora*, with sweet-scented blossoms in June, is the ❻ **Orto Botanico** (Botanical Gardens), part of the gardens Queen Christina loved so much. There are three tropical greenhouses, a sandy desert area, a Japanese garden, fountain and large basin of water, trees from all over the world of venerable height, and an orchid fair every spring. A lovely place to walk and bask in the sun.

❼ **Palazzo Torlonia.**
Via della Lungara, 2.

Used to house Prince Torlonia's priceless private collection of ancient Roman busts and sculptures. The Torlonia family ancestor, a cloth merchant from douthern France, came to Italy under Napoleon to find his fortune. Ennobled to princes and marquises, the family in the 19c made even more money draining swamps they bought for a trifle, and selling the land for double. Today it is a private apartment building. The Torlonia collection, which was moved out of Rome during an altercation with city officials, will reopen elsewhere sometime in the future.

Via della Lungara, 233. Tel. 066819121. **John Cabot University**. Formerly the Monastery of the 100 Priests. This building houses what is arguably the best U.S. college abroad. It has a fine academic staff and professor/student ratio; BA degrees in business, international affairs, political science, art history, literature, economics, humanistic studies and Italian studies.

❽ **Porta Settimiana**. A gate built by Pope Alexander VI Borgia marks where Rome stopped for the first couple of millennia! Throughout the Middle Ages, the area from here to the Vatican was outside the walls, defenseless. If you look up you can

soon asked for land in payment. Within a short while they conquered Sicily and Calabria for themselves (today many southern Italians are blond and tall). Pope Leo IX took arms against them, lost and was taken prisoner. As they were devout Catholics, the pope used their strength in pursuit of Church reform.

• **1027 King Canute** of England and Denmark, famous for *not* being able to stop the sea's tide when he ordered it back, came to Rome to show fealty to both the Catholic Church and the Holy Roman Emperor.

• **1054 Byzantine church broke off** from the pope's authority, formalizing a long-standing division.

• **1059 Nobles excluded from Church business**. At the Council of Lateran the Normans insisted that papal elections be in the hands of the cardinals; Roman nobles would no longer have any say. Much-needed reforms had begun,

against such prevalent customs as married clergy and the sale of valuable bishoprics.

• **1075 Laymen forbidden priesthood**. Pope Gregory VII forbade laypeople being invested into the Church, and excommunicated Holy Roman Emperor Henry IV for opposing this. The pope had to call in the Normans again to save himself from the emperor and his Lombards. While "helping" the pope, the Normans sacked Rome and a furious populace would have killed His Holiness had he not escaped south to Salerno.

• **1077 Emperor Henry "went to Canossa,"** as the expression goes, walking barefoot and in shirtsleeves through the snow to beg pardon of the pope, who kept him waiting three days before granting absolution.

• **1096 The First Crusade**. A monk from Cluny, France, became Pope Urban II. He started the Crusades – holy wars against

see where the portcullis descended, and note the massive hinges on either side. Lucky are the people who live in the tiny apartment carved out of the thickness of the wall. On both sides under canopies are religious frescoes that have seen better days.

Now you enter Trastevere proper.

Romolo Restaurant. The baker's daughter *La Fornarina*, Raphael's beautiful mistress and model for many paintings, lived here in the 16c. Still a tavern today, called Romolo (see Restaurants, page 291), it stretched round the corner, incorporating what is now **Sarti Ceramic Art** (see Specialty Shops, page 221).

Diagonal walls are characteristic of medieval buildings, such as those on your right.

Piazza della Scala. Look at *No. 54*, an ancient farmhouse. This area was a fief of the Stefaneschi family in the Middle Ages – and some of the women were so powerful the *men* had to take the women's names in marriage and not vice versa!

Islam to make it safe for pilgrims to visit the Holy Land. Jerusalem was their Mecca. Over the next 200 years, these crusades intermittently succeeded in wresting the Holy Lands from the Muslims. Even today crusader castles are dotted around the Middle East, sentinels of former grandeur and belligerence. The crusaders usually traveled by boat, so Italians along the Adriatic coast cleverly profited from these wars: boat building became the biggest money maker with fleets hammered out every day. Popes and emperors squabbled over whether the Church had sole right to make ecclesiastical promotions.

• **1154 Holy Roman Emperor marched on Italy**. Barbarossa (AKA Red Beard), the newly elected Holy Roman Emperor Frederick I of Hohenstaufen, conquered large areas of southern Italy. In Rome, the first and last English pope, Hadrian IV, with Barbarossa's help squashed the -

Diseases The populace of medieval and Renaissance Rome was constantly being decimated by a variety of diseases: bubonic plague (brought on by the bite of a flea who had first bitten an infected rat); dysentery (widespread through dirty food); typhus (from contaminated drinking water, often due to the Tiber floodings, which brought water mixed with sewage into the streets); and malaria, which occurred regularly every summer when the mosquitoes could breed happily in the stagnant ponds or moats around the city.

Our favorite in the Museo di Roma: painting *Festival of the Moccoletti in Via del Corso* by Ippolito Caffi (1809-1866), showing the locals playing the game of extinguishing each other's candles during Carnival.

❾ **Vecchia Farmacia della Scala** (1523, Carmelite monks). The monks invented a special "Acqua della Scala" to fight plague. In the 16c alone there were four plagues: 1523, 1527, 1538, 1558. The old *farmacia* on the upper floor still looks much as it did, with marble urns where the decoctions were stored.

Piazza della Scala, 23. Tel. 065806217.

Chiesa di Santa Maria della Scala. Built in 1592 to house a miracle-working image that had hung on the staircase (*scala*) of a medieval house across the square. The pretty altar canopy with columns (Carlo Rainaldi) was added in 1650. Caravaggio's *Death of the Virgin*, now in the Louvre, was originally commissioned, and rejected, for the side chapel.

❿ **Museo di Roma – Trastevere.** Formerly a Carmelite monastery and then a folklore museum, the current museum's permanent collection recalls Trastevere's history on the upper floor. The ground floor houses temporary exhibitions honoring local artists, poets and traditions.

Piazza Sant'Egidio, 1B. Tel. 065816563.
Fee - Open Tuesday to Sunday 10 am-6:30 pm except July-August: 10 am-1:30 pm. **Closed** Monday.

Piazza Santa Maria in Trastevere. The heart of this *simpatico* quarter of Rome, essentially unchanged since the 1600s. The fountain was upgraded by Carlo Fontana in 1692. To the left of the church: Palazzo Moroni, used by the Benedictine monks when their monastery became infested with mosquitoes every summer. To the right of the church: *No. 26* in the piazza: above the door "Fons Olei," celebrating the miraculous fountain of oil. Across the piazza, at Vicolo Santa Maria in Trastevere, 23, is charming Palazzo Leopardi.

⓫ **Chiesa di Santa Maria in Trastevere** (AD 1140). Established in the 3c when St. Calixtus was pope and

movement headed by Arnaldo da Brescia to make Rome a republic.
• **1200 Papal States largest ever**. Under Pope Innocent III (1198-1216) the Papal States grew as far north as the Po River and as far south as Ceprano – threatening the emperor's Sicilian

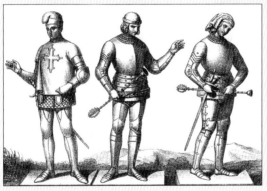

state. Three successive popes wrestled for power and territory with Barbarossa's grandson, **Emperor Frederick II Hohenstaufen** (1194-1250), at one point excommunicating him for not starting a crusade on time. He retaliated, signing a treaty with the sultan of the Holy Land allowing Christian pilgrims entry to the holy sites and crowned himself king of Jerusalem. Guelphs (papal faction) and Ghibellines (emperor's faction) fought on and off for 30 years, until the waning of imperial power with the death of Frederick. Hailed as *Stupor Mundi* (wonder of the world), he left an empire that hemmed in the Papal States to the north and south.

named for him after his martyrdom, which took place nearby (he was thrown headfirst from a window into a well – quite a shot). It was soon dedicated to the Virgin Mary, the first Marian church in Rome. Keepers of taverns here, including Taberna Meritorio for legionnaires, were not thrilled with the idea of a Christian church, feeling it would dampen jollity, and they claimed ownership of the land. But Emperor Alexander Severus decided in favor of the Christians, saying, "better God should be worshipped in whatever form" there than have taverns and boozy soldiers.

Facade. The unforgettably beautiful mosaic high up is 12-13c, portraying the presentation of gifts to the Virgin and Christ child, whom she is suckling (note her bare breast). Around them are grouped 10 virgins. At the base of the belfry is an 11c mosaic of the Virgin and Child. Many more majestic mosaics are peppered around inside. Richly robed figures fill the half dome at the end of the apse – its 12c Byzantine derivation is evident in the dark lines around face and form. Between the windows below is the life of the Virgin and

In **1598** the Tiber burst its banks and Trastevere was inundated by 5.5m (6 yards) of water; 1,096 people died.

History AD
• **3** Allegedly at the time of Christ's birth this was the site of a "miracle spring" which spouted oil for one whole day. There was so much oil it flowed down to the Tiber. The current theory is that the so-called oil was actually black water from a break in the tubing

• **1266 France dominated southern Italy.** Prince Charles d'Anjou of France, encouraged by the French pope Urban IV to curb the Hohenstaufens' power to the south, killed Frederick's brilliant successor and illegitimate son Manfred. The papal party thus triumphed and Charles became king of Sicily (1266-85). French influence dominated in the south of Italy, even in art and architecture. Giotto and Cavallini worked for the French in Naples on the Church of Santa Chiara. Excesses of the previous centuries when women had wielded enormous powers, now caused a reaction against them. **Nuns were forced into "clausura," "segregatio."** The female counterparts of St. Francis's monks, the "Clares," were named after his friend whom he inspired to take vows and form an order of nuns to help the poor. However, the Church at that time did not allow women to go out to the people so Clare and her followers were forced to stay inside their convents. Even during religious services nuns were "secluded," behind the altar in some churches or up on a loggia in others. Pope Boniface VIII was the strictest. In those days men were all-important, considered "hot and dry," while women were perfidious, and considered "cold and damp."

• **1300 Boniface VIII Caetani proclaimed this the first Jubilee Year.** The custom came from the Jews. Boniface allowed too many statues of himself and was accused of idolatry. When he excommunicated King Philippe IV, **French troops stormed the papal hideaway** at Anagni and the famous "schiaffo," or slap, from the Frenchman de Nogaret followed, with the imprisonment of the pope. Boniface died in Rome soon after.

• **1303 Pope Benedict XI moved to Perugia.** Rome was a hotbed of intrigues. He stalled on convening a

of the aqueduct of Augustus, which was known to be polluted. This "miracle" was one of three that, according to medieval legend, were believed to have occurred in Rome – thus confirming the miraculous Virgin birth.

• **222** Under Pope Calixtus I a *titulus*, or meeting place, for the Christian community of Trastevere was built here.

• **1140** The present church was built during the reign of Pope Innocent II, of Trastevere's Papareschi family, with materials from the Baths of Caracalla.

• **12c** The mosaic facade was started. Restored in the 14c.

• **1702** The portico with statues of popes was added by Carlo Fontana; in it are fragments of antique carvings.

Christ by Maestro Pietro Cavallini in comic-strip form, an example of Roman-style mosaics.

Don't miss the pavement of Cosmati marble geometrics (see Santa Maria in Cosmedin, page 43). Two sarcophagi of cardinals have noteworthy carving. Five popes are buried under the altar. The ancient building to the right housed a *Schola Cantorum* (Liturgical Singing School).

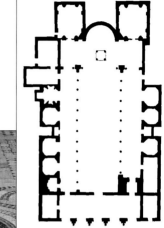

general council to condemn the late Pope Boniface and dithered between sanctioning and pardoning the French. A weak man, he died of dysentery in Perugia.

• **1309 Papacy moved to Avignon**. The next pope, Clement V, a Frenchman, took his marching orders from King Philippe, opening a 68-year papal exile. Although he felt the papacy should return to Rome, Clement, weak and ill, never left Avignon.

• **1316** Another Frenchman became **Pope John XXII**; almost all his newly appointed cardinals were French. Highly unpopular for turning against the Franciscans and burning some at the stake (read *The Name of the Rose* by Umberto Eco).

• **1369** The Byzantine emperor came looking for help, as Turks were threatening his borders. He even abjured the Orthodox faith to get help (though his clergy did not).

• **1370 Election of the sixth Frenchman: Pope Urban V**. With the promised escort of the Holy Roman Emperor Charles IV's army, Urban V **moved back to Rome** halfway through his papacy. He camped in the Vatican, since the Lateran had burned.

• **1370** Pope Urban dreamed that the Holy Spirit ordered him to **return to Avignon**. Despite Saint Bridget's pleas, he did so, but soon died. The same year the last of the Avignon French popes was elected, Gregory XI. Though he said Rome was the proper

Proceed down Via San Callisto to the right toward **Via dell'Arco di San Callisto** and glance to the right to see the high arch over the street. Turn left onto Via dell'Arco di San Callisto and immediately on the right are three medieval houses: *No. 42* with stair and fresco; then *Nos. 43* and *44*. Aren't they gorgeous? Go to the end of the road and turn left on Piazza Santa Rufina with the medieval church tower of the **Convento delle Suore di Santa Rufina e Seconda**. The two martyrs lived here. In 1026 it was the palace of Pope John XIX. Turn right on Via della Lungaretta. Walk to Viale Trastevere and reach…

place for a pope, lack of money made the move impossible. Also, the England-vs.-France **100 Years War** would have to end before the launching of another crusade, so dear to the papal hearts.
• **1377 Papacy returned to Rome**. Ending the 68-year *Babylonian captivity*, Pope Gregory XI moved into the Vatican Palace. Antipopes (elected by a rival faction) had become a tradition in papal politics. With the popes back in Rome, the French faction continued this fiction, precipitating the *Great Schism* (1380-1417), as they installed **successive antipopes at Avignon**. This habit had gone on for 1,000 years!
• **1400** The Holy Roman Emperors' power waned. The papacy survived.

Viale Trastevere, corner of Piazza Sonnino.

⓬ Basilica di San Crisogono (facade 1863, covering a 17c restoration by G. B. Soria). There is precious little left of the early church except the 12c belfry. Inside are 22 ancient Ionic marble columns, 4 yellow alabaster and 2 large porphyry columns, with a Cosmatesque floor (12c). In the apse behind the altar, Pietro Cavallini (13c), who also did the mosaics of Santa Maria in Trastevere, created this one of St. Chrysogonus with Jesus and the Virgin.

Through the sacristy, down spindly steps, you can see (for a fee) a horseshoe-shaped *Confessio* from the 8c as well as vestiges of frescoes in the earlier apse.

History AD
• **2c** The first building complex was 6 m (6½ yards) below and adjacent to the present church.
• **3c** On top, an enormous assembly hall with beautiful frescoes was built.
All of this has been covered up.
• **5c** The present church, situated at a level above the hall.
• **1122** First restoration.
• **1623** Cardinal Scipione Borghese commissioned Giovanni Battista Soria to rebuild the church in the late-Renaissance/early-Baroque style.

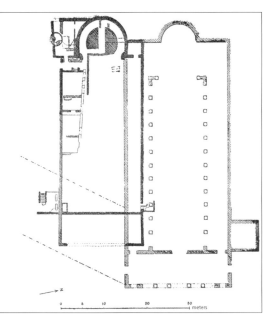

⓭ "Dante's House," Torre degli Anguillara (12c, see Medieval Towers, pages 128-29).

Viale Trastevere, corner of Piazza Sonnino.

Behind Dante's house go to the little square **Piazza del Drago** (Dragon Square). Now take the tortuous **Vicolo del Buco**.

On your left is a medieval house built into the back of **⑭ Chiesa di San Salvatore della Corte**. Early in the 20c a nearby ammunition dump blew up, damaging the facade, and the 1914 repairs were not too faithful. Luckily the 12c belfry tower survived, though it is difficult to see. The apse and the transept shape are 12c, but not the decoration.

Vicolo del Buco, 24, was formerly an English hospice. On the wall is a small plaque in abbreviated Latin: "coll. Angl. m num. 52 e 53" (Collegium Anglicanus).

Near the church is **Eredi Baiocco,** a well-known *stucchi* (plaster artworks) shop.

Via della Luce, 16A. Tel./fax 065818854.

Turn right onto Via della Luce and walk past *No. 41*, a medieval house and courtyard on your right, and *No. 7*, a religious edifice on your left. This used to be a simple mensa for the locals, who only half a decade ago could still have a glass of house wine and bring their own food.

Turn second left on **Via dei Tabacchi**, and first left on **Via Anicia** for a medieval treat.

⑮ Confraternita di San Giovanni dei Genovesi (15c cloister). A cloister untouched since it was built in 1482 is hidden behind a nondescript facade. Calm, beautiful, full of sweet-smelling flowers. Why have we lost the knack of creating patches of heaven on earth? The cloister was part of a hospital "for sick sailors or needy ones," started with the largesse of a nobleman from Genoa. Patients were visited twice daily by the doctor. Sheets, food, drink and medications (they ground up herbal potions here) were provided. Patients who died without a will left their effects to the Confraternita. When it ceased to be a hospital it remained a charitable institution.

History AD
• **3c** This was the site of a Roman hall, dedicated to Santa Bonosa.
• **985-996** Documents prove there was a small church here in the reign of Pope John XV, who lifted the ban on excommunication, but not the death sentence on the infamous **Marozia** (see "Dark Millennium," page 113), who had been the lover of one pope, the mother of another, as well as the aunt of one and the grandmother of a fourth.
• **1121** Papal bull of Calixtus II mentioned this church as already functioning "for the troops" (*curti* meaning "cohorts," the Roman squadrons). This bears out information about soldiers living in this area (see Chiesa di Santa Maria in Trastevere, page 117).

Chiesa di San Giovanni Battista. A flowery late-Baroque interior (18c), but with generous proportions. The treasures are kept in the inner sanctum to the left through the far door. Silver statues, Rococo processional torches, and relics, all carried in the religious mega-processions which different confraternities would lead round their *rione* (quarter) on "high days and holidays."

Via Anicia, 12.

Open Tuesday and Thursday; summer 2-4 pm, winter 3-6 pm. No photography. A donation is appreciated.

Out of the Confraternita turn right, then first left on **Via Madonna dell'Orto**. At the end of the road you can see gigantic **⑯ San Michele a Ripa Grande**, a building now belonging to the Ministry of Culture. Originally built in 1693 by Cardinal Odelscalchi to train street children for jobs, it has been a prison and hospital. After WW II many artists invaded the place and made their studios there. The courtyard with orange trees is attractive. Often there are art shows and conferences in the main building.

Via di San Michele.

*Piazza di Santa Cecilia,
22. Tel. 065899289.*

The frescoes and also ancient houses **can be seen** (donations expected) Tuesday and Thursday 10-11:30 am, Sunday 11:30 am-noon.

History AD

• **Circa 3c** Cecilia converted Valerian, her husband, to Christianity and they lived in chastity together. During the persecutions he was killed when he would not sacrifice to idols. She also was condemned to death by suffocation in her own bath house. Singing hymns, she survived several days – and thus became patron saint of music. The executioner then tried to chop off her head, but he botched the job so badly, she lingered on for three days, making conversions before she eventually gave up the ghost.
• **5c** A shrine was built here, though both she and Valerian had been buried in the Catacombs of San Callisto on the Via Appia as no bodies could be interred in Rome for health reasons.
• **820** Pope Pascal I searched for their tomb, and brought both bodies into Rome to be buried under her own baths where she had been tortured (see the heating tubes on the wall). Some contemporary mosaics have Pascal with a square halo, showing that he was alive at the time the mosaics were created.
• **12c** Bell tower, porch and mosaics added.
• **1293** Di Cambio designed the baldacchino over the altar.
• **1393** Tomb of English cardinal Adam Easton.

Turn into Via Santa Cecilia and continue straight toward Basilica di Santa Cecilia, past a medieval complex of buildings on your right. Notice fake "medieval restaurants."

⓱ Basilica di Santa Cecilia in Trastevere. A tranquil spot with an ancient fountain and lilies in the garden, and a superb fresco of multicolored winged angels in the convent.

(17)

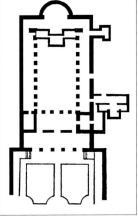

Interior. Crypt. In 1599 Maderno sculpted Cecilia's statue (to be sure it was a likeness, they opened the tomb so he could sculpt from "life").

Diagonally opposite the church at **Piazza di Santa Cecilia, 19**, is another lovely medieval house with columns and an arched extension with a travertine course running along the whole facade.

122

The Last Judgment, an extraordinary fresco (1293) by Maestro **Pietro Cavallini** (the artist who created the mosaics in Santa Maria in Trastevere), was rediscovered in 1900 in the nuns' private dining room. The angels' wings, with graduated multicolored feathers in pinks and reds, and the pleated robes are gorgeous.

Pietro Cavallini's masterpiece. Note the wings' color gradations.

Continue up the *Via di Santa Cecilia* and turn left on *Via dei Genovesi*, and immediately right on *Vicolo dell'Atleta*.

🔞 **Vicolo dell'Atleta, 14**, is a jewel of Dark Ages architecture, as are the houses next to it. Hebrew writing on the central column identifies this as an ancient **synagogue**, founded by the leading medieval lexicographer, Nathan ben Jechiel (1035-1106).

Two fabulous antique sculptures were found under these buildings a century ago: *Apoxyomenos*, a marble athlete holds a *strigil* (a tool to remove excess oil from the body); this Roman copy of the Greek original by the master sculptor Lysippus, is now in the Vatican Museums (see page 88).

Greek bronze found at Vicolo dell'Atleta, 14.

The bronze horse is a Greek original (probably dating from the 4c BC) now in the Musei Capitolini. This former synagogue now operates as the restaurant Spirito di Vino (see Restaurants, page 292).

Now turn left on **Via dei Salumi**, and continue to **Via dell'Arco de' Tolomei** – another ancient arch, though widened 150 years ago. Go through the arch and up the hill; on your left at *No. 1* is a **medieval tower** of great height incorporated in the present building. All the houses on the left are easy on the eye, and venerable. ❶ **Palazzo Mattei** is in the center of **Piazza in Piscinula**, at *No. 1*, a block of exquisite antiquity (though heavily restructured) with medieval casements, windows, doors, bricks, columns. Instructive in showing how people lived back then (see the heavy wrought iron on the windows), it is one of the most important apartment houses surviving since the Middle Ages.

Our walk has now ended, though in this same neighborhood there are more old treats to discover for yourself.

Janiculum Hill

❶ Chiesa di San Pietro in Montorio

[H 3/4]
Piazza di San Pietro in Montorio, 2.
Tel. 065813940.

Getting there
Bus 115.

Open 9 am-12 noon and 4-6 pm.

History AD
• **Late 15c** Built on top of a medieval church by Ferdinando and Isabella of Spain soon after they had thrown the Arabs out of Spain.
• **16c** Richly decorated by outstanding artists. (The Raphael and other fine paintings later disappeared into the Vatican Museums.)

The Renaissance church of St. Peter on Golden Hill (1499-1502) is a possible site of St. Peter's crucifixion. The view of Rome from the parapet is lovely; and lucky Spanish students can study in the Spanish Cultural Academy right next to the church.

The facade has simplicity, almost austerity. But inside! **1ST CHAPEL RIGHT** Sebastiano del Piombo painted in 1518 a superb Flagellation from drawings by Michelangelo. **4TH CHAPEL RIGHT** Ceiling fresco by Vasari (1511-1574, more famous for his chronicles of Renaissance artists), who slipped in his own portrait in black on the left.

Unmarked tomb of Beatrice Cenci (see page 48). **5TH CHAPEL LEFT** Michelangelo's star pupil, Daniele da

Volterra, 1509-1566, painted the Baptism of Jesus. **2ND CHAPEL LEFT** Bernini and pupil (F. Baratta). Within the church courtyard is

❷ Tempietto

One of the jewels of early-Renaissance architecture (Bramante, 1499-1502). Notice the perfect proportions and the classic orders inspired by ancient Roman buildings. Medieval saints' tombs were often circular and pilgrims could easily spot them and come to pray. It's very popular today for weddings.

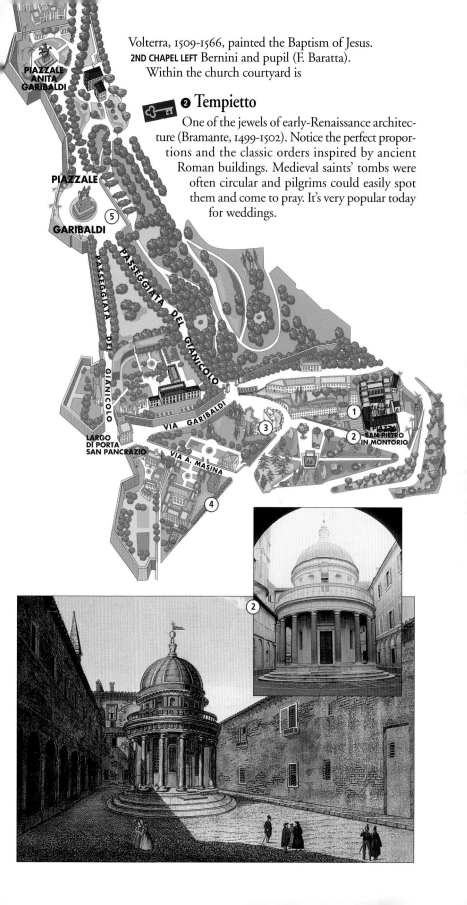

PIAZZALE ANITA GARIBALDI

PIAZZALE

GARIBALDI

PASSEGGIATA DEL GIANICOLO

PASSEGGIATA DEL GIANICOLO

VIA GARIBALDI

VIA A. MASINA

LARGO DI PORTA SAN PANCRAZIO

PIAZZA SAN PIETRO IN MONTORIO

- **98-117** Trajan had water from Lake Bracciano channeled to Rome, in a mostly subterranean aqueduct.
- **Dark Ages** Water in the aqueduct was cut off during the barbarian invasions of Rome.
- **1612** Pope Paul V Borghese had the aqueduct repaired, and it was named after him.
- **1690-98** C. Fontana pillaged marble from the Roman Forum and Forum of Nerva, and used six columns from the old St. Peter's, to build this monumental "Mostra," modeled on a triumphal arch.

❸ Fontanone dell'Acqua Paola

Used to bring water to Trastevere, the Vatican and Via Giulia, this is one of the most magnificent fountains of the city because you feel so refreshed watching the enormous force of water gushing down, and because the view over Rome is spectacular from here. You can see this Baroque fountain (1612) from most parts of Rome, it is so huge. In summer there is usually an outdoor bar and cinema in the square.

❹ American Academy in Rome (McKim, Mead and White, 1912)

One of the leading American centers abroad for independent study and advanced research in the arts and humanities. Since 1894, the U.S. has had

Via Angelo Masina, 5.
Tel. 0658461.

Veduta del Castello dell'Acqua Paola sul Monte Aureo

126

an institution – like other national academies such as the French Academy and the British School at Rome – offering support in an inspiring environment to some of America's most gifted artists and scholars. The American Academy is the only one that is privately funded, and its juries select up to 30 lucky individuals, out of the 1,000 or so who compete annually to win the coveted Rome Prize. Thanks to the academy's generous patrons, these lucky Fellows get to live, study and create in a beautiful setting, working independently and exchanging ideas. Public events include exhibitions, concerts and lectures. By appointment you can visit the beautiful Sid and Mercedes Bass gardens.

❺ Giuseppe Garibaldi monument

KIDS His equestrian statue dominates a terrace with the best view over Rome for grown-ups and entertainment for kids. Nearby is Garibaldi's wife, Anita, the only equestrian statue with a woman wielding both her gun and her suckling baby.

Piazzale Giuseppe Garibaldi.

Medieval Towers

Medieval towers sprouted all over Rome from the 7c to the 13c. They denoted power; their height showed the importance of a family. Rome probably had more than the Tuscan town still famous for its medieval skyscrapers, San Gimignano. Now as you pursue this layered city, see if you can spot the ones that didn't come down:

Torre dei Caetani
The remains of a medieval castle belonging originally to the Pierleoni. *On the Tiber Island* (see page 49).

Torre dei Frangipane
or Torre della Scimmia *Monkey tower* (15c)

At the top of the tower the picture of the Virgin (always lit) is in thanks for the safe return of a newborn babe which had been snatched by a monkey and taken up the tower. After some time in prayer, the father whistled, and monkey with babe came down.
Corner of Via dei Pianellari and Via dei Portoghesi.

Torre dei Margani (12c)
and Torre degli Annibaldi
These two fortified towers were part of a large castle of the Annibaldi family.
Torre dei Margani has been incorporated into the bell tower of San Francesco di Paola church. The other tower in *Via Fagutale* is still inhabited. *Bottom right corner Piazza San Pietro in Vincoli.*

Torre dei Borgia
Off Via Cavour in an 8c fortified palace of the bishops of Tivoli. Fabric of flint stones and black stones in alternating layers. Adjacent to the house where **Pope Alexander VI Borgia** kept **Vannozza Caetani,** the mother of his children. *Halfway up the stairs called Via San Francesco di Paola leading to San Pietro in Vincoli Church* (see page 176).

Torre del Grillo (1223)
Connected by a *bridge of sighs* to the 17c palace of Marquese Cosimo del Grillo. On the tower's top the marquis left his mark. *Going down Salita del Grillo on righthand side.*

Torre de' Conti (13c)

Built by Pope **Innocent III**, son of **Count Segni** from Anagni (south of Rome), for guarding the papal processions to the Lateran. Made of detritus and marble from the edge of the Forum of Nerva. **Petrarch** called it "unique in the whole city." It was twice as big until it semidestructed in the great 1348 earthquake. *Corner of Largo Ricci and Via Tor de' Conti.*

Torre delle Milizie (1227)

Built by **Pope Gregory IX**, another son
of another **Count of Segni**, on the slopes of
Quirinal Hill, then a heavily fortified area.
Largest and most remarkable of the baronial
towers, where now two eagles live. *On Largo
Magnanapoli behind Foro Traiano.*

Torri Capocci (5c)
The two towers, in medieval times part of the
Capocci family fortress, are now divided by
Via Giovanni Lanza. The freestanding tower is
part of the Augustine Monastery; the other is
engulfed by the Convent of the Daughters of
Our Lady of the Garden.
Piazza San Martino ai Monti.

Tor Millina
Ancient tower restored in 1492 by Pietro
Millini, who incorporated it into his palace.
*Corner of Via di Tor Millina and Via Santa
Maria dell'Anima.*

Torre Orsini in Palazzo Taverna
A smaller tower where the authors used to live but which is more famous for
being mentioned in Dante's *Inferno*. The 13c fortress of the powerful Orsini family
was rebuilt in the 15c, but this tower became an elevator shaft after WW II.
Courtyard of Via Monte Giordano, 36.

Torre Vecchiarelli
Vestiges of a medieval tower were subsumed in this 17c palace built by Cardinal
Odoardo Vecchiarelli.
Via dei Vecchiarelli, 37.

Torre del Papito
or **Torre dei Boccamazzi** (14c)
When the subterranean Area Sacra di Largo Argentina was cleared of all buildings
in 1925, only this one tower was left standing, along with its adjoining portico.
Largo di Torre Argentina, corner of Via Florida and Via San Nicola de' Cesarini.

Torre della Moletta

Another tower of the Frangipane family,
who built right into the Circus Maximus ruins.
Via dei Cerchi, corner Viale Aventino.

Torre degli Anguillara
or **Casa di Dante**

The fortified feudal castle of the
Anguillara family. Legend says Dante slept
here. Today only part of the tower remains
but it's enough to give us a feel for
medieval times. *Viale Trastevere and
Piazza Sonnino.*

Aventine Hill

❶ Rose Garden ❷ Orange Garden
❸ Basilica di Santa Sabina
❹ Chiesa di Sant'Alessio
❺ Priorato di Malta
❻ Chiesa di Sant'Anselmo
❼ Chiesa di Santa Prisca
❽ Basilica di San Saba

[I 7/8]
Getting there
Bus 75, 175, 715 or
B Metro Circo Massimo
stop.

One of the seven hills of ancient Rome, where the top brass moved when the emperors took over the Palatine Hill. Today it is still an attractive residential area and there are some great private houses hidden among the pine trees, as well as a fine church or two.

❶ **Rose Garden.** Two gardens stuffed with roses, and a splendid view of the Palatine ruins across the Circus Maximus. Massive blooming occurs in late April through May, with perfume wafting in the air as you walk under the bowers.

❷ Orange Garden (Parco Savelli). These 10c walled fortifications were later made into the stronghold of the Savelli family (13c), which dominated this hilltop. The bucolic garden has views across the river to the Janiculum Hill and St. Peter's.

❸ Basilica di Santa Sabina. An authentic early Christian church. Although much of the original decoration has gone, dignity and generous proportions make this a gem of the Aventine.

Early vestiges: **Main door** of carved wood from the original 5c church, with scenes from the Old and New Testaments. Top left panel shows the Crucifixion without the cross (death on the cross was then considered too painful to be shown). **Interior**. The 5c blue and gold mosaic over the front door depicts Jews who converted to Christianity; 13c mosaic monument to a Dominican master general in the middle of the nave.

*Piazza Pietro d'Illiria, 1.
Tel. 0657941.*

Open 7:30 am-noon
and 3:30-6 pm.

❹ Chiesa di Sant'Alessio (Church of St. Boniface and St. Alexis, originally 1217, modernized after 1750 and more substantially in 1846). Of the 13c church only the campanile and the Cosmatesque doorway and floor remain. **Facade**. Tommaso De Marchis, 1750. **Interior**. Immediately to the left of the entrance is a sculpture of St. Alexis. That diagonal beam over him is a remnant of the wooden stair under which he lived and died after he fled his bride-to-be; he returned 17 years later as a beggar and slept here unrecognized by his parents.

*Piazza di Sant'Alessio, 23.
Tel. 065743446.*

Open 8 am-8 pm
(ring the bell
if the door
is closed).

❺ Priorato di Malta. The residence of the grand master of the Order of the Knights of Malta. Famously grand view of St. Peter's through the **keyhole** of the outer wooden door. These Maltese knights were already busy running hospitals in Jerusalem when the crusaders arrived in 1099.

*Piazza Cavalieri
di Malta, 3.*

Fee
Open group tours
only, Saturday 10
and 11 am (can also
reserve by phone
0667581234).

❻ Chiesa di Sant'Anselmo (1892-96). Pope Leo XIII built this as the chapel of a large international college for the Benedictines. Their Gregorian chants are enchanting. The Dalai Lama has stayed in the monastery wing.

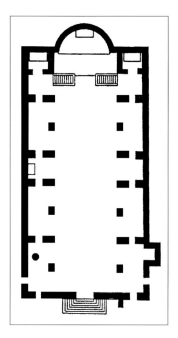

❼ Chiesa di Santa Prisca (reconstructed 17c and 19c). St. Peter stayed here with his fellow Judean tent maker Aquila and his wife Priscilla (or Prisca), as St. Paul mentioned in his *Epistles*. A Christian cemetery was built in the early 5c; a church was added two centuries later.

In those days this was an important church and its priests attended Church councils in 499 and 595. It was one of the 20 abbeys of medieval Rome. **Facade.** 1660 Baroque, by Carlo Lambardi. **Interior.** The 17c frescoes by Passignano show St. Peter baptizing Prisca as well as a ferocious lion licking her toes instead of eating her. **Beneath the church.** Some 1c houses have been found here, possibly belonging to Emperor Trajan, as well as a nymphaeum. Small museum and crypt. In 1933 a 2c temple of the military god Mithras was discovered. Frescoes and a statue of Mithras killing the bull were found 15 years later.

Via Santa Prisca, 11. Tel. 065743798.

Cult of Mithras   By the beginning of the Roman Empire, worship of the Persian god Mithras was widespread among the legionnaires returning from overseas service in the Near East. The soldiers considered Mithras their special patron, who therefore was seen as the protector of the empire's stability. Bas- reliefs in Rome's many Mithraic temples show the god wearing trousers, a short tunic and a Phrygian cap.

Central to the cult was the ceremonial slaughtering of a bull by an adept who had risen through the seven levels of initiations. As the bull's neck was stabbed by a short dagger, a snake and a dog licked its blood while a scorpion bit its testicles. A particularly expert way of killing the bull, shown in some ancient bas-reliefs, is to put one's fingers into its nostrils, making it easy to pull back its head, as the flesh inside the nose is so highly sensitive that the animal is immobilized, and then slicing its neck. This rite symbolized the universal cycle of renewal and therefore fertility.

Worshippers of Mithras witnessed the sacrifice and participated symbolically by eating bread and drinking wine. One can easily imagine the early Christian fathers emulating this "communion" Mithraic worship. Certainly they worked hard to root out what they considered the pagan cult of Mithras, which had been Christianity's main rival in the early years.

❽ Basilica di San Saba. Church with a motley history. **Exterior.** Portico 13c. Last reconstruction 1943. **Interior.** On the left is a fresco of the life of St. Nicholas of Bari. One scene shows three young maidens lying naked in bed. They were of a good family and their penniless father was in despair seeing no future for his dowerless daughters. St. Nicholas, aware of their predicament, one night threw a bag of gold through their window, thus giving them dowries – and giving us **Santa Claus!**

Piazza Gian Lorenzo Bernini, 20. Tel. 065743352.

133

Gem Churches

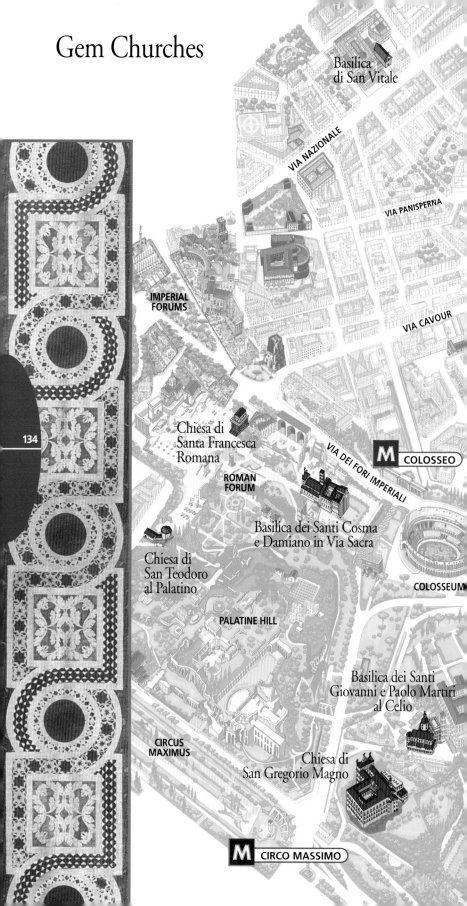

Basilica
di San Vitale

VIA NAZIONALE

VIA PANISPERNA

VIA CAVOUR

IMPERIAL
FORUMS

Chiesa di
Santa Francesca
Romana

VIA DEI FORI IMPERIALI

M COLOSSEO

ROMAN
FORUM

Basilica dei Santi Cosma
e Damiano in Via Sacra

Chiesa di
San Teodoro
al Palatino

COLOSSEUM

PALATINE HILL

Basilica dei Santi
Giovanni e Paolo Martiri
al Celio

CIRCUS
MAXIMUS

Chiesa di
San Gregorio Magno

M CIRCO MASSIMO

134

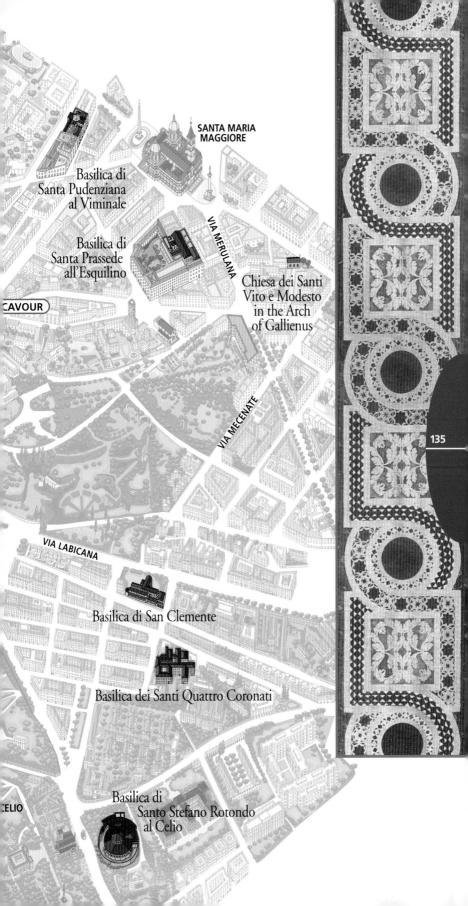

SANTA MARIA
MAGGIORE

Basilica di
Santa Pudenziana
al Viminale

VIA MERULANA

Basilica di
Santa Prassede
all'Esquilino

Chiesa dei Santi
Vito e Modesto
in the Arch
of Gallienus

CAVOUR

VIA MECENATE

135

VIA LABICANA

Basilica di San Clemente

Basilica dei Santi Quattro Coronati

CELIO

Basilica di
Santo Stefano Rotondo
al Celio

Via Nomentana, 349.
Tel. 068610840.

Getting there
Bus 36, 60, 337.

Fee for catacombs
Open 9 am-noon
and 4-6 pm.
Closed Sunday morning
and Monday
afternoon.

The **mausoleum** is
open the same
hours as catacombs,
above.

History AD
• **Circa 300** During Emperor **Diocletian**'s persecutions, this land be-
longed to the family
of Agnes ("pure" in
Greek), a Christian
teenager who spurned
advances of a praetor's
son and was martyred
for her freedom of
choice. Thrown naked
into Domitian's arena,
her hair miraculously
grew to cover her
shame (see Piazza Na-
vona, page 146). They
botched an attempt to
behead her before
finishing her off.
• **324** Emperor
Constantine built
a church over Agnes's
tomb here to honor
his daughter Costan-
tina's baptism (see her
mausoleum, below.)
• **625** In an epoch no-
table for decadence,
Pope **Honorius I**, an in-
dustrious savior of
Rome's imperial glory,
rebuilt this little jewel
the way you see it,
which – unlike most
of the city's churches –
miraculously escaped
later revamping.

Basilica di Sant'Agnese fuori le Mura and Mausoleo di Santa Costanza

About a mile beyond Porta Pia is this marvelous early church complex, where in addition to these two buildings there was originally an enormous basilica attached to the mausoleum.

Basilica di Sant'Agnese (7c).
Entering from the Via
Nomentana side, the tour-
ist descends a long flight
of stairs to the church level;
the entrance to the cata-
combs is opposite the bottom stair. Services on
Sundays at Sant'Agnese are
crowded – unusual these
days, and allegedly because
of the miraculous statue of
the Virgin in the grotto
outside. Notice the fine 7c
Byzantine mosaic behind
the altar. The women's
gallery over the nave is

unique. The complex has a sports club for the parish; its *bocce* pitch, soccer, tennis and clubhouse make the church lively.

Catacombs. Saint Agnes is buried under the church, in the 7 km (4 mile) long catacombs. They started as tufo quarries, then became burial places (uncremated bodies had to be buried outside the city) and a site for worship during persecutions.

Mausoleo di Santa Costanza (AD 351). For us mosaic freaks, among the world's most satisfying artworks are the mosaics completely covering these vaulted ceilings.

Truly fine 4c Roman-style mosaics, with an attempt at perspective, they were created before the fall of Rome, and decadence.

The "putti" crushing grapes to make wine are charmingly alive and colorful – combining pagan and Christian subject matter. These mosaics have perfect

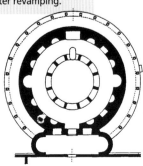

harmony and bring an uplifting religious quality to the building, especially if there is a wedding ceremony with the melodious full-bodied tones of an organ filling the air (the hall has perfect acoustics). The magnificent casket of salami red porphyry in a niche opposite the door is a copy of the original, now in the Vatican Museums.

The old basilica (now the adjacent walled garden) was absolutely vast: 98 m (107 yards) long and 40 m (44 yards) wide. Sant'Agnese is tiny in comparison.

Basilica dei Santi Quattro Coronati

Down a little side street off Piazza San Giovanni, you are suddenly back in the Middle Ages visiting this gem-like medieval enclave. It is part of a convent, surrounded by giant fortifications that offered sanctuary to early popes from assaults by the powerful Roman nobles and other barbarians.

Today nobody knows anything about the four crowned martyrs for whom it was named, except they were killed for refusing to worship the pagan god of medicine, Asclepius (see Tiber Island, page 49).

Since the original church was twice as long and twice as wide, the rounded apse and the overhead **women's gallery**, reconstituted from the earlier building, look awkwardly large in this tiny basilica.

Note the lovely 12c Cosmatesque floor and an exquisite 15c Renaissance tabernacle next to the last column on the left. The Baroque frescoes were added in the 17c. There are usually a few nuns at prayer behind the

History AD
• **4c** Emperor Constantine's daughter Costanza converted to Christianity because, while praying at Saint Agnes's tomb, her wounds were miraculously healed. She died in 354; her body was sent back from Asia Minor to this mausoleum.

[I 11]
Via SS.Quattro Coronati, 20. Tel. 0670475427.

Getting there
Bus 81, 85, 87, 93, 186 or **B Metro** Colosseo stop.

Open 6:15 am-12:30 pm and 3:15-8 pm.

Our favorite
The nuns are Augustinians, a cloistered order; when you ring to enter the adjoining chapel of St. Silvester (to the right side of the first outer courtyard), the key will be passed to you through a rotating wooden hatch that prevents you from seeing the nuns inside their convent. But what you do see in the chapel are fabulous frescoes of St. Silvester's life.

.TEMP. SS. QVATVOR. COR.

[H 10/11]
Via Labicana, 95.
Tel. 067740021.

Getting there
Bus 81, 85, 87, 93, 186 or
B Metro Colosseo stop.

Open daily 9 am-1:30
pm, 3-6 pm.
Fee to excavations.

forbidding bars that cut off the altar and its surrounding area. Be sure to ring the bellpull on the left wall to visit the wonderfully mystical 12c cloister: like the contemporary cloister of St. Paul Outside the Walls, a truly spiritual garden.

Basilica di San Clemente

In this wonderfully preserved medieval basilica, you will experience an amazing whirl through three different layers of Rome's history, thanks to the Irish, who again saved civilization.

❶ The **present church** was started during the time of Pope Pascal II (1108) and built exactly over an earlier larger one. Salvaged from the old church, and still in use, is the superb **choir**, that marble enclosed area in the center of the church. The bishop's throne behind the high altar is 12c, as are the Cosmatesque floor and mosaic spiral candlestick. Arnolfo di Cambio (13c) sculpted the wall tabernacle; 14c frescoes below the apse mosaics complete that colorful wall.

❷ The **lower Christian church**, dating from 385, can be visited through the sacristy. It was rebuilt in the 5c, restored in the 8c-10c and heavily damaged during the 1084 Sack of Rome (by the dreaded Robert Guiscard, whose marauding Normans had occupied Sicily). Wonderful **6c frescoes** show St. Clement's exile and death as well as Sinnius, prefect of Rome, blinded when coming to arrest his wife for attending Mass here. Pick out Pope **St. Leo IV** with a square halo (meaning he was still alive at the time of the painting). This and the exciting finds below it were discovered in 1857 by Father Mullooly, prior of the church's custodians, the Irish Dominicans. In 1967 on this level a total-immersion **baptismal font** was discovered. In 1989 Professor Guidobaldi discovered the 6c sacristy where Pope Gregory I (died AD 604) prepared himself for Mass. The floor is a lovely inlay of colored marbles, a technique predating the intricate Cosmatesque floors of the 12c.

❸ At 10 m (11 yards) deep in the earth, directly below the two superimposed churches, you can visit a **Roman street** with two AD 1c houses. One was a Temple of Mithras, inserted into an earlier family *domus* with finely stuccoed ceilings.

The rite of going into the water up to one's neck was prevalent in the early Church, especially with adult converts, to wash away their sins.	**Our favorites** **Mosaics** from the 12c on the back wall behind the altar are replete with paschal sheep (the flock) and doves (the apostles) amid leafy bowers. Christ is on a triumphal arch with Saints Peter and Clement and their boats; the river of paradise flows from the cross. In **St. Catherine's Chapel** are frescoes (pre-1430) by the founders of the Renaissance, Masaccio and his teacher Masolino. A true gem. Ignore the less interesting 18c frescoes on ceiling and wall, and the busy Baroque stucco work. The **Irish Dominicans** have taken tender loving care of this marvelous basilica since 1667 and present delightful summer concerts and operas in the colonnaded courtyard, which was the medieval entrance. A recent production was Andrew Lloyd Weber's *Jesus Christ Superstar*!

[G 8]
*Piazza di Santa
Francesca Romana, 4.
Entrance from
Via dei Fori Imperiali.*
Tel. 066795528.

Open 10 am-12 noon
and 4-6 pm.

Chiesa di Santa Francesca Romana

The church of St. Frances of Rome, 8c, is mainly a wedding church in the Roman Forum, which occasionally has sacred music concerts. Santa Francesca is the patron saint of motorists. Taxi drivers throng here on March 9,

"Feeding the Chickens," detail from the apse mosaics.

139

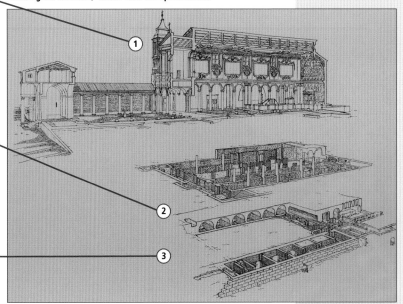

the saint's day, when her mummified body is paraded. **Facade**. Now Baroque, it was "ameliorated" by Carlo Lambardi in 1615, during the frenzy of the Counter-Reformation. **Interior**. A 17c **coffered ceiling**. **Two paving**

• **1611** (Pietro da Cortona) Restructured in part, with the charming semicircular porch and the facade added, though da Cortona's piazza plans were not completed.

stones from Via Sacra show imprints of St. Peter's knees as he prayed hard while the magician Simon Magnus performed wizardry by flying around him (behind a grille in the south wall). A 12c **altar painting** was discovered underneath a 19c one during restoration in 1950. In the sacristy is possibly the oldest Christian painting ever (5c), discovered underneath the 12c one. The **apse** has a Byzantine **mosaic** of the Madonna and saints (1161), full of bright colors.

Bell tower (*campanile*, 12c). This one is a real beauty. Always easy to tell a *Romanesque* (10-13c) steeple by its 3, 5 or 7 stories, and slim marble column lookouts and porphyry discs or ancient plates embellishing the facade. A wedding-cake look!

Basilica dei Santi Cosma e Damiano in Via Sacra, AD 6c

[G 9]
Largo G. Gatti
Via dei Fori Imperiali, 1.

Open 9 am-1 pm
and 4-7 pm.

Built out of two Roman edifices, Romulus's Temple and a hall in Emperor Vespasian's Forum of Peace. Redecorated in the 17c with Baroque curlicues. Don't miss the 18c Neapolitan Nativity scene off the courtyard.

Our favorite
The large restored 6c mosaic covering half the dome behind an uninteresting baldacchino altar.

140

Chiesa di San Teodoro al Palatino

[G 8]
Via di San Teodoro.
Tel. 066786624.

Open 9:30 am-noon.

Tucked into the side of the Palatine Hill, the emperor's great grain supplies were stored here in the Horrea Agrippiana. After Christianity was legalized (AD 313), these storehouses were transformed by the creation of this church, as well as several "Diaconia," houses for needy Christians.

St. Theodore was a soldier who patrolled Turkey, on the eastern frontiers of the empire. As a Christian he was martyred in AD 306.

Exterior. Down some steps to a tiny oval courtyard, a pagan altar at its center; concerts are given here on summer evenings. The church facade in brick is very welcoming, and the restorations in 1453 changed the building into a perfect circle while preserving the apse inside.

Interior. Under the octagonal dome are the most comfortable plush seats in any church!

Don't miss the dark but finely executed 6c mosaic in the apse. Excavations under the church can be visited. Named after a Greek prelate, this recently became a Greek Orthodox church.

Chiesa dei Santi Vito e Modesto in the Arch of Gallienus

This sleepy church nestles in one of the arches of the Porta Esquilina, built in AD IC and later incorporated into the Servian wall.

[F 11]
Via Carlo Alberto, 47
(Via di San Vito).
Tel. 064465836.

Open 5-7 pm.

The span over the road has an AD 262 inscription to Emperor Gallienus.

Basilica dei Santi Giovanni e Paolo Martiri al Celio, AD 410

A veritable thriller is told of the lost bodies of these two brothers, officers in the Imperial Roman Army, murdered when they converted to Christianity during the brief reign (AD 361-363) of Emperor Julian the Apostate, who tried to turn the clock back to pagan worship. Their bodies were hidden in their 20-room apartment house overlooking the Colosseum. Two other people were

[H 9] Piazza Santi
Giovanni e Paolo, 13.
Tel. 067005745.

Open 8:30 am-noon
and 1:30-6:30 pm.

murdered when they spread the word of the missing brothers. A century later the house became a church. Restored in the 5c after Alaric the Hun's damage and again in the 11c after Robert Guiscard's destruction. Medievalist Richard Krautheimer wrote about a row of Romanesque windows: "the Lombard or Rhenish dwarf's gallery placed atop the Early Christian apse . . . remains forever an alien body" (see page 94). Titular church of New York's cardinal.

Portico (12c). The entrance door is surrounded by tiny mosaics and a pair of carved lions.

Interior. The high altar columns of alabaster are Egyptian. The church was prettily redecorated in the 18c.

Monastery garden. Large substructures, *vivaria*, "are the remains of cages that housed wild animals destined to die in the Colosseum."

[H 9]
Clivo di Scauro.
Tel. 0670454544.

Fee
Open Thursday to Monday 10 am-1 pm and 3-6 pm.

Ancient Roman House
Down under the basilica, visit this vast, private, 4c home with marvelous frescoes, converted from 3c shops

[I 10]
Via Santo Stefano, 7.
Tel. 0670493717.

Open Tuesday to Saturday 9 am-1 pm and 3:30-6 pm.
Closed Sunday and Monday.

Basilica di Santo Stefano Rotondo al Celio

Built in a tranquil setting next to a blip in the nearby ancient aqueduct stands St. Stephen's church in all its circular magnificence, umbilically joined to the Missionary Sisters of the Sacred Rib.

Exterior. Charming ancient brick edifice with a columned portico entrance.

Interior. Three concentric circles with columns create an impressive interior with a feeling of spaciousness and light. The original design of four entrances through the four mosaicked chapels at each corner has long since been lost. The central altar was created in 1580. The frescoes show scenes of martyrdom, and a feeling of austerity is palpable, probably due to so many invasions and so much destruction.

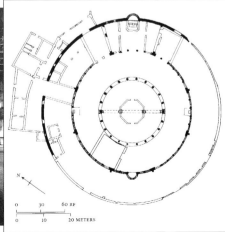

Chiesa di San Gregorio Magno, AD 575

[H 9]
*Piazza San Gregorio, 1.
Tel. 067008227.*

Open 8:30 am-12:30 pm
and 1:45-6:30 pm.

The church of St. Gregory the Great is a large complex, with a small building occupied by the nuns of Mother Teresa of Calcutta on the left side of the church, and a monastery of Armenian monks overlooking a charming courtyard on the right. A beautiful small square with cypresses houses Roman vestiges believed to be the wall of Gregory's house. A shop in the outbuilding below the stairs sells products from the Monastery of Camaldolesi near Arezzo: honey, natural products for hair and skin, and marvelous flower scents.

Basilica di San Vitale,
AD 402

Buried down a steep staircase, this large church was cut in half in 1475 by Pope Sixtus IV della Rovere, who also rebuilt the facade.
Interior. Restored in the 19c and desperately needing a face-lift today. The four large statues around the altar have fine carving.

·TEMPL·S·GREGORII·

[E 9]
*Via Nazionale, 194B.
Tel. 064823338.*

Open 7:30 am-12:30 pm and 4:30-7:30 pm.

Basilica di Santa Pudenziana al Viminale,
Rebuilt AD 384, Pope Siricius

[F 10]
*Via Urbana, 160.
Tel. 064814622.*

Open 8 am-noon and 3-6 pm.

143

Set deep in the ground, this very old church has a long unbroken history of worship. The ancient building is beautiful, and if you're lucky you might be able to see the Roman Baths (behind the *Custode* door on the left).
Facade. Fine medieval frieze in marble over the weathered original door.
Interior. 4c mosaics glitter, covering the wall behind the altar. Wallowing in water, on either side of the figure of Christ, are a winged bull and lion, the lion's face strangely similar to that in *The Wizard of Oz*.
It is now a Filipino church; if you visit during a fair, sample some of their delicious food.

Basilica di Santa Prassede all'Esquilino, AD 822

[F 11]
*Via Santa Prassede, 9A.
Tel. 064882456.*

Open 7:30 am-noon and 4-6:30 pm.

Pope St. Paschal built the church to honor his mother, Theodora. St. Zeno's chapel, halfway down the nave, is the best example of Byzantine art in Rome. Cosmatesque pavements pattern the floor, with a marble porphyry disk commemorating where St. Praxede hid early Christian martyrs' bodies. Though the reshoring of an oft-sagging building altered the original structure, the 9c mosaics are intact and in profusion, as are two sisters depicted in them. Look for a woman with a square halo (called a nimbus); it indicates that she was still alive at the time of the mosaic.

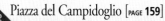

145

Noble edifices, combining taste and beauty with imposing proportions, would immensely conduce to the exaltation of the Chair of St. Peter. Pope Nicholas V

Poussin sculpted Ganges), prompted Innocent X to levy a tax on bread; from then on he was reviled with slogans attacking him and his sister-in-law Olimpia (whose name was distorted into "Olim Pia" the Latin equivalent of "she *was* virtuous").

Fontana del Moro (1653, Bernini). At the south end of the piazza, opposite Palazzo Pamphili, the central figure of an African cuddling a dolphin was added by Bernini to the 1575 fountain designed by Giacomo della Porta. Indefatigable Bernini often had assistants sculpt his designs. At the north end of the piazza, the third fountain was redesigned in the 19c to match the Moro Fountain.

Chiesa di Sant'Agnese in Agone (1657, Borromini). Look carefully at the front of this church to appreciate Borromini's inventive use of rippling in-and-out curves that give depth to the thin facade he transformed into a grandiose papal monument. Borromini's plans always call for sober, basically white interiors, so you will be surprised by the somewhat overpowering richness you find inside. Bernini's use of warm-colored marble predominates, and he ordered the frescoes in the dome (1670-90, Ciro Ferri) and pendentives (1662-72, Baciccia). The church's monumentality is Borromini's, its flamboyancy Bernini's.

Piazza Navona.
Tel. 0668192134.

...ting Innocent X's not-so-innocent favorite and sister-in-law, Olimpia Maidalchini, to dangle a solid silver model of this fountain before the eyes of the pope – and then give it to him.
• **1652** Pope Innocent X Pamphili commissioned Girolamo Rainaldi and his son Carlo to make a glorified family chapel incorporating St. Agnes's much revered shrine.
• **1653** Innocent replaced the Rainaldis with Borromini, who pulled down their front wall and designed the complex plasticity you see in the facade. He also lightened the cramped interior.
• **1667** Bernini took over, but did not modify the unity of Borromini's masterpiece except by gilding, sculpting and using colored marble.

NEARBY

Palazzo Braschi (1792, Cosimo Morelli). This was the last palace erected in Rome for the nephews of a pope, in this case Pius VI Braschi's. Napoleon deposed and deported Pius VI, who died imprisoned at Valence, where his death certificate reads: "Name: Citizen Jean Braschi. Trade: pontiff."

Inside is the **Museum of Rome**. Even a short visit gives you a feeling for the glorious days and nights enjoyed by the popes, their families and courtiers from the Middle Ages to the 19c. Paintings show Piazza Navona with the nobles' carriages axle-high in water during August (their version of air conditioning), and also Queen Christina of Sweden being feted by the Barberini family during her first Carnival in Rome.

[F 5]
Piazza San Pantaleo, 10.
Tel. 0667108346.

Getting there
Bus 30, 40, 46, 62, 64, 70, 81, 87, 116, 492, 628.

Fee
Open 9 am-7 pm.
Closed Monday.

• **1651** Pope Innocent X held a contest to choose the sculptor who should crown his great piazza with a central monument. Originally, a much less elaborate fountain was to be created by the pope's protégé, Borromini. But his archrival Bernini managed to steal the commission away, by get-

Under the obelisk is a huge, empty grotto, a mannerist architectural trick which makes the enormously heavy obelisk appear to be floating in air.

The Nile, the Danube, the Ganges and the Plata represent the four corners of the world. The immense cost of this complicated design, involving four other sculptors who did the individual river gods (Claude

[F 5] *Corso Vittorio Emanuele, 166. Tel. 0668806848.*

Fee
Open Tuesday to Sunday 9 am-1 pm; Tuesday and Thursday 5-8 pm.

Museo Barracco or **Piccola Farnesina** (1523). A small, cozy museum containing Giovanni Barracco's superb collection of Assyrian, Egyptian and Greek artifacts, but his Etruscan and Roman art is not as good as what you can see at Villa Giulia and Palazzo Massimo. This elegant Renaissance townhouse, complete with classical courtyard, was built for Father Leroy, whose coat of arms, including the French lily, is on the facade. People believed he was of the Farnese family, whose lily is similar, so it was dubbed "Little Farnese Palace."

Corso Vittorio Emanuele, 141.

Palazzo Massimo alle Colonne (1536, Baldassarre Peruzzi). The seat of the Massimo family, which claims to be descended from a Roman emperor. It was built at the height of the Renaissance by Peruzzi, one of the finest architects of that epoch, on the site of the ancient **Odeon of Emperor Domitian**. The curved facade of the palazzo follows the semicircular shape of that small AD 1c theater. The lofty portico has six Doric columns.

Every March 16 the palazzo is open to commemorate the miraculous cure of Paolo Massimo, who in 1583 was brought back from the dead by **St. Philip Neri**. You may or may not lend credence to miracles, but the Renaissance luxury you will observe if you visit Palazzo Massimo on March 16 will be hard to believe.

Piazza Sant'Andrea della Valle. Tel. 066861339.

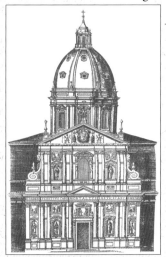

Basilica di Sant'Andrea della Valle (1665, Carlo Maderno, Carlo Rainaldi, Carlo Fontana). The dome is the second highest in Rome, after St. Peter's. The hero of Puccini's **Tosca** is painting in this church in the opening scene of that opera. Enter, and compare the ceiling paintings by **Domenichino** (1581-1641) with those of his rival, **Giovanni Lanfranco** (1582-1647). The latter did the brilliant and innovative trompe l'oeil fresco of the Glory of Paradise in the dome, the earliest 17c illusionist cupola painting, which influenced subsequent Baroque masters. Domenichino had previously executed the fresco cycle of the life of St. Andrew in the vault of the choir, in a very traditional, static style. But after he had seen Lanfranco's exuberant dome, Domenichino painted the pendentives of the dome with frescoes of the four Evangelists in a style so vigorous that they have been compared to Michelangelo's Sistine Ceiling.

The famous feature of the facade is the single stone angel halfway up the left side, of which there is no pendant on the other side to provide symmetry. The sculptor **Ercole Ferrata**, hearing that Pope Alexander VII had criticized his first angel, swore, "If he wants another, let him make it himself!"

Courtyard of Cardinal Andrea della Valle's 1517 palazzo, showing his famous art collection, one of the earliest.

Palazzo Madama (1610, Paolo Maracelli and Ludovico Cardi). This palace replaced one where **Catherine de' Medici** lived before going off in 1533 to Paris, where she married **Henri** II and introduced fine cuisine to the transalpine barbarians. It is named after the illegitimate daughter of Emperor **Charles** V of Austria, who married Alessandro de' Medici but whose title was simply *Madame*. The stunning Baroque facade and enlarged wings surround an ornate chamber which has housed the Senate of the Italian republic since unification in 1871.

[F 5] *Piazza Madama (Corso Rinascimento).* Tel. 0667061.

Open first Saturday of each month 10 am-6 pm.

Decoration in the Senate dome.

Chiesa di Santa Maria della Pace (15c, Baccio Pontelli). FIRST CHAPEL RIGHT On both sides of the arch are Raphael's sinuous "Sibyls" (1514), commissioned by Agostino Chigi (see page 110) for this, his chapel.

[E 5] *Piazza della Pace.*

SECOND CHAPEL RIGHT Architecture by Antonio da Sangallo the Younger (1483-1546). Sculptures of candelabra and escutcheon by Simone Mosca with marble stolen from the Temple of Jupiter on Capitoline Hill. FIRST CHAPEL LEFT Baldassarre Peruzzi (1481-1538) painted the glorious fresco of the Virgin with Saints Bridget and Catherine. OCTAGON Above the altar the sacred image by Carlo Maderno of Mary the Peaceful (Madonna della Pace).

Adjoining the church is a cloister of beautiful proportion by Bramante (1500).

Santa Maria della Pace.

Three Renaissance Palazzi and Campo de' Fiori

Palazzo della Cancelleria, Palazzo Farnese, Palazzo Spada

[F 5]
Piazza della Cancelleria.
Tel. 0669887566.

Getting there
Bus 44, 46, 62, 64, 70,
81, 87, 90, 186, 492.

History BC
• **Underneath** this palace lie a Roman consul's tomb and other ancient remnants.

History AD
• **366-384** Pope **St. Damasus** built, and gave his name to, a church and his archival library.
• **1486** Cardinal Raffaele Riario, Pope Sixtus IV della Rovere's nephew, built this vast edifice thanks to the gains from one night's gambling with another pope's nephew. The elegant design has been variously attributed to the Lombard Andrea Bregno, Bramante and an unknown architect trained in Urbino.
• **1495** Cardinal Riario for his titular church had **Bramante** completely rebuild as part of the palazzo the 4c **Basilica di San Lorenzo in Damaso** – the entrance is on the right side of the facade.
• **1513** The palace was finished just in time for the installation of the first Medici pope, Leo X, who proceeded to seize it from the owners, punishing them for their part in the bloody assassination plot against the Medici elders.
• **1798** The church was used as a stable during France's occupation of Rome and was completely restored in the 19c.

At the inception of the Renaissance in Rome, the scholar-pope Nicholas V, who organized the great Jubilee of 1450, called for fine buildings to awe simple people into accepting Catholicism: "Noble edifices, combining taste and beauty with imposing proportions, would immensely conduce to the exaltation of the Chair of St. Peter."

Nicholas V and his architect, Leon Battista **Alberti**, decided to replace the crumbling Basilica of St. Peter's with a megachurch in the Renaissance style. In the succeeding two centuries, few churches were constructed in Rome other than St. Peter's, while enormous fortunes and energies were expended by cardinals and bankers on their private residences. They wanted to impress each other and the masses – including the Jubilee pilgrims sleeping in the porticoes of Rome churches and in the vineyards outside the walls. Renaissance architectural buffs had no qualms about recycling ancient monuments the Church considered pagan. In the year Nicholas V launched a building spree, his contractors robbed 2,522 cartloads of travertine from the Colosseum! Half a century later, **Raphael**, painter, architect and ultimate Renaissance man, asked Pope Leo X Medici, "How many popes have allowed the destruction of ancient temples, statues, arches, and other buildings, the glory of ancient Rome?"

Palazzo della Cancelleria (1486-1513) and Basilica di San Lorenzo in Damaso (1495, Bramante)

This was the first large palazzo in Rome built entirely in the Renaissance style, made of gleaming white travertine, much of which was stripped from the nearby Theater of Pompey (see page 55). Over the centuries it has housed

154

many VIPs, including a cardinal-duke, brother of Scotland's Bonnie Prince Charlie. It is now the papal chancellery and is an exclave of the Vatican, not subject to Italian sovereignty.

The long facade with its double pilasters is Florentine in conception. Don't miss the Riario family roses on the upper windows and on the pavement inside. The inner court is a Renaissance masterpiece of perfectly harmonious proportions – despite the building plot's lack of symmetry and vast size.

With special Vatican permission you could view the enormous fresco that Vasari painted in a record 100 days. When he boasted of this to Michelangelo, the great master quipped, "It looks it."

Palazzo Farnese (1514-89, Sangallo the Younger)

Most people consider this the ultimate Renaissance palace: big, beautiful and brimming with art. **Michelangelo** was the final architect here, responsible for the overhanging Florentine roof and the heightened cornice just below it, as well as the exuberant central loggia-window right over the entrance.

During the two decades Michelangelo directed this gigantic building project, he created the top floor, with taller-looking windows and higher ceilings than his predecessor, Sangallo, had used in the lower two floors. So the inventor of Mannerism broke with the tradition that upper floors are given less importance than the lower ones. By giving the top of the palace added height, he saved the endlessly long facade from seeming as monotonous as the front of the nearby Cancelleria. The Mannerist conception he shared with Raphael was of turning the classical rules of architecture upside down

[F 5] *Piazza Farnese.*

Not open
to the public.

Our favorite
Look up at this window at night when the light is still burning here in the French ambassador's beautiful office and you will see the glorious ceiling painting.

History AD
• **1514** Alexander Farnese, a cardinal with lady friends, and well-endowed nephews ordered an "adequate lodging" from Antonio de Sangallo the Younger. He had been made cardinal at 25, thanks to his sister Giulia, then Pope Alexander VI Borgia's official companion.
• **1534** Farnese became Pope Paul III and ordered the palace progressively enlarged, as a showplace for his family. He greeted Michelangelo's return to Rome with, "For thirty years, I've been looking forward to employing you," and commissioned him to do, first the *Last Judgment* in the Sistine Chapel, and finally the family palace. Michelangelo also designed a private bridge so the Farneses could stroll across the Tiber to Villa Farnesina. Only the span across Via Giulia was ever constructed.

to introduce tension, a disturbing note, into their buildings. Recently cleaned, the gleaming facade shows irregular, decorative brickwork.

Since the French ambassador lives and works here, you cannot enter without an invitation. This denies you a view of the monumental inner courtyard, and the state dining room whose frescoes by Annibale Carracci (1560-1609) portray the sort of mythical love-play among pagan gods that you would expect to find in a French boudoir. Looking at the palace from the sumptuous square in front, you would never imagine that to the left of the ambassador's office is one enormous room – so gargantuan that it rises two stories to include not only the six windows next to the ambassador's, but also all six windows above! Such Mannerist distortions foreshadowed Rome's Baroque. In the square, the two fountain basins match the palace's scale. Brought here from the Baths of Caracalla, they remind us that giganticism was one of the things being revived by the Renaissance.

The "Farnese Bull."

Annibale Carracci frescoes.

[G 5]
Piazza Capo di Ferro, 13.
Tel. 066874896.

Getting there
Bus 44, 46, 62, 64,
70, 87, 90, 186, 492.

Fee
Open Tuesday to
Saturday 9 am-7 pm
Sunday 9 am-1 pm.
Closed Monday.

Palazzo Spada

(1540-50, Giulio Merisi da Caravaggio)

Don't miss the sculpted surfaces of this building, both inside and out. The facade is covered with decorative or representational carvings, going a step further than earlier buildings whose outer walls were adorned with paintings or mosaics.

Pop in, and if there is enough light, see the magnificence of this palazzo that marks the transition

from Renaissance to Baroque. It was designed only half a century after Palazzo Farnese was started. If Farnese is partly Mannerist, Spada is the epitome of Mannerism, this slightly wicked style reacting against the austerity of early-Renaissance classicism. The stuccoes on the facade include statues of famous antique personalities; above these are garlands and medallions, as well as inscriptions relating to the figures below. In the courtyard, the decor is even more frivolous: cavorting centaurs and tritons, among festoons of flowers and fruit.

The **Galleria Spada Museum**, up the steps at the rear of the palazzo, contains four delightful rooms which house the family art collection, including paintings by Brueghel, Andrea del Sarto and Titian.

On the first Sunday of the month, with reservations (*Tel. 066832409*), you can visit the salons, as well as

corridors full of stuccoes and the magnificent throne room where popes were received royally when they dropped in for elegant soirees.

This palazzo gives you a feeling of those exciting times when cardinals whirled around the dance floors, beautiful women flirted with the monsignors and everybody tried to forget about the 1527 Sack of Rome and the threat of Protestantism.

History AD
• **1549** Designed by Michelangelo Merisi da Caravaggio for Cardinal Capo di Ferro.
• **1556-60** Giulio Mazzoni decorated the facades with stucco work.
• **17c** Cardinal Spada bought the palazzo and had it spruced up by his great friend **Borromini**, who designed the garden wall and added the trompe l'oeil gallery.
• **21c** Now the seat of the Italian Council of State.

Our favorite

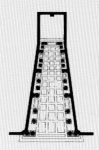

Trompe l'oeil gallery, the high point of superfluity, designed by dour **Borromini**. Through the glass wall

of the library and on the other side of a small formal garden is what appears to be a long colonnade leading to a life-size statue. Closer examination (and a tip to the guard might permit you to step nearer) shows it is about a quarter as long as it looks, and the statue is tiny. Borromini reduced the dimensions of this colonnade in careful proportion as it recedes. When you visit the Vatican you can decide if Bernini copied his monumental Scala Regia staircase with its gradually foreshortened columns from his rival, Borromini.

The restored fountain in front has a more modest version of the seminude female shown here, spouting water from her ample bosom.

[F 5]
Campo de' Fiori

The world's most gorgeous food market is onstage every weekday from before breakfast until lunchtime. Vegetable and fruit in season are displayed super fresh and lovingly (and reluctantly when they are out of season). Bargaining is de rigueur after midday when the crowds thin and prices tumble. Fish is by the Farnese movie theater, while flowers (which give the place its name) are at the other extreme, where Via dei Baullari intersects. The central sad statue is **Giordano Bruno**, burned for heresy here on February 17, 1600, a child of the Renaissance condemned by the Inquisition. A Dominican monk at the age of 15, he accepted God only as the unifying logical force dominating a world in which man has no obligation to pray but rather to live according to moral virtues: Truth, Prudence, Wisdom, Law and Universal Judgment. Even at the height of the Renaissance enlightenment, this was unacceptable, so he was tracked down in Venice, imprisoned and sentenced to the stake. **Clement VIII** Aldobrandini, pope from 1592 to 1605, increased the severity of the Inquisition, which in his reign sent 30 "heretics" to the stake. His Jubilee of 1600 brought hordes of pilgrims to Rome – and some stayed to witness Bruno's auto-da-fe.

A century earlier the 1500 Holy Year had netted vast sums from the sale of indulgences. About that time **Vannozza Cattanei** moved into *Via del Pellegrino, 58* (Pilgrim's Way, now an artisan street). It was a narrow muddy lane, but her great and good friend **Pope Alexander VI Borgia** widened, straightened and paved it. Here she gave birth to the irascible **Cesare Borgia.** When the pope's attention strayed

to the equally beautiful **Giulia Farnese** (see Palazzo Farnese, page 158) Vannozza and her third husband became respectable proprietors of a Roman hotel chain, of which the flagship was **La Vacca** at the western corner of Campo de' Fiori. Don't miss the cow's head sculpted on a cornerstone and over *Vicolo del Gallo, 13*, an escutcheon uniting the armorial quarterings of Vannozza and her husband, and the crest of the Borgia pope who had encouraged this entrepreneurial venture by exempting her taverns from the wine tax.

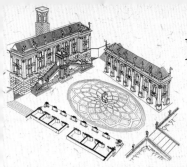

Piazza del Campidoglio

Capitoline Museums,
Basilica di Santa Maria in Ara Coeli

Michelangelo in 1536 designed this magnificent stage set to crown the Capitoline, smallest of ancient Rome's seven hills, but the most important since it was the seat of power. From busy Piazza Aracoeli you mount graciously sloping stairs (the *Cordonata*) and step off into the sudden hush of his geometrically delineated piazza, with his three low and harmonious buildings as a dramatic background.

Michelangelo was inspired by the two millennia of Rome's glorious history that revolved around this hilltop. Being a sculptor, he used it to showcase great classical Roman statues, notably the equestrian statue of Emperor Marcus Aurelius, apparently in amicable conversation with the populace.

In terms of dramatic symmetry, this space is rivaled only by Piazza San Pietro, laid out over a century later by Bernini, who considered himself a follower of Michelangelo. This was Rome's first planned piazza. It is just how Michelangelo originally conceived it – though Marcus Aurelius's statue is a copy; the original (with its gold leaf partially intact) is inside the Museo Capitolino.

History BC
• **6c** Two centuries after Rome's founding on this and the adjacent Palatine Hill, the enormous Temple of Jupiter was built, making it the holiest part of this holy city. Traitors were hurled from the hill, including a woman who let the Sabine enemy forces into Rome.

History AD
• **166** In the fifth year of Marcus Aurelius's rule (161-180), an unknown sculptor produced this bronze equestrian statue of the emperor and philosopher.
• **Middle Ages** Unlike most similar statues, the bronze Marcus Aurelius escaped being melted down for scrap. Taken to be **Constantine**, Rome's

first Christian emperor, it was placed beside Rome's cathedral, St. John Lateran.

• **1536** Pope Paul III Farnese decided to flatter Emperor **Charles V** by according him a triumphal procession like those of the victorious generals of ancient Rome. Charles had just triumphed over the infidels in North Africa, but the pope probably seized the opportunity in order to efface memories of the Sack of Rome of 1527, when Charles's troops defeated and imprisoned the previous pope, **Clement VII Medici**. Embarrassed by the wretched appearance of Rome, Pope Paul asked Michelangelo (busy painting the *Last Judgment* in the Sistine Chapel), to beautify the final destination of the emperor's triumphal procession, Capitoline Hill (which for good reason was then known as the "Hill of the Goats"). Only the base for Marcus Aurelius and his horse was ready in time for the imperial triumph. His revolutionary plan turned the square's entrance toward St. Peter's.

• **1564** Michelangelo died, and only the double staircase at the back of the square had been built. His master plan was finally completed a couple of centuries later.

Our favorite
The dramatic impact of this roomlike ensemble is underlined by the famous trapezoidal markings on the ground, which Michelangelo conceived of as if to remind us that this is the center of the world – once and forever.

Michelangelo drew formal Renaissance facades for both the medieval **Palazzo Senatorio** at the back, and **Palazzo dei Conservatori** on the right, and added the **Palazzo Nuovo** on the left, a mirror-image of the Conservatori, making two symmetrical arms gathering you into Rome's city center.

From a 12c guide book *Mirabilia Romae*: "The Capitol was the head of the world, where the consuls and senators abode to govern the earth." And the U.S. Congress and Senate building took its name, the Capitol, from here.

Musei Capitolini (Capitoline Museums)

The **Palazzo dei Conservatori** (1564, Michelangelo, Giacomo della Porta) is on the right – river side – of the square, as you face the Senator's Palace. Your ticket is valid for this museum as well as its twin on the left.

[G 7] *Piazza del Campidoglio, 1.* Tel. 063997800.

Fee
Free admission last Sunday of the month.
Open Tuesday to Sunday 9 am-8 pm.
Closed Monday.

Courtyard. The first thing that meets the eye is the gargantuan head, knee, leg, hand, arm, and two feet from a marble statue of Constantine the Great. This used to be down in the Roman Forum in his basilica (Maxentius started the building; Constantine finished both it and him). The dressed parts of the body were in wood covered in gilded bronze, and have been lost in the mists of time. The seated figure measured 12 m (13⅛ yards). The other large head and hand you see are probably of his son Constantius II. On the left are bas-reliefs from Hadrian's Temple, personifications of foreign provinces. Above these is an inscription from AD 51 about Emperor Claudius's conquest of Britain. This part of the museum is free.

Now pay your entrance fee, good for both buildings.

History AD
• In the **Middle Ages** these were the magistrates' chambers and halls.
• **1450** Pope Nicolas II Parentucelli built new public halls.
• **1471** The ancient bronze statues given by Sixtus IV della Rovere as an extraordinary gift to the people of Rome were placed here, making it the first public museum in the world.
• **1561**. The facade was remade in accordance with Michelangelo's plan.
• **1801** Napoleon stole many ancient statues for the Louvre.
• **1821** When the statues were returned, the building was restored.
• **Today** it is the Municipal Registry. (Do you want to get married?)

The museums are vast, so *flow along*, stopping to admire some pieces that are priceless. Upstairs: on the first landing are four magnificent deep panels from triumphal arches. Three are of Marcus Aurelius; the one on the right is **Sacrifice to Jupiter**, at his temple on this hill.

La Lupa.

ROOM I has frescoes from the 16c, and two large statues of popes. In **ROOM II**, also frescoed, starts the collection of ancient Roman and Greek statues. Admire the (1643) deeply carved wooden doors separating these papal chambers. **ROOM III** **Junius Brutus** (3c BC). Bronze head. This head with ivory and glass eyes perhaps is not his. It has been stuck on a 16c bust. **Spinario** (1c BC). Bronze. The famous statue of a young Greek boy pulling a thorn from his foot. These two came from Pope Sixtus IV's 15c donation. **ROOM IV** **La Lupa** (She-Wolf, 5c BC). Bronze. Another famous statue, probably Etruscan, it depicts the legend of Rome's founding: the wolf who suckled Romulus and Remus. *They* were added 2,000 years later by Antonio Pollaiolo, in that curious Renaissance custom of embellishing an existing work. The mosaic floor is not old but *so* attractive.

ROOM VII Room of the Tapestries. Made by 16c and 17c children who were scooped up from the street and taught a trade. **ROOM XV** **Esquiline Venus** (1c BC). Marble. A priestess of the Temple of Isis. Small and beautiful.

Bust of Commodus as Hercules (AD 2c). The effete likeness of Emperor Commodus stares vacantly, his hair pompadoured, with a lion skin over his head – not

Esquiline Venus.

Caravaggio's *Fortune Teller*.

messing one curl. **ROOM XXIV** Hall of the bronzes. **Head of Constantine** or perhaps his son Constantius II; and an exquisite antique **Roman bed**, reconstructed from separate fragments. **ROOM XXV** All the ancient goodies discovered in art patron Maecenas's garden. The head of his friend Emperor **Augustus** (27 BC) is interesting. **Painting collection.** Pinacoteca, which has recently been beautifully renovated. Up the stairs are 10 rooms of mostly religious paintings from 15-17c, with some works by Veronese, Tintoretto, Rubens, Velasquez. On the right at the entrance is the long Galleria Cini with an extraordinary collection of historic porcelain. On the far left is the Sala Petronilla, dominated by Guercino's enormous masterpiece of the burial and apotheosis of St. Peter's daughter Petronilla. In the same room are two memorable paintings by Caravaggio: **The Fortune Teller** (1595). The young man half listens as the gypsy palm reader tries to get his attention – and his ring! **St. John the Baptist** (1602), profane and sensual. Michelangelo was the first to depict St. John as a young man. Caravaggio, however, went further, painting him nude and at play with a ram.

New wing. More ancient Roman discoveries. Especially interesting are

ROOM III Statues of **three emperors:** Claudius, Domitian and Trajan.

ROOM XIII Bust of Faustina, faithless wife of Antoninus Pius. Bust of Sabina, ignored wife of Hadrian.

Palazzo Nuovo, or **Museo Capitolino** (1644-55, Michelangelo, Girolamo Rainaldi). The New Palace is on the left of the square when facing the central Senator's Palace.

Courtyard. The center fountain of a reclining statue named Marforio was one of the "talking statues" in Rome, originally located on one of Rome's streets. When the people were dissatisfied they hung a sign around the statue's neck with their complaint,

Our favorite
Imagining the huge statue of Constantine reassembled and presiding again in his huge basilica in the Roman Forum.

History AD
• **1603** Work began; it was completed 50 years later with funds from Pope Innocent X Pamphili. Michelangelo's drawings were followed for the facade, so that the piazza would have a united look. Another museum for antiquities was needed, since more ancient Roman artifacts came to light as they cleared away centuries of rubble.

Our favorites
The real Marcus Aurelius on his favorite horse, and the Dove Mosaic (see page 164).

often in rhyme. Glass bay on the right. Equestrian **Marcus Aurelius** (AD 2c). This glorious statue of the emperor with hand outstretched has been restored to its former beauty, much of its gold leaf still shining dully. Once mistaken for Constantine, this statue survived, and gives us an idea of how fabulous ancient Rome must have been with statues of such quality. To see it without a glass reflection, go to the small window on the right.

One floor up

HALL 1 Dying Gaul (3c BC). Marble. There is pathos in this finely wrought figure found in Sallust's orchard (see page 230). **Hadrian's friend** and love, Antinous, is

• **1734** Pope Clement XII Corsini opened this museum, allowing the public access to these collections of antique sculptures. Additions were made later by successive popes.

the handsome young man in white marble on the right, with a bruised knee (in reality just a blemish in the marble).

HALL 2 Hadrian as Mars (AD 2C). Emperor Hadrian was soldier-philosopher-architect. Perhaps another portrait of **Antinous** is on his right. Many of the statues here came from Hadrian's Villa in Tivoli.

HALL 4 Hall of the Philosophers. There are three statues of **Socrates**, one of **Homer** and three of **Cicero**. The central statue of a young warrior is **Marcellus**, after whom that wonderful Teatro di Marcello, near the Tiber Island, was named (see page 45).

HALL 5 Hall of the Emperors. Has 65 busts, but not all of them are of emperors. Roman portraits did not idealize their subjects, and this room certainly shows that. **Nero**: young with a fringe, doesn't look crazy at all. On a column, a sensitive portrait of young **Augustus** (1C BC). His wife **Livia** is in the right-hand corner, second shelf, and has a grand headdress and pursed lips: a strong woman. Portrait of a **Flavian lady**, on a column (AD 1C). Fine artistic work, fine hairdo, but it must have taken hours every day.

Octagonal room on left returning to staircase: **Capitoline Venus** (AD 2C). Marble. An ancient Roman copy of a Praxiteles original. Modest Venus surprised at the bath. The room has copies of Roman frescoes to give flavor. Very successful.

GALLERY 35 Part of the long corridor. **Drunken old woman** (3C BC). She's gripping her wine flask, just like a Chianti bottle!

HALL 8 Dove Mosaic. This beautiful mosaic of doves drinking from a golden bowl is from Hadrian's Villa. It was copied 1,000 times during subsequent centuries – but none is more beautiful. This too is a copy, probably an AD 2C Roman reproduction of a 2C BC Greek original, or maybe the prototype itself.

Basilica di Santa Maria in Ara Coeli (591). Up 122 steep steps from the piazza of the same name, this rare Rome example of a Romanesque church first belonged to the Benedictines and then to the Franciscans. The wooden Christ child in the sacristy worked medical miracles. It is moved to the nativity scene in the second chapel to the left at Christmas when children are encouraged to recite prayers. You can also enter from the top of the Capitoline Hill.

[G 7]
Piazza Aracoeli.
Tel. 066798155.

Getting there
Bus 44, 75, 95, 160, 170, 628, 710, 716, 719.

Open 9 am-noon and 3-6 pm.

Palazzo Venezia

This massive and venerable building dominates the square of the same name. Mussolini harangued the crowds in the 1930s from the central balcony (and then stepped back into his gigantic office for a gallant encounter with Clara Petacci, his adoring young mistress).

Museum. The memorable Map Room and other major rooms contain works from the Barbo family's private collection. The ne'er-do-well nephew Lorenzo Cybo lost the fortune that permitted the building of the Cancelleria by his foe, the winner Raffaele Riario. Rotating large exhibitions are frequently blockbusters.

Piazza Venezia

Palazzo Venezia,
Victor Emmanuel Monument
and Palazzo Doria Pamphili

[F 7]
Via del Plebiscito, 118.
Tel. 066798865.

Getting there
Bus 46, 60, 62, 64, 70, 492.

Fee
Open 9 am-2 pm.
Closed Monday.

History AD
• **1455** Half Renaissance palace, half fortress, with a tree-filled courtyard. The Basilica of San Marco, in the corner, started in AD 336, has some fine 9c mosaics in the apse. Pope Paolo II Barbo started the present construction and dedicated the complex to his Venice home.
• **1564** It became the Venetian ambassador's residence.
• **1814** Austria, conqueror of the Veneto, had *its* ambassador living here.
• **1916** The state repossessed the building, which became Mussolini's offices. To impress Hitler, he had the medieval quarter between here and the Colosseum torn down so the great symbol of Rome's imperial might would be visible from the balcony.

Piazza Venezia.
Tel. 06328101.

Getting there
Bus 46, 60, 62, 64, 70, 492.

Open Tuesday-Saturday 8:30 am-7 pm.

Victor Emmanuel Monument (*Vittoriano*, 1885). Dubbed deprecatingly "The Typewriter" or "Wedding Cake," it was inspired by Roman imperial buildings. Officially the "Altar of the Fatherland," it celebrates Italy's unification in 1870 and is dedicated to the first

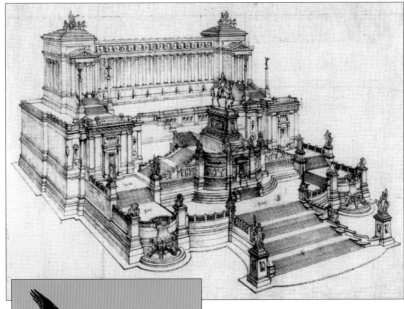

king, Victor Emmanuel II. The flying horses and chariots at the top are what any self-respecting public building would have had in ancient Rome. Do climb those stairs, when open, for the splendid view from the upper level. Many Romans wish it would sink under its own great weight. Guarded by smartly uniformed troops, it houses the Tomb of the Unknown Soldier with its eternal flame – reminiscent of the House of the Vestal Virgins (see page 24). Within it are the Museo Centrale del Risorgimento and the Ala Brazini (see Museums, page 263).

Palazzo Doria Pamphili. This immense home still belongs to the Doria Pamphili family. The elegant 17c entrance is by Antonio del Grande (1660). The palace has had a potpourri of noble owners: Pope Julius II della Rovere gave it to his nephew, the duke of Urbino. It was sold to Cardinal Pietro Aldobrandini, whose heir Donna Olimpia married Innocent X's nephew Camillo Pamphili. Then it passed to the princely Doria family. From this entrance you can glimpse the large inner garden and visit the important family art collection (see Museums, page 262).

[F 7] *Piazza del Collegio Romano, 2. Tel. 066797323.*

Getting there
Bus 56, 181, 640, 713.

Giovanna d'Aragona, Princess Colonna,
by an unknown artist clearly
influenced by the *Mona Lisa's* smile.

Fontana di Trevi

Trevi Fountain, 1762

The water spurts and gushes – one could almost believe the larger-than-life sea horses are splashing through waves, especially after dark with the spectacular lighting. It takes genius to create an enormous fountain in a relatively small space.

In the 1950s and 1960s Rome became *Hollywood on the Tiber* and the Trevi fountain, designed by Nicola Salvi, became the icon of pleasure-seeking in the Italian capital: in the Fellini film *La Dolce Vita*, paparazzi, Anita Ekberg getting her body parts drenched. To ensure good luck and an early return to Rome, toss a coin over your left shoulder into the fountain (in the old days one drank a glass of its sweet water for the same reason). It has become a MUST to visit. And why not come when it is most beautiful – at night?

The custom in imperial times of building a monument where the new water arrived in Rome was copied by the

[E 7]
Piazza di Trevi.

Getting there
Bus 56, 58.

History BC
• **19** With the help of a virgin, Roman technicians found a source of pure water only 22 km (14 miles) from the city. This **Aqua Virgo** (in Latin) was piped over Rome's shortest aqueduct directly to the Baths of **Agrippa**. Rebuilt, it is now called **Acqua Vergine** (in Italian).

History AD
• **476** Fall of the Roman Empire. Vandals, Visigoths, Goths and Huns all had their part in this. The real coup de grâce came 50 years later when a thoroughly demoralized Rome had its

aqueducts cut by the Goths.
• **1453** Pope Nicholas V Parentucelli mended Acqua Vergine and built a simple basin to herald the water's arrival.
• **1629** Pope Urban VIII Barberini asked **Bernini** for drawings. When the pope died the project was abandoned. But Bernini moved the fountain to its present site – facing the Quirinal Palace.
• **1730-40** Competitions to redesign buildings, fountains and even the Spanish Steps had become the rage. Two popes had organized competitions for this monumental project – with no winners. Pope Clement XII Corsini organized another contest, which Salvi lost – though he got the job anyway.
• **1751** Salvi died, with his masterpiece half-finished; but before he went he made sure a stubborn barber's unsightly sign would not spoil the ensemble. He hid it behind a sculpted vase.

later popes, and some of Rome's fanciest fountains were the result. These were called *Mostre* (Shows), and were also a monument for whichever pope built them. The Trevi fountain is perhaps the showiest of the *Mostre*. The building behind was purposely left with a blank wall to accommodate the fountain.

The figures are Abundance on the left; Good Health on the right; Ocean in the middle, controlling the sea horses, with Tritons riding on their backs. Run, don't walk.

Palazzo del Quirinale

As the chief of state's residence, this huge palace has changed its loyalties like a chameleon. Originally it was a summer palace for the popes; Napoleon altered it so he could strut around here, but he never came to his "Second City." After another half century of popes it was inherited by the kings of Italy. It is used currently by the presidents of the republic.

Being at the top of the highest of the city's seven hills, it is free of the deadly mosquitoes the pontiffs feared. From the fall of the Roman Empire until recently, Rome had *malaria* (literally, bad air) as a serious summer disease to contend with. Around Rome were undrained marshes, and in Rome's low-lying areas (like the moat around Castel Sant'Angelo), mosquitoes bred happily in summer, and malaria decimated the population. With the invention of DDT these worries became a thing of the past as the U.S. Armed Forces blanket-sprayed every conceivable puddle of stagnant water in 1945.

Palazzo del Quirinale and Fontana dei Dioscuri

[E 8/9]
Piazza del Quirinale.

Getting there
Bus 64, 70, 71, 170.

Quirinale Palace can only be visited by special permission.

History BC
• Here in **ancient times** was the Temple of Quirinus, part of a Sabine encampment.

History AD
• **1574** Pope Gregory XIII Boncompagni added a bucolic retreat to the villa and vineyard of Cardinal d'Este (of Tivoli fame).
• **1733** Pope Clement XII completed works commenced by two preceding popes with architect Ferdinando Fuga.
• **1798** General Bonaparte's troops conquered Rome, declared it a republic, deposed and expelled Pope Pius VI, who died in exile in France.
• **1808** Napoleon declared himself king

of Italy and started planning to visit Rome.
- **1811-12** Emperor Napoleon's architects made alterations to the Quirinale, which he saw as his second palace for ruling his newly created empire.
- **1814** The pope repossessed it when Napoleon lost the Battle of Waterloo and his empire – and his chance of ever coming to Rome, where his mother spent her remaining years.
- **1870** Italy was united and this became the palace of its kings.
- **1947** Italy became a republic and its new president took over the vast palace and grounds.

Tapestry of the labors of Hercules.

The papal apartments are rich in tapestries, sculpture and paintings. The large chapel is the same size and shape as the Sistine Chapel. Most valuable of the collections are antique Chinese vases, but most interesting are the French clocks from the 16 to 17c, all presents to His Holiness. The Room of Hercules has a superb Gobelin tapestry, **The Labors of Hercules**, his buttocks robustly delineated. The gardens – where an ancient Roman villa was unearthed in 1999 – are vast, but closed. On a cold November night in 1870 Vittorio Emanuele di Savoia came from the north to take possession of his new residence. The pope's suite had not left the key to the locked palace – so at 11 pm there was a frantic chase to find a locksmith to open the door of the Quirinale for the new king of Italy. **Stables**. These have been converted into a museum for fine art exhibits (see page 261).

Our favorite
In the Room of the Ambassadors, the marble floors with bird mosaics, stolen away from Hadrian's Villa. The joyous colors make them look as if they were created yesterday.

Fontana dei Dioscuri

In front of the Quirinale are the colossal and magnificent ancient Roman sculptures of Castor and Pollux and their gorgeous steeds. The original models for these statues were Greek (5c BC); these pale Roman copies are circa AD 2c. They were moved to this site in 1587 from the nearby Baths of Constantine (now a private palace).

The obelisk came from in front of the Mausoleum of Augustus; it was moved here in 1786. And the large water basin used to be a cattle trough in the Forum.

PVS PRAXITELI   OPVS FIDIAE

Baroque Beauties

A rule of thumb is that the Renaissance in Rome was from 1450 to 1600, whereas Baroque was from 1600 to 1750. Mannerism was the final stage of the Renaissance, circa 1525-1600, leading to Baroque.

The **Renaissance** literally meant the "rebirth" of the classical styles of ancient Greece and Rome in all the arts: literature, music, architecture, sculpture and painting. The advent of the Renaissance meant mankind was emerging from the Middle Ages; the papacy had returned to Rome after three quarters of a century in Avignon; artists and patrons were in a celebratory mood. The ancient Roman edifices that had been pillaged or neglected for a millennium seemed perfect prototypes for the buildings of this exuberant age. Pope Martin V (1417-31) is credited with launching the Renaissance in Rome with his vast program of reconstructing the city, including its ancient buildings, as well as restoring the early churches. Pomponius Leto, historian and professor, was accused of holding orgies during his costumed banquets in the catacombs, but protested that he was just trying to recapture the spirit of the early Christians. This movement culminated in the High Renaissance (1500-1520) when the three giants – Leonardo, Michelangelo and Raphael – were spreading their enlightenment in Rome.

Baroque art, and especially architecture, emphasizes decoration and movement, using classical elements but in an exaggerated manner meant to inspire religious spirituality. It reached its apogee here in Rome with the palaces, fountains and sculptural tableaux of Bernini, as well as his churches, and those of the apprentice who surpassed him in architecture, Borromini. This style, too, erupted at a period of enthusiasm and optimism, the Counter-Reformation, when the Catholic Church

❶ Chiesa di Santa Susanna
❷ Chiesa di Santa Maria della Vittoria
❸ Basilica di Santa Maria degli Angeli

had emerged from the ugly skirmishes with Protestant antagonists and the popes were eagerly spending the Holy See's riches to enhance their families and their fame. The zenith of the Baroque was the Roman Festivals (*Feste Romane*), when extraordinary floats, sculptures and large temporary edifices were created, from which fireworks exploded. Taking weeks to build, and sometimes rising as high as 20 m (22 yards), these fanciful constructions enchanted not only the ruling Vatican hierarchy but also the Roman populace with momentary but acute gratification.

❹ Basilica di San Pietro in Vincoli a Collie Oppio
❺ Chiesa del Gesù
❻ Chiesa and Piazza di Sant'Ignazio di Loyola
❼ Chiesa di San Luigi dei Francesi

❽ Chiesa di Sant'Ivo alla Sapienza
❾ Chiesa Nuova and Oratorio dei Filippini

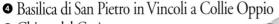

[D 10]
Piazza San Bernardo.
Tel. 064827510.

Getting there
Bus 60, 61, 62, 95, 137,
492, 590 or
A Metro Repubblica stop.

Open Monday to Sunday
9 am-12 noon and
4-7 pm.

❶ Chiesa di Santa Susanna (1603, Maderno)

The facade is considered Carlo Maderno's masterpiece of early Baroque that influenced the later, more flamboyant churches of Bernini and Borromini. It is the last of a series of religious buildings on this site that go back to the original home of little Susanna, a 3c girl (daughter of a Christian priest) who gave up her life to save her virginity. She was put to death by Emperor Diocletian for refusing to marry his heir and adopted son. Both she and her martyred father, St. Gabinus, are buried here. Pope Benedict XV in 1922 gave Rome's American Catholic community this church.

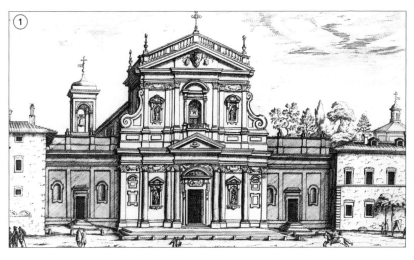

[D 10]
Via XX Settembre, 17.
Tel. 0642740571.

Getting there
Bus 16, 36, 37, 60,
61, 62, 910 or
A Metro Repubblica stop.

Open Monday-Saturday
8:30 am-noon and
3:30-6 pm; Sunday
3-3:30 pm.

❷ Chiesa di Santa Maria della Vittoria
(1612, Maderno)

St. Mary of Victory, completed after Maderno's death, was originally plain and monochromatic on the inside. But in 1646 Maderno's disciple, the great **Gian Lorenzo Bernini** (1598-1680), transformed the interior by installing in the **Cornaro Chapel** his multimedia production combining sculpture, architecture, painting and lighting to recreate an emotion.

Bernini's Ecstasy of St. Theresa. The saint's excitement when her heart was pierced by an angel's spear is unabashedly sensual. Her palpitating body is rippling with delight, her half-open mouth groaning in pleasurable pain. The handsome angel smiles down at his ravished conquest. St. Theresa of Avila was a 16c Spanish nun who reacted so emotionally to her vision of the angel spearing her that she founded the extremely ascetic Order of Discalced Carmelites (they wore sandals rather than shoes), which now serves this church.

❸ Basilica di Santa Maria degli Angeli

(1561, Michelangelo; 1749, Vanvitelli)

Interior. This Renaissance church was made out of the core of the AD 4c Baths of Diocletian (see page 59). The facade (1) is the back wall of the now-vanished *Caldarium* (hot baths). You first enter the vestibule (2), formerly the luke-warm *Tepidarium*, and then the vast transept (3), formerly the *Frigidarium*, which runs from left to right. Crossing at the center is breathtaking; Michelangelo made minimal changes, respecting the lofty ceiling and elegant proportions of the ancient baths. Vanvitelli moved the high altar from the left transept (4) to its present position opposite the entrance, at the end of the new nave (5) that he extended into what had been the baths' *Natatio* (open-air swimming pool).

In the vestibule is a fine statue of St. Bruno, founder of the Carthusian order which maintains the church, by Jean-Antoine **Houdon** (1766). Many of the oil paintings were brought here from St. Peter's when they were replaced with mosaics (see page 81). This is the titular church of the cardinal of Baltimore. Italian American glass artist Narcisus Quagliata created the dome of the right transept chapel.

[E 10]
Piazza della Repubblica.
Tel. 064882364 or 064870690.

Getting there
Bus 60, 61, 62, 64, 70, 115, 136,137, 170, 640 or
A Metro Repubblica stop.

Our favorite
The curious *meridian* (1703), a sundial on the right side of the transept (6), which for a century and a half was used to determine midday for the city of Rome. Light comes in through a carefully placed opening high up on the wall and falls across a brass strip in the floor, the exact north-south meridian of Rome. When the sun's rays line up precisely along the strip, that's high noon.

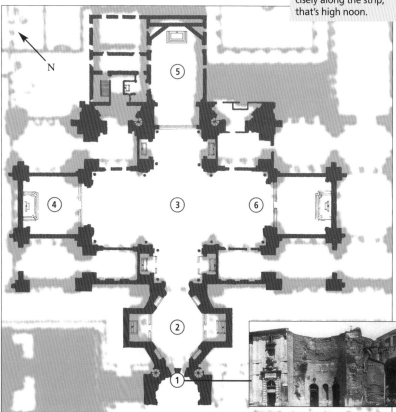

N

During the Christmas and Easter seasons there are concerts of religious music.

Piazza della Repubblica.
Tel. 064880812.

Via Romita, 8.
Tel. 0639960700.

Free
Open Tuesday to
Sunday 9 am-2 pm.
Closed Monday.

[G 9/10] *Piazza*
San Pietro in Vincoli, 4A.
Tel. 064882865.

Getting there
Bus 11, 27 or
B Metro Cavour stop.

Open 7 am-12:30 pm
and 3:30-7 pm.

History BC
• **534** Etruscan king
Servius Tullius's
daughter Tullia had
husband **Tarquin** de-
pose her father, over
whose wounded body
she drove her chariot
on what is now Piazza
San Pietro in Vincoli.
• **1c** BC-AD **1c**
Believed to have
been the site of a
republican-era
tribunal.

History AD
• **Circa 64** Reputedly
Emperor **Nero** added
a torture chamber for
Christians (discovered
in the 1950s) and
his court here con-
demned St. Peter.

Aula Ottagonale (Octagonal Hall, AD 298-306). This handsome building, to the right as you leave the church, was the southwest corner of the main section of Diocletian's Baths (and later a planetarium). Today it is a museum of 19 beautiful classical sculptures, several of them found in these baths, most of them larger-than-life-size nude men. Two of these, in the center, are original bronzes: 2c BC **Hellenistic Prince** and 1c BC **Seated Boxer** (see page 260).

❹ Basilica di San Pietro in Vincoli a Colle Oppio

(rebuilt 443, 1475 and 1575)

To reach St. Peter in Chains church, climb up Via San Francesco di Paola, also known as Salita dei Borgia or Vicus Sceleratus (crime alley), a long flight of stairs through a tunnel, from Via Cavour to Piazza San Pietro in Vincoli. This gives you the atmosphere of the place. (Visitors can also circumnavigate the hill, by car or foot around Via Terme di Tito and left to Piazza San Pietro in Vincoli.)

Michelangelo started out life as a sculptor who despised painting. This is the best place in Rome to see what he could get out of a block of stone.

Pope Julius II's Tomb. Michelangelo and the pope constantly quarreled about the design of what was meant to be the tomb to end all

---

BERNINI VS BORROMINI
A Walkabout

Chiesa di Sant'Andrea al Quirinale
Chiesa di San Carlo alle Quattro Fontane
Palazzo Barberini
Tritone Fountain and Fountain of the Bees

One of the inexhaustible games one can play in Rome is "Bernini or Borromini – who is Mr. Baroque?" Everybody in Rome, from the late mayor, whose previous experience happened to be as art critic for communist periodicals, to the barman at your hotel, has a strong opinion on this burning topic. Even two days of sightseeing in Rome entitles you to take sides and challenge any contrary opinion. These two supreme architects of Rome's Baroque splendors were born within a year of each other, started their professional lives as friends working side by side on lavish building

projects, but soon became bitter enemies competing fiercely for architectural commissions. They converged on Rome from opposite ends of Italy, reflecting the diverse characters of their regions: the southerner, Bernini (1598-1680), was an exuberant Neapolitan, whereas the northerner, Borromini (1599-1667), was a dour Lombard. Borromini, wracked with paranoia, finally killed himself, vilifying his rival in his final years, as he saw Bernini becoming ever more famous while he himself remained unknown, unsung and usually unemployed. In his own time, especially as he outlived and out-produced his northern competitor, Bernini would have gotten the most votes, but today Borromini has at least tied, if not out-polled, his southern rival.

You can decide whom you prefer by visiting some masterpieces of both in an easy hour's walkabout:

tombs. This gargantuan project, which Michelangelo called a "tragedy of a sepulcher," was unfinished when Julius died, and subsequent popes would not permit Michelangelo to complete it. Forty statues were planned, of which several are dispersed around the world, but the pope reposes in St. Peter's Basilica unloved. The three larger-than-life statues here that Michelangelo made for the tomb are not arranged according to his plan for Julius's tomb: **Moses**. A virile Moses, muscles rippling, looks

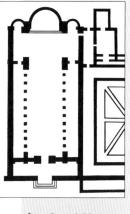

• **440** Byzantine empress Eudoxia in Constantinople received two chains that had bound St. Peter, one from Jerusalem, the other from Rome's Mamertine Prison (see page 36). She sent one to her daughter, wife of Emperor Valentinian III, who built this church to house it. Later the other chain was sent to Rome, and the two chains magically fused together.
• **1475** Facade modified with an elegant portico by **Pope Sixtus IV**'s nephew (who became Pope Julius II in 1503), as part of Sixtus's efforts that

BERNINI
Chiesa di Sant'Andrea al Quirinale
(1658-71)

[E 9] Via del Quirinale, 29.

Reputedly Bernini's favorite original building, this small church turned religious architecture 90 degrees layed out as an oval with the longest dimension stretching sideways and the short axis leading from the entrance door to the high altar. The **facade**, recessed in a curved proscenium for dramatic effect, is made up entirely of classical architectural elements: Greek egg-and-dart motif, Corinthian pilasters, Roman half-circles and triangles. They are, however, squeezed into a vertically elongated shape and dominated by a large escutcheon of papal prince Camillo Pamphili, who commissioned the church. The **interior**, known as "the pearl of the Baroque," is an almost Rococo dramatic

transformed Rome from a medieval into a Renaissance city. (But top-heavy upper story added a century later.)

• **1492-1503** Next door, straddling the steep staircase with a balcony over it, is the so-called Borgia Palace, home of Vannozza Cattanei, the mistress of Pope Alexander VI and mother of his two children: Cesare Borgia (who killed his half brother the duke of Gandia) and Lucrezia.

imploringly to God as he clutches the newly received commandments. The emotional and spiritual intensity of this sculpture has been felt by millions of admirers in the last half millennium.

Rachel, one of Jacob's two wives, symbolizing the active life; and the other wife, **Leah**, the contemplative life. St. Peter's two highly venerated chains, now joined, repose under the main altar.

St. Sebastian from San Pietro in Vincoli.

[**F 7**]
Piazza del Gesù.
Tel. 06697001.

Getting there
Bus 46, 60, 62, 64, 70, 81, 87, 115, 186, 492, 628, 640, 810.

178

History AD
• **1540** With the approval of Pope **Paul III Farnese**, a Spanish soldier called **Ignatius Loyola** (canonized in 1622) founded the Society of Jesus, devoted to zealous missionary

❺ Chiesa del Gesù

(1568-84, Vignola and Della Porta)

The Church of Jesus is the mother church of the Jesuit order and architecturally represents a step in the transition from Renaissance sobriety to Baroque excess.

The Jesuits, militant as well as spiritual, wanted a church in keeping with the decisions of the Council of Trent. Under the politically astute Pope **Pius** IV, the council favored reforming the Church in order to negate the accusations of the Protestants and to fill the laymen's need for personal attention from the clergy.

Architecturally, this church satisfied the requirements of the Council of Trent since its broad nave accommodates the hordes of faithful being preached to, there is a clear separation between the congregation and the priests, and the main altar's central position is emphasized as the spot

play of light and shade. Rising toward the soaring dome is a sculpted ensemble with a crucified St. Andrew over the altar looking up toward an effigy of himself ascending into heaven.

BORROMINI
San Carlo alle Quattro Fontane (1634-67)

[**E 9**] *Via del Quirinale, 23.*

Thanks to Bernini, whom he then took as mentor, Borromini got his first commission: to design a monastery and church on a tiny plot of land for an obscure religious order, the Spanish Discalced Trinitarians. Perhaps no church in the world so clearly demonstrates the pulsating drama of movement that is the objective of Baroque architecture. From the exterior you cannot imagine how the inside might appear since every part of the **facade** is undulating S curves except the door. The entrance is in the central bay, which curves forward in a convex line and then flows into concave bays on either side. The eye never comes to rest on any dominant element as it would on a flat Renaissance wall. The **interior**

where the laity receive the mass from the clergy.

The facade, by Della Porta (along with the rejected plan by Vignola), has been widely copied. Those heavy lateral scrolls embracing Greek columns solve the problem posed for designers of church facades by the fact that the center nave is much higher than the two side aisles. This became the model, often

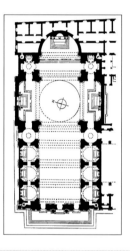

and preaching activity. This was one arm in Catholicism's fight against Protestantism.

• **1545** Paul III, Renaissance humanist, sought to promote Christian unity and reform the Church by calling a general council, which convened in Trento, Italy.

• **1552** Pope **Julius III** Ciocchi del Monte, a pleasure-loving, indolent pontiff, had to suspend the council meetings due to hostility between the Austrian Holy Roman Emperor and the French king.

• **1564** Pope **Pius IV** Medici (no relation) concluded the Council of Trent with reformist policies designed to fight Protestantism, including ordering bishops to leave Rome and work in their dioceses. He reined in the Inquisition and curtailed the Index of Forbidden Books, but finessed Emperor Ferdinand's demand that priests be allowed to marry, as they had in the early years of Christianity.

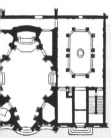

is shaped like an oval football pinched in at its four corners. The dome above is less a reflection of the floor below than an explosion into the firmament. As in all Borromini's work, the church interior is pure white. Its entire form would fit into one of the four piers supporting the dome of St. Peter's. Be sure to come at a time when you can visit the adjoining monastic cloister where Borromini demonstrates his devotion to Michelangelo's Mannerist style by such subtle, disturbing tricks as having no columns in the four corners – the weight of the upper story is carried by pairs of columns topped with arches that seem more concerned with providing openings than with weight bearing.

BERNINI & BORROMINI
Palazzo Barberini (1633)

[**E 9**] *Via Quattro Fontane.*

Inside this giant pile you can confront the two giants of Baroque. The entrance to the wing on the left will bring you to Bernini's huge square staircase. Borromini's smaller oval staircase is just inside

called *Jesuit style*, for Baroque churches all over the world. Contrasting with the church's external sobriety is the later, and overly ornate, High Baroque interior.

Don't miss the **Cappella di Sant'Ignazio** (in the transept on the left), where the saint is buried under the altar, his sleek silver statue surrounded by dazzling lapis lazuli columns.

Bernini sculpted the furiously praying St. Robert Bellarmino statue on the left in the choir.

[E/F 7]
Piazza Sant'Ignazio.
Tel. 0667944061 or
066794560.

Getting there
Bus 62, 81, 85, 95, 160,
175, 492, 628.

Free concerts of
religious music are
often held here dur-
ing religious festivi-
ties and at 9 pm
Sunday evenings.

❻ Chiesa and Piazza di Sant'Ignazio di Loyola

Piazza Sant'Ignazio (1727, Filippo Raguzzini). A Barocco-Happening. Our favorite square in Rome has the stylish whimsicality of a *Commedia dell'Arte* stage set, perhaps influenced by **Palladio**'s famous 16c Teatro Olimpico at Vicenza, where trompe l'oeil perspective was used to give depth to the scenery. This whole piazza, enclosed by five small buildings, was commissioned by the Jesuits as a jewel-like setting for their church, built 100 years earlier in pure Baroque style.

The piazza is in a style midway between Baroque and Rococo which architecture historians call *Barocchetto Romano*. Other examples are the **Spanish Steps** and the church of the **Maddalena**. In this style purely abstract curvilinear shapes are used to give a feeling of limitless space in a relatively cramped situation. They give some light relief in a city where the grand palaces tend to be classic and heavy. Here Raguzzini's facades follow the curves of three intersecting oval shapes, creating a series of concave and convex surfaces that delight the eye with their elegant movement.

Chiesa di Sant'Ignazio (1626-50, Father Orazio Grassi). Cardinal Ludovico Ludovisi, nephew of Pope Gregory XV (1621-23) built this Baroque beauty to honor the founder of the Society of Jesus, whom his uncle had canonized. The design follows that of the nearby **Chiesa**

Palazzo Barberini.

the entrance to the right wing. Borromini had been working as chief assistant to the original architect of the palazzo, Carlo Maderno, whom, along with Michelangelo, he considered his inspiration. Thirty-one-year-old prodigy Bernini took over on Maderno's death and inherited Borromini. Bernini was the most talented sculptor and decorator of his day, but knew little of architecture and had to rely on Borromini to solve the problems that such an immense construction presented. The square staircase is certainly impressive as it thrusts around 90-degree turns, but the subtlety of the rounded oval stairway demonstrates Borromini's ability to endow small spaces with monumentality. Outside, as you look at the main facade, notice the details of Borromini's windows on the top floor: the seven central ones are topped by false-perspective arches to look as if the windows were set far

back into the building; the smaller windows, one on either side of those seven, broke with all previous architecture by combining flat and rounded elements on top of the window in the pediment – the ends of which thrust out diagonally from the building like birds' wings. This palazzo may represent a glorious moment when the two artists worked in harmony, as they did on the baldacchino in St. Peter's (see page 79).

The palazzo also houses the **Galleria Nazionale d'Arte Antica** (see Museums, page 262) in some of the great rooms, with a permanent collection of fine

del Gesù, mother church of the society, and shows the influence of Algardi, Domenichino and Maderno.

The church's final architect, Grassi, was a Jesuit priest, as was also Father Andrea Pozzo, who painted the church's unforgettable ceiling frescoes. The most famous of these is the false perspective at the crossing, showing a soaring dome. Pozzo painted it to replace the cupola Grassi designed before Ludovisi's money ran out. Be sure to stand on the disk halfway up the nave to get the full force of these trompe l'oeil perspectives that show in glorious 3-D the triumphs of St. Ignatius Loyola (1491-1556) – apparently bursting into the sky.

paintings such as **Raphael's** *Fornarina* (left), **Caravaggio's** *Judith Cutting off the Head of Holofernes* (below) and **Holbein's** *Portrait of Henry VIII*.

Via Quattro Fontane, 13.
Tel. 064814591.
Fee
Open Tuesday to Sunday
9 am-7 pm. **Closed** Monday.

Getting there
Bus 70, 81, 87, 90, 116, 186, 492.

Open 8:30 am-12:30 pm and 3:30-7 pm.
Closed Thursday pm.

History AD
• **1478** Rome's French colony acquired a small church in this quarter of Rome, which is still identified with Gallic culture.
• **1518** Cardinal Giulio de' Medici, future Pope Clement VII, laid the cornerstone.
• **1589** San Luigi was consecrated as the official church in Rome for the French, dedicated to their King Louis IX, who led two crusades and was made a saint.
• **1597** Caravaggio started his five-year cycle of paintings.

❼ Chiesa di San Luigi dei Francesi

(1589, Fontana)

The French church – the Caravaggio church. The facade is almost too clean for Rome, and the whole atmosphere is pompous, a very un-Italian quality. But follow the crowds to the fifth chapel on the left, just before the altar, and you will be entranced with three paintings by Michelangelo Merisi (1571-1610, from the north Italian town of Caravaggio, from which he took his *nom de peintre*, Caravaggio).

The facade is usually attributed to Giacomo della Porta, but the ensemble is probably the work of Domenico Fontana. Caravaggio's three masterpieces in the Contarelli chapel represent **St. Matthew and the Angel** (over the altar), the **Calling** (on the left) and the **Martyrdom of St. Matthew** (on the right). Notice the exaggerated but lifelike positions of the figures, and the drama built up by the illumination coming from a single source, like a theatrical spotlight. Caravaggio started the Neapolitan school of painting in which the poor and the sick were

BERNINI
Triton Fountain
and *Fountain of the Bees*

Just down the hill from Palazzo Barberini is the piazza of the same name,

dominated by the famous Triton Fountain (1642). Here Bernini broke with tradition by excluding virtually all architectural elements and creating a purely sculptural fountain. The merman (or Triton) is blowing a high spout of water

subjects. He launched "reality" (notice the dirty soles of the feet). Painting had come a long way since the more classic works of Michelangelo and Raphael.

Caravaggio was banished to Naples because he had killed a man in a knife fight. Walking back to Rome as a penance without knowing that the pope had pardoned him, he died on the beach.

❽ Chiesa di Sant'Ivo alla Sapienza

(1642-60, Borromini)

Our favorite Baroque church: the finest masterpiece by the finest architect of Roman Baroque. Borromini built this church in the courtyard of the

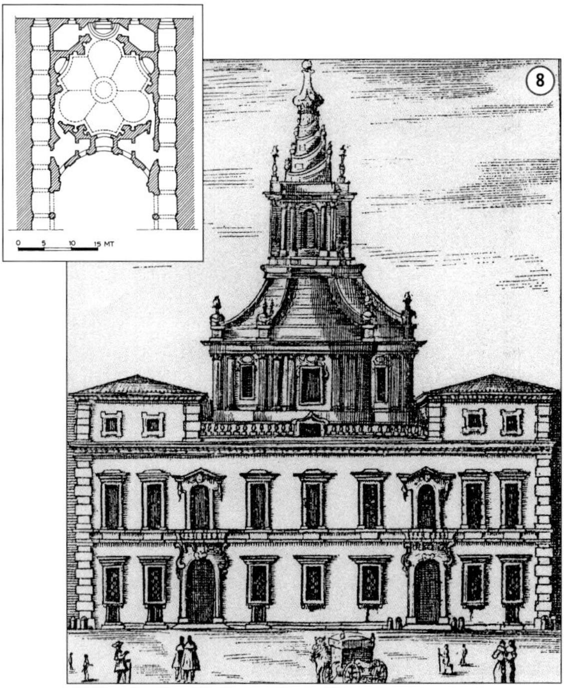

[E 5]
*Largo della Sapienza
and Corso Rinascimento,
40. Tel. 066864987.*

Getting there
Bus 70, 81, 87, 115,
116, 186, 492, 628.

Open Sunday for Mass
10 am-noon.
Closed July and August.

History AD
• **1303** Pope Boniface VIII (who invented Christian Jubilees) founded Rome's university.
• **1575-87** Giacomo della Porta completed the university building with its large courtyard, the Palazzo della Sapienza (wisdom palace).
• **1599** Francesco Castelli was born at Bissone, in Italian Switzerland.
• **1620** Castelli, changing his name to Borromini, worked as stone carver under Bernini in St. Peter's. Neurotic, he fell out

183

out of his conch shell while kneeling on two scallop shells held up by four dolphins. At the corner of Via Veneto, Bernini's Fountain of the Bees (Fontana delle Api, 1644) honors his patron Pope Urban VIII Barberini, whose family symbol was, appropriately for such a busy swarm, the bee. It features three giant insects crossing a scallop shell to drink at the large fountain.

YOUR CHOICE?
Stand in this vast square. Glance up the Via delle Quattro Fontane at the corner of Borromini's Church of San Carlo. Study the two glorious Bernini fountains. Look up at the Palazzo Barberini hovering above the

square. Dream that you are a 17c cardinal and favorite nephew of the pope having to decide who will be your family architect – Bernini or Borromini? Or, why not, both?

with Bernini and considered himself spiritual heir of Michelangelo.

• **1642-48** Borromini's design for the church was carried out, but the interior decoration took another couple of decades and was completed after his death.

St. Ivo's dome.

existing Renaissance **Palazzo della Sapienza** (1575, Giacomo della Porta), the original site of Rome's university, "La Sapienza."

He enlivened the end of this courtyard by surmounting it with a giant drum above which a spiral cone seems to have been upended. A Middle Eastern ziggurat is the only architectural precedent for this twisted lantern top, a soaring leap of artistic, as well as spiritual, faith.

The interior is even more unexpected. You enter a dazzling white space, curved and narrow below, but soaring up to a well-lit and gilded dome. Movement, a central characteristic of the Baroque, is dramatic: the walls are fluted, covered with niches of alternating shapes and dimensions; concaves and convexes are everywhere.

Outsized Corinthian pilasters carry your eye up to the dome's base, which echoes the rounded hexagon of the floor plan, except that the limbs of the upper hexagon are alternately curved and rectangular.

The ribs of this tentlike dome are accentuated with eight-pointed stars that look like starfish swimming up toward the lantern. And the lantern at the very top seems to be disappearing into heaven. Top British architect Lord (Richard) Rogers says St. Ivo's "blows my mind."

[E/F 4] *Piazza della Chiesa Nuova.*

Getting there
Bus 46, 62, 64.

❾ Chiesa Nuova and Oratorio dei Filippini

These twin buildings were new in the 17c, and the church is still called NEW (*nuova*). The Franciscans (who wanted a return to simplicity), built it because they needed a larger church.

The more famous of the two is the oratory, constructed for the order of St. Philip Neri Oratorians: the Declaimers (founded 1561). In the wake of the Protestant movement, the Catholic Church launched the Counter-Reformation, from which emerged Baroque Art.

Chiesa Nuova or **Santa Maria in Vallicella** (1575-1605). Cardinal Cesi initiated a competition won by Marino Longhi to transform the original church of San Giovanni (12c). The later facade was by F. Rughesi (1605).

Poor austere Filippo Neri did not get his wish for a simple place of worship. His decrees were ignored since the inside is positively redolent with Baroque busyness.

Church Baroque is all exuberance; and such is the splashy ceiling painting by Pietro da Cortona. Rubens painted the three pictures around the altar, on *slate* to prevent reflections.

Oratorio dei Filippini (1662, Borromini). Son of a master mason from Lake Lugano, Switzerland, Borromini served his apprenticeship at Milan's cathedral, where his father was sculpting on the roof of the dome. He had envisioned undulating waves for the oratory facade, but financial constraints watered down the design. Borromini was a brick enthusiast, admiring the long, thin, ancient Roman examples. He had special bricks used for this oratory, but unfortunately economies led to cancellation of the deep waves of convex and concave curves he had projected for the facade.

Visit the 17c library upstairs with its massive oak bookcases and extraordinary books.

Piazza dell'Orologio with clock tower.

Via Giulia

[**E/F 4 - G 5**] *Via Giulia.*

Getting there
Bus 46, 62, 64,
98, 116, 870, 881.

Piazza dell'Oro.
Tel. 0668892059.

Another Pilgrims' Way. Named for Pope **Julius II della Rovere** (1503-13), who imposed an urbanization plan on medieval Rome, transforming it into a Baroque city with broad straight avenues for the glorification of the Catholic Church. Via Giulia was for pilgrims to reach St. Peter's Square without having to weave their way through back alleys. It quickly became, and remains today, Rome's smartest address.

❶ **Basilica di San Giovanni dei Fiorentini** (1620, Sansovino, Antonio da Sangallo, Carlo Maderno). Despite the uninspiring 18c facade, this is a Baroque church in which several accomplished 17c architects participated. Pope Leo X Medici built it for his Florentine compatriots who filled this area, but unfortunately he did not accept the plans which were submitted by either of the great geniuses of the High Renaissance, Michelangelo and Raphael. More recently there were weekly masses to which you could bring your household pets for a blessing.

❷ Raphael's House. *Via Giulia, 85.*
So called because he owned the land, like other artists who snapped up nearby plots on the new street. But he died too soon and the house was built after his death.

PIAZZA DELL'ORO

PONTE AMEDEO SAVOIA AOSTA

LARGO DEI FIORENTINI

VIA DEI CIMATORI

VIA GIULIA

VICOLO SUGARELLI

VICOLO DEL CEFALO

VIA DEI BRESCIANI

VIA DEL GONFALONE

LUNGOTEVERE SANGALLO

VIA SAN FILIPPO NERI

VICOLO DELLA MORETTA

LARGO PEROSI

PONTE MAZZINI

LUNGOTEVERE DEI TEBALDI

VIA DI SANT'EGGIO

VIA DEI FARNESI

VIA DEL MASCHERONE

VICOLO DEL POLVERO

VIA GIULIA

❸ **Palazzo Sacchetti** (1542, Antonio Sangallo and Nanni di Baccio Bigio). Sangallo, architect of the Palazzo Farnese, built it for himself. After his death it first passed into the hands of Cardinal Giovanni Ricci, who had Baccio Bigio enlarge it, then to the Sacchetti family, who still live in it. This vast Renaissance block has a courtyard in the center and a garden in back that originally sloped down to the river's edge. Since the late 19c construction of the Lungotevere embankment road, the Sacchettis do not get flooded regularly like their predecessors, but the formal Italian garden is much abbreviated and its giant antique sculpted heads look out of proportion. Don't miss the ruined fountain on the corner of Via Giulia and Vicolo del Cefalo, where that boy on a dolphin used to make water in the most natural way.

Via Giulia, 66.

❹ **Chiesa di San Biagio** (facade 1730, G. A. Perfetti). The Armenian community church is named after the Armenian bishop St. Blaise (martyred in 316), protector of the throat. On his feast day, February 3, after an Armenian choral mass, each participant is given a small loaf, *pagnotta*, giving this church the name "San Biagio della Pagnotta."

❺ **Sofas of Via Giulia**. These are the huge unfinished travertine blocks that extrude from the buildings on the right side of the street, the ground-floor remains of an unfinished court **Bramante** designed for Pope Julius II.

Via Giulia, corner of Via del Gonfalone.

❻ **Oratorio di Santa Lucia del Gonfalone**. Down the little Vicolo della Scimmia (Monkey Lane) is the entrance to this guild hall of the medieval confraternity of flag carriers. Blood sports in the Colosseum were superseded in the Middle Ages by extravagant religious processions with floats and flags organized by the many confraternities (see San Giovanni Battista, page 121). Concerts are still held in the main oratory hall, which has a cycle of 12 beautiful frescoes of the *Passion of Christ* painted in 1573 by Federico **Zuccari** (see page 207) and others.

Via del Gonfalone, 32A.
Tel. 066805637.

Via Giulia, 52.

❼ Carceri Nuove (New Prisons) (1655, A. del Grande). Pope Innocent X had this built as a model prison, and it served as such until the end of the 19c, when it was replaced by the huge and ugly **Regina Coeli Jail** just across the river. The sign on the facade reads "for a safer and more humane imprisonment of the guilty" (on nearby Via del Gonfalone another prison, built 200 years later, was exclusively for children, but is also now abandoned).

❽ Chiesa di San Filippo Neri (1728, F. Raguzzini). Mussolini wanted to destroy all the buildings in this area so that a wide road could lead from Ponte Mazzini to the Chiesa Nuova on nearby Corso Vittorio Emanuele. But a public uproar actually forced the dictator to abandon his plan before he could tear down this disemboweled church's facade. In 1999 the facade was restored and the remaining rooms behind it turned into a private association.

❾ Chiesa del Santo Spirito dei Napoletani (1700, Carlo Fontana). The flamboyance of Neapolitan Baroque at its height. Recently restored, including monuments to the last two rulers of the Kingdom of the Two Sicilies, which included Naples and its *Campagna Felix* territory. The facade and absidal arch frescoes are 19c.

Pietro Gagliardi's frescoes, the Holy Spirit descending on the apostles.

Via Giulia, 146.

❿ Palazzo Ricci (front facade 1634). At the rear facade of this lugubrious building, don't miss the Renaissance grisaille frescoes executed in the mid-16c by the minor Renaissance artist Polidoro da Caravaggio (opposite the restaurant Pierluigi).

Via di Sant'Eligio.
Rarely open.

⓫ Chiesa di Sant'Eligio (1516). Raphael was the first architect of this little jewel down a side street, which is the church of the gold- and silversmiths (Eligio was a goldsmith). Although the vault and dome were altered in the 17c, art expert Anthony Blunt considered this one of the purest expressions of the spirit of the Renaissance.

⓬ Chiesa di Santa Caterina da Siena (1526, Baldassarre Peruzzi). Like the churches of the Florentines and the Neapolitans on upper Via Giulia, this is Siena's community church in Rome, as indicated by the crest on the sober Renaissance facade.

⓭ Palazzo Falconieri. In 1638 Orazio Falconieri of Florence commissioned **Borromini** to unite two buildings he had acquired from the Odescalchi and Farnese families. The

Via Giulia, 1.

result is impressive, if somewhat austere. The master's touch is visible in the lovely sun-drenched loggia overlooking the river at the rear, and in the falcon heads on elongated female busts overlooking the street.

⓮ Chiesa di Santa Maria dell'Orazione e Morte (1576, rebuilt 1737 by Ferdinando Fuga). Yet another confraternity, this one devoted to picking up the bodies of the unclaimed dead and giving them a decent burial. There used to be spacious storage halls for the corpses and several openings over the river at the rear. Here they hauled in the bodies that were found each morning floating in the Tiber, showing that the Tiber has always been polluted. Winged skulls are the macabre motif on the doorways, along with the reminder, *Me today, thee tomorrow!*

⓯ Arch of Palazzo Farnese (1603). Designed by **Michelangelo** as part of a bridge that was supposed to continue across the Tiber so the Farnese family could use a private aerial street to go from its palazzo on this bank to its **Villa Farnesina** property across the river without having to mix with the hoi polloi.

⓰ Fountain of the Giant Mask. A grotesque face drooling water into a giant's bathtub: two marble objects left over from ancient Rome. For centuries this Baroque fountain spurted wine during festivals.

Palazzo Altemps,

15-16c

[**E 5**] *Piazza Sant'Apollinare, 44.* Tel. *066897091.*

Getting there
Bus 70, 81, 87, 90, 115, 116, 186, 492, 628.

Fee
Open Tuesday to Sunday 9 am-7 pm.
Closed Monday.

History BC
This served as a marble warehouse, near a Temple of Apollo.

History AD
• **Dark Ages** Part of a fortification between two rival families: Orsini and Colonna.
• **1477** Girolamo Riario built a town house. The Riario family (cousins and nephews of Pope Sixtus IV della Rovere) cornered Rome real estate: Raffaele Riario built the Cancelleria and Pietro Riario started Palazzo Corsini.
• **1511-23** Cardinal di Volterra Francesco Soderini added refinements.

Presenting an important collection of ancient Roman statuary in a harmonious setting, this beautifully restored Renaissance palace is a delight to visit.

Here, and at the Villa Borghese Museum, you can see what leading 16c and 17c families collected as their contribution to the "rebirth" of classical culture.

The museum is organized according to criteria similar to those adopted in the 16c for the display of Altemps sculptures. At the same time, through the sculpture, this allows an image to be presented that is close to the 16c appearance of the palace itself. The ancient marbles gathered at the beginning of the 17c and the rooms finished at the same time, after more than a century of work, complement each other. It is an original attempt to suggest the setting within which the taste for antiquity and especially the interest in classical sculpture developed in Rome.

Adriano La Regina
FORMER SUPERINTENDENT OF ROMAN ANTIQUITIES

Sculpture Museum. Many pieces are gone from Cardinal Altemps's original collection, scattered in museums around the world. The remaining Altemps pieces are enhanced with sculptures from the Ludovisi collection, and other works that serve to fill the palazzo. The sculptures are clearly identified by their name tags, and many have drawings next to them showing how the statue had been broken in the past, and which part was restored. Most of the statues are larger than life and very imposing.

Courtyard (Sangallo, Peruzzi and Longhi). One is immediately struck by the discreet elliptical awning (like the shade that must have been over the Colosseum), protecting the patio and adding a luminous quality to the old stone, marble and colorful frescoes. In the center of one wall is a mosaic fountain made mostly of seashells. The panel of miniature cockleshells and pebbles shows

Aphrodite Bathing.

• **1568** The reluctant Cardinal Marco Sittico Altemps finished the building as a fitting place to show off his magnificent collections of books and antique sculpture. This great connoisseur became a cardinal despite strong inclinations in other directions (he had a son, Roberto, to prove it). In aristocratic European families the first son inherited the family castle, the next became a military officer, and the third went into the Church. They had little choice.

Room of the Painted Views: ceiling (left). Room of the *Sideboard* fresco (bottom).

an art form that defies patience. Don't miss the Altemps coat of arms (lightning hitting a bridge) in colored sand and lime.

GROUND FLOOR The **arcading** is perfectly proportioned for the statuary.

Hall of the Portraits. Among the busts of emperors, Julius Caesar, the action man, looks mousy and Marcus Aurelius, the philosopher, looks mighty.

Hall of the Tower. Look down at parts of the ancient Roman houses on which the palazzo's foundations reside. **Hall of the Entrance to Palazzo Riario.** Aphrodite, just out of her bath, looks beautiful and vulnerable.

Halls of Athena. In both statues the goddess looks unbeautiful and invulnerable.

UPSTAIRS South loggia. Don't miss the first bas-relief on the left wall, dating from AD 2c. It shows several gods and goddesses at play on Mt. Olympus. Vulcan, having just caught Mars in flagrante with his wife Venus, gathers Apollo, Hercules, Bacchus, Mercury, Mars and Luna to witness her infidelity.

The **first two rooms** house Egyptian and Syrian pieces; the striated marble bull has a noble look. In the next small room is a marble copy of a Greek bronze satyr

Our favorite
The **Room of the Sideboard** has a dark fresco showing some furniture groaning with silver platters; it is masterly. In 1477 Girolamo Riario and Caterina Sforza were married, some believe in this room, and originally on all four walls were paintings of the wedding presents and greeting cards.

by Praxiteles (4c) that once stood on a street in early Athens and was copied all around the ancient world.

Note the ribbon holding the pipes of Pan, so fine it seems to move in the wind – but it's really marble. **Room of the Painted Views**, a sunny corner room, has frescoes all over the walls and up to the ceiling. Columns with trompe l'oeil tapestries of landscapes give a richness, and the views are stunning. Above these is a painted balcony, just under the ceiling, stuffed with jolly fat cherubs. **Hermes Longhios** is a beautiful white marble statue. A glint of red in his hair shows it was once gilded.

Room of Moses has a frieze of the story of Moses high up on the walls. Here is a most famous ancient marble carving, the **Ludovisi Throne** (5 BC), thought by some experts to be one of a pair, the other decorated with men. A relief sculpture of Aphrodite being born out of the waves, helped by two handmaidens, shows her transparent dress clinging to her body in wet folds leaving little to the imagination. Dug up from the Ludovisi gardens at the end of the 19c, the throne has a fascinating past. First, the mythology: Cronus cut off his father Uranos's testicles with a diamond and threw them into the sea. Thus Aphrodite *Urania* is born from his sperm/foam. Originally in Epizephiris (*Gentle Breezes* in ancient Greek), Magna Graecia, it was too beautiful not to be stolen from its temple setting and ended up in Julius Caesar's garden here (he had many other gardens, though never got to enjoy them much). Then it disappeared until it was discovered about 100 years ago.

Sala della Duchessa. **Aphrodite Bathing** with Cupid offering a towel (see page 190) is a Roman marble copy of a famous 3c BC Greek bronze by Doidalsas.

Cardinal's bedchamber. Frescoes here are vivid, and the wooden ceiling charmingly painted. The large, red-marble, flat sculpture of Dionysius with round holes for eye and mouth makes one wonder if wine flowed instead of water from this fountain. Under the sculpture and to the right is a little cupboard used by the cardinal as a "convenience for urinating."

Room of the Fireplace. A gigantic fireplace dominates this room, which used to go up two stories (the present ceiling is modern). Also dominating the room is a giant statue of **Galatea's Suicide**, showing realistic marble drops of blood where he is plunging his sword into himself. On the right is an enormous **sarcophagus** (3c), carved from a single piece of marble. Romans battle barbarians all over the place. Particularly fine renditions of a Roman general's skirt which seems to be flying (center), a coat of mail on a Roman soldier (right corner), and all the horses – frightened and neighing – make this an exciting work of art. The **private chapel** is in stark contrast to the ornate **Chiesa di Sant'Aniceto Room**, which is richly frescoed and marbled. Don't miss some more cherubs having a fine old time on the ceiling. Altemps was bitterly grieved when Pope Sixtus V killed his son Roberto as an example to the other rowdies and perhaps named his own place of worship, in a defiant mood, after an obscure pope who wasn't a martyr (Anicetus, circa 155-166).

North loggia. Facing due south and drenched in sun, this charming space is rich in scrumptious frescoes of pergolas and climbing plants. Here were placed the obligatory busts of the 12 Caesars (that every self-respecting connoisseur should have). The small fountain has glass mosaics, cupids, two Altemps rams, and two girls with water urns.

To leave, you have to go back through the rooms you just admired, as the exit is at the entrance.

Asclepius with
a satyr in the foreground.

RENAISSANCE ARTISTS AND ARCHITECTS

Stop and consider for a moment the number of fine artists and sculptors living at one time. What propelled this flowering of the arts? Was it the social climate (an enlightened society and rich patrons)? Was it simply the need to decorate new buildings? Or was it a natural blossoming of talent? Note that half of those listed below were alive when Columbus sailed the ocean blue in 1492.

1267 - 1337	Giotto
1284 - 1344	Simone Martini
1290 - 1348	Bernardo Daddi
1383 - 1447	Masolino (Tommaso di Cristoforo Fini)
1386 - 1466	Donatello (Donato di Betto)
1387 - 1445	Fra Angelico (Giovanni da Fiesole)
1406 - 1469	Filippo Lippi
1415 - 1492	Piero della Francesca
1420 - 1497	Benozzo Gozzoli
1431 - 1498	Antonio Pollaiolo
1431 - 1506	Andrea Mantegna
1444 - 1514	Donato Bramante
1445 - 1510	Sandro Botticelli
1445 - 1523	Perugino (Pietro Vannucci)
1449 - 1494	Domenico Ghirlandaio
1452 - 1519	Leonardo da Vinci
1454 - 1513	Pinturicchio (Bernardino di Betto)
1475 - 1550	Luca della Robbia the Younger
1475 - 1564	Michelangelo Buonarroti
1477 - 1549	Sodoma (Giovan Antonio Bazzi)
1481 - 1536	Baldassarre Peruzzi
1483 - 1520	Raphael Sanzio
1483 - 1546	Antonio da Sangallo the Younger
1486 - 1570	Sansovino (Jacopo Tatti)
1490 - 1576	Titian (Tiziano Vecellio)
1499 - 1546	Giulio Romano (Giulio Pippi)
1500 - 1571	Benvenuto Cellini
1507 - 1573	Vignola (Jacopo Barozzi)
1511 - 1574	Giorgio Vasari
1528 - 1588	Veronese (Paolo Caliari)
1540 - 1602	Giacomo della Porta
1562 - 1629	Pietro Bernini (Father of Gian Lorenzo)
1573 - 1610	Caravaggio (Michelangelo Merisi)
1596 - 1669	Pietro da Cortona (Pietro Berrettini)
1598 - 1680	Gian Lorenzo Bernini (the Great)
1599 - 1667	Francesco Borromini

Villa Borghese and Museum

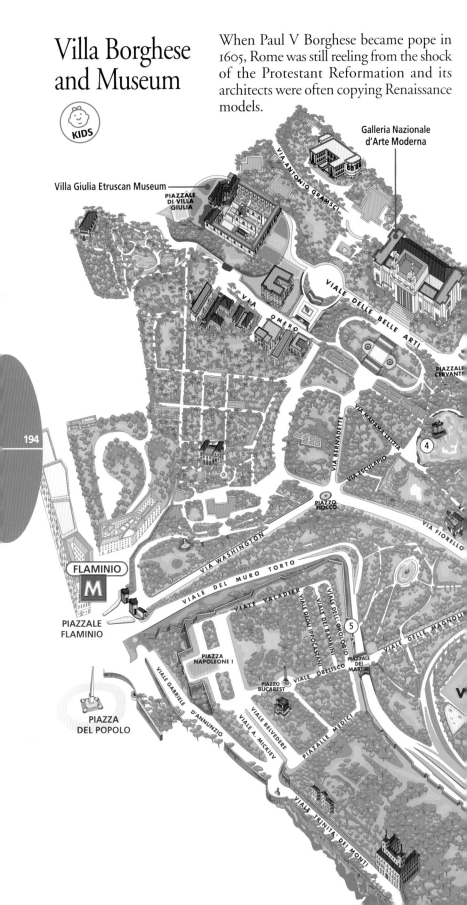

When Paul V Borghese became pope in 1605, Rome was still reeling from the shock of the Protestant Reformation and its architects were often copying Renaissance models.

KIDS

Galleria Nazionale d'Arte Moderna

Villa Giulia Etruscan Museum

PIAZZALE DI VILLA GIULIA

VIA ANTONIO GRAMSCI

VIA OMERO

VIALE DELLE BELLE ARTI

PIAZZALE CERVANTI

VIA MADAMA LETIZIA

VIA BERNADETTE

4

VIA ESCULAPIO

PIAZZO FIOCCO

VIA FIORELLO

VIA WASHINGTON

VIALE DEL MURO TORTO

VIALE VALADIER

VIALE DEGLI IPPOCASTANI

VIALE DEL OROLOGIO

VIALE DEI BAMBINI

5

VIALE DELLE MAGNOLIE

FLAMINIO
M

PIAZZALE FLAMINIO

PIAZZA NAPOLEONE I

PIAZZO BUCAREST

VIALE OBELISCO

PIAZZALE DEI MARTIRI

V

PIAZZA DEL POPOLO

VIALE GABRIELE D'ANNUNZIO

VIALE A. MICKIEV

VIALE BELVEDERE

PIAZZALE MEDICI

VIALE TRINITA' DEI MONTI

History AD

- **1605-21** Pope Paul V Borghese (former Chief Inquisitor) reigned, and his nephew Cardinal Scipione exploited this situation adroitly.
- **1607** Scipione confiscated the paintings he coveted by Cavalier d'Arpino (Caravaggio's teacher). To make sure he got the portrait of Diana the Huntress he imprisoned its painter, Domenichino.
- **1803** Napoleon thrust his sister Pauline on the weak Prince Camillo Borghese and plundered the prince's father's ancient statue collection, sending it to the Louvre. In exchange, he gave him worthless land in north Italy.
- **1805** Princess Pauline had her famous nude likeness sculpted by Canova. Her outraged husband had it locked away and they separated soon after.
- **1997** The museum reopened, restored to splendor beyond what it had ever known. Luxurious honey-colored travertine dominates the basement entrance (ticket booth, shop and snack bar) and a floor above on the garden side is the world's most sumptuous public lavatory!

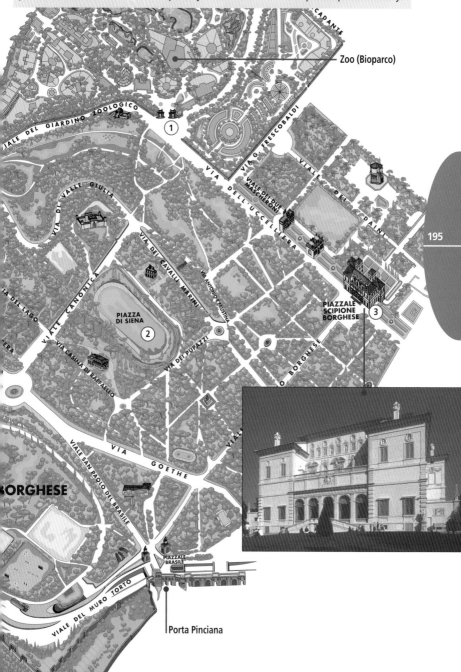

Zoo (Bioparco)

Porta Pinciana

By the end of Paul's unusually long (16-year) papacy, the new exuberant spirit of Roman Baroque had been launched, partly due to the largesse of the nephew on whom he squandered papal favors. Cardinal Scipione Borghese did for Rome what the Medicis had done for Florence a century earlier. Villa Borghese was the showplace for this 17c artistic flowering – *villa* for Italians refers to a country estate, not just its main building, which frequently is called a *casino* (whether or not it is the scene of gambling). The cardinal imported Jacob More from Edinburgh to landscape this vast area. The English-style park is 6 km (4 miles) in circumference, Rome's greenbelt. It contains statues, great trees, ❹ a lake with rowboats, vistas and even ❺ a water clock.

Don't miss the Baroque birdcage pavilion, with twin domes in wire netting in the garden to the left of the museum's entrance. The cages are empty, but see Kids' Rome (pages 266-67) for information about ❶ the **zoo**. In the spring, ❷ **Piazza di Siena** (named after the Borghese hometown) is the spectacular scene for international horse shows the last week of May.

[**B 9**] *Piazzale Scipione Borghese, 6.* Tel. 0632810, fax 068555952.

Getting there
Bus 52, 53, 95, 116, 490, 495, 910.

Fee
  Open Tuesday to Sunday 9 am-7 pm.

Advance reservations essential.

❸ **Galleria Borghese** (1614, Giovanni Vasanzio, real name Jan Van Santen, Dutch). In the formal inner garden lies

this beautiful mansion built by Cardinal Scipione Borghese. Beyond the walls of Rome, the *black* aristocracy (ennobled by popes) built their pleasure palaces on farmland surrounding the city.

The cardinal's exquisite taste can be admired in the superb statuary and paintings; but also in the highly decorated rooms, which are positively groaning with rosy-cheeked revelers cavorting all over the ceilings – *each* of the ceilings and in EVERY room! The richness is indescribable: chocolate cake with whipped cream! There are even some jokes: a trompe l'oeil personage disappears behind a door, which in fact is a fresco on the wall. Evening visitors may find the harsh spotlighting excessive. In the old days, with only hundreds of candles, this must have been a lush environment. The decor is so strong it almost overpowers the oil paintings. If you are interested in learning all the names of all the ceiling paintings, buy the guide to the Borghese Gallery; it has a map with names and descriptions for each ceiling. The rooms have recently been renamed after the ceiling paintings.

Any artwork with Cardinal Scipione's coat of arms on the name tag means this was part of his original collection.

Our favorite
Behind the antique Roman statues on either side of the front door, be sure to admire the lush damask silk curtains. On closer inspection they are brilliantly painted in trompe l'oeil.

⑤

Water clock.

GROUND FLOOR CENTER ROOM (AD 320). The Roman mosaics of gladiators and beasts on the floor, found at Torre Nuova near Rome in 1834, even have some of the famous gladiators' names. Above the central door is a panel of a horse seemingly careening in full flight out of the wall. The horse was sculpted in Greece AD 1-2c; the cardinal added the rider, sculpted by Gian Lorenzo's father, **Pietro Bernini**. (The elder Bernini was a fine sculptor and master of detail. See his "four seasons," where even the sculpture of Autumn has carefully carved body hair. But he was outstripped by his son, a true genius. The rich and famous rushed to Gian Lorenzo's studio; his portrait busts were called "speaking likenesses," so well did he get under the personage's skin.)

Going counterclockwise: **ROOM I, FRONT RIGHT** Walk around the (in)famous statue of **Pauline Borghese**, Napoleon's spoiled sister, posing nude as Venus, by **Antonio Canova** (1805). Her skin looks like satin, as do the cushions. (It once had a motor in the base, turning the statue.)

ROOM II Sala del Sole, **MIDDLE RIGHT** The cardinal felt he discovered the talented younger Bernini and collected many fine works by him: **David** (1623/24), sculpted when Gian Lorenzo Bernini was in his 20s, is supposedly a self-portrait. David is readying himself to send a stone into Goliath's face, his body twisted on itself like a spring.

Rape of Persephone.

ROOM III Sala di Apollo e Daphne **BACK RIGHT**. **Apollo and Daphne** (1624, Bernini). Virtuous Daphne escapes from love-struck Apollo by turning into a laurel tree. Note the wispy leaves forming out of her hair. Bernini was a year older than when he created David.

ROOM IV Sala degli Imperatori, center back. The **Rape of Persephone** (Proserpina in Italian, 1622). In Bernini's earlier representation of masculine desire, the pursuit is all the more blatant. Locks of hair spiral out from the sculpted heads, and Pluto's fingers plunge into Persephone's luscious thigh.

ROOM V Sala dell'Ermafrodita, small cubicle left of large center room. The **Hermaphrodite** (AD 1C), half male, half female, lies face down. The cushion was added in the 16c. In the middle of the room is a charming Roman mosaic of two fishermen in a boat (AD 1C).

ROOM VI Sala del Gladiatore, far left back. **Aeneas and Anchises** (1618-20, Bernini, when he was quite young, with a little help from his father, Pietro). Aeneas flees from the burning city of Troy carrying his father, who holds the sacred household gods. Also, two later works by Bernini: **Truth**, a woman with the sun in her hand, and **Pietas Romana**.

ROOM VII Sala Egiziana, center left. Everything here is inspired by Egypt. The ceiling, floor and walls have hieroglyphs and Egyptian motifs.

Peplofora (5c BC), statue of a wonderfully static antique woman with flat folds in her dress. **Isis** (AD 150), female statue, her dress black marble, her face white.

ROOM VIII Sala del Fauno, left front. Caravaggio's works:

Madonna de' Palafrenieri (1605), Christ as a young boy almost steps on a snake. St. Anne looks on as Mary pulls him back. Dramatic background. This painting was banned from an altar in St. Peter's for *lacking decorum*. Cardinal Borghese scooped it up.

St. Jerome (1606) is writing with a skull on his desk. Darkness swirls about him. The famous self-portrait (1593) as a sick Bacchus (a hangover?), holding fruit, with grape leaves in his hair.

Boy with a Basket of Fruit (1594) – perhaps one of his lovers?

John the Baptist (1609), a languorous lad, sits awkwardly, naked, staring at the painter. **David with the Head of Goliath**: This painting was sent to the pope asking for pardon when Caravaggio, suspected of murder, fled Rome. (He died before learning he was pardoned.) **UPPER FLOOR The Galleria** (Painting Gallery). Not to be missed: **ROOM VIII** Small entrance vestibule. Two mosaic portraits of Cardinal Borghese by Provenzale, the most gifted mosaic artist since the 13c. The one of Scipione as Orpheus dates from 1608, the other from 1621.

Room IV. Sala degli Imperatori.

ROOM IX Sala di Dido, middle room right side, the room of Raphael.
The Deposition, taking Christ from the cross (1507). Admire the movement, and feel the weight of Christ's body. Also see Raphael's **Portrait of a Man** (1502) and his **Lady with a Unicorn** (1506), a delightful, whimsical, spoiled young lady and pet.
ROOM X Sala di Ercole, front room right side. Formerly called Room of the Sleep, it was a bedroom with a 17c four-poster bed.
ROOM XI, XII, XIII Three small rooms next to the vestibule.
ROOM XIV La Galleria di Lanfranco, center room back. Now we see what Cardinal Scipione Borghese looked like in the two **Bernini busts** (about 1632). A second one was commissioned after a colored vein in the marble emerged when the cardinal's forehead was being given its final polishing. Scipione was not amused: "Do it again Gian Lorenzo!" These sculptures show a fat man, with intelligent eyes and a self-conscious wispy beard. Don't miss the two **Bernini self-portraits** in oil: one as a young man(1623), the other older and more gaunt (1635).
On the table in the middle: a Bernini model for the famous sculpture of Louis XIV (1669) which the Sun King wanted at the top of the Spanish Steps (see page 202).
ROOM XV Sala dell'Aurora. The master of Ferrara, Dosso Dossi dominates this room. The best painting is **Madonna and Child** (1525), with a new treatment for both halos.
A brilliant **Last Supper** (1546-47) by Jacopo Bassano shows the disciples as barefoot fishermen snoozing after lunch. Christ asks who will betray him and the light passes through the glass of wine, staining the tablecloth blood red.
ROOM XVI **The Nativity** (1546) by Giorgio Vasari, more famous for his book on the lives of the Renaissance artists.
ROOM XVII An unusual painting here is **Antique Dealer's Gallery** (1620) by Franz Francken the Younger. Also here is Gaspare Landi's 1806 portrait of Canova, sculptor of the wild **Pauline Bonaparte**, which may be seen downstairs (see page 197).
ROOM XVIII A masterpiece by Rubens, **Christ's Deposition from the Cross** (1602). Don't miss Mary Magdalene looking quite pre-Raphaelite with her breasts peeping out.
ROOM XIX Sala di Paris e Elena, middle room left. Two by Domenichino: **Sybil** (1616) looks like a society lady. Joyful **Diana the Huntress** (1617), with her troupe of merrymakers (for which Domenichino languished in jail until he gave it to Scipione), and the contorted face of Antonio Carracci's **The Laughing Youth** (1583).
ROOM XX Sala di Psyche, front room left. The **Titian** room. His most famous painting, **Sacred and Profane Love** (1514), with Profane Love looking far more attractive than her pious friend. Other works to see are Titian's **Venus Blindfolding Cupid** (1565), **Christ Scourged** and **St. Dominic**; Antonello da Messina's smiling **Portrait of a Man** (1475); and Lorenzo Lotto's **Madonna** (1508) with a refreshingly obstreperous child.

Our favorite Cranach's splendid **Venus and Cupid** with a honeycomb (1531), shows Venus with elongated medieval body and small breasts, much in vogue in the 1500s. Don't miss her elegant hat.

SHOPPING and
THE GRAND TOUR

200

Spanish Steps
and Piazza di Spagna

[D 7]
Piazza di Spagna.
Getting there
Bus 116, 119, 590 or
A Metro Spagna stop.

Trinità dei Monti.
Getting there
Bus 119, 590.

Spanish Steps
History AD
• **1564** Giacomo della Porta was the first architect to come up with a design.
• **1578** The hill, a private vineyard, was expropriated by Pope Gregory XIII to make room for the stairs.
• **17c** The hill had a double line of shade trees. Three popes squabbled with the French kings about what to do with the site. Prime Ministers Colbert and Mazzarin pushed for a solution, championing the Convent of the Minim's wish for all-weather access. Mazzarin offered to pay on condition that there be a statue of the French king. The pope refused. There were four projects, all topped by a colossal Louis XIV statue. The Vatican was adamant. Until the deaths of Clement XI and Louis XIV, the situation was stalemated. Construction was finally triggered when French envoy Gueffier, a gentleman of the pope's bedchamber, left a "considerable sum" for the stairs.

In the 18c English lords and their retinues came to Rome in droves, rounding off their formal education with a visit to the cradle of Western civilization. So pilgrims were joined by scholars, artists, poets and big spenders on "the Grand Tour."

This was Rome's periphery, just inside Porta Flaminia, the main entry to the city, and thus the obvious spot for their carriages to stop. Fine places to stay and eat sprang up, many with foreign names that still abound: hotels called Londra, Parigi, Inghilterra, Carriage. The Ciociaras, girls from nearby hill-towns, came to Rome dressed up in their finery and loitered on the Spanish Steps, hoping to catch the eye of a painter looking for a model, or of rich but lonely foreigner. And then came shops of ever newfangled "*Tour*-ists" not only with a way of spending also with a new commodity: souvenirs and gifts to take h

Before plunging into the latest version of these shops in the eye-filling beauty of this centuries-old piazza, starting

Chiesa della Trinità dei Monti (1495). King Charles VII after a trip to Rome. Its location is breathtaking, its arc paintings by Federico Zuccari (1540-1609). The church is p **the Minims – Order of the Sacred Heart**, founded in 149 BC palace. Ironic that this Minim order ("Sacred Perpetua this maximalist site. Lucullus was famous as the greatest go time. At his table you sampled roasted swan, oysters from C relays of runners in four days), plus exotica of every sort between courses. He gave us the word *Lucullan*, still used

When deathly ill, Louis XI (1423-1483) was nursed back of this order. He helped them found the convent: the sta

_ kind: stores to provide these
_heir time and their money but
_me.

_he adjacent Golden Mile, enjoy
_our tour from the top.

of France founded this church
_itecture French, with dazzling
_rt of the next-door **Convent of**
_ on the site of Lucullus's   ıc
_ Lent" for them) should be on
_rmet and gourmand of Caesar's
_olchester, England (brought by
including theatrical interludes
_o describe a fabulous feast.
to health by the French monks
_ of French influence in what is
misleadingly called the Spanish
Steps area. Today a French
school is in the garden.

Obelisk (ıc bc). From the
gardens of Julius Caesar's
colleague Sallust.
     This is a Roman copy of
the Egyptian obelisk that is
now in nearby Piazza del
Popolo.

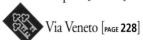

201

O Rome! my country!
city of the soul!

Lord Byron

[D 7]
Piazza di Spagna, 26.
Tel. 066784235,
fax 066784167.

Fee
Open Monday
  to Friday 9 am-1 pm;
  Saturday 11 am-2 pm
  and 3-6 pm.
Closed Sunday
  and public holidays.

Keats and Shelley Memorial House (early 18c). Coming here with his friend the painter Joseph Severn in 1820, Keats hoped the dry (!) Roman air would cure his tuberculosis. He was depressed by criticism of his poetry, and by the distance (both miles and her indifference) between him and the girl he loved. He coughed his way to death – which followed swiftly in this house early the next year. He was 27. Shelley was inspired to write a poem lamenting the death of his friend Keats, but he, too, died young, in a boat tragedy near La Spezia a year later in 1822, leaving behind his disconsolate widow, Mary Wollstonecraft, author of *Frankenstein*. Their fellow Romantics Byron, Browning, and Tennyson all came to Rome for inspiration, delving into the classics and soaking up Rome's ancient beauty.

The museum has a good library, Keats's death mask, engravings, atmosphere.

[D 7]
Via di Propaganda, 1.

Collegio di Propaganda Fide (1622, Bernini and Borromini). The two rival geniuses of Roman Baroque architecture designed various parts of this pile, but with indifferent results.

The facade over the piazza is signed Bernini, whereas Borromini designed the convex and concave entrance facing Via di Propaganda – in 1667 just before he committed suicide.

Borromini's window.

Colonna dell'Immacolata. In 1857 Pope Pius IX, despite the almost unanimous opposition of his advisers, proclaimed that the Virgin Mary was herself born free of sin. He commemorated this controversial dogma with a statue of the Virgin placed on top of an ancient Roman (pagan) column.

The event is celebrated December 8, when the mayor of Rome and the pope meet here amidst public rejoicing.

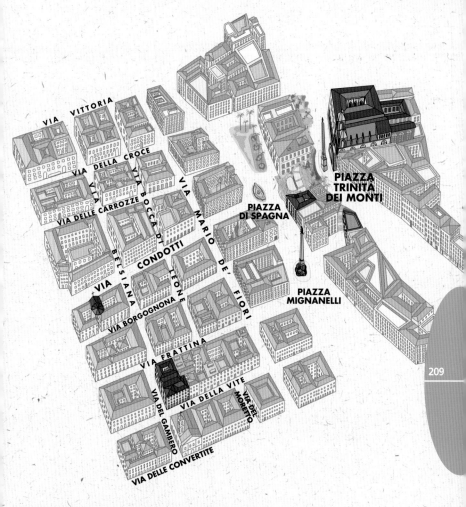

World-famous fashion stores identified on the map on pages 210-11 are not listed here. Shops noted in this section are listed by address number under the name of each street or square.

> **[D 7]**
>
> **Getting there**
> **Bus** 119, 590 or
> **A Metro** Spagna stop.

Piazza di Spagna

11 **Frette**. Superb bath and bed linens. *Tel. 066790673.*

35 **Blunauta** (formerly Baloon). Attractive clothes for men and women in silk, cotton and cashmere. *Tel. 066780110.* (Also behind Saddlers Union, *Via Condotti, 29,* and *Piazza San Anastasia near Circo Massimo.*)

52 **Rossati**. Inexpensive lace and lingerie. *Tel. 066790016.*

53 **Sergio di Cori**. Gloves. *Tel. 06678443.*

61 **Sermoneta**. Gloves are coming back – big. *Tel. 066791960.*

65 **Shaki**. Good kitchen kitsch. *Tel. 066786605.*

85 **Sportstaff**. Ladies' trendy prêt à porter. Moderate. *Tel. 066781599.*

VIA VITTORIA

63   65   68   46

75

VIA DELLA CROCE

VIA   13   27

15   39

VIA DELLE CARROZZE   18   53   37

Mila Schön-87   85A   85   81   26   28   29

BELSIANA

49-Trussardi

51-Dolce & Gabbana

26   26-Versace

44-Ferragamo Men

67-Hermes

68-Gucci

73-Ferragamo Women

73   67

77-Armani

79-La Perla

5   47   56   58   61A

BOCA DI LEONE

LARGO GOLDONI   **VIA CONDOTTI**   24

13-Valentino

32   27   26   15-Vuitton

20-Max Mara

4C-Ungaro

4H-Crisci

69B   14   5

D-Gucci

D4

VIA BORGOGNONA

33   28   31

43-Laura Biagiotti   42B-Mandarina Duck

67   52

32A-Moschino

21-Givenchy

22-Gattinoni

25-Versace

86   90   93

VIA FRATTINA   114

18   67   115

16   67   56   52   51   25   22

133   138

14   31   33   57

22   **VIA DELLA VITE**

VIA DEL GAMBERO

VIA DEL MORETTO

VIA DELLE CONVERTITE

Floodwater Height Plaque
Water from the swollen
Tiber River reached this
height (22 cm, or 4 ft.) in
December 1870.
Via Borgognona, 33.

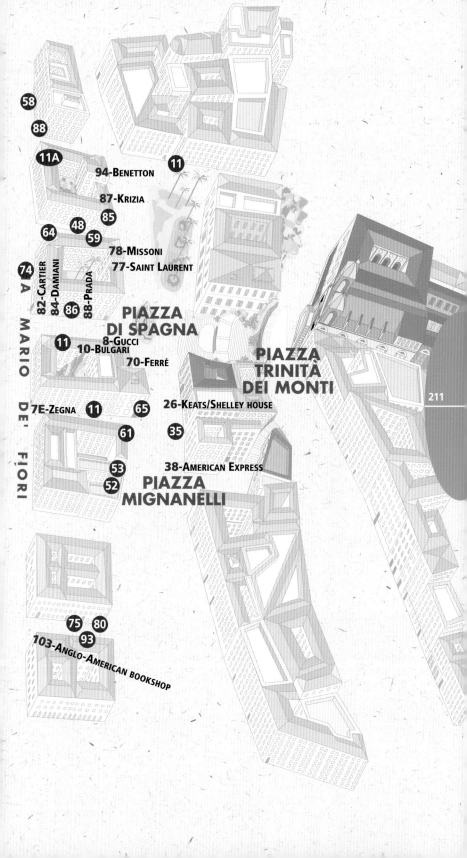

58

88

11A

11

94-Benetton

87-Krizia

85

64 48 59

A 74

78-Missoni

77-Saint Laurent

82-Cartier

84-Damiani

88-Prada

86

PIAZZA
DI SPAGNA

11

8-Gucci

10-Bulgari

70-Ferré

PIAZZA
TRINITÀ
DEI MONTI

211

M
A
R
I
O

D
E'

F
I
O
R
I

7E-Zegna 11 65

26-Keats/Shelley house

61 35

53

38-American Express

52

PIAZZA
MIGNANELLI

75 80

93

103-Anglo-American bookshop

Via Belsiana

13 **Fabris**. Leather goods. Moderate. *Tel. 066784944.*
15 **Sorelle Macalle**. Classic and casual clothing. *Tel. 066784284.*
26 **Dotti**. Candy-colored reptiles in superb bags and shoes. *Tel. 0669920456.*
52 **Domus**. Classic shoes. Moderate. *Tel. 066789083.*
67 **Beauty Point**. Jazzy makeup. *Tel. 0669190754.*
69B **Beretta**. Top sports clothes. *Tel. 066784843.*

Via Bocca di Leone

28 **Mariella Burani**. Her own boutique designs. *Tel. 066790630.*
46 **Thé Verde**. China, tea and fine textiles. Sip and shop. *Tel. 0669923705.*
53 **Corradini**. Prizewinning goldsmith and jeweler. *Tel. 066793487.*

Via Borgognona

5 **Malo**. Ladies' knitwear, shoes and bags. *Tel. 066791331.*
31 **Loro Piana**. Divine knits, jackets, coats and pants for men and women. *Tel. 0669924906.*
33 **Massimiliano Sermonetta**. Men's clothes. *Tel. 066787680.*

Via delle Carrozze

18 **Firmastock**. Big, big fashion names at half price! *Tel. 0669200371.*
26 **Quetzalcoatl**. Mouth-watering homemade chocolates. *Tel. 0669202191.*
28 **Fragiacomo**. Unusually comfy, but expensive, shoes. *Tel. 066798780.*
29 **i cinque**. Everything for ladies: unusual scents, makeup, plus leather goods and a coiffeur. *Tel. 066794331.*
48 **Alcozer**. Bijoux. *Tel. 066791388.*
59 **Agostini**. Antiques. *Tel. 066784052.*
64 **Siragusa**. Superb design, ancient style. Beaten gold bracelets wrapped around carved stones, antique coins, beads. *Tel. 066797085.*
73 **Il Portone**. Pandora's box for men. Shirts, ties, belts, cufflinks and boxer shorts in matching *pochettes* (little pouches). *Tel. 066793355.*
81 **Marisa Padovan**. *Pareo* wraps and swimwear. Expensive. *Tel. 066793946.*
85 **La Peonia**. Wine, olive oil, sweets, *bottarga* caviar. Fine Sardinian products. *Tel. 06678842.*
85A **Dolci & Doni**. Gooey cakes, rosy atmosphere, pretty pics, friendly waiters, two-star coffee. *Tel. 0669925001.*

Fresco literally means "fresh," referring to the fact that frescoes were painted while the plaster was still wet, as opposed to *seccos*, which are painted when the plaster is dry. The procedure involved a combination of artistic skill, timing and patience. The lines of the drawing were transferred to the rough plaster ceiling and walls by puncturing heavy paper with holes and blowing a red powder through these holes. This image was called the *sinopia*. (A notable exception is the Sistine Chapel. Recent renovations have revealed that Michelangelo painted directly onto the wet plaster without making a drawing first.) Next, a wet plaster mix was placed onto the area to be painted on a section-by-section basis.

Via Condotti – Most elegant of Rome's shopping streets

11 Sergio Valente. Beauty queens have it all done here: hair, pedicures, manicures, massages, waxings, facials. (2nd floor.) *Tel. 066791268.*

24 Modigliani. Designer tableware. *Tel. 066785653* (USA: *888-259-7988*).

26 Saddler's Union. Traditional fine leather goods: saddles, whips, bags and moccasins. *Tel. 066798050.*

27 Burma. They claim they make the best copies of any piece of jewelry. *Tel. 066798285.*

32 Buccellati. Each piece of jewelry is a work of art, and most have the Florentine finish. *Tel. 066790329.*

47 Rogani. Seven different sizes of Kelly bags, not for the fainthearted. *Tel. 066784036.*

56 Furla. Ladies' shoes and leather goods. *Tel. 066791973.*

58 Campanile. Men's shoes. *Tel. 066783041.*

61A Battistoni. Finest men's shirts in the world, plus great tailoring for men and women in fabulous fabrics. (In the inner courtyard.) *Tel. 066976111.*

Via della Croce

11A Pelletteria Fiorentino. Handbags, rubber Kelly bags and so on. *Tel. 066790301.*

27 Fabbi. Fabulous Italian victuals. *Tel. 066790612.*

63 Caruso. Crinkled silk scarves and original dresses and hats. *Tel. 066990929.*

65 Romis. Men's clothes. *Tel. 0667995984.*

68 Flavio Trancanelli. Well-made shoes, one of a kind. *Tel. 066791503.*

75 Vasari. Specs and trendy sunglasses. *Tel. 066794160.*

88 Xandrine. Glorious designs: beautiful necklaces; strapless tops that transform dowdy suits into dream looks. *Tel. 066786201.*

The painter needed to wait until the mixture reached its optimum consistency – part humid, part dry – to prevent the paint from disappearing into the absorbent mix. When the mixture reached this desired state, the painter worked swiftly to create the full effect of the flow of paint and plaster together.

If the mixture dried and hardened before the painter could get the design painted, the unique effect vanished. The painter also needed to account for seasonal changes; in the winter the plaster dried more slowly but the daylight was shorter, while the reverse occurred in the summer.

Via Frattina

22 **Pollini**. Men's and women's fashion and bags. *Tel. 066798360.*

25 **Tusseda**. Lingerie, swimwear. *Tel. 066793576.*

52 **Castelli**. Hair jewelry and coiffures. *Tel. 066780066.*

56 **Stilvetro**. Wonderful pressed glassware in rainbow colors; cutlery; plastic clocks: beautiful bric-a-brac. *Tel. 066790258.*

67 **Micci**. Inexpensive sweaters and jackets. *Tel. 066790561.*

86 **Yamamay**. Colorful bras and thongs! *Tel. 0669190260.*

90 **King Gold**. Jackets, fun skirts and tops; walking sticks. *Tel. 066792742.*

93 **Demoiselle**. Undies and swimsuits. Expensive. *Tel. 066793752.*

114 **Artestile**. Porcelain, silver, crystal. *Tel. 066991143.*

115 **Roxy Ties**. Inexpensive ties and Roxy's own colognes. *Tel. 066796691.*

133 **F & F**. Glass and silver. Bridal registries. *Tel. 066780105.*

138 **La Cicogna**. *Bambini* (baby) clothes. *Tel. 066791912.*

PALAZZO BORGHESE
(1578)

Monsignore Tommaso del Giglio used **Giacomo da Vignola**, fellow Bolognese, to design this palazzo near the Tiber. A few years later Cardinal Camillo Borghese bought it. When he became pope in 1605, construction started in earnest. Carlo Rainaldi worked on the river side of the palace, making this end look like a great galleon moored next to the wide and graceful steps of the Porto di Ripetta. Inside the inner courtyard great antique statues loom.

And on the *piano nobile,* where the exclusive Caccia Club is, ceilings reach new heights, with frescoes and gold in profusion.

Largo Fontanella Borghese, 19.

Via del Gambero

16 **Valambert**. Linen clothing for women (also for men at Via Campo Marzio, 45). *Tel. 066789220.*

18 **Pitran**. Men's clothing in large sizes (also for women at Via Merulana, 5). *Tel. 0667994012.*

Largo Goldoni

5 **Fendi**. Megastore of all Fendi – shoes, bags, furs, accessories, ready-to-wear and *alta moda*! *Tel. 0633450886.*

Via Mario de' Fiori

58 **Tramontano**. Customers Woody Allen and Alberto Sordi may be funny, but these Naples leather goods are serious. *Tel. 0669380373.*

74 **Libano Agostino**. Cameo center. *Tel. 066788480.*

Via della Vite

14 **Senzacqua**. Watch repair. *Tel. 066789437.*

22 **Noblet**. Men's fashion. *Tel. 066798383.*

31 **Helio**. Desirable shoes for all occasions. Their specialty: little ballerina-style flats. Original designs. *Tel. 066790837.*

33 **La Porcellana Bianca**. Lacy china and pressed glass. *Tel. 0669200745.*

57 **Silvany**. Corduroy pants and more for men. *Tel. 066781442.*

75 **Silvana del Plato**. Clothes for kids, birth to eight years. *Tel. 066786596.*

80 **Calico Lion**. Silky christening robes for under-eights. *Tel. 066784626.*

93 **Lili la Tigresse**. Feminine and funky clothes. Moderate. *Tel. 066789086.*

BASILICA DI SAN LORENZO IN LUCINA

A charming church in a triangular square, bathed in sunlight. In the square are two nice bars and some interesting shops. And under the building on the left of the church was found the sculptured blocks of marble from the **Ara Pacis** (see page 50). The church is 4c, though the bell tower is 12c, added when the fabric was rebuilt. The loggia has six antique columns. Inside is a piece of the gridiron on which poor Saint Lorenzo was grilled alive. Also the tomb of French painter Nicolas Poussin (1594-1665).

Underground Roman relics on various levels dating from AD 2c, 3c and 4c can be visited with a guided tour on the last Saturday of each month at 4:30 pm.

Piazza San Lorenzo in Lucina.
Tel. 066871494.

The Trident Area

The twin churches St. Mary of Miracles and St. Mary of the Holy Hill prettily stand guard, gathering together three avenues in a big bow: *Via Babuino, Via del Corso* and *Via di Ripetta*. Until recently, this trident-shaped area was the bastion of Rome's artists, but now flashy stores have crept in among the galleries and antique shops.

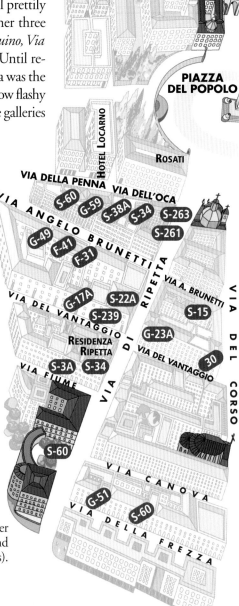

PIAZZA DEL POPOLO

A Great Place to Shop and Visit Galleries

Shops are listed by address number under the name of each street and square (see this map for locations). So now . . .

Via del Babuino

20 **Touring Club Bookshop**. Guidebook heaven. *Tel. 0636005281.*

25 **Bonucelli**. Very upmarket antiques. *Tel. 063610963.*

29 **Anna d'Ascanio**. Fine upstairs art gallery. *Tel. 0636001730.*

34 **Barilla**. Moderately priced, chic shoes. *Tel. 0636002654.*

NOTE: Letters preceding street numbers refer to particular types of business establishments, as follows:
S = Shop (see listings)
A = Antique store
G = Gallery
A street number without a letter in front of it indicates something other than a shop, antique store or gallery. For more information, see listings under street names on the following pages.

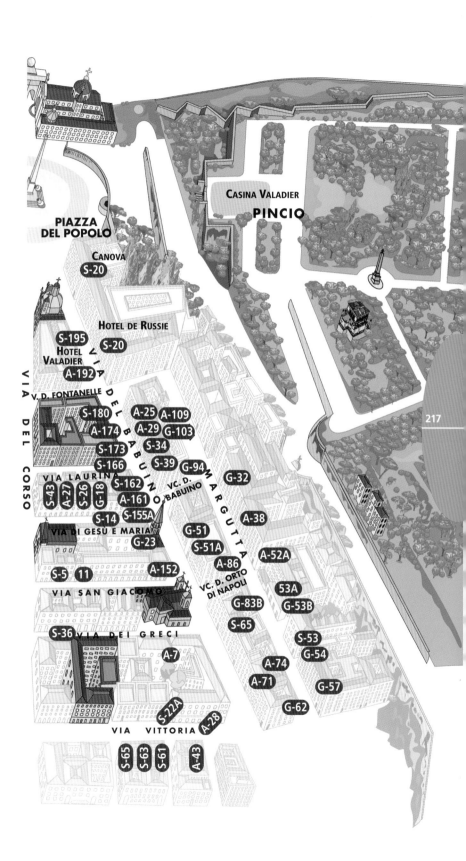

CASINA VALADIER
PINCIO

PIAZZA
DEL POPOLO

CANOVA
S-20

HOTEL DE RUSSIE
S-195   S-20
HOTEL
VALADIER
A-192

V. D. FONTANELLE

S-180   A-25   A-109
A-174   A-29   G-103
S-173   S-34
S-166   S-39   G-94

VIA LAURINA   G-32
S-43 A-27 S-26 G-18 S-162
VC. D.
A-161   BABUINO
S-14 S-155A   A-38

VIA DI GESÙ E MARIA
G-23   G-51
                S-51A
S-5 11   A-152   A-86   A-52A

VIA SAN GIACOMO
                VC. D. ORTO
                DI NAPOLI   53A

S-36 VIA DEI GRECI   G-83B   G-53B
                       S-65

                A-7   S-53
                              G-54
                A-74
                A-71   G-57

S-22A
        A-28   G-62

VIA   VITTORIA

S-65 S-63 S-61   A-43

217

VIA DEL CORSO

VIA DEL BABUINO

MARGUTTA

39 **Feltrinelli**. Books, some in English. *Tel. 063001842.*

51 **Il Cortile**. Luce Monachesi's avant-garde art gallery gem. *Tel. 063234475.*

51A **Bottega Verde Erborista**. Herbal store. *Tel. 063218162.*

65 **Babuino Novecento**. Art as furniture. *Tel. 0636008344.*

71 **Aldo di Castro**. Antique prints and icons. *Tel. 063613752.*

152 **Lampronti**. More polished mahogany antiques. *Tel. 0636001839.*

155A **TAD Concept Store**. Jewels/lunch/plants/hair/fashion. *Tel. 0632695122.*

161 **Armi Antichi**. Old weapons. *Tel. 063614158.*

162 **Mario Lucchese**. Wonderful men's sport clothes. *Tel. 063614159.*

166 **Maria di Ripabianca**. Gorgeous women's cashmeres. *Tel. 0636000037.*

173 **Fabriano Papeterie**. Fine stationery. *Tel. 0632600361.*

174 **Cesare Lampronti**. Old master paintings. *Tel. 063210624.*

180 **La Tessitura d'Arte**. Luxurious upholstery fabrics. *Tel. 063265214.*

192 **Carlucci**. Antiques: museum pieces. *Tel. 063610542.*

195 **Cesari**. Fine linens. *Tel. 063207854.*

Via Angelo Brunetti

15 **Mastrofini**. Handmade shoes. *Tel. 063610204.*

31 **Fersini**. Framer. *Tel. 063217053.*

41 **Maurizio Desideri**. Better frames. *Tel. 063219247.*

49 **Fidia Arte Moderna**. Art gallery. *Tel. 063612051.*

Via del Corso

One long shopping street with sexy clothes for the junior set.

Via Fiume

3A **Arte 3**. One of the best art supply shops. *Tel. 063219240.*

Via della Frezza

51 **Il Gabbiano**. Sandro Manzo's contemporary art stars. *Tel. 063227049.*

60 **BBK**. Design, furniture, housewares, giant candles. *Tel. 063244259.*

Via Gesù e Maria

14 **Discount dell'Alta Moda**. Name designers' outlet store. *Tel. 063225006.*

23 **Galleria La Vetrata**. Changing young art scene. *Tel. 063265007.*

Via dei Greci

7 **Pachera**. Antiques: less mahogany, more fruitwood. *Tel. 063613770.*

36 **Lion Bookshop and Café**. Browse and booze. *Tel. 063265007.*

Via Laurina

18 **Stop**. Contemporary art and design. *Tel. 0632111453.*

26 **Il Narciso**. Attractive drawings and prints. *Tel. 063207700.*

27 **Gussio**. Old tiles and plates restored and sold. *Tel. 3614156.*

43 **Bacillario**. Hell's Angels-type clothes. *Tel. 0636001828.*

Via Margutta – "Art Alley"

- **32** **Marchetti**. Small, contemporary gallery. *Tel. 063204863.*
- **38** **Nuovo Fauro**. Unusual antiques. *Tel. 063203965.*
- **52A** **Consorti**. Very contemporary art. *Tel. 063614053.*
- **53A** Don't miss the ancient-style mosaics in the front yard.
- **53B** **Galleria Alessandri-Margutta**. Art shows to hire. *Tel. 063614006.* Also here is **La Bottega del Marmoraro**. Marble sayings, newly sculpted. *Tel. 063207660.*
- **54** **Valentina Moncada**. Best in this courtyard of galleries. *Tel. 0632069.*
- **57** **Monogramma**. Signora Morabito's taste in art. *Tel. 063265o297.*
- **62** **De Magistris**. Painter at work. *Tel. 063207686.*
- **74** **Brando**. Tidbits of art from the past. *Tel. 063200727.*
- **83B** **Il Saggiatore**. Weird art. *Tel. 063207709.*
- **86** **Francesco Sensi**. Classical antiques. *Tel. 063207643.*
- **94** **Vittoria Cusatelli**. Sculptor at work. *Tel. 0632652960.*
- **103** **Galleria Vittoria**. More mahogany. *Tel. 063242599.*
- **109** **Maurizio Grossi**. Marble, antique or modern, and gifts. *Tel. 0636001935.*

Via dell'Oca

- **34** **Fatto a Mano**. Handmade silks. *Tel. 063612184.*
- **38A** **Souleiado**. Cote d'Azur prints, housewares, dresses. *Tel. 063610402.*

Via della Penna

- **59** **Studio S**. Siniscalco shows superb Italian/international modern art. *Tel. 063612086.*
- **60** **Bang**. One-of-a-kind, unusual clothes. *Tel. 063212201.*

Piazza del Popolo

- **20** **Borsalino**. Those world-famous hats. *Tel. 0632650838.*

Via Ripetta – Youthful jewelry

- **22A** **Tais**. Gold, silver, perfume. *Tel. 063202915.*
- **34** **L'Olfattorio**. Perfume sampling, not buying. *Tel. 063612325.*
- **60** **Non Solo Arte**. Art supplies and more. *Tel. 063216987.*
- **239** **Il Mare**. International book and coffee shop. *Tel. 063612155.*
- **261** **Nicole Caramel Pret à Maman**. Maternity clothes. *Tel. 063612059.*
- **263** **Botteghe della Soliderieta**. Ethnic bowls, soap. *Tel. 0636006600.*

MOSAICS

Eighth-century BC mosaics, as an art form using black, white and red pebbles, started in Greece. By the time they reached Rome, they had been refined and had become decorative pictures of cut marble.

Later, pieces of glass were added, or used alone, in harmonious compositions on the floor and to decorate walls. These were called *Emblemas*. After the fall of Rome, the Church kept the tradition alive, inspiring a new flowering (Byzantine mosaics), notably in Ravenna.

Via San Giacomo

5   Shop **El Charro**. Cowboy boots: Texan and Spanish. *Tel. 0636002209.*

11   School **Scuola delle Arti Ornamentali**. Art school plus crafts. *Tel. 0636001843.*

Via del Vantaggio

17A   Art gallery **Galeria Incontro d'Arte**. Prince of prints. *Tel. 063612267.*

23A   Art gallery **l'Archimede**. "Far-out" art shows. *Tel. 063260934.*

30   Gym **Platinum Palace**. Fitness and break dancing. *Tel. 063006723.*

Via Vittoria – One-off clothes and shoes, among other things

22A   Shop **A-di Supermercato GS**. Groceries. *Tel. 065530II77.*

28   Antiques **Diana Marchetti**. Good, inexpensive prints. *Tel. 063220916.*

43   Antiques **Antiquariato Visco**. Unusual antiques. *Tel. 066794859.*

61   Shop **Boticelli**. Outlandish shoes. *Tel. 066991507.*

63   Shop **Gallo**. Velvet espadrilles, knitted silk ties. *Tel. 0669940682.*

65   Shop **Dal Co'**. Historic shoes. *Tel. 0669940682.*

Specialty Shops

Antiques

Rome's antiques streets are *Via Giulia, Via Margutta, Via del Babuino* and *Via Coronari*.

Bath and Bed Linens

The best buys in town for towels, sheets, table linens and fabric. *Largo Argentina and nearby Via delle Botteghe Oscure and Via Arenula.*

Bread/Biscotteria

Innocenti. Fresh, beautiful biscuits daily. *Via della Luce, 21. Tel. 065803926.*

TIME LINE

BC

753	Romulus and Remus found Rome
715	King Numa Pompilius of Sabina
509	Republic of Rome declared
396	Romans destroy Etruscan city of Veii
390	Gauls sack Rome; Romans consolidate power
378	Servian Wall built around Rome
312	Appian Way and first acqueduct
270	Rome fights Magna Grecia in the Battle of Taranto
216	Hannibal crosses Alps, almost destroys Rome
197-148	Wars against Philip V of Macedonia, Greece
149-146	Third Punic War: Carthage destroyed
146	Destruction of Corinth, Greece
90-88	Social War – Italians want same social rights as Romans
89-82	First civil war between *Populares* and *Optimates* (nobles)
73-71	70,000 rebelling gladiators led by Spartacus defeated
60	Julius Caesar forms First Triumvirate with Crassus and Pompey
44	Caesar stabbed to death
31	Egypt conquered; Anthony and Cleopatra commit suicide
27	Augustus becomes first emperor

Panella. Claims to know "the art of bread." The biggest in town: *Largo Leopardi, 2. Tel. 064872344* (near train station).

Candy and Chocolate

Confetteria Moriondo e Gariglio. Freshly made chocolate. *Via del Piè di Marmo, 21-22. Tel. 066990856.*
G. Giuliani. Fresh chestnuts with or without chocolate. Mmmm! *Via Paolo Emilio, 67. Tel. 063243548.*

Ceramics, Terracotta and Plaster

Beatrice Palma's Creazione in Gesso. Need any statues, busts or friezes? *Francesco di Sanctis, 13. Tel. 063701817.*
Eredi Baiocco. Plaster, friezes and Roman themes. *Via della Luce, 31A. Tel. 065818854.*
Persioni. First-rate assortment of terracotta objects large and small. *Via Torino, 92. Tel. 064883886.*

Clothing, Fabrics

2 Myricea. Wearable fashion and china and glass. *Piazza del Parlamento, 38. Tel. 066873643.*
A & M. Chic men's sweaters and separates. *Via della Stelletta, 28. Tel. 0668301576.*
De Clercq e De Clercq. Exclusive and refined knits. Restrained and pretty. *Via dei Prefetti, 10. Tel. 0668136826.*
Fabindia. Exquisite Indian imports for men and women; also fabrics. *Via del Banco di Santo Spirito, 40. Tel. 0668891230.*
Ferrari. T-shirts, jackets and all the paraphernalia of the great racing cars. *Via Tomacelli, 149. Tel. 0668136330.*
Lisa Corti. Her fabrics never cease to amaze. *Via di Pallacorda, 14. Tel. 0668193216.*
Lisio. Beautiful fabrics and house furnishings. *Via Sistina, 12. Tel. 064880518.*
Milo. Hand-embroidered dresses from Florence. *Via Sistina, 103. Tel. 066792282.*

Via Coronari – The Real Antique Center
Stroll along this street chock-a-block with beautiful artisans' creations from the past. Three shops sum up the mood:
Casali. Old lithographs of views, and modern ones of flowers. Reasonably priced. *Via dei Coronari, 115. Tel. 066873705.* (Also at Piazza della Rotonda, 81A.)
La Chiocciola. Anna Maria Quattrini specializes in Empire and Biedermier beauties. *Via Coronari, 185. Tel. 0668801954.*
Marmi Line. Superb marbles, whether sculptures, intarsia (inlay) or mosaics from the past and present. *Via dei Coronari, 145. Tel. 066893795.* (Cheaper marble gift shop at 141 Coronari.)

221

continued on page 222

Framing, Prints

Carlo Desideri. Exceptional rich frames in his father's tradition. *Via Plinio, 48* (Prati area). *Tel. 066874090.*
Muccifora Stampe. Prints of Rome, old and new. *Via Cuccagna, 19* (*Piazza Navona*).

Hairdressers

Bianca Nevi e I Sette Nani (Snow White and the Seven Dwarfs). Children's hairdresser with animals to sit on! Fun! *Via Metastasio, 17. Tel. 066865409.*
Carlo and Viviana. Ask for Aldo for style cut and color. *Via della Purificazione, 87. Tel. 064743506.*
Eraldo and Alberto Caprani. Great colorists and cutters. *Via della Stelletta, 13. Tel. 066868907.*
Mirella Razzia. Cut and color. *Vicolo Doria, 5A. Tel. 066789650.*
Sandra Kelly. Great haircuts. *Via di Santa Cecilia, 10. Tel. 065895793.*

Herbal Shops
Herbs for health and beauty, even perfumes and soaps.

Ai Monasteri. Liqueurs, honey, marmalades, facial creams and shampoos. *Corso Rinascimento, 72. Tel. 0668802783.*
Antica Erboristeria Romana. *Via di Torre Argentina, 15. Tel. 066879493.*
Antica Farmacia dei Monaci Camaldolesi. *Piazza San Gregoria al Celio, 1. Tel. 067008227.*
Erboristeria Barberini. *Via della Purificazione, 12. Tel. 064825034.*
Le Erbe del Boschetto. *Via del Boschetto, 28A. Tel. 064820816.*

Jewelry

Bigiotteria "fai da te." Wonderful selection of costume beads and pearls. Make your own necklace. *Via Sora, 17. Tel. 066868685.*
Carlo Maria Biagiarelli. Superb icons rescued from the Soviet Union. *Piazza Capranica, 97. Tel. 066784987.*

SPECIAL CLOTHING
Extra Large (men). *Via Barberini, 52.* Tel. 0642884377. *Via delle Mercede, 58.* Tel. 066793760.
Sweaters. A high concentration of sweater shops on *Via dei Giubbonari* (Campo de' Fiori area).
Wild Fashion. One-of-a-kind, unusual clothing on *Via Governo Vecchio*.

800	Charlemagne emperor of Rome, crowned by Pope Leo III
962	Otto I founds Holy Roman Empire, at the request of Pope John XII
1084	French and Normans invade Rome
1309-77	Popes sequestered in Avignon; anarchy in Rome
1492-1503	Pope Alexander VI Borgia
1503	Pope Julius II starts to rebuild St. Peter's
1508	Michelangelo starts to paint the Sistine Ceiling
1520	Martin Luther triggers the Protestant Reformation
1545-63	Council of Trent, the Counter-Reformation
1623-44	Pope Urban VIII Barberini presides over the Baroque era
1667	Bernini completes St. Peter's Square
1721	Spanish Steps
1762	Trevi Fountain
1798	Napoleon's army occupies Rome
1806	End of the Holy Roman Empire
1820-61	Garibaldi, Mazzini and Cavour lead the Risorgimento
1870	Rome becomes Italy's capital after the pope surrenders
1904	Main synagogue built
1926-43	Mussolini
1929	Lateran Treaty creates separate Vatican State
1940-45	Italy enters WW II against the Allies, ends it with them
1946	Republic established by referendum
1962	Pope John XXIII initiates reforms in Second Vatican Council
1979	John Paul II, first non-Italian pope since 1523

Claudio Tacchi. Original designs, handmade jewelry. *Via della Mercede, 12A. Tel. 066787546.*

Diego Percossi Papi. This artist designs exquisite, unusual jewelry. He can take your old stones and reinvent them. *Via Santo Eustacchio, 16. Tel. 0668801466.*

Etnici. Unusually beautiful ethnic jewelry at reasonable prices. *Via del Pellegrino, 66. Tel. 0668309111.*

MMM. A jewel of a jewel. Two artists create stunning interpretations of ancient Roman jewelry. *Via dell'Orso, 57. Tel. 066869188.*

Magic

Eclectica. Tricks and antique paraphernalia. *Via in Aquiro, 70. Tel. 066784228.*

Mosaics

Petochi. Fabulous 19c micromosaics from the collection of the Petochi family, jewelers since 1884 (by appointment to the royal Savoia family). More a museum than a shop. *Piazza di Spagna, 23. Tel. 066793947.*

Savelli. The most complete choice of mosaics of all sizes – including the miniature mosaic work of two 13c popes, Alberto Bruzzese and Paola Frascarelli (members of the Savelli family). *Via Paolo VI, 27. Tel. 0668307017.*

Perfumes

Amorvero Profumo and **Aqua di Profumo**. Specially created for (with fragrances sold only at) the Hassler Hotel, with Lorenzo Dante Ferro and Astrid Wirth blending 208 aromatic ingredients of essential oils and absolutes. *Piazza Trinità dei Monti, 6. Tel. 06699341.*

L'Olfattorio. (See Trident area map, page 216.) *Via di Ripetta, 34. Tel. 063512325.*

Shoes

Grilli. Men's and women's classics. Beautifully made. *Via del Corso, 166. Tel. 066793650.*

Petrelli. Custom-made shoes in the great tradition. *Vicolo Scanderbeg, 107. Tel. 066783842.*

Orthopedic shoes. Birkenstocks and more. *Via del Teatro Valle, 38. Tel. 06687589.*

Smoked Edibles

Pompili Francesco. Wild smoked salmon, duck, goose and more, for that aperitif in your hotel room before you go out to dinner. *Via della Gatta, 1. Tel. 06 6783842.*

Stationery Stores

Blank Books. Handmade on the premises. *Via della Stelletta, 20B.*

Buffetti. Office supplies – locations everywhere.

Imperiale. Next best thing to handmade books. *Via Metastasio, 10. Tel. 0668802045.*

Vertecchi. Fine assortment of paper products and pens. *Via della Croce, 70.*

Yoga

Yoga Center. In Trastevere. *Via della Pelliccia, 3. Tel. 065812871.*

Joan Geller. Private and small groups. *Tel. 065803377.*

RELIGIOUS ARTICLES
For the Clergy
Indulge yourself with that embroidered lace cassock you've always fancied – or a pair of puce cardinals' socks. *Via dei Cestari (off Largo Argentina).* **Medals, rosaries, religious statues and mosaics** can be found on *Via della Conciliazione and Piazza San Pietro.*

Galleria Alberto Sordi
Rather like the covered shopping arcade in Milan, a mélange of shops and cafés and even a tinkling piano at the cocktail hour. *Via del Corso, opposite Piazza Colonna.*

Piazza del Popolo,

1816-20

[C 6]
Getting there
Bus 95, 490, 495, 926 or
A Metro Flaminio stop.

Favorite architect and town planner of two popes, Giuseppe Valadier reshaped the square and enlarged it into an oval, surrounding the central obelisk with four lion fountains. On one side, he created a French-type vista leading up to the Pincio Gardens, with sphinxes on the first tier, statues of men in Phrygian caps on the second and an arcaded fountain above. The elegant neoclassical square with towering obelisk made a gracious first vision for pilgrims and tourists in the pre-train, pre-plane era. Outside the gate, a winding motorway, *Muro Torto*, leads up to Porta Pinciana and Via Veneto.

History BC
• **1c** Already 1,000 years old, the obelisk was brought from Egypt by Emperor Augustus to adorn the Circus Maximus. The largest in Rome, it was moved here in 1589.

History AD
• **1c** Nero's mother Agrippina had her pyramid tomb here. Famous for poisoning unwanted enemies, including her own husband, Emperor Claudius, she helped corrupt her son with her wicked ways (incest is best).
• **15-18c** Monastery buildings with their kitchen gardens spilled into the square.

Porta del Popolo (old Porta Flaminia) (1562)

The 3c Aurelian walls are intercepted by a massive gate, built by Pope Pius IV Medici to impress pilgrims arriving from the north. Don't miss the Medici crest: six large pills (!) on a shield. When Queen Christina of Sweden, having abdicated and converted to Catholicism, arrived

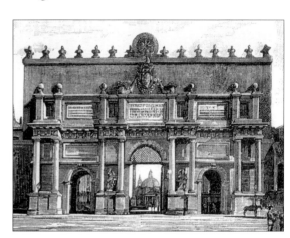

224

here in 1655, Pope Alexander VII Chigi had Bernini redecorate the inner face of the gate with garlands and his crest (two trees and two papal hills with stars).

Basilica di Santa Maria del Popolo (1099)

Tucked into part of the ancient Roman walls. The malevolent ghost of Nero, considered the Antichrist because of his persecutions, used to haunt the area from his nearby pyramid tomb. At popular demand Pope Pascal II (1099-1118) exorcised the area by chopping down a walnut tree which had grown over Nero's tomb, throwing the tomb into the river and building a church here. The exorcism is depicted in the image on the right of the chancel arches, in gilded stucco. Another pyramid had existed on the other side of the square (near Rosati's café) housing Nero's mother's remains. This church, an excellent example of early-Renaissance architecture, was rebuilt in 1472-77 by Sixtus IV della Rovere. Baroque (17c) stucco (type of plaster) statues were added above the nave's arches.

Tel. 063610836.

Open Monday to Friday 7 am-noon and 4-7 pm; Sundays and holidays 8 am-1:30 pm and 4:30-7 pm.

.TEMP·DIVÆ·MARIAE·POPVLI·

Our favorite

Superb paintings by Caravaggio, the master of chiaroscuro (bright light and heavy shadows), can be found in the Cerasi Chapel – first on the left when you reach the altar. One painting is *The Conversion of St. Paul on Horseback on the Road to Damascus*; in the other, *The Crucifixion of St. Peter*, three men raise a fourth tied to a cross. Pinturicchio's frescoes dominate the church.

Piazza del Popolo.
Tel. 063610250.

Open 6 am-1 pm
and 4:30-8 pm.

Chiesa di Santa Maria dei Miracoli
and Chiesa di Santa Maria di Monte Santo

Carlo Rainaldi designed these Baroque churches with a little help from his friends Bernini and Fontana (1679). They look like identical twins but differ in size and shape. One is round, the other elliptical, and they have different-shaped domes. Masterful architecture.

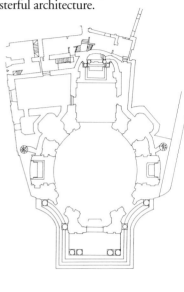

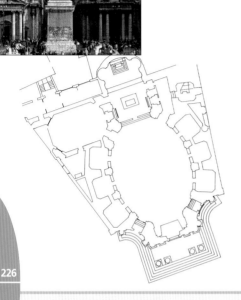

DRINKING FOUNTAINS

Roman fountains, spurting water from the aqueducts, were first and foremost where the populace got their water to drink and wash with. Apart from the myriad metal drinking fountains dotting the city (gift of an American philanthropist) there are some beautiful and sweet-watered fountains.

Fountain of the Three Papal Hats
St. Peter's area
Largo Colonnato
Fountain della Barcaccia
Shaped like a low boat
Piazza di Spagna
Fountain of Moses
Acqua Felice
Four lions flank Moses
Piazza San Bernardo
Fountain della Pigna
Shaped like a pine cone
Piazza San Marco
Fountain of Old Man with a Wine-Keg
Palazzo Madama, Via degli Staderari
Fountain under the Obelisk
Piazza San Giovanni in Laterano
Fountain Acqua Paola
Large triumphal arch with many spouts
Janiculum Hill
Fountain of the Bees
Via Veneto-Piazza Barberini

Fountain of the Soup Tureen
(used to be in Campo de' Fiori)
Corso Vittorio-Chiesa Nuova

BEAUTIFUL FOUNTAINS
NOT MENTIONED ELSEWHERE

Fontana delle Naiadi
Mario Rutelli (ex-Mayor Rutelli's grandfather), 1885-1912. The girls are lying about in various stages of abandon. When unveiled, these graceful art nouveau figures were considered highly improper. *Piazza della Repubblica.*
Quattro Fontane
To highlight the giant cross of two intersecting streets he considered particularly holy, Sixtus V asked Domenico Fontana to design something artistic. The pope, town-planner extraordinaire, had already marked the extremities of this "street-cross" with obelisks: one in front of the Quirinal Palace, one behind Santa Maria Maggiore and one at the top of the Spanish Steps (Porta Pia marked the base of the cross). Fontana (aptly named) placed fountains at the four corners of this cross roads – representing the rivers Arno and Tiber and the goddesses Diana and Juno.
*Corner of Via XX Settembre
and Via Quattro Fontane.*

ART AND THE CITY

Whether copying graceful Greek statues, bringing mosaics to a high art form, or inventing the Futurist movement in the early 20th century or the neo-classicism of de Chirico and his pals, Rome staggers under the weight of its artistic history. When Rome was the dolce vita capital there was a flowering of artists and galleries. Though quiescent now, there are still bustling galleries, art supply shops and artists throughout the city.

A FEW NOTEWORTHY GALLERIES

Trident area:
Studio S. Where a vernissage draws the "crème de la crème" from the art world as well as high society. Carmine Siniscalco, dean of the Roman art galleries. *Via della Penna, 59. Tel. 063612086.*
Il Cortile. Luce Monachesi, daughter of the famous painter, shows mostly minimalist art. *Via del Babuino, 51. Tel. 063234475.*

Other areas:
Galleria Giulia. *Via Giulia, 148. Tel. 0668802061.*
Galleria della Tartaruga (views of Rome). *Via Sistina, 85A. Tel. 066788956.*

Sala Uno (abstract). *Via di Porta San Giovanni, 10. Tel. 067008691.*
Stefania Miscetti. *Via delle Mantellate, 14. Tel. 0668805880.*
Il Segno. *Via Capo le Case, 4. Tel. 066791387.*
2 RC. Modern prints, and books. *Via delle Mantellate, 15. Tel. 066868878.*
Studio d'Arte Alessi. Have your portrait painted in the manner of Balthus, Picasso or an old master. *Via Francesco Crispi, 24A. Tel. 064741644.*
Eduardo de Giorgio. Wooden balls and pyramids painted by the artist with miniature scenes of Rome and Capri. Beautiful blues. *Via Monserrato, 13. Tel. 066833108.*
Wooden sculptures. Codognotto wood sculptor can put your name in oak. *Via dei Pianellari, 14.*

ART SUPPLY SHOPS

For paints and brushes to capture those Roman views. **Arte 3**. *Via del Fiume, 3A. Tel. 063619240.* **Poggi**. *Via Pie' di Marmo, 40-41. Tel. 066793674.* **Vertecchi** (art supplies plus boxes and cute paper). *Via della Croce, 70. Tel. 066790155.*

ART LESSONS

Accademia del Superfluo. Roberto Lucifero, a Bernini of the 20c who can transform any space into beauty, presides over this brilliant school for decoration (marbling, tromp l'oeil and frescoes for your walls). Want to have a custom-made fresco in your home, club or office? Order a painted ceiling with cherubs kicking each other, as some famous hotels have done. *Via di Grottapinta, 21. Tel. 0668308770 or 066877965, fax 0668307356.*

SOME PAINTABLE CORNERS OF ROME

Piazza Margana, Via Sant'Angelo in Pescheria, Piazza Sant'Ignazio.

Via Veneto

[C/D 8/9] *Via Veneto*.

Getting there
Bus 52, 53, 95, 116, 490, 495 or
A Metro Barberini stop.

History BC
• **1c** This was a gigantic vineyard, orchard and working farm extending from the present Villa Borghese to Via Flavia belonging to Julius Caesar. At his death it was bought by the powerful and newly rich Sallust, Caesar's friend.

History AD
• **271 Aurelian Walls** Emperor Aurelian launched the 10-year project of surrounding the city of Rome and its seven hills with massive fortifications because the barbarians were knocking at the door, and not politely. At their apogee, the walls had 383 towers, 5 principal entryways, 116 latrines and 2,066 catapult openings.
• **403 Porta Pinciana**. Emperor Honorius built the massive gates.
• **1614** These gates were used by the Borghese family to enter their vast villa gardens.
• **1870** After 16 centuries of tending and defending, the Aurelian Walls were breached by **Garibaldi**, the papal guard fled and Italy's unification was completed. The new government decided to raze the walls. Luckily, a few diehard Romans banded together, squatted in the crevices of the walls and kicked up such a fuss that the authorities gave up – and these historic walls were saved for posterity.

228

In the roaring 1950s this was the epicenter of the dolce vita, where famous stars (Anita Ekberg, Jimmy Stewart, Ingrid Bergman, Marcello Mastroianni, Ursula Andress) glowed with fame and notoriety, and unknowns glowed with the ambition to be famous. They sat all day in the elegant cafés hoping to be photographed. Two of these, Restaurant Doney and Café de Paris, are still here. So are the elegant hotels (see pages 286-87) and shops.

Glass-enclosed outdoor restaurant areas succeed each other down the street like circus elephants holding each other's tails.

At the top end of Via Veneto you will see **Porta Pinciana**, a gate in the monumental **Aurelian Walls** that have surrounded Rome for seventeen centuries (see also the Museum of the Walls of Rome, page 66).

When the Aurelian Walls were built, Rome's decline had already started. For the several centuries before that, Rome's protective barrier had been at the outer edges of the empire: Spain, Syria and northern England (where Hadrian's Wall is still today an imposing sight like the Wall of China).

In the last quarter of the 19c the Ludovisi princes, who owned the whole Via Veneto area, took advantage of the real estate boom to carve up their estate into the upper-middle-class blocks you see today. They laid out Via Veneto with a wide curve to help the carriage horses make it up the hill from the piazza of their neighbors, the Barberini. The last vestige of the Ludovisi family (descended from Pope Gregory XV) is not open to the public: the original Villa Ludovisi (illustrated below) is hidden behind Palazzo Margherita, the American embassy.

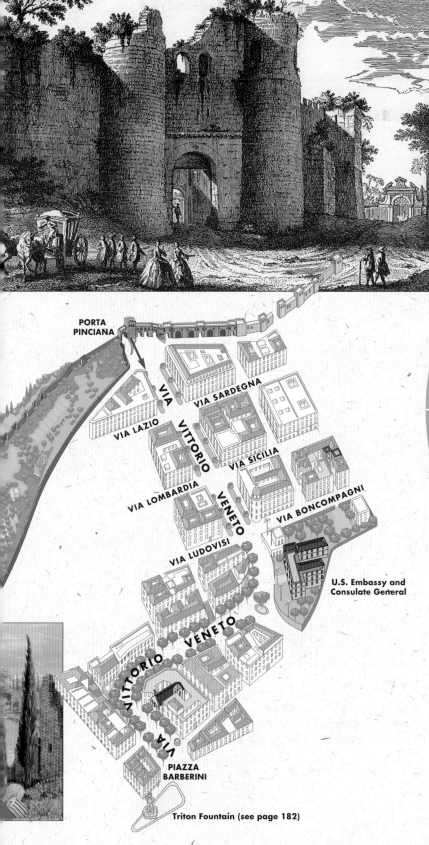

PORTA PINCIANA

VIA LAZIO

VIA SARDEGNA

VIA VITTORIO

VIA SICILIA

VIA LOMBARDIA

VENETO

VIA BONCOMPAGNI

VIA LUDOVISI

U.S. Embassy and Consulate General

VITTORIO VENETO

VIA

PIAZZA BARBERINI

Triton Fountain (see page 182)

Here are the three historic cafés of Via Veneto:

Harry's Bar. This is not part of a chain of the Venetian original (and best). Wood paneling and comfortable chairs, like an exclusive club. So relax and have a Bellini (champagne and peach juice). **Closed** Sunday. *Via Veneto, 150. Tel. 06484643.*

Restaurant Doney. An elegant coffee and food bar with sumptuous buffet dinners and sidewalk café. Attached to the Excelsior Hotel. This was *the* place for movie stars during the '50s and '60s ("Sophia Loren and Errol Flynn drink with Audrey Hepburn and Anthony Quinn"). **Closed** Monday. *Via Veneto, 145. Tel. 0647082783 or 0647082805.*

Café de Paris. It claims to be Via Veneto's most popular café, and it very well may be. Have a *frullato di frutta* (fresh fruit shake) or dinner at the sidewalk café. **Closed** Wednesday during winter. *Via Veneto, 90. Tel. 0642012257.*

U.S. Embassy and Consulate General (1886, Gaetano Koch)

The embassy itself is impregnable, but you can line up to enter the consulate building at Via Veneto, 123A. The whole of this area used to be the fief of the Ludovisi family, extending to the Aurelian Walls. Palaces, gazebos, the Bird Palace, the moated Gothic castle, the Labyrinth of the Statues and thousands of trees were destroyed to make way for the builders after Rome became the capital of Italy (1871), with princes scrambling in an ugly rush to sell to the property developers. The old palace, originally the Orsini family's, was remodeled for Prince Ludovisi in 1887 into the heavy building you see today. At the turn of the century, Queen Margherita, who gave her name to the palazzo, lived here for 26 years, after her husband, King Umberto I, was killed. He was the son of reunited Italy's first king. You mourn for a few years, and then you become a merry widow. Romans beat a path to her door for the smashing parties she gave. *Via Veneto, 119A. Tel. 0646741.*

[OFF MAP]
Piazza Sallustio.

Getting there
Bus 52, 53,
60, 61, 62, 910.

NEARBY
Orti Sallustiani
(42 BC - AD 130)

Sallust's Orchard. Worth noticing, and even visiting with a special permit, this mysterious place is 14 m (42 ft.) *below* ground level, a palace built against the Pincian hill. Pretty manicured gardens lead down to it. One explanation for the difference between the old and the present-day levels of Rome is that rubble from the ruins (and garbage) little by little filled up the whole of the ancient city. This place really is very deep down. Perhaps there was an earthquake too, which might have made such a difference of height in the ground level!

The circular hall can be seen from the road. This large

History BC
• **49** Sallust, praetor, historian and politician, was coerced to join Julius Caesar in his North African campaigns, and when Numidia (part of today's Algeria) fell Caesar made him governor there.
• **44** Sallust bought this farmland at Caesar's death, hurrying away from Numidia as fast as he could. The Numidians had risen up against him and sent a delegation to Rome to complain about his severe taxation. So he was happy to settle down here to live.
• **34** Sallust died, willing the property to his nephew, who left no heirs. So it passed into imperial hands.

History AD
• **126** The house was refurbished by Hadrian.
• **410** When Alaric swept into Rome near the present Porta Pia, he destroyed most of the house. It had only lasted 450 years.

and comfortable house had many rooms with mosaics and frescoes and, since Sallust was a rich and important man, a private lavatory. Hadrian's Hall (AD 127) has just been restored in the most interesting and innovative way.

KIDS

[D 9]
Via Veneto, 27.
Tel. 064871185.

Getting there
Bus 52, 53, 61, 62, 95, 492,
A Metro Barberini stop.

Open 9 am-noon and 3-5 pm.

Chiesa di Santa Maria della Concezione

(Church of the Immaculate Conception, 1625).

This unassuming church facade hides a macabre art show: thousands of human skulls and arm and leg bones of long-gone Capuchin brethren, woven into "attractive" tableaux. A must – for the strong stomachs!

The church's founder, Cardinal Antonio Barberini (brother of Pope Urban VIII), had this motto placed in the chancel: *Hic jacet pulvis, cinis et nihil* (Here lie dust, cinders and nothingness).

Historic Roman Bridges

Ovid's Long-Lost Villa Discovered
The Roman poet's opulent BC villa, with mosaics, was unearthed in 2000 on the banks of the Tiber, near the Ponte Milvio.

Pons Milvius (109 BC, Ponte Milvio). *Still in use today*. Largely rebuilt, but the middle four arches are original. A graceful brick and marble construction with a 15c *keep*. The Battle of Ponte Milvio (AD 312) was a turning point in Christian history, when the pagan Maxentius was defeated by Constantine – who on the eve of battle saw a vision of a glowing Christian cross. Maxentius came across this bridge from Rome to fight his enemy, but Constantine's cross-bearing troops seized the bridge, cutting off Maxentius from his base. Constantine went on to legitimize Christianity, build several basilicas and convert to Christianity on his deathbed. In 1850 Garibaldi blew up part of this bridge to stop the French invasion.

Pons Aelius (Ponte Sant'Angelo). *Still in use today*. Emperor Hadrian (whose family name was Aelius) built a bridge here (AD 137) to cross the river to his mausoleum (now Castel Sant'Angelo). It collapsed in the Holy Year 1450 when the vast crowd panicked. Rebuilt, it was the scene of Beatrice Cenci's execution (see page 48). Bernini and his school embellished the bridge with 10 statues of angels (1598-1660). The three central arches are the ancient ones.

Pons Nerone (about AD 60). Already in lamentable condition in the 15c, today nothing remains except two stone piers visible at very low tide near the present Ponte Vittorio Emanuele II. The mad emperor built this to connect the city center with his circus and with Via Triumphalis (hence also Pons Triumphalis).

Pons Aurelius, now **Ponte Sisto**. *Still in use*, this bridge with the doughnut hole is one of the city's loveliest. An ancient Roman bridge (Pons Aurelius), from which early Christian martyrs had been hurled into the Tiber, had fallen down by 792. The present bridge was built by Pope Sixtus IV for the 1475 Holy Year to connect the parallel pilgrim routes on either side of the river, Via Giulia and Via Lungara. The gracious Baroque fountain at the Trastevere end is the little sister of the great

Ponte Milvio.

Acqua Paola, visible from the bridge, way up on the Janiculum Hill (with the best view of Rome); both were planned by Pope Paul V Borghese. This one, Fontana di Piazza Trilussa, was originally at the other end of the bridge and moved here only a hundred years ago with the construction of the embankments.

Pons Fabricius (62 BC). The oldest and best preserved bridge *still in use today*, and in constant use by pedestrians, it joins the left bank to the Tiber Island. Inscriptions on either side of the central span attribute this construction to Roads Commissioner Lucius Fabricius. Another inscription attests that it was satisfactorily repaired after the great flood of 23 BC. Pope Innocent XI added the parapet in 1679. Added to the parapet in the 1840s are two ancient herms of the four-faced Janus, giving this bridge the name *Ponte dei Quattro Capi*.

Pons Cestius (46 BC, L. Cestius). *Still in use today* but so extensively altered that it is not considered ancient. Joining the island to the Trastevere bank, it is in constant use (even by cars). In AD 370 huge amounts of marble were stolen from the Theater of Marcellus to repair the bridge. In 1888 when the embankments were built, one arch was destroyed and the central span was restored to its original form.

Pons Aemilius (Ponte Rotto). This structure is all that remains of Rome's first bridge, constructed of wood in the 3c BC. The second construction, by Aemilius Lepidus and Fulvius Nobilior in 179 BC, had stone piers; it became the first stone bridge over the Tiber in 142 BC, when stone arches were added by Scipio Africanus and Minucius. One end was swept away in 1598 by the raging river. Its death knell was dynamite blasting used to make the embankments in the 1880s. Now its single arch, with foundations dating back to Emperor Augustus (1c BC), sits forlornly in the middle of the river.

Pons Sublicius (about 600 BC). Ancus Marcius, king of the Romans on the Palatine and the Etruscans in Trastevere, built this to honor the peace between them. Farther down the river Horatius had previously won the epic battle against the Etruscans after he hacked down the then-wooden bridge, as Thomas Macaulay celebrated in his 19c "Lays of Ancient Rome." It was near the present Ponte Aventino Sublicio.

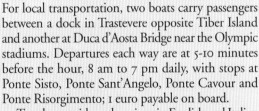

Boating on the Tiber River

For local transportation, two boats carry passengers between a dock in Trastevere opposite Tiber Island and another at Duca d'Aosta Bridge near the Olympic stadiums. Departures each way are at 5-10 minutes before the hour, 8 am to 7 pm daily, with stops at Ponte Sisto, Ponte Sant'Angelo, Ponte Cavour and Ponte Risorgimento; 1 euro payable on board.

Tour boats with explanations in English and Italian leave the dock opposite Castel Sant'Angelo at 10 and 11:30 am and 3:30 and 5 pm daily, returning there one hour and 15 minutes later; 10 euro payable on board, or by telephone or online with credit card. Dinner boats leave that dock at 8 pm Sunday to Tuesday and 9 pm Thursday to Saturday for a glorious cruise, booze and schmooze of 2 hours and 15 minutes; 40-60 euro payable by telephone or online. *Tel. 066789361; www.battellidiroma.it.* Private parties: *Tel. 0669380264.*

EUR

[OFF MAP]

Getting there
Bus 30, 160, 628,
714 or **B Metro**

EUR, today an elegant satellite town on the south side of Rome, was a product of Mussolini's planning. Like the Olympic stadiums to the north, with naked statues and admirable black and white mosaics, these buildings represent the best of fascist architecture.

EUR was originally conceived for the World's Fair of 1942, which never took place because Italy entered WW II in June 1940. Don't miss the fine 1930s mosaics on the buildings' walls.

Museo della Civiltà Romana boasts the complete model of ancient Rome and is well worth a visit. Hundreds of minor and major Roman personages stand mournful in their dusty togas – plaster copies of the statuary of ancient times. There is also a life-size walk-in Roman library and many fascinating models: oil presses, country houses, kitchens, and so on.

In the next square, toward Via Cristoforo Colombo, is **Museo Nazionale delle Arti e Tradizioni Popolari**, a folklore museum with each province's traditional costumes, and wooden farm implements on the ground floor. There are occasionally special exhibitions.

Across this piazza is the **Museo dell'Alto Medioevo** (late medieval), on the second floor – mostly jewelry, ceramics and horses' bridles – with the cleanest bathrooms in town.

Next door is the **Museo Preistorico ed Etnografico Luigi Pigorini**, which has the actual vestiges of a Roman barge shown as discovered underwater (in Lake Bracciano). (See Museums, page 265, for hours and addresses.)

Our favorite
The most harmonious building is without question the so-called **Colosseo Quadrato** (properly, Palazzo della Civiltà del Lavoro), which sits atop hundreds of white stairs, its arches playing shadow games with the sun, as though in a Giorgio de Chirico painting. There is also a gigantic domed church, Santi Pietro e Paolo, a modern conception reminiscent of both the Pantheon and St. Peter's.

234

DAY TRIPS

Outskirts outings in 100 km (60 mile) radius of Rome

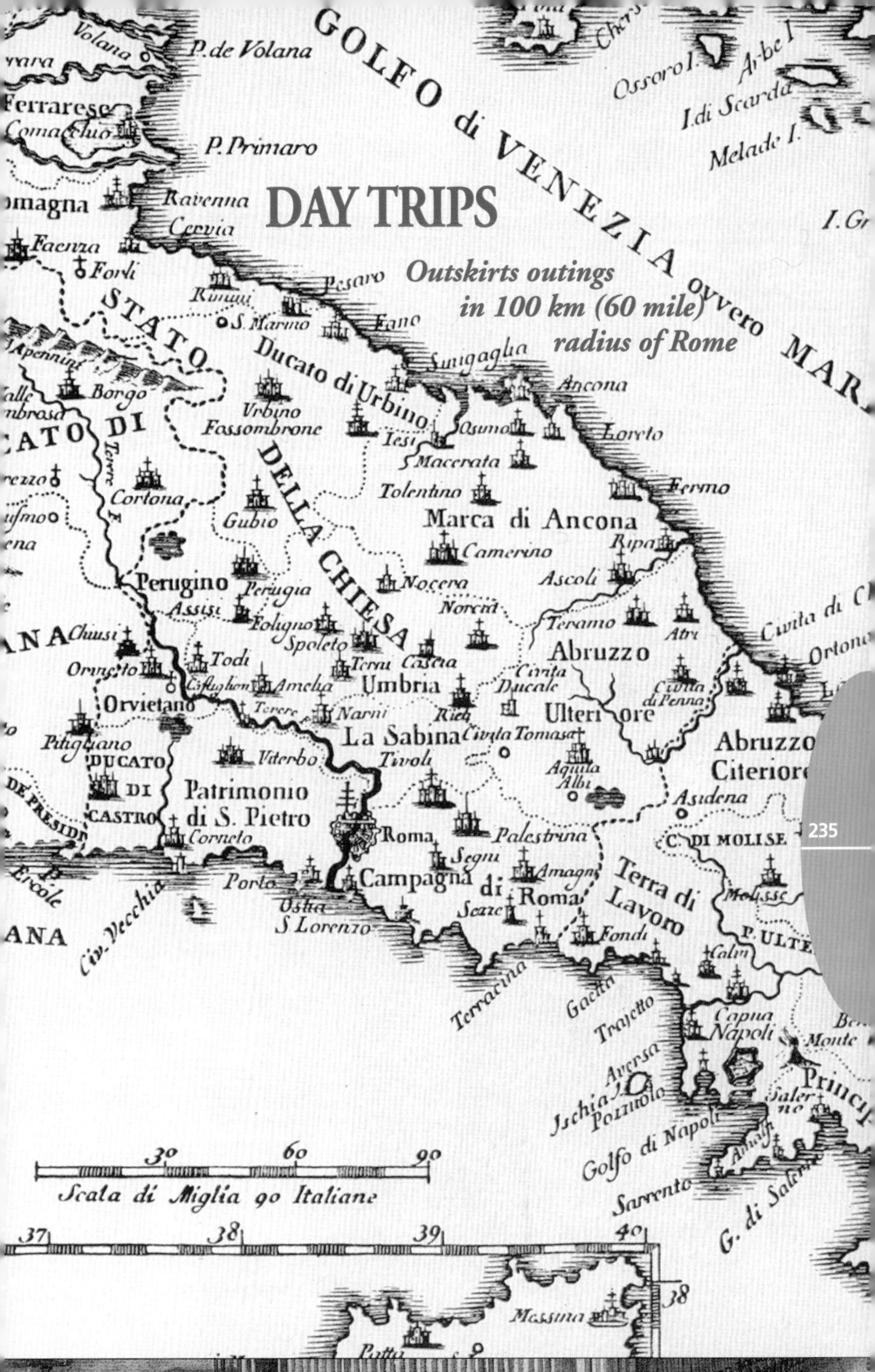

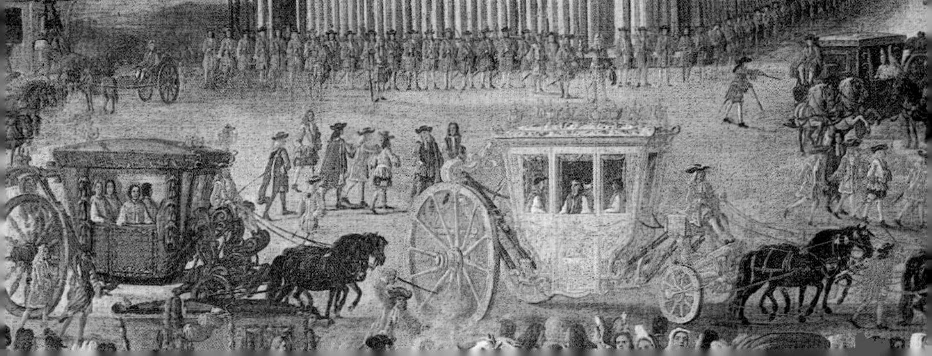

Bomarzo and Viterbo

 Villa Lante

KIDS

North from Rome 92 km (55 miles).
Getting there
By car: take **Via Cassia** and follow signs for Bomarzo and Viterbo, or take the highway (autostrada **A1**, direction Florence).

North from Rome
102 km (63 miles).

Bomarzo Monster Park
(1525-83)

Used to be called the Sacred Wood. Situated in the Orsini Palace grounds, the land slopes away like a natural amphitheater in a series of terraces. Gigantic animals, sirens, a children's dream house, which looks as though it is falling over, and giant stone monsters one can climb onto or into. A room in Hades' mouth, a dragon, a two-tailed goddess.

Tel. 0761924029. **Fee - Open** 8 am-8 pm in summer and 8 am to sunset in winter.

Nearby in **Bagnaia** is **Villa Lante della Rovere** (1578, Vignola), famous for its beautiful garden. Piped spring water, cascading fountains of great ingenuity. The crayfish symbol of owner Cardinal Gambera is on fountains, sculptures and railings. All this, together with the two small Renaissance pavilions, is as formal as the Bomarzo Monster Park is wacky. *Via Jacopo Barozzi, 71.*

Tel. 0761288008. **Fee - Open** 9 am-6:30 pm in summer and until 4:30 pm in the winter months. **Closed** Monday.

Villa Lante, the gardens.

Viterbo

This medieval **walled** city with few 19c overtones was once Etruscan; the Necropolis is under Piazza San Lorenzo. The **cathedral** is 12c, and the **Papal Palace** 13c. The **hot springs** were once renowned and have recently reopened.

One of Bomarzo's monsters.

Terme dei Papi. Huge outdoor pool with hot water at 36 degrees C (95 degrees F); mud treatments optional. Self-service restaurant. **Closed** Monday.

Hotel
Nicolò V is adjoining. *Strada dei Bagni, 12 (toward Tuscania). Tel. 07613501.*
Restaurants
In Viterbo: **Il Grottino**. *Via della Cava, 7. Tel. 0761308188.* Reserve. **Closed** Tuesday. Or **Enoteca La Torre**. *Via della Torre, 5. Tel. 0761226467.* **Closed** Sunday.

Villa Lante, the fountain.

Palazzo Farnese (1530)

North from Rome
76 km (47 miles).

Getting there
By car: take **Cassia Bis**, exit at signs for Caprarola.

This insignificant town falls away on either side of the main street, leading down from the imposing gates of the great palace at the top of the hill. It was planned as a fort by architects Sangallo and Peruzzi to house Pope Paul III Farnese's armies. Farnese (who had a son by his mistress before becoming pope) elevated his grandson to cardinal when the lad was only 12 years old, and 10 years later the young man, Alessandro Farnese, commissioned Vignola to create this pleasure palace, abounding in beauty and humor. Though the building is pentagonal outside, the inner courtyard is round. It was decorated by the brilliant Zuccari brothers (see House of the Grotesque Masque, page 207), one of whom, in the fresco, can be seen holding the canopy over the pope and King François I of France. Taddeo Zuccari (buried in the Pantheon) depicted himself and Vignola as saints in the small chapel. In the corners of some rooms, trompe l'oeil pillars and candelabras seem to pop out at you. You can still see the hooks in the private rooms where tapestries, brocade and silks hung. Alessandro had a **whispering room**, where a murmur in one corner could be heard clearly by a person in the opposite corner. Most important in the magnificently laid-out gardens (also by Vignola) – with water courses winding down hills, green parterres, and bridges – are the grottoes, where at the push of a button the playful cardinal could drench his visiting ladies with water spraying from tiny spouts in the mosaic floors.

Fee - Open 9 am-6:30 pm. **Closed** Monday.

Hotel in Ronciglione
Il Cardinale. *Via Casia Cimina, km 19.*
Tel. 0761624051, fax 0761612377. Located near Lago di Vico.

Restaurant in Ronciglione
Stella. *Viale Garibaldi, 122*. *Tel. 0761625066*. Superb pasta *alla crema di tartufi bianchi* (cream of white truffles), grilled meat on a wood fire, great home-made digestives (*limoncello, nocino*).

Palazzo Farnese and its courtyard.

Lago di Vico

World Wildlife Fund reserve. A stone's throw up the road is this tiny volcanic lake, with dense hazelnut trees farmed around the perimeter, and few human encroachments.

Restaurant
Cavallino Bianco. You can ride a horse and then have a country meal near the lake. *Tel. 0761612034*. **Closed** Monday.

Farfa

North from Rome
50 km (35 miles).

Getting there
By car: take **Via Salaria**;
  exit at signs for Farfa.

Magnificent frescoes from 1625 adorn the walls of the little church in this superb 6c Benedictine monastery. Shops abound in this tiny hamlet: the church's herb shop, an antique shop and, across the road, hand-woven towels and sheets.

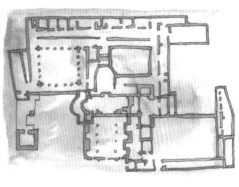

Restaurant
Trattoria Lupi. *Tel. 0765277008*. **Closed** Wednesday.

Lago di Bracciano

KIDS

North from Rome

Getting there
By car: On the **Cassia bis**
take the exit for Bracciano.

This volcanic lake, a mere 40 km (22 miles) north of Rome, has three towns: Bracciano, Trevignano and Anguillara. In 1804, when Napoleon crowned himself emperor of the French, a giant *mongolfiera* (hot air balloon) was launched from Paris. It finally collapsed in Lake Bracciano.

Visit medieval *Castello degli Orsini*, on a rocky hill. One can even rent it for a posh wedding. First mentioned in 1234, it became an Orsini castle in 1470. It then passed to two of the other great families of Rome, the Colonnas and Odescalchis. Scholars agree this is one of the most interesting of Renaissance castles in Italy because it is so well preserved and still has its original furniture.

Bracciano. *Tel. 0699804348*. **Fee - Open** 10 am-noon, 3-5 pm. One-hour guided tours.

Restaurants
Piccola Trattoria. Tasty fish from the lake, as well as pasta with porcini mushrooms or truffles. *Via G. Tamburri, 7. Tel. 0699804536*. **Closed** Tuesday and all of August.
Vino e Camino Wine bar; also serves cold cuts, cheese plates, bruschetta, soups and meats. *Via delle Cantine, 11. Tel. 0699803433*. **Closed** Monday.

Trevignano

The site of Etruscan town Sabate, hence the Roman name for the lake, Lacus Sabatinus. There is a romantic ruin of the old castle Rocca degli Orsini, destroyed in 1496 by Giovanni Borgia. A small museum with some Etruscan artifacts is in Palazzo Comunale.

Windsurf boards can be rented at the lake.

> **Restaurant**
> **Grotta Azzurra**. *Piazza Vittorio Emanuele III, 18.* Tel. 069999420.

Anguillara

On a small promontory with a charming public garden. Ruins of buildings from imperial Rome have been excavated near Acqua Claudia, a freshwater spring.

> **Restaurant**
> **Chalet del Lago.** Great location; a bit pricey but worth it. *Viale Reginaldo Belloni.* Tel. 0699607053. **Closed** Thursday and Sunday night.

Lago di Martignano

A nature reserve, where you have to park your car and walk down to the small, unpolluted volcanic lake for a swim. Paddle boats, kayaks, sailboats, chairs, beach umbrellas, sandwiches, drinks and ice cream available.

Etruscan Day

It's difficult to get away from the Etruscans; they were everywhere north of Rome – *before* the Romans. Romans did a good job of ethnic cleansing by either destroying Etruscan civilization or assimilating it and pretending it was theirs. A few places still exist where we can glean a bit about them. Etruscans seem to have had their women on an almost equal footing (women reclining in funerary statuary are the same size as their men). Games and sports were important (mirror handles and urn covers had exquisite acrobatic figures as handles). Having parties with delicious food seems to have been paramount (based on frescoes of banquets in tombs).

KIDS Veio Cerveteri Tarquinia

Getting there
By car: take either the **Via Aurelia north** in the direction of Civitavecchia or the highway (autostrada **A12**) in the same direction and exit accordingly.

Veio (8c-6c BC)

Etruscan capital, rivaling Athens in its day, with beautiful public buildings and a well-laid-out city, with a surrounding wall 11 km (4 miles) in circumference. For a while it was unclear as to whether Etruria or Rome would prevail. But after a 10-year siege in 396 BC, those belligerent Roman sheep farmers tunneled through the rock and destroyed Etruscan Veio; it was too close to Rome for comfort. Etruscan towns were typically built on cliffs or precipices for defensive purposes. Veio was no different. Today this terrain offers a country walk over a clear, gushing river, and a climb up a steep ravine in pretty oak woods to some high fields. Beautiful discoveries such as the Apollo of Veio are housed in Rome's Villa Giulia Museum (see page 70). Remains of Apollo's temple are visible, and the site is sparse but big. There are guides for hire. **Fee.**

North from Rome
25 km (15 miles).

Country lane leading to Veio.

North from Rome
45 km (27 miles).

Piazza Santa Maria.
Tel. 069941354.

Fee
Open 9 am-7 pm.
Closed Monday.

Cerveteri

Go immediately to the magical **Necropolis** (8c-3c BC) – signposted but not too clearly. This amazing town of the dead, with its strange tombs like manicured conical hills, stretches deep into the unexcavated fields. It served as a cemetery for the Etruscan city of **Caere**. The local name "Necropoli della Banditaccia" refers only too well to the tomb robbers who for centuries have despoiled tombs rich with gold, statuary and carved utensils. These gigantic tomb-houses, laid out on streets, are conical mounds carved in the soft tufa rock, which hardens only after contact with air. Large earth hills were heaped atop these tombs, now covered with grass. The most unusual landscape we have ever seen. Many tombs are open for viewing, though the useful or beautiful objects the dead needed to take with them to the otherworld (cooking and eating utensils, precious ornaments) have been stolen and sold. The celebrated **Sarcophagus of the Married Couple** is in Villa Giulia Museum. Ask to see the **Tomba dei Rilievi** (relief sculptures), the finest tomb but often closed.

240

In the medieval town of Cerveteri (built on top of old Caere) is the **Museo Nazionale Cerite**, housed in the refurbished Castello Ruspoli (16c). The wealth of Etruscan artifacts from the nearby Necropolis are presented clearly in glass cases.

Restaurant
You can sample the light, delicious Cerveteri wine at **Antica Locanda Le Ginestre**. *Piazza Santa Maria, 2. Tel. 069940672.* **Closed** Monday.

Tarquinia

This Etruscan city, "Tower Tarxuna," is beyond the 100 km (60 mile) radius from Rome, up the Via Cassia, but deserves mention for its archaeological wonders from the 9c BC (though believed to be as old as the 13c BC). Seventy-five years after Rome conquered Veio, it vanquished Tarquinia and the 800 square km (480 sq. miles) of territory in an Etruscan enclave of Sutri, Caere, and Vulci, in 311 BC.

Necropolis of Monterozzi: of the 40 tombs open for viewing in the necropolis, 11 have wall paintings. This site is crowded in the busy tourist season. **Fee.**
Palazzo Vitelleschi (15c), a beautiful Gothic edifice with Renaissance overtones, houses the exceptional **Museo Nazionale Tarquiniese**.

Piazza Cavour. Tel. 0766856036. **Fee - Open** 8:30 am-7:30 pm. **Closed** Monday.

Restaurant
Arcadia. *Via Mazzini, 6. Tel. 076635550.* **Closed** Monday and the month of January.

Etruscopolis. Presumably a tomb robber has gone straight and opened this artificial necropolis, where he has reproduced Etruscan wall paintings in a cave formerly used for mushroom growing.

Via delle Cave di Pietra. Tel. 0766855175. **Fee - Open** Thursday-Tuesday 9:30 am-6 pm.

On a slope between the high hills of Tivoli and the sea is the perfect place for a house. Hadrian built here (AD 118-134). His genius was to realize that this position halfway up would protect him from icy blasts in winter and still provide wafting sea breezes in summer. It was the richest, most sumptuous of the imperial villas, with startling innovative palaces at every bend, two bathing establishments (one for summer, in a cool location; one for winter, letting in the low rays of the sun), a theater, a brooding place, vast gardens and ornamental ponds, and guest quarters with superb floor mosaics. Not to mention the *cryptoportici,* where the servants would run *unseen underground* to their master's beck and call.

Hadrian's personality was a strange mix of contrasts, and he was often depressed, needing to be

Tivoli

Hadrian's Villa

West from Rome 27 km (16 miles).
Via di Villa Adriana.
Tel. 0774382733.

Getting there
By car: take the **Via Tiburtina** from Rome and follow signs for Tivoli.
By bus: take the **B Metro** to Rebibbia stop and then board a **bus** for Tivoli and then **walk** 3 km from Tivoli to Hadrian's Villa.

Fee
Open daily. Winter 9 am-4 pm; summer 9 am-7 pm.

Restaurant
Adriano. Having moved up-market, this restaurant is not the place for unruly youngsters or bargain hunters, but its elegant decor and good food – and especially its location – make it the obvious place for a meal. *Via di Villa Adriana, 194. Tel. 0774382235.*

alone. He didn't get much enjoyment from the place inspired by his thousands of miles of travel. Becoming sick at 62, he retired to Baia (promontory of Naples) and died in AD 138, some say of a broken heart when his lover Antinous drowned mysteriously, perhaps throwing himself into the Nile. His rejected wife Sabina probably spent more time at the villa than he.

The falls of Tivoli.

Tivoli

The patricians all had their summer houses up here, above Hadrian's pleasure dome.

A pre-Roman town had existed for centuries. In Augustus's reign a seer from the **❶ Temple of Sibilla** (located in the ancient heart of Tivoli) predicted the birth of Christ.

Temple of Sibilla.

Restaurant **Antico Ristorante Sibilla**. *Via della Sibilla, 50. Tel. 0774335281.*

❷ Villa d'Este (1550, Pirro Ligorio). Cardinal d'Este, of the Ferrara family (and therefore a relative of Lucrezia Borgia, due to her marriage to the Duke of Ferrara), created this glorious garden. The cardinal pillaged Hadrian's marbles, especially his fountains, which are terraced down the hill in amazing profusion. This Tivoli garden is a MUST visit – if possible, at night, when the fountains are lit and some of them play music.

The palace has some beautiful Mannerist frescoes, painted by the students of the Zuccari brothers.

Tel. 0774333404. **Fee - Open** daily. Winter 9 am-4 pm; summer 9 am-7 pm.

Palestrina

Jewel of the Roman campagna. The ancient *Praeneste* was founded in **7c BC**, as you will see in vestiges of city walls built of giant interlocking polygonal blocks. After 200 years of intermittent wars, its Latin populace joined Rome around **82 BC**.

Victorious General **Sulla** destroyed the city and rebuilt what was probably the largest temple in the Italian peninsula, a soothsayer's mecca – now a fine museum.

Tempio della Fortuna Primigenia (Temple of the Goddess Fortune, 2c BC). This temple originally occupied an enormous triangular area (the base is three football fields wide), including the area of the attractive medieval town. Imagine a vast temple cascading down in south-facing terraces, the size of St. Peter's Square plus the whole of Via della Conciliazione. The masterful architecture joined two

Palestrina
and
Zagarolo

West from Rome
37 km (22 miles).

Getting there
By car: take **Via Prenestina**.

Archaeological Museum of Palestrina
Tel. 069538100.
Fee
Open daily 9 am-7 pm.

Mosaic Annex
Piazza Regina Margherita.
Fee
Open daily 9 am-4 pm.

A model of the temple.

earlier temples, the other one being the Temple of the Goddess Isis. The Roman invention *opus cementium* (the first cement) transformed the Greek squareness with flights of fancy and imposing colonnades. This can still be seen today and the ancient Roman cement is still holding up. In the province of Lazio there are three other gigantic 2c BC temples dedicated to divinities: Hercules at Tivoli, Diana at Nemi, and Jupiter at Terracina.

The *whole* and *sole* commerce of the place was to predict the future! The fortunetellers used wooden tablets (rather like Tarot cards – unlike with Etruscan predictions, which were done with the squirming entrails of just-sacrificed animals). There was a hall for finding out if

Our museum favorite
Dating from AD 1c is the mosaic of finely cut marble depicting Nile scenes from its source in Uganda to the delta and Alexandria. Boat scenes, animals, birds and fishes, warriors, a woman doing her wash, people lazing under a bower having a picnic – all quite beautiful and illustrative of those times. Executed by Greeks from Alexandria, copying another, far older Ptolemaic mosaic.

one's wishes had been granted, a sacrificial temple with a Greek round temple to balance it on the same terrace level, and a wishing well – all this to get the visitor to part with his money.

Horace called it "cool Praeneste" and nobles built their summer houses near the temple to get away from the city's heat and take advantage of views sweeping out to islands in the Mediterranean.

It was built on six levels with majestic stairways connecting each level with fountains and statues. Via degli Arconi is the lowest level. On the next level is the Duomo (cathedral), with many pieces from the temple in its facade. To the east was the grotto into which one threw the divining tablets. Continuing upward past Via del Tempio one reaches Piazza di Cortina. The golden goddess's shrine was here, now the Colonna-Barberini palace which houses the newly restored museum. You cannot see the lost statue of the goddess Fortune, but there are sculptures, vases and toilet articles from 4c BC tombs, as well as a model of the shrine.

For its first half millennium it was the oracle of oracles, famous for miracles, with everyone from the known world wanting to go there. In WW II the town was bombed (1943), but this brought to light the skeleton of the temple.

Restaurants

Trattoria Piscarello. Large enough for bus loads, it serves good food; spaghetti *al ragu* (meat and tomato sauce), pasta with *tartufo bianco* (white truffle), *misto caccia* (venison, goose and rabbit) and divine ice cream from Sorrento – walnut, sweet chestnut, plum, and so on, served in their shells and skins. *Via del Piscarello, 2. Tel. 069537751, 069574326.*

Antica Palestrina. Specializes in mouse-tail-shaped gnocchi. *Piazza Santa Maria degli Angeli, 9. Tel. 069538540.* **Closed** Thursday.

Pizzeria. *Piazza Santa Maria degli Angeli, 3,* in the central square.

Taverna Tre Fontane in the square below the Duomo.

Zagarolo

Near Palestrina and 33 km (20 miles) from Rome.

One enters this charming 12c town, perched on a thin, long hilltop – like so many here in the Castelli Romani wine area – through a great 17c gate from the time of the Rospigliosi control of the town. The castle is ugly, and empty. But fragments of Roman buildings are everywhere, including a sarcophagus made into a fountain. The slopes are covered with grapes and its wine is light and refreshing. The area probably started life as a fort in Roman times, with some large farms dotting the plains. Then came a village where the "tunic makers" lived; and survivors of the massacre of Gabii fled here. Habitations of the 6c have been uncovered. In AD 970 the Crescenzi family built a series of fortresses in a circle on the various hills around and about to defend their land from the Saracens. After the 11c the Colonna family and the popes wielded influence alternately. By the 16c Pope Pius V created a dukedom for the Colonnas. And then came the Rospigliosis. In the 19c Zagarolo was given the status of "town."

Restaurants

Il Giardino. A garden hangs on the slippery walls; **La Lampada**; and **Osteria Vicolo della Rosa** (*Vicolo della Rosa, 1. Tel. 069524179.* **Closed** Monday). Off the main street. All serve the fine light wines of the region.

Frascati and Grottaferrata

21 km (15 miles) from Rome.
Getting there
By car: take Via Tuscolana.

The Alban Hills are a volcanic excrescence with many small and attractive towns, and the countryside has the undulating beauty of hill and dale. From here you can start to trace the **aqueducts**.

You can go on a picnic in one of the wild woody areas which can still be found near Rome. For example, **Ponte Lupo** is an aqueduct built in 144 BC, by Quintus Marcius Rex. The Senate asked

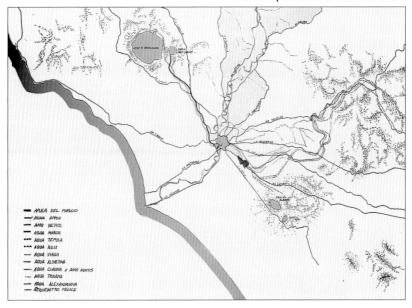

him to repair two old aqueducts and build a new one! This one was repaired in every reign of every emperor, and still stands in part today. Off Via Polese at the 31 km mark, down a dirt road in the calm and silence of the countryside, it is a marvel of massive antique Roman construction, and it brought water to Rome for 1,000 years!

Frascati

Famous for its white wine. The hillsides are dotted with vast Renaissance and Baroque villas, the size of palaces, that were built beginning in the 16c by the grand papal families as summer estates. In the center of town is **Villa Torlonia** and visible above it, with a road rising through a manicured tunnel of trees, is ❶ **Villa Aldobrandini**; ❷ **Villas Falconieri**, **Lancellotti**, **Mondragone**, all 16c and only visitable occasionally. Even higher on the hill is one you can sleep in: **Hotel Villa Tuscolana**.

Via Tuscolo (km 1.5). Tel. 06942900.

Tuscolo. The ruins of the house in *Tusculum* where the famous Cato the Censor was born (2c BC) are 5 km (3 miles) away, set in some dense woods.

Grottaferrata

Visit the **Abbazia di San Nilo**, an abbey founded in 1004 by St. Nilo from the Greek part of southern Italy who was fleeing the Arab invasion. You can pick up a demijohn of the monk's wine right in their grotto, part of a pre-Christian Roman villa.

Guided tours Saturday and Sunday at 4:30 pm. *Tel. 069459309.*

Restaurants
The best bottle in town is the one you drink with a delicious meal featuring local mushrooms at **Restaurant da Nando**, *Via Roma, 4. Tel. 069459989.*

Or stay the night on one of the great 16c estates of the Roman nobility, **Park Hotel Villa Grazioli**, *Via Umberto Pavoni, 19. Tel. 06945400.*

Nemi and Castel Gandolfo

Southeast from Rome 35 km (21 miles).
Getting there
By car: take the **GRA** (ring road) exit at **Via Appia Nuova** and follow signs for Marino and then Castel Gandolfo.

The dark Lake Nemi, imbued with its ancient pagan rites, gives this area great mystery even today. A small volcanic lake surrounded by thick woods, it was called the Mirror of Diana because the imposing temple of Diana the Huntress was nearby. He who would change the order and become priest himself had to creep up the slope and surprise and kill the incumbent priest. So says Fraser's *Golden Bough*. Fear, violence . . . and rape. Emperor Caligula (AD 37-41), who kept two floating palaces here, proclaimed himself the god who would marry a local Diana. This little fantasy was to get fresh nubile girls, with whom Caligula's rites were all too earthy. Engineers in Mussolini's time ingeniously drained the lake to see if there was any truth to this legend. To their amazement they found the two enormous boats perfectly preserved in the mud on the bottom. Sadly, they were firebombed in their museum by retreating Germans toward the end of WW II (for the remaining artifacts see page 256). The hardy can walk up the steep cliff to the medieval town on the top. Castle Ruspoli is worth a visit, and the plunging views from its garden down to the lake are breathtaking. If you come here during

247

the wild strawberry season (which seems to be stretching to almost half a year nowadays), this delicacy, grown on the crater's sides, is not to be missed.

Restaurants

Up in the town, **Specchio di Diana** has just been refurbished; reserve at weekends. *Via Vittorio Emanuele, 13. Tel. 069368805.* **Closed** Wednesday.

Capriccio sul Lago offers dining on the lake's edge amongst the bulrushes. **Closed** Monday. *Via del Lago di Nemi. Tel. 0693953002.*

Castel Gandolfo

The pope's summer place, this 18c town is poised on the lip of a larger crater, Lake Albano. Italy's *spina* is peppered with extinct volcanoes – and some not so extinct. The pope spends the hottest summer months here, and at midday on Sundays blesses the crowd from his palace on the little square. Occasionally he holds a general audience in the summer at Villa Cybo (tickets can be arranged in Rome through the Prefettura della Casa Pontificia: *Città del Vaticano, 00120, Tel. 6982*).

Lake sports. Pedal boats (leave a document as guarantee) and swimming. Lakeside snacks are available.

Restaurants

Gardenia. Spacious rooms with a view of the lake from on high. Freshwater fish as well as fish from the sea. *Viale Bruno Buozzi, 4. Tel. 069360001.* **Closed** Monday (open daily in summer).

Bucci. This simple family-run restaurant has great terrace dining overlooking the lake. *Via de' Zecchini, 31. Tel. 069323334.* **Closed** Wednesday.

Taverna dei Cacciatori. Much game is served here. Dining on the terrace gives you a great view of the lake below. *Via de' Zecchini, 1. Tel. 069361203.* **Closed** Tuesday.

Ostia Antica

This was the most important **port** in the ancient world, with myriad goods coming in (staples and exotics) to placate the plebs or pander to the patricians. Started in republican (300 BC) times, it was finally abandoned because of malaria and the silting up of the port and waterway (AD 5-6c).

At its height 100,000 people lived and worked in this commercial hub. Apartment buildings were not allowed to be higher than the requisite five stories. They had mica windows – light entered but people could not see in. And shops nestled cozily under them on the ground floor, tucked into the arcading, as did taverns, brothels, dry cleaning establishments, the works. There were few private houses in Ostia, but one or two of

them seem to have perfect proportions for a house today (and they had the luxury of a *private* latrine under the stairs). There were two fire stations, a barracks and a courthouse. And around the main square where the theater abuts were the corporations' offices, each one with a mosaic outside the door, depicting its specialty. The theater could house 3,500 spectators. There were many public lavatories, and numerous public baths where the citizens bathed once a day in beautiful surroundings. Hot water was piped through special brick tubing, so that one could have a convivial soak, but also hot air was used to heat the marble floors. There were massage facilities, cold dunking pools and snacks served. The architecture was always elegant, and embellished with black and white mosaic floors, columns and capitals. Religion was taken seriously, and temples to Rome and Augustus, Venus, Vulcan, Fortuna, Mithras and Ceres, as well as Egyptian gods, dotted the town; better to be safe than sorry. Roman garrison towns were designed in the same way, rigorously laid out. The Decumanus Maximus was always the main street, and close to it would be the theater, public baths and temples; so all over the empire a citizen couldn't get lost as towns built by the military always had that grid.

Isola Sacra (Sacred Island)

An interesting insight into how the ancients were buried: some with ornate, large tombs, others very small and humble. For 250 years the inhabitants of Trajan's Port were buried here. As it is surrounded by water (sea canal and river), they felt any dangers of sickness from the dead bodies were minimized. The entrance is indicated by a signpost on the right 1 km beyond Ostia Antica in the direction of Fiumicino. **Fee**.

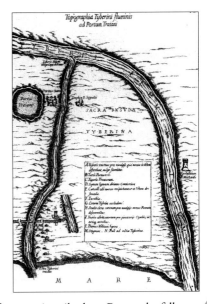

Trajan's Port

Because the mouth of the Tiber kept getting silted up, Emperor Claudius started digging a new port which Trajan finished in AD 103. This precisely hexagonal basin is very pleasing in shape. The channel to the sea contained some large sunken ships on which was built the lighthouse, and which protected the port from getting silted up. But, at the fall of the empire, without the Romans' diligence, the port soon became inoperable, filled with silt, and the sea receded. Trajan's Port is far along on the right, on the road leading to Fiumicino. **Fee**.

And in nearby **Fiumicino** visit the **Museo delle Navi Romane**, which houses ancient ships found here during construction of the airport. *Via A. Guidoni, 35. Tel. 066529192.*

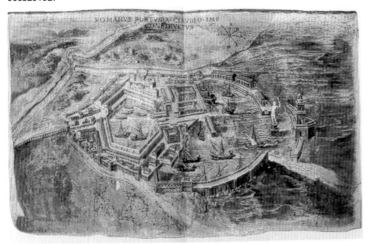

Restaurants

At the 15c castle in "new" Ostia Antica is the restaurant **Il Monumento**; good, but reservations are necessary on a weekend. *Piazza Umberto I, 8. Tel. 065650021.*

At the entrance of Ostia Antica is the kitschy, but good, **Allo Sbarco di Enea**. Book a table before you tramp around the sites. *Via dei Romagnoli, 675. Tel. 065650034.*

Fiumicino is known for its fish *restaurants*. Here are a few of the best: **Gina**, giant table of seafood hors d'oeuvres and great pasta. *Viale Traiano, 141. Tel. 066583143.* **Closed** Monday. **Il Pescatore**, good spaghetti *al cartoccio* (cooked in greaseproof paper with tomato, prawn and maybe a lobster tail). Reserve on a weekend. *Via Torre Clementina, 154. Tel. 066505189.* **Closed** Thursday. **Bastianelli al Molo**, large and bustling with a view of the sea. Reserve on a weekend. *Via Torre Clementina, 312. Tel. 066505358.* **Closed** Monday.

Nearby is the famous **Oasis of Macchiagrande**, the only Mediterranean wetlands in the region, now a World Wildlife Fund (WWF) reserve. It formed part of the famous marshes that surrounded Rome and made travel in the summer so dangerous for so many centuries because of the malarial mosquito.

Ninfa
KIDS

South from Rome
77 km (48 miles).
Getting there
By car: take **Via Appia Nuova** south to Cisterna di Latina, then next left to Doganella. Over the crossroads continue to Ninfa.

History BC
• **320** Ninfa came under Roman domain. A megavolcano exploded in prehistory – and Ninfa became part of the marsh below. The Romans drained the marshes and 23 towns dotted the plain; Roman chronicler Pliny wrote that after drainage Ninfa was "where people danced and sang." Three consular roads passed nearby: Via Appia, Via Setina and Via Corana. There were hostelries every 8 km (5 miles), with changes of horses as well as beds and meals available for travelers.

History AD
• **500** As the Roman Empire declined and fell, marshes took over. Malaria ruled. Barbarians pillaged.

Nature Trail in a Medieval Town's Ruins
Botanical Garden and World Wildlife Fund Sanctuary

Over 1,850 hectares (750 acres) of botanical magic with a bewildering variety of birds, fish and animals, this WWF reserve is inside an ancient town, vestiges of which appear around every bend of the river: a stand of bamboo and close by, an ancient bridge; a grassy knoll with the shell of a 12c church, the frescoes now faint. Tall trees, meadows, walls and rare flowers (springtime is best).

Fee
Open April 1 to October 30 the first Saturday and the first Sunday of every month. Tickets should be bought in Rome, at **World Wildlife Fund**, *Via Po, 25C. Tel. 06844971*, or **Caetani Foundation**, *Via delle Botteghe Oscure, 32. Tel. 066873056.*

Norma, Sermoneta, Sabaudia and Circeo

Getting there
By car: from **Ninfa** travel east on the road between Doganella and the Abbey of Valvisciolo. Turn south and follow signs for Sermoneta.

Norma

This town up on the cliff is also worth a visit to get the dramatic view from the top of the old volcano.

Madonna of the Angels by Benozzo Gozzoli.

Restaurants
Near Ninfa, in Borgo Grappa: **Trattoria Giggetto**. In the center of Borgo Grappa, opposite the Carabinieri office. *Tel. 0773208007.* **Closed** Monday and Tuesday.
In Cori: **Trattoria Zampi**. *Via Leopardi, 17. Tel. 069679688.* **Closed** Monday.

- **743** Byzantine emperor Constantine V gave Ninfa to Pope Zacharias.
- **880** Saracens invaded, installing water mills to crush grain, olives and grapes.
- **1000** Swamps inundated Via Appia after the Arabs were expelled, but Ninfa flowered: nobles, soldiers, artisans, peasants all lived in a town boasting 10 churches, 2 hospitals, 4 monasteries, 4 bridges across the river, 5 principal gates and a double wall to repel invaders.
- **1159** Alexander III was installed as pope in Ninfa because Holy Roman Emperor Frederick Barbarossa had made Rome unsafe. Ninfa suffered Barbarossa's rage.
- **1492-1503** Pope Alexander VI Borgia confiscated Ninfa and Sermoneta for his adored daughter Lucrezia, but died shortly after, and the towns returned to the Caetani family. Ninfa's heyday was short. Fighting broke out amongst the Caetani brothers and jealous towns joined in. Roman canals stagnated and the fertile plain was waterlogged. Fever and death followed. Ninfa became a ghost town and slowly crumbled away.
- **1765** Repairs initiated; water mills used in winter when mosquitoes died out.
- **1920** Last male Caetani descendant, Prince Gelasio, started the long uphill struggle to save Ninfa. His British son-in-law, the Honorable Hubert Howard, made it into a magic garden, with rare bamboo, flowering trees and medieval ruins. He got the water moving again by cleaning the rivers and draining the marshes: paradise reborn.

Sermoneta

South from Ninfa.
4 km (2.5 miles).

Ancient Roman settlement of Sulmo, but not Ovid's birthplace. This small town with its castle has charm. There is a music and art festival in the summer.

Sabaudia and Circeo

White sandy beach: children's paradise. Waves are not dangerous. Public beaches have free access, and beach chairs, beds and umbrellas can be rented. Food and drink are available.

At the end of those 20 km (12½ miles) of sandy beach is the promontory of **Circeo**, where legendary Ulysses was tempted by the sweet singing of the Sirens, who tried to lure him onto the rocks. Circeo is a medieval town worth a visit, but be careful of the nymphs.

Getting there
From Rome take **Via Pontina**; turn off at signs for Terracina and Sperlonga. Follow signs for Sabaudia. From Ninfa follow signs for Latina and then take the coastal road to Borgo Grappa and on to Sabaudia 26 km (16 miles).

The promontory of Circeo seen from Sabaudia's dunes.

Restaurants
On the beach before Monte Circeo is the well-known (and perhaps overpriced but the atmosphere is great) **Saporetti Restaurant**. *Tel. 0773596024*. In the other direction (about 5 km [3 miles] down the coastal road) are three restaurants, one right after another.

Terracina
and
Sperlonga

South from Rome
108 km (62 miles) to **Terracina**, 16 km (9 miles) more to Sperlonga.

Getting there
Take **Via Pontina**; follow signs for Terracina and further on for Sperlonga.

Tiberius's Villa

One passes through this medieval town with the BC **Temple of Jupiter Anxur** spectacularly sited high on the hill. The panorama of the Fondi plains and Mount Circeo to the northwest and even the island of Ischia on a clear day to the southwest is rewarding. This temple guarded Terracina from the wrath of the gods. Further along are salt and freshwater lakes where one can hire a boat. The attractive old town of **Sperlonga** (*spelunca* means "cave") on a rocky promontory precedes an attractive beach at the end of which is Emperor Tiberius's villa.

Praetorium Palace (AD 14-37). **Tiberius**'s palace and reception cave were discovered in 1954. Archaeologists could not believe their luck, as for centuries the palace had been known only from ancient books. Waves, but also the unexploded mines and artillery shells of WW II, made the dig dangerous.

The infamous cave was where the emperor liked to dally (although falling rocks were always a danger). He fancied both boys and girls, but if a youth or maiden did not succumb to his pleasure he or she was thrown to the crocodiles. A reflecting pond had elegant statues around the circumference, while another kept the fish alimented with clean sea water, a system of locks protecting baby fish. Some rooms were as close to the sea as the cave, so Tiberius could catch fresh fish from his bed. The gardens were formal, with walkways where two-wheeled carriages could be pulled, and the carrying-litters of the rich and famous jostled for space. Also to be found there were Greek *thinking pavilions*, shooting lodges, multiple dining rooms, libraries, gymnasiums, theaters, parks, observation points, and shady pergolas.

But the pièce de résistance was the giant **Laocoön** statue, placed in Tiberius's time at the center of the pool network and found five centuries ago in myriad pieces. **Homer**'s *Odyssey* tells of **Ulysses** and his sons being attacked by Scylla, in the form of a monster snake. Three Greek sculptors from Rhodes, **Pliny** wrote, carved the amazingly sensitive human forms, where muscle is visible under skin. But the group is very fragmented. Which is the older or finer of the two Laocoön statues, this one, or the one in the Vatican Museums (see page 88)? The experts cannot agree.

Visit the **Museo Archeologico Nazionale di Sperlonga** (National Archaeological Museum of Sperlonga).

Via Flacca, km 16.2. Tel. 0771548028. **Fee - Open** 9 am-4 pm daily.

Restaurant
Il Fortino. *Via Flacca. Tel. 077154337.*

Tiberius's cave.

ESSENTIALS

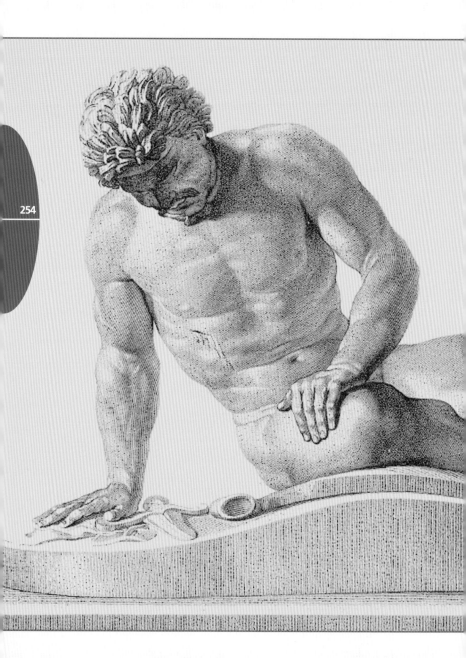

255

Museums

[E 11]
*Largo di Villa Peretti
(Piazza dei Cinquecento).*
Tel. 0648903500.

Getting there
Bus 3, 4, 9, 16, 36,
38, 64, 170, 175,
640, 910 or
A Metro Termini stop.

Fee
Open Tuesday
to Sunday 9 am-7 pm.

The museum is orderly
and very accessible. It is
the Superintendent for
Ancient Art Adriano
La Regina's masterpiece.

Museo Nazionale Romano di Palazzo Massimo

Across from the central train station, Rome's newest museum houses magnificent ancient sculpture, superb mosaics and historic coins.

GROUND FLOOR/ROOM VIII Afrodite Pudica, Greek sculpture by Menophantos, IC BC; unlike Paris's Venus de Milo, she has arms. **ROOM VII** Equally perfect is Wounded Niobid in gently shining marble. **GALLERY III** Mosaic emblem from republican times shows a cat and a pair of ducks.

ROOM V The imperial era is ushered in by a commanding figure of Augustus as chief priest with his head covered, 20 BC. Also see portrait heads of children and women.

MIDDLE FLOOR Imperial sculptures in marble are mostly copies of much earlier Greek bronzes. In **ROOM V** Nero's villa at Subiaco and Hadrian's villa at Tivoli are well represented by sculptures, mostly of human bodies.

ROOM V and **ROOM VI** have marble statues of Apollo, copies of bronzes by famous Greek sculptors, the latter looking Etruscan.

ROOM VII features a hermaphrodite lying on his/her stomach, but just raised enough to be revealing. Also a sculpture, in bronze, is Dionysus, fished out of the River Tiber (see traces of paint).

ROOM X has all that was salvaged from the Museum of the Boats at Lake Nemi – the two enormous barges that Caligula had built to dally with his dollies; superb handles and doorknobs with fierce animal heads and the bronze balustrades from the boats' railings with double-headed figures. Also here are a couple of Eros figures with wings. **ROOM XIV** is sarcophagus heaven. Don't miss the perfect one in deep relief. Spot the one head that's turning (AD 180).

TOP FLOOR *Guided tours only* **ROOM II** Be amazed by the nature fresco (IC BC) from Livia's underground summer dining room in the outskirts of Rome; trees, flowers, birds hovering – all impart an atmosphere of coolness, green and peaceful.

ROOM III-IV The lost frescoes of the ancient villa of the Farnesina (IC BC) where some scholars surmise that Caesar may have lodged Cleopatra. Witness the fine brushwork,

the Egyptian decorations, the love motifs (Aphrodite reigns in two of the rooms), the knockdown elegance. Here are a dining room in shiny black with little views in pale green; a beige bedroom with stuccoes in fine relief; a red bedroom showing a woman and two leopards. **GALLERIES I AND III** Here starts the thrilling mosaic collection: thin, thin, tiny mosaic tesserae composed into beautiful pictures (2c BC-AD 4c). **ROOM VIII** In a cubicle is the grotto from Nero's maritime villa at Anzio with a reclining Hercules done in shells, glass and pumice. **BASEMENT** Ali Baba's cave of gold coins and jewelry is here. Coins are displayed with moveable magnifying glasses so that you can follow the entire course of Rome's history. The jewels of a young Roman girl are touchingly arranged against the background of her life and death.

Galleria Nazionale d'Arte Moderna e
Contemporanea (Museum of Modern Art)

Houses Rome's most important collection of 19c and 20c Italian art; also many other European artists (Monet, Cézanne, and so on). It is enormous, with 73 rooms. The collection was started in 1883, the building constructed in 1911 and enlarged in 1933 by architect Cesare Bazzani. Recently refurbished, it now has two shops, a restaurant and a bar, with a very pleasant terrace for summer dining. The two massive halls, on the left and the right, house late-18c and 19c paintings – the one on the left from 1770 to 1880, and the one on the right from 1880 to 1910. The 20c artists are in the two modern galleries on the left and right in the back (Fontana, Burri, Capogrossi, and so on). Exhibitions are held regularly of famous artists, both foreign and Italian.

[A 7]
*Viale delle Belle Arti, 131.
Tel. 06322981/3298302.*

Getting there
Tram 19 and 30.

Fee (free entrance for the under-18s or over-60s).
Open Tuesday to Sunday 9 am-7 pm.
Closed Monday.

Foreign academies are nearby. **The British School at Rome** has an exceptional library and stages many exhibitions featuring the work of its fellowship students. *Via Gramsci, 61. Tel. 063264939.*
The **Egyptian Academy** and **Romanian Academy** are across the road.
Two notable foreign academies are the **Japan Cultural Institute** on *Via Gramsci, 74,* and the **Danish Academy** on *Via Omero, 18.*

Museo Nazionale Romano

Italy's state-owned collection of ancient Roman art is distributed among the four museums listed below. Information and reservations: *Tel. 0639967700.*

I Palazzo Massimo alle Terme (see pages 256-57).

II Palazzo Altemps (see page 190).

Piazza Sant'Apollinare, 48. Tel. 06480201.
Fee
Open Tuesday-Sunday 9 am-7 pm.

III Terme di Diocleziano Baths of Diocletian (see pages 63, 175). We call this "the Museum of the Tombs." The most exciting tomb inscription is that of Nero's slave (then a freedman), Epafrodito, who helped Nero plunge the dagger into his own throat when Nero was forced to commit suicide. (Large marble plaque, gallery on the right, first floor up on left-hand side.)

GROUND FLOOR In the gallery on the right, center stage, are three noteworthy ladies of leisure (not pleasure) in terracotta. One of them is holding a little pet pig. These are from Ariccia, 4c-3c BC. The artist gloriously captures their seriousness.

ONE FLOOR UP Left at the top of the stairs is the area devoted to the god Mithras. God of light, protector of justice and agreement, he was once a rival to Christ and Christianity. He was important in the pantheon of gods in ancient Rome, where every house had a little altar (*aedicola*) of the household gods. There are two statues of Mithras, one marble with the original lurid paint and gold leaf intact, found buried under Santo Stefano Rotondo Basilica.

TWO FLOORS UP There are two new wings at the top of the stairs. Straight ahead: the most coherent explanations of the pre-Roman civilizations of the Latins (11c-8c BC), south and east of Rome. On the right: Bronze Age peoples 1700-1300 BC. Don't miss tombs 482 and 483 from the Necropolis of Osa.

CLOISTER AND GARDEN Enormous; designed by followers of Michelangelo, with giant ancient statues clustered around the central, trickling fountain. On the left wall as you walk out is a memorable painting in trompe l'oeil of a monkey in a doorway.

Via Enrico de Nicola, 79. Tel. 0639967700.
Fee
Open Tuesday-Sunday 9 am-7:45 pm. Bookshop.

IV Crypta Balbi. Lucius Cornelius Balbus, Spanish general under Emperor Augustus, won such a key victory in Libya in 13 BC – and made so much money out of it – that he could build what was only the third permanent theater in Rome. It rained so hard on opening day that the Tiber burst its banks, and people were paddled to the theater in boats!

Nothing remains of Balbus's theater except the ruins of its annex under this museum. Its cloisterlike porticos were so dark as to merit the name "crypt."

Here you see Rome as a "palimpsest," changing gradually but radically over centuries as one layer was built over another, with evidence of what happened in the Dark Ages (end of AD 5c to 10c): street levels rose by about half a meter (a bit more than a yard) per century (due to dumped rubbish, earthquakes and mudslides after torrential rains); earlier Rome had shrunk to half its size, the population almost down to zero.

Rome's museums are closed Monday, except the following:

Museo del Palatino:
Open daily

Museo Preistorico Etnografico L. Pigorini:
Open daily

Keats and Shelley Memorial House:
Closed Sunday

Museo Comunale Birreria Peroni:
Closed Sunday

Musei Vaticani:
Closed Sunday

Galleria Doria Pamphili:
Closed Thursday

Jewish Community Museum:
Closed Saturday

Museo Nazionale di Palazzo Venezia:
Closed Sunday and holidays

Tomb and Museum of Cecilia Metella:
Closed Sunday.

GROUND FLOOR The exquisite marble altar in the front window, found nearby, was carved by a 1C BC sculptor as his tombstone. The first panels (in Italian and English) show how Balbus's theater became the shell in which medieval churches and shacks were built and finally spawned a Renaissance convent: the Confraternity of St. Catherine's Pitiful Virgins, cast-off daughters of prostitutes. Look down on the theater's ruins on your right (including the actors' latrines).

Beyond the computer room see the fine models of buildings that used to be in this area. You progress from 1C BC through the Middle Ages, witnessing how this part of Rome changed six times during different centuries, from ancient Roman houses through four intermediate phases to the Renaissance monastic complex.

ONE FLOOR UP Here are amphorae – beautiful terracotta jars with different shapes for oil, wine, fish sauce, spices; fragments of 8c frescoes, history of the Byzantine occupation; glass mosaics jumbled up in a display case; room of the two papal chairs.

TOP FLOOR Models of the forum with medieval houses and farms supplanting the ancient spaces.

Guided visits are offered to the Exedra and the Roman-period basement.

Via delle Botteghe Oscurre, 31. Tel. 064815576.
Fee
Open Tuesday-Sunday 9 am-7:45 pm. Bookshop.

Domus Aurea (Nero's Golden House; see page 17)

Vestiges of the mad emperor's luxury palace.

Via Labicana, 136. Tel. 0639749907; information and reservations 0639967700.
Fee
Open 9 am-8 pm. Reservations required. Visits limited to 25 people every 15 minutes; tour lasts one hour.

Museo del Palatino (Palatine Museum; see page 30)

Gems of Roman art. Think drapery, never better sculpted than these: Ninfa (left of entrance); Aphrodite (in almost transparent cloth); Dancer (deep pleats delineating her breasts); Artemis (scarf draped nonchalantly); three black marble herms (thumbs in skirts); Hera Borghese (copy of 5c BC statue). Also see intarsia wall paneling in super bright marble from Nero's house (AD 54-68).

LOWER GROUND FLOOR Early beginnings of Palatine Hill, shepherds' huts; also republican mansions with decorations of griffins.

Two entrances to the Palatine: Piazza Santa Maria Nova, 53 (near Arch of Tito), and Via di San Gregorio, 30. Tel. 066990110; information and reservations 0639967700.
Fee Admission includes Palatine Hill.
Open daily 9 am-7 pm; 9 am-4 pm in winter.

Museum of the Villa of the Quintilii

Until their untimely deaths in AD 182 the Quintilius brothers, Condianus and Valerius Maximus, lived grandly with their families on this vast estate, apparently a palace of baths. Both were consuls, famed for culture, wealth and military prowess – provoking Emperor Commodus's jealous wrath. On charges of plotting to kill him (actually fomented by his sister Lucilla), Commodus put them to death, along with one of their sons. He snatched for himself this property, and it became his favorite and remained an imperial palace until the fall of the empire.

The entrance – on the Via Appia Nuova, not the Appian Way – has a small museum with exquisite marble statues and interesting fragments of wall decorations. Excavations continue; who knows what treasures will emerge!

Walking uphill from the museum you skirt around giant baths: caldarium, tepidarium and frigidarium, with walls over 30 m (98 ft.) high. A sort of theater-in-the-round is next, and then the residence's public rooms, with a large rectangular courtyard and water cistern. Four richly decorated rooms, with colorful marble floors and painted walls, were heated by *hypercausts* (terracotta tubes) in the floors and walls.

In the private quarters a domed chamber still has high walls. Off the open-air atrium, notice how tiny are the three bedrooms, just cubicles; but all were heated. Behind these were the private baths with hot-water sprays in the sweating rooms. According to Seneca, a contemporary, these rooms had glass ceilings, and mirrors on the walls (polished black marble) alternated with white marble and fine paintings, with precious marbles underfoot. Also gushing fountains and statues were at every corner.

Beyond the servants' area (with latrines and bathing) is another bathing complex – the fourth!

Via Appia Nuova, 1092. (No longer entered on Via Appia Antica.) Tel. 0639967700.
Getting there Archeobus from Piazza Venezia.
Fee
Open Tuesday-Sunday 9 am to an hour before sunset.

Tomb and Museum of Cecilia Metella (see page 68)

A small museum, attached to the tomb, houses several beheaded marble sculptures. The cave area shows this was a quarry. Inside the tomb, see the incredibly thick walls and fabulous brick construction.

Via Appia Antica, 161. Tel. 067844271; information and reservations 0639967700.
Getting there Archeobus from Piazza Venezia.
Fee
Open Monday-Saturday 9 am-6:30 pm. **Closed** Sunday.

Ara Pacis (see page 50)

Richard Meier has enveloped this great masterpiece of ancient sculpture in a modern frame, along with a new auditorium and reading room.

Lungotevere in Augusta (corner of Via di Ripetta). Tel. 0636010385.

Aula Ottagonale (Octagonal Hall; see page 176)

Nineteen classical sculptures are beautifully installed in this ancient setting.

Via Romita, 8. Tel. 064870690.
Fee
Open Tuesday to Saturday 9 am-2 pm; Sunday 9 am-1 pm.

Capitoline Museums (see page 160)

Ancient sculpture in the left building, sculpture and painting on the right.

Piazza del Campidoglio, 1. Tel. 0639967800.
Fee
Open Tuesday to Sunday 9 am-8 pm. **Closed** Monday.

Castel Sant'Angelo (see page 91)

This ancient mausoleum-turned-medieval fort was later a Renaissance palace.

Lungotevere Castello, 50. Tel. 066819111.
Fee
Open Tuesday to Sunday 9 am-7 pm. Entry up to one hour before closing.

Dying Gaul.

Centrale Montemartini (ACEA)

The "Gas Works" harbors one of the world's most unforgettable museums. Ancient Roman art is framed by equally classical machinery in an early-20c power station.

Via Ostiense, 106. Tel. 066991191.
Fee
Open Tuesday to Friday 10 am-6 pm; Saturday and Sunday 10 am-7 pm.

Delle Mura, Porta San Sebastiano (The Walls of Rome; see page 66)

This museum is situated in and on the battlements of an ancient city gate.

Via di Porta San Sebastiano, 18. Tel. 0670475284.
Fee
Open Tuesday to Saturday 9 am-7 pm; Sunday 9 am-2 pm.

261

Galleria Borghese (see page 196)

Here you will find an extraordinary 17c art collection in its original setting: the sumptuous villa of a cardinal's estate.

Piazzale Scipione Borghese, 6.
   Tel. 0632810, fax 068555952.
Fee
Open Tuesday to Saturday 9 am-7 pm;
   Sunday and holidays 9 am-1 pm.
   (Advance reservations essential.)

Paolina Borghese, by Antonio Canova, 1805.

Galleria Colonna

In one of Rome's largest and most opulent private palaces, built in 1730, this museum contains the private collection of the Colonna family, which traces its ancestry to a Roman emperor. An enfilade of golden rooms stretches out in front of you with 18c painted mirrors – magnificent though sadly starting to chip. Hundreds of mirrored wall sconces reflect the candlelight. The velvet throne of Martin V (1417-31), the scholarly family pope, was moved to this palace when it was built two centuries after his death. Notable paintings include Annibale Carracci's **Peasant Eating Beans** and Tintoretto's **Narcissus**.

Via della Pilota, 17. Tel. 066794362.
Fee
Open Saturday only, 9 am-1 pm.

Galleria Doria Pamphili (see page 166)

A city within a city, this vast pile is resplendent in its grandeur. Statues by Algardi line the monumental stairs by Antonio del Grande. The Galleria di Specchi rivals Versailles. Three portraits of the Pamphili pope, Innocent X (see Piazza Navona, page 146) – by his protégé Bernini – alongside the portrait by Velázquez characterize this family museum. Titians, Caravaggios, Brueghels, and Lorrains share the glorious galleries with Algardi's portrait bust of Donna Olympia Maidalchini, the pontiff's "sister-in-law," who acted as his first lady and more.

Café Doria. Plashing fountain, elegance, refinement. Tea room, cakes and snacks. *Via della Gatta, 1A. Tel. 066793805.*

Piazzale del Collegio Romano, 2. Tel. 066797323.
Fee
Open Friday to Wednesday 10 am-5 pm. **Closed** Thursday.

Galleria Nazionale d'Arte Antica di Palazzo Barberini

(see pages 180-181)

The collection of 13c-17c art is up the stairs on the magnificent *piano nobile* (main, or "noble," floor), totally restored and doubled in extent. To the right are mostly religious paintings, including those by Philippo Lippi, Peruzzi, Sodoma, Bronzino, Tintoretto, El Greco and the Maestro of the Manchester Madonna. Four rooms have superb frescoed ceilings. Don't miss Raphael's sensuous portrait of his great love, *La Fornarina,* and Holbein's bombastic Henry VIII. To the left is a vast darkened room with a domed ceiling covered with frescoes, and some 17c paintings, culminating in Caravaggio's **Judith Cutting Off the Head of Holofernes**. In the 18c room are two charming Bouchers, and Pierre Subleyras's almost-modern **Nude**.

Special visits: The private apartments (where the family lived until 1960) remain as decorated in 1740-70, mostly small rooms with wall paintings in oil. The leafy loggia once overlooked vast gardens.

Via Quattro Fontane, 13. Tel. 0632810.
Fee
Open Tuesday to Saturday 9 am-7 pm; Saturday until midnight in the summer; Sunday and holidays 9 am-1 pm.

Galleria Nazionale d'Arte Antica di Palazzo Corsini

(see page 112)

Grand family palace with its original library; paintings by Rubens, Caravaggio, Murillo.

Via della Lungara, 10. Tel. 0668802323.
Fee
Open Tuesday to Friday 9 am-7 pm; Saturday 9 am-2 pm; Sunday and holidays 9 am-1 pm.

Jewish Community Museum (see page 48)

Ritual objects used in Roman synagogues over the last 300 years. Part of Rome's "Babylonian-style" Great Synagogue.

Lungotevere dei Cenci, 15. Tel. 0668400661.
Open Monday to Thursday 9 am-5 pm; Friday 9 am-2 pm; Sunday 9 am-12:30 pm. **Closed** Saturday.

Keats and Shelley Memorial House

See the home of poets John Keats and Percy Bysshe Shelley and of Mary Shelley, who wrote *Frankenstein*.

Piazza di Spagna, 26. Tel. 066784235.
Fee
Open Monday to Friday 9 am-1 pm; Saturday 11 am-2 pm and 3-6 pm. **Closed** Sunday and public holidays.

Museo Barracco (see page 152)

Small private palace with Middle Eastern art as well as some middling Greek and Etruscan.

Corso Vittorio Emanuele II, 168. Tel. 0668806848.
Fee
Open Tuesday to Friday 9 am-7 pm; Sunday and holidays 9 am-1 pm.

Museo Centrale del Risorgimento and Ala Brazini (see page 166)

Inside the Victor Emmanuel Monument are two museum spaces, entered from the two opposite ends of this so-called Vittoriana. **Museo Centrale del Risorgimento** includes memorabilia from the years leading up to Italy's unification in 1870 and from WW I: busts, letters, swords and guns. Shops, café and elevator. **Ala Brazini** exhibit space houses occasional megashows.

Museo Centrale del Risorgimento: Piazza Venezia. Tel. 066780664.

Ala Brazini: Via di San Pietro in Carcere. Tel. 066780664.
Fee
Open Tuesday to Sunday 9 am–6:30 pm.

Museo Comunale Birreria Peroni

They stopped making fine beer and started showing fine art: exhibits of contemporary Roman painters and sculptors.

Via Cagliario, 29. Tel. 066710932.
Fee
Open Tuesday to Saturday 10 am-7 pm; Sunday and holidays 9:30 am-1:30 pm.

Museo d'Arte Contemporanea Roma (MACRO)

One of Rome's main showplaces for 21c art. Frequently changing exhibits.

Via Reggio Emilia, 54. Tel. 06671070400.
Fee
Open Tuesday to Sunday 9 am-7 pm; Sunday and holidays 9 am-2 pm.

Museo della Civiltà Romana (see pages 234, 269)

Piazza G. Agnelli, 10 (EUR). Tel. 065926041.
Fee
Open Tuesday to Saturday 9 am-2 pm.

Museo Nazionale delle Arti e Tradizioni Popolari (see page 234)

Traditional Italian crafts, clothes, music making.

Piazza Marconi, 8 (EUR). Tel. 065926148.
Fee
Open Tuesday to Sunday 9 am-8 pm (except July-August: 9 am-2 pm).

Museo delle Cere (Wax Museum)

Piazza Santi Apostoli, 67 (inside Palazzo Colonna). Tel. 066796482.
Fee
Open daily 9 am-8 pm.

Museo di Roma – Trastevere (see page 116)

Local artists, poets and traditions are remembered in this very medieval quarter.

Piazza Sant'Egidio, 1B. Tel. 065816563.
Fee
Open Tuesday to Saturday 10 am-6:30 pm (except July-August: 10 am-1:30 pm).

Museo Napoleonico

Dedicated to Napoleon, who never made it to his "second capital," Rome.

Piazza Ponte Umberto, 1. Tel. 0668806286.
Fee
Open Tuesday to Saturday 9 am-7 pm; Sunday and holidays 9 am-1:30 pm.

Museo Nazionale delle Paste Alimentari

(National Museum of Pasta Foods)

Ever wondered who invented macaroni? (Answer: Oretta Zanini de Vita.) Located near the Trevi Fountain, this unusual museum will edify you on pasta making through the ages.

Piazza Scanderberg, 117. Tel. 066991119.
Fee
Open daily 9:30 am-5:30 pm.

Museo Nazionale di Palazzo Venezia

Museum in the palace from which Mussolini harangued the throngs. Check the banners outside for the current art shows.

Via del Plebiscito, 118. Tel. 06699941 or 0632810.
Fee
Open Monday to Saturday 9 am-2 pm. **Closed** Sunday and holidays.

Museo Nazionale Etrusco di Villa Giulia (see page 70)

The wonderfully remodeled Etruscan Museum, filled with treasures.

Piazza Villa Giulia, 9. Tel. 063201951.
Fee
Open Tuesday to Saturday 8:30 am-7 pm; Sunday and holidays 9 am-2 pm.

Museo Praz

Art connoisseur Praz's private house with beautiful Neoclassical furniture.

Via Zanardelli, 1. Tel. 066861089.
Fee
Open Tuesday to Sunday 9 am-1 pm and 2:30-6:30 pm.

Museo Preistorico ed Etnografico Luigi Pigorini (Prehistoric and Ethnographic Museum; see page 234)

A recent addition to this very specialized museum is an 8,000-year-old boat recently excavated from the bottom of Lake Bracciano, 30 km (18.6 miles) from Rome.

Piazzale Marconi, 14 (EUR). Tel. 06549521.
Fee
Open daily 9 am-8 pm.

Musei Vaticani (including Sistine Chapel; see page 85)

World-class museum, especially, but not exclusively, for Italian art.

Viale del Vaticano. Tel. 0669883041.
Fee
Open Monday to Saturday 8:45 am-3:20 pm. **Closed** Sunday, except last Sunday of each month. Entry up to one hour before closing.

Palazzo delle Esposizioni

No permanent collection, but often has fine temporary shows. Cafeteria and gift shop are good.

Via Nazionale, 194.
Tel. 064885465.
Fee
Open Wednesday to Monday 10 am-9 pm. **Closed** Tuesday.

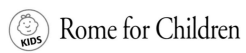
Rome for Children

Getting there
Bus 75, 81, 85, 87 175, 186,
Tram 30 or
B Metro Colosseo stop.

Roman Forum and **Palatine** (see Ancient Rome, page 27)

The world's biggest and most ancient jungle-gym. Children can hide behind the 2,000-year-old ruins, run on the grassy mounds near Julius Caesar's temple and have fun at the Vestal Virgins'. The Palatine, above, is one of the seven hills of ancient Rome, the first place the earliest Romans settled. The hordes you encounter down in the Forum seem to disappear and suddenly you are alone. Picnics are theoretically illegal; part of the beauty of this area is its cleanliness.

Getting there
Bus 95, 490, 495, 590 or
A Metro Flaminio stop.

Villa Borghese (see Renaissance, page 194)

This central park, once the private gardens of the Borghese family, offers some fun for kids. For tiny tots, near Porta Pinciana, right at the top of Via Veneto, one can get a pony ride or take a few turns on the merry-go-round. The Pincio is a favorite place for Rollerblading, skating and skateboarding; quite a few young people show up on weekends to strut their stuff. Near the Pincio you can rent bicycles, Rollerblades and scooters. A prestigious horse show is held in May in the graceful Piazza di Siena arena. Take a boat ride on the small lake just below.

266

Via della Navicella, 12.

Getting there
Bus 81, 628, 671, 673.
Open 7 am to dusk.

Getting there
Bus 319.
Open 7 am to dusk.

Playgrounds

For young children, Rome offers two possibilities: **Villa Celimontana**, right up the street from the Colosseum, with a fully equipped outdoor playground plus a skating rink – free of charge. This park is a great place for a picnic and offers pony rides, too. Not big but very well kept and central. **Villa Ada**, northeast of central Rome, offers more open spaces. Vast fields lend themselves to soccer games. There is a small playground and also a skating rink. Again, perfect for a picnic.

Piazzale Giuseppe Garibaldi (see Christian Rome, page 127)

Above Trastevere on the rim of the Janiculum Hill, in front of the mounted statue of national hero Garibaldi, is one of the places from which to view the city. Pony rides and a merry-go-round are nearby. A puppet show in Italian runs from 4 to 7 pm Monday to Sunday, as well as from 10:30 am to 1 pm Saturday and Sunday. There is no charge, but donations are welcome. At noon sharp you will be scared out of your wits by the firing of a cannon just below this lofty square, a tradition dating back 100 years, when it signaled lunch time for the workers.

Getting there
Bus 870.

Villa Pamphili

The largest park in Rome lies northwest of central Rome, with its main entrance not far from Piazzale Garibaldi. There are pony rides and endless walks.

Getting there
Bus 710, 870.
Open 7 am to dusk.

Orto Botanico

(Botanical Gardens; see Christian Rome, page 114)
Take your babe for a quiet walk and and lots of fresh air in the Botanical Gardens in Trastevere. In the greenhouse are an orchid collection, a cactus collection and other tropical plants and trees. No picnicking, biking or dogs allowed.

Largo Cristina di Svezia, 24
Tel. 066864193.
Getting there
Bus 23, 280, 870.
Fee - Open 9 am-6:30 pm.
   Closed Sunday.

Bioparco (Zoo)

Rome's zoo is tucked into a corner of Villa Borghese, and is becoming more animal friendly. Kids age 3 and under enter free. Senior citizens (60 years) are free on Wednesday.

Viale del Giardino
Zoologico, 20.
Tel. 063608211.

Getting there
Bus 52, 53, 910 or
Tram 19, 30.

Open Monday to
   Sunday 8:30 am-
   5:00 pm.
   Ticket office closes
   at 4:15 pm.

Carriages

For a special treat hire a horse and buggy to take you around the city center. Most drivers speak English and are good guides. Prices are to be negotiated *before you start your ride*. Carriage stands can be found at the Spanish Steps, the Pantheon, the Colosseum, the Trevi Fountain and St. Peter's Square.

Circus

If the little brutes are getting really out of hand, there's usually a circus in town. Posters are put up all over the city – so keep your eyes open. Also check the local newspapers.

Via delle Tre Fontane.
Tel. 065914401.

Getting there
Bus 160, 714.

Open Monday
to Friday 3-8 pm;
Saturday 3 pm-2 am;
Sunday 10 am-1 pm
and 3-10 pm.

Luna Park (Lun EUR)
Rome's version of Coney Island amusement park is in
EUR (off Via Cristoforo Colombo, which leads southwest
out of the city). Ferris wheels, bumper cars, the works.

Monuments
Taking children to see the "sights" can often be difficult for all involved. Here are
a few monuments which could capture their attention:
Catacombs (There are many; see page 105). These underground dark labyrinths
are spooky enough to delight and perhaps even frighten most kids. Tours are with
guides only. Be sure to keep your eyes on your children because it is very easy to
lose one's way in this maze.

Via Appia Antica area: Catacombs of San Callisto, Catacombs of Domitilla,
Catacombs of San Sebastiano.

Via Salaria area: Catacombs of Priscilla.

Via Nomentana area: Catacombs of Sant'Agnese.

Getting there
Bus 75, 85, 87, 175, 186,
Tram 30 or
B Metro Colosseo stop.
Fee
Open 9 am-1 hour
before sunset.

Colosseum (see Ancient Rome, page 10)
Tell your kids the tales about gladiators and wild beasts
and they will certainly want to make a trip to see this
amazing stadium. Tell them the thumbs-up and thumbs-
down signs originated here as the crowds signaled freedom
(thumbs up) or death (thumbs down) for the gladiators.

Getting there
Bus 62, 64, 70, 81, 87,
115, 186, 492, 628.

Piazza Navona (see Renaissance, page 146)
There is much street entertainment going on in this
square, including mimes, puppet shows, music and
sometimes fire eaters. It is also one of the best places to
get an ice cream and to people-watch.

Getting there
Bus 23, 34, 49, 64, 87,
280, 492, 926, 990.

Castel Sant'Angelo (see Christian Rome, page 91)
A prison complete with winding, dark, scary corridors,
secret passageways, real cannons and cannonballs. It
provides a good opportunity to capture kids' imagination
and tell tales of adventure, courage and battles. There is
a small weapons museum.

Via Veneto, 27.
Getting there
Bus 52, 53, 56, 58, 95,
116, 204 or
A Metro Barberini stop.
Free
Open daily 9 am-1 pm
and 3-7 pm

Church of the Immaculate Conception (see page 231)
A spooky place which just might fascinate the older kids!
The bones and skulls of thousands of Capuchin monks
have been crafted into decorative tableaux. No photographs
allowed.

Remember, it is a church, so have respect and dress
properly. A small donation given to the friar who
accompanies you is appreciated.

Bocca della Verità (The Mouth of Truth; see Ancient Rome, page 43)
Remember the scene with Audrey Hepburn and Gregory Peck in the film *Roman Holiday*? For fun, show the kids the first lie detector, which is located in the portico of the Church of Santa Maria in Cosmedin. According to a medieval legend, if you put your hand into the mouth and tell a lie you will be bitten!

Piazza della Bocca della Verità, 18.

Getting there
Bus 23, 44, 81, 95, 170, 715, 716.

Open daily 9 am-1 pm and 3-6 pm.

Museums suitable for kids

Centrale Montemartini (Art Center ACEA; see page 261)
Sunday free entrance for kids 12 and under. They will also receive material for drawing what they have seen.

Viale Ostiense, 106. Tel. 065748030.

Getting there
Bus 95 or
B Metro Piramide stop.

Guided tours for kids.

Museo dei Bambini di Roma
(Children's Museum – Explorer)
A museum-laboratory for kids 12 and under, accompanied by adult. An entire city for kids has been constructed here.

Via Flaminia, 82. Tel. 0636005488 (phone to book visit)

Getting there
Bus 88, 95, 117, 119, 204, 231, 491, 495, 618, 916,
Tram 2, 3, 19 or
A Metro Flaminio stop.
Closed Monday

Museo della Civiltà Romana
(see page 263)
Located in EUR (near the amusement park Luna Park and the open-air swimming pool Piscina delle Rose). See the detailed scale model of ancient Rome.

Piazzale G. Agnelli. Tel. 065926135.

Getting there
Bus 160, 714.

Swimming Pools

Piscina delle Rose
This is the only public outdoor pool in Rome. Open daily May 10 to September 30, 9 am-9 pm.

Some major hotels away from the center of Rome have pools that can be used by non-hotel guests, although they tend to be very pricey:

Viale America, 20 (EUR). Tel. 065926717.

Getting there
Bus 714 or
B Metro EUR Marconi stop.

Aldrovandi Palace
Located near the zoo, on the far side of Villa Borghese.
Via Aldrovandi, 15. Tel. 063221430.
Getting there
Bus 52, 53 or **Tram** 30.

Parco dei Principi
Expensive. At the far east end of Villa Borghese.
Via G. Frescobaldi, 5. Tel. 06854421.
Getting there
Bus 52, 910.

Cavalieri Hilton
Luxurious. On the hill in Monte Mario, north of central Rome.
Via Cadlolo, 101. Tel. 0635091.
Getting there
Bus 990, 991.
Open May-September 9 am-7 pm.

Shangrila
EUR area.
Viale Algeria, 141. Tel. 065916441.
Getting there
Bus 705 or **B Metro** Eur Fermi stop.

Hotel Giancolo
Atop the Janiculum Hill.
Piazza Tavani Arquati, 104. Tel. 065811052.

Lake and Beaches

EUR. You can hire boats on the Laghetto Artificiale, and paddle boats.

Ostia. This is the closest beach to Rome and the most crowded. Take the B line subway to either Pirammide or Magliana. Here catch the local train to Ostia Lido. The entire trip will take about 40 minutes. Get off the train, cross the street and you are on the Mediterranean coast.

The shore is lined with private "stabilimenti," where you must pay an entrance fee and can rent chairs, chaise longues and umbrellas. For a free beach, take the local bus from Ostia Lido heading south and get off at the public beach Castel Porziano; beaches near Rome have dark gray volcanic sand. Here you find food, showers and other facilities but no entrance fee.

Fregene. More up-market than Ostia, but still gray sand. You need a car to get there. Swim in the pool, as the seawater is not clean.

Sabaudia. Further afield to the south. Breathtakingly white sand and no dangerous waves. Beautiful views of Circeo – and the Sirens (see Day Trips, page 252).

Food

Are the kids getting cranky because they are hungry? Try a few quick ways to appease their appetites without having to sit down at a table:

Pizza a taglio. Italians' answer to *fast food* is "pizza a taglio," slices of pizza sold by weight. More types of pizza than you can possibly imagine, but not the pepperoni pizza – it doesn't exist here! These shops are all over the city and are a favorite snack for Romans as well.

Gelato. Ice cream is an all-time favorite with all ages, and the Italian version is the original and probably the best in the world. There are ice cream places everywhere, open year-round. Avoid buying from street vendors if you can – the quality is not as good. And we tend to favor places that make their own: watch for the sign *produzione propria*.

If worse comes to worst and your kids need a taste of a Big Mac, don't worry; there are more than 29 **McDonald's** restaurants in Rome.

Also, Rome has a **Hard Rock Cafe**.

Via Veneto, 62A. Tel. 0642012760.

Haircuts

Matteucci, a hairdresser for children, has prancing animals for the little ones to sit on.

Via Metastasio, 17. Tel. 066865409 (see also Specialty Shops, page 222).

Tip: For other child-oriented activities, see Day Trips, page 235.

Castroni sells imported groceries at these central locations:
*Via Cola di Rienzo 196.
  Tel. 066874383.
Via Flaminia 28. Tel. 063611029.
Via delle Quattro Fontane 38.
  Tel. 064882435.
Via Ottaviano 55.
  Tel. 0639723279.*

Rome by Night

Some think Rome is most beautiful at night when its important monuments are artistically lit up and the traffic has thinned out. We have a few walks to suggest where you can really see the regality and elegance of the "eternal city."

Moonlight Walks

Ancient Rome

Start off at **Piazza Venezia** and proceed along **Via dei Fori Imperiali**, where on your left is **Trajan's Column** and on your right the **Roman Forum**. In the background rises the majestic **Colosseum** and to its right the **Arch of Constantine**. Turn right and take **Via di San Gregorio** until you reach **Via dei Cerchi**. Turn right: on your

MUSIC - WHERE AND WHEN

Classical Music

🎼 **Accademia Filarmonica Romana**
Concerts at Teatro Olimpico.
Piazza Gentile da Fabriano, 17.
Tel. 063201752.
Getting there - Bus 628.

🎼 **Arts Academy**
Concerts in the Sala Accademica.
Via G. A. Guattani, 17. Tel. 0644252303.

🎼 **Concerti del Tempietto**
Concerts in Sala Baldini.
Piazza Campitelli, 9.

🎼 **Istituzione Universitaria dei Concerti**
Concerts in the Aula Magna at the
Università La Sapienza.
Piazzale Aldo Moro. Tel. 063610051.
Getting there - Bus 9, 71, 310, 492.

🎼 **Oratorio del Gonfalone**
Concerts in the Oratorio del Gonfalone.
Via del Gonfalone, 32A. Tickets tel.
0685301758.

🎼 **St. Paul's Within the Walls**
Via Nazionale, corner Via Napoli.
Tel. 064826296.
Getting there - Bus 60, 64, 170, 640;
A Metro Repubblica stop.

During Christmas and Easter holidays
many churches have concerts. Check local
listings and billboards on the streets.

Opera

🎼 **Teatro dell'Opera**
Piazza B. Gigli.
Tel. 06481601 (tickets: 064881755).
Getting there - Bus 60, 64, 70, 71, 170, 640;
A Metro Repubblica stop.
www.opera.roma.it.

🎼 **Chiesa Valdese**
Piazza Cavour. Tel. 0665795117.
Getting there - Bus 34, 49, 87, 280, 492.

🎼 **St. Clemente Church**
Operas staged here during June and July.
Via Labicana, 95. Tel. 0670451018.
Getting there - Bus 85, 87; Tram 30;
A Metro Manzoni stop.
B Metro Colosseo stop.

🎼 **St. Paul's Within the Walls.**
Via Nazionale, corner Via Napoli.
Tel. 064826296.
Getting there - Bus 60, 64, 170, 640.
A Metro Repubblica stop.

Rock, Jazz, Folk, Country and Other

Big rock concerts are held in big places
such as **Palazzo dello Sport, Stadio
Olimpico** and **Stadio Flaminio.**

Akab
Via di Monte Testaccio, 69.
Tel. 0657250585. (Mixed Music)

Alexanderplatz
Via Ostia, 9.
Tel. 0639742171. (Jazz)

Alpheus
Via del Commercio, 36.
Tel. 065747826. (Mixed Music)

Big Mamma
Vicolo San Francesco a Ripa, 18.
Tel. 065812551. (Blues)

Caffè Caruso
Via di Monte Testaccio, 36.
Tel. 065745019. (Mixed Music)

Caffè Latino
Via di Monte Testaccio, 96.
Tel. 065744020. (Mixed Music)

The Club
Via Cagliari, 25.
Tel. 0697603944.
info@theclub.it. *(Jazz)*

Fonclea
Via Crecenzio, 82A.
Tel. 066896302. (Folk and Country)

Ippodromo Capannelle
Via Appia Nuova, km 12.
(Summer Latin American Music Festival)

La Palma
Via G. Mirri, 35.
Tel. 0643566581. (Jazz)

New Mississippi Jazz Club
Borgo Angelico, 18A.
Tel. 0668806348. (Jazz and Blues)

Palaeur
Piazzale dello Sport.
Tel. 063224969.
www.palaeur.com. *(Major Pop Concerts)*

left you will see the **Circus Maximus** and on your right rise the magnificent palaces of the **Palatine Hill**. Walk the length of the circus and turn right onto **Via di San Teodoro**. On your left is the **Arch of Janus** and further ahead on your right, **Chiesa di San Teodoro**. Follow the street around until you reach **Piazza della Consolazione**. Take the stairs leading up to the **Campidoglio,** but before you actually reach Michelangelo's square, stop and enjoy the view.

Christian Rome

Begin your walk by crossing over **Ponte Sisto,** which connects Trastevere to city center. After a few minutes you come into **Piazza Farnese,** now home of the French embassy. Walk through **Piazza Campo de' Fiori** onto **Piazza della Cancelleria** and then across the main street to **Piazza Navona**. Cross the river on the **Ponte Sant'Angelo** and look at the marvelous **Castel Sant'Angelo**. The highlight and end of your walk will be **St. Peter's Basilica,** a really breathtaking vision.

Renaissance and Baroque Rome

Your walk begins at the newly refurbished **Piazza del Popolo**. Stroll down the antique-dealer street of **Via del Babuino** for a few blocks and then take a left onto the unique **Via Margutta** – the location of many artists' studios. Federico Fellini lived here. At the end of Via Margutta you reach the **Spanish Steps**. From Via Due Macelli go down Via del Tritone and follow signs on your left for the **Trevi Fountain (Fontana di Trevi)**.

Nightclubs

Night life starts around midnight. Almost all the clubs are listed online at www.2night.it.

Pubs: Scottish, Irish and English

St. Andrew's Pub (Scottish)
Vicolo della Cancelleria, 36. Tel. 066832638.

Druid's Den (Irish)
Via San Martino ai Monti, 28. Tel. 0648904781.

Fiddler's Elbow
Via dell'Olmata, 43. Tel. 064872110.

HOMESICK?

American Restaurants

For those craving American cooking, Rome has its **Hard Rock Cafe** (*Via Veneto, 62A. Tel. 064203051*), with restaurant and merchandise store, and 29 **McDonald's**.

Jeff Blynn's. Out of the center, run by a Yank. Frequented by Italian stars for its New York look and beautiful bar. Italian *cucina* and U.S. favorites: baked potatoes, T-bone steaks, cheesecake, apple pie. Live entertainment in the evenings; summer dining in the garden. Sunday brunch. Reserve. *Viale Parioli, 103C. Tel. 068070444.*

Piedra del Sol. Mexican food. Good, not great, but mood is Mexican, especially the mariachi players. Downstairs can get noisy – quieter on the ground floor.

Open until 2 am. Reserve. *Vicolo Rosini, 6 (near Parliament). Tel. 066873651.*

Oliphant. Only authentic TexMex in town. Buffalo wings, stuffed baked potatoes, huge salads and mild Mexican fare. Great songs from the '60s and '70s on a jukebox, and American sports events on a big screen. *Via delle Coppelle, 31-32 (near Piazza Navona). Tel. 066861416.*

Internet

Rome has several Internet cafés. Biggest and busiest is **Space Web** (formerly Easy) in Piazza Barberini. Open daily 7-1 am. *Via Barberini. Tel. 335462086.* Info@ spacewebsrl.com.

Movies in English

Tired of films dubbed in Italian? These theaters show movies in original version:

Trinity College

Via del Collegio Romano, 6. Tel. 066786472.

Birreria Marconi (English)

Via di San Prassede, 9C. Tel. 06486636.

The Beefeater Pub

Via G. Benzoni, 44. Tel. 065730030.

The John Bull

Piazza Sant'Andrea della Valle. Tel. 066871536.

A Private View of Italy
Looking for a very special private tour guide? Contact "A Private View of Italy," a group of young people from Rome's titled families, who take visitors on quite superior tours. Because of their familial connections, these descendants of the ruling class can get you into the princely palazzi, and they really know their art history. Contact *Stephano Aluffi Pertini, Tel. 39064941988, apvoi@tin.*

Latest and Coolest

Art Café. Hot disco in Villa Borghese gardens. Open Tuesday and Friday all year, plus Thursday in summer, when it is absolutely lovely.

Via del Galoppatoio, 33. Tel. 0636006578.

Bloom. Restaurant on the ground floor and sushi bar above, it becomes a dance club on Friday, Saturday, Monday and Tuesday.

Via del Teatro Pace, 30. Tel. 0668802029.

La Maison. Arguably the most "with-it" club for the moment. Goes gay on Sunday. Closed Monday and Tuesday.

Vicolo dei Granari, 4. Tel. 066833312.

Young

The ancient Testaccio neighborhood is jammed with hot spots; as Caesar would say, go, see and choose for yourself. Two suggestions are

Bush. Hi-tech dance club with big-screen monitors and house music.

Via Galvani, 46. Tel. 0657288691.

Caffè Latino. Attracts a thirtyish crowd with dancing, an occasional live music performance and a separate music-video room and bar.

Via di Monte Testaccio, 96. Tel. 0657440020.

Alcazar. Monday nights. Numbered tickets, and no one enters after the film starts. You can book ahead but must pick up your tickets 20 minutes before show time. *Via Merry del Val, 14 (off Viale Trastevere). Tel. 065880099.* Getting there - Tram 8.

Pasquino. In the heart of Trastevere with only English-language films, three theaters with four daily showings each. *Piazza Sant'Egidio, 10. Tel. 065815208.* Getting there - Bus 23, 280 and Tram 8.

Metropolitan. English-language films frequently shown. *Via del Corso, 7. Tel. 063200933.*

English Bookstores

Anglo-American Book Co. *Via della Vite, 102. Tel. 066795222, fax 066783890.*

The Almost Corner Bookshop. Open 10 am-1:30 pm and 3:30-8 pm. *Via del Moro, 45. Tel. 065836942.*

The Lion Bookshop and Café. English books of all kinds, as well as English magazines and newspapers. Cake and cookies, coffee and tea; relax and read your newspaper or guidebook. Open 10 am-7 pm. *Via dei Greci, 33 (near the Spanish Steps). Tel. 0632650437, fax 0632651382.*

The Open Door Bookshop. Mostly used paperback novels. *Via della Lungaretta, 23. Tel. 065896478.*

Feltrinelli Internazionale. Across the street from the St. Regis Grand Hotel. Go downstairs for the English books, but all guidebooks are on the street level. Open 9 am-8 pm. *Via V. E. Orlando, 84-86. Tel. 064827878, fax 064827873.*

Less Young

For the young more in heart than in limb, these institutions are dependable.

Bella Blu. Glitzy spot for the world of politics, commerce and showbiz. Supper club with disco dancing and piano bar. Suit and tie. Closed Monday.
Via Luciani, 21. Tel. 063218749.

Black Out. Stark postindustrial style leaves plenty of room for young rockers to enjoy themselves. Separate off-music room for chilling out.
Via Saturnia, 18. Tel. 0670496791.

Gilda. Sophisticated nightspot near the Spanish Steps. Piano bar, restaurant and dance floors with live and disco music. Jackets required. Closed Monday.
Via Mario de Fiori, 97. Tel. 066797396.

GOA. Best Italian DJs show their stuff here, especially Thursday. Closed Monday, Tuesday and Wednesday.
Via Libetta, 13. Tel. 065748277.

Jackie O'. The stars have no trouble getting past the doorman, but common mortals are advised to reserve. Restaurant, piano bar and disco (Friday and Saturday), all dressy. Closed Monday.
Via Boncompagni, 11. Tel. 0642885457.

New Scarabocchio. Been around forever, so it must be doing something right.
Piazza Ponziani, 8C. Tel. 065800495.

Piper. In the Trieste district: dance music, live groups, pop videos and a dance floor surrounded by intimate seating areas. Open Saturday and Sunday.
Via Tagliamento, 9. Tel. 068555398.

Qube. Rome's biggest underground disco, a veritable sea of young bodies dancing till they drop. Open Thursday through Saturday.
Via di Portonaccio, 212. Tel. 064385445.

Suite. Reproduction of a luxurious, futuristic hotel suite in neutral tones with warm lighting. Studio 54 has a frivolous seventies and eighties theme on Wednesday, when the crowd tends to be in the early thirties. Sushi in the private lounge.
Via degli Orti di Trastevere, 1. Tel. 065747826.

Gay/Lesbian

Check www.gayroma.it/locali.htm.

Alpheus. Newest addition.
Via del Commercia, 36. Tel. 06574826.

Edoardo II. Restaurant and cabaret. Different theme nights include Spanish night Wednesday, with paella and sangria. Friday: striptease night. Live music. Closed Wednesday.
Vicolo Margana, 14. Tel. 0669942419. www.edoardosecondo.it.

Extasia Excess Baths. The morning after. Sauna for men only Friday and Saturday.
Via Ombrone, 1. Tel. 068558398.

Hangar. American bar. Closed Tuesday.
Via dei Selci, 69. Tel. 0648813971.

L'Alibi. Gay bar for both sexes.
Via Monte Testaccio, 44. Tel. 065743448.

Yes - No	*Si - No*
Please	*Per favore, prego*
Thank you	*Grazie; grazie mille*
Excuse me	*Mi scusi*
Okay - Yes, no, maybe	*D'accordo; va bene - Si, no, forse*
It is very kind of you	*È molto gentile da parte sua*
Exchange	*Cambio*
I have a credit card	*Ho una carta di credito*
Check - Payment	*Assegno - Pagamento*
Where is the nearest bank, please?	*Per favore, dov'è la banca più vicina?*
Toilet	*Toilette, bagno*
When? - At what time?	*Quando? - A che ora?*
One minute - One hour	*Un minuto - Un'ora*
Half an hour - Quarter of an hour	*Mezz'ora - Un quarto d'ora*
1, 2, 3, 4, 5,	*Uno, due, tre, quattro, cinque,*
6, 7, 8, 9, 10	*sei, sette, otto, nove, dieci*
Arrival - Departure	*Arrivo - Partenza*
Fast - Slow	*Veloce - Lento*
Danger	*Pericolo*
Stop - Let's go	*Fermata, stop - Andiamo*
Full - Empty	*Pieno - Vuoto*
Good - Bad	*Buono, bene - Male*
Near - Far	*Vicino - Lontano*
Open - Closed	*Aperto - Chiuso*
Small - Large	*Piccolo - Grande*
Right - Left	*Destra - Sinistra*
Now - Later	*Adesso - Più tardi*
Before - After	*Prima - Dopo*
A little - A lot, much - Too much	*Poco - Molto - Troppo*
How much?	*Quanto?*
How much does it cost?	*Quanto costa?*
Enough	*Basta*
Always - Never	*Sempre - Mai (pronounced my)*
Where?	*Dove?*
Less	*Meno*
Of course!	*Certo!*
That's better - That's worse	*Questo è meglio - Questo è peggio*
What a pity!	*Che peccato!*
Sales - Discount	*Saldi - Sconto*
Easy - Difficult	*Facile - Difficile*
Why?	*Perché?*
The bill	*Il conto*
Do you speak English?	*Parla inglese?*
I understand - I don't understand	*Capisco - Non capisco*
Can you repeat that?	*Può ripeterlo?*
Who are you?	*Lei chi è?*
I love you - F*** off!	*Ti amo - Vaffan*****
Leave me alone - Go away	*Lasciami in pace - Vai via*
Good morning - Good evening	*Buon giorno - Buona sera*
Good night	*Buona notte*
Hello, goodbye	*Ciao (pronounced chow)*
Happy birthday - Congratulations	*Buon compleanno - Congratulazioni*
Help	***Aiuto***

Basic Facts

Emergencies

24-hour emergency phone numbers

If you are robbed or need help call the *carabinieri* (national police) at **112** or the *polizia* (local police) at **113**. Dial **118** for an ambulance and **115** in case of fire. If you are lost you can always ask a *vigile urbano* (traffic police officer) for directions. Many are multilingual. If you have a health problem, ask your hotel concierge (*portiere*) for a doctor or a hospital. Last, but not least, contact your embassy.

General Information

General Rome info   Tel. 060606

A fabulous telephone number that will give you, in Italian or English, any information about anything in Rome. If you need help, the person who answers will connect you with whatever municipal office is needed. The following numbers and websites are also very useful:

Tourism	*Tel. 0636004399* www.romaturismo.it	**Bus/Tram/** **Metro**	*Tel. 800431784* www.atac.roma.it
Train	*Tel. 06892021* www.trenitalia.com	**Hotels**	www.romaturismo.it www.romeby.com
Plane	*Tel. 0665951* www./adr/ot		hr@hotelreservations.it

Using the Telephone in Rome

At the beginning of all Rome phone numbers, 06 must be dialed, except for the two Freephone series, 800 and 199, as well as local assistance numbers. The same is true of all Italian numbers, which now begin with what used to be the area code, such as 02 for Milan. In addition, cell phones for all of Italy start with the number 3.

For international calls dial 00, and then the country code + area code + local number. These calls can be placed from any public phone. You can dial direct almost anywhere in the world from Rome pay phones. Most phones only accept phone cards, so buy a 5 euro or 10 euro card, sold at tobacco shops (look for signs with a big white T against a black background) and at some newsstands.

PUBLIC TRANSPORTATION

Getting to and from Airports

From the airport to the center of Rome, you can
• take a white cab from the taxi stand, costing about 45 euro;
• go upstairs to the train station (*Stazione Ferroviaria*) across the street (look for the picture of a train). The ticket office is on the right before the tracks, or use the green automatic ticket machines.

One train goes directly to the central railroad station (*Stazione Termini*). The 30-minute ride costs 9.50 euro. Departure approximately every half hour.

Another train stops at stations on the outskirts of the city: Trastevere, Ostiense, Tuscolana, Tiburtina and Fara Sabina, taking from 30 to 40 minutes depending on where you get off. Departures every 15 minutes. Tickets cost 5 euro.

From Rome to **Fiumicino Airport**, you can

• take a taxi, costing about 45 euro;
• take the train from the *Stazione Termini* (train station), 30 minutes non-stop to the airport for 9.50 euro. Departs every half hour, 6:50 am-9:20 pm;
• take the local train, which makes various stops before reaching Fiumicino Airport, for 5 euro. Train makes stops every 15 minutes at the following stations in Rome: Tiburtina (on Via Tiburtina), Tuscolana (on Via Tuscolana), Ostiense (near the Piramide: pyramid), Trastevere.

To and from **Ciampino Airport** (charter flights and budget airlines). The older and smaller airport on Via Appia Nuova just outside of the GRA (ring road).

Take the subway **A** line and get off at the last stop, Anagnina. Then catch a Cotral bus (blue), which goes to the nearby Ciampino Airport. Buses leave every half hour. Buses connecting Ciampino with the center of Rome stop running at 11 pm. A taxi into the center of the city costs about 45 euro.

ATT access: *8001724444*.
International telephone directory: *4176*.

Help with foreign calls: *170*.
National telephone directory: *412*.

Best idea: bring a cell phone into which you can insert a SIM card, or rent one in Italy through your hotel concierge, or telephone *063720700*.

Beware of . . .

Although Rome may look like a movie set, it's a big city. Therefore, please,

Ladies, keep your handbag close to your body. In some parts of the city teenagers on mopeds drive along and snatch unclutched purses.

Gents, keep your wallet in your front pocket unless you're determined to have it snatched. Be especially careful of **pickpockets** on buses, trams and subways (especially those used by tourists). They can spot an unsuspecting tourist a mile away. Their latest tactic is, working in couples, for one to push you from behind to distract you while the other picks your pocket – as they slip out the door.

Gypsy children seem cute and harmless but are the best pickpockets in town. In their classic act one of them pushes a cardboard sign at you while others surround you and pick your pockets and bags.

Automobile drivers who offer their services in the airport or station. These are not registered cabdrivers. Taxis in Rome are white, with a sign saying "TAXI" on top and a dependable meter inside.

Mano morta. This disease is dying out in the modern world. On the bus or other crowded place, a man will leave his arm down, with hand ever so gently cupped over the female tourist's bottom. In a jolt of the bus, he will squeeze!

Hours

In a word, arbitrary. Some shops downtown are open nonstop from 10 am to 7 pm, while others close at 1 pm for lunch and reopen from 3:30 pm (4 pm in summer) until 7:30 pm (8 pm in summer). Saturday afternoons during the summer many shops, not just food stores, are closed (the Romans all go to the beach). On Monday mornings food stores are open; virtually all others are closed – except in summer. Museums: 90% are closed on Monday; for those that are open that day, see page 258, or call *0639967700*.

Banks. Open 8:30 am-1:45 pm and 2:45-3:30 pm.

ATM. Machines are on almost every corner, open 24 hours.

American Express. *Piazza di Spagna, 38. Tel. 0667641*; open Monday to Friday 9 am-5:30 pm, Saturday 9 am-12:30 pm.

Subway, Bus and Tram

The BIT ticket costs 1 euro and can be used for subway, bus and tram. You can change buses/trams (punching the ticket every time you get on a bus) until 75 minutes from the first time stamped on your ticket. However, the Metrobus ticket can be used for only one subway ride plus as many bus-tram rides as you can fit into 75 minutes. ATAC tickets can be purchased in tobacco stores (look for the sign with a big white T on a black background), at newsstands and from machines in the subway stations.

Subway (Metro)
• The orange **A** line crosses Rome from the northwest corner (Mattia Battistini) to the southeast corner (Anagnina).
• The blue **B** line runs from northeast corner of Rome (Rebibbia) to the southwest corner (Laurentina). The two lines cross at the Termini train station, where you can change subway lines.

Taking the subway is easy and painless. However, both lines are packed at rush hours, so avoid 8:15-9:15 am and 6:00-7:00 pm if you can.

The metro stations on Line **A** do not have facilities for the physically challenged, but there is the 590 bus line, which follows the same route and has wheelchair access. All metro stations on Line **B** have facilities for the physically challenged except for the Circo Massimo, Colosseo and Cavour.

Bus and Tram (Italian: Autobus, Tram)
You can get all over town by bus and tram in Rome but sometimes you must have patience, since some lines do not run frequently. The most popular bus, number 64, goes from the Termini railroad station to St. Peter's Basilica and runs very often.

Enter the bus through the rear doors and exit through the middle doors (on the new, large buses and trams you can

Rome Tourist Office. *Via Parigi, 5 (next to the St. Regis Grand Hotel). Tel. 06488991.*
Tourist information kiosks. Green octagonal booths are dotted about the city with free maps, free information and attendants who speak English.
Pharmacies (open all night)
Farmacia Corso Rinascimento, *Corso Rinascimento, 44. Tel. 0668803760.*
Farmacia Arenula, *Via Arenula, 73. Tel. 0668803278.*
Farmacia Internazionale, *Piazza Barberini, 49. Tel. 06485456.*
Post offices. The **central post office** in *Piazza San Silvestro* (open 8 am-8 pm) or the **Vatican post office** (mail with Vatican stamps must be posted in the Vatican). Telephone information: *803160.*
Toilets. One of Rome's few public toilets is under *Piazza San Silvestro*. Others, located throughout the city, are marked **WC**. Every bar and restaurant in Italy has a toilet for its customers. Carry tissues just in case, and don't expect a lock on the door.
Climate
NOVEMBER-FEBRUARY: Cold and rainy, rarely freezing. A few days of sun at a time.
MARCH-MAY: Springlike weather, though the last half of May can be hot.
JUNE-SEPTEMBER: Hot and humid with afternoon thunderstorms in late July-August.
OCTOBER: Indian summer with the cold showers creeping in.

Daily and Monthly Specials

SUNDAY – Porta Portese. 7 am-1:30 pm. Antiques, furniture, prints, clothes, shoes: the good, the bad, the passable. Entrances: for clothes Piazza Porta Portese and Viale Trastevere; for bric-a-brac Piazza Ippolito Nievo (one of the first on the right is **India Antica**).
Papal blessing. **Piazza San Pietro at noon**. If in Rome, the pope blesses the crowd from his window high up on the right (north) side of the square.
MONDAY TO SATURDAY – Piazza Campo de' Fiori. **7 am-2 pm**. Glorious fruit, flowers and vegetable market.
Piazza Borghese. Old prints and book stalls. Some bargains.
San Giovanni Flea Market. **Via Sannio**. Mostly new clothes, shoes and suitcases.
WEDNESDAY – Mass and papal blessing. **Piazza San Pietro**. Pilgrims crush into the square

also enter at the front). Punch your ticket upon entering, but of course not everyone does. You might be tempted not to, but inspectors do get on the buses/trams (and trains) to check tickets, and fines are rather high.

♿ **Bus line 590** is for the physically challenged and has the same route as the Metro A line. Runs every 90 minutes. Check schedule at bus stops.

Night buses. More than 20 bus lines run from 12:30 to 5:30 am. The main terminal stations are Termini (railway station) and Piazza Venezia. Buses leave from these two locations about every 30 minutes. Look for the blue owl at the bus stop, which indicates the night lines. For info on schedules phone toll-free *800431784* Monday to Saturday 8 am-8 pm. Contact them at their website, **www.atac.roma.it**, or email **clienti@atac.roma.it** to get schedule info.

Archeobus. A new service: Buses leave Piazza Venezia at hourly intervals 9:50 am-4:30 pm for a jump-on/jump-off tour of archaeological sites, principally on Via Appia. *Tel. 0646950414.*

Trains
Going directly to the station is the best way to purchase your tickets, though there are long lines. Most agencies issue train tickets or buy them from the ticket machines at the train station (credit cards accepted). There are two main stations in Rome: **Stazione Termini** (Piazza dei Cinquecento) and **Stazione Tiburtina** (Circonvallazione Nomentana at Via Lorenzo il Magnifico). For information call *891021*. Some operators speak English. You can also purchase tickets online at www.trenitalia.com.
Reminder: to avoid being fined you must validate your ticket at yellow boxes before boarding the train. True for all tickets except Eurail pass and Eurostar.
More about **Termini train station**: Here you have access to the two metro stations as well as the largest bus terminal in Rome. You can also find here:
Luggage storage: open 7 am-midnight.
Tourist Office
Police and carabinieri station. If you have lost luggage or documents (or have had them stolen) on the train, report it here.
24-hr store. Not the greatest place at night but it has food, drinks and other

and the pope addresses them, when possible, in their own languages. If it's raining this mass is held in the Nervi Auditorium to the left of the colonnade. See St. Peter's Basilica (page 82) for info regarding tickets.

SATURDAY AND SUNDAY – Gardens of Villa Medici. Guided tours at 10:30 and 11:30 am. Fee. *Tel. 0667611.*

JANUARY: 6 - Epiphany. End of toy fair in Piazza Navona. **MID-JANUARY - FEBRUARY**: Sales!

FEBRUARY: Carnevale (Mardi Gras). Children dress up and parade through the streets.

MARCH: 16 - Visit of Palazzo Massimo chapel (see page 152).

MARCH-APRIL: Holy Week and Easter. On Good Friday the pope holds a stations of the cross ceremony at the Colosseum.

APRIL: Spanish Steps covered with azaleas.

21 (753 BC) - Rome's birthday. Candles on the Campidoglio and fireworks.

MAY: May 1 - May Day rock concert. Piazza San Giovanni.

International horse show. Piazza di Siena, Villa Borghese.

Rose show. Aventine Hill Gardens. Art fair. Via Margutta.

JUNE: 23-24 - Feast of Saint John. San Giovanni. Street parties with music and dancing.

Summer music festival - June-August: see Music entry.

JULY: Tevere Expo - Italian products on the riverbanks between Ponte Margherita and Ponte Sant'Angelo. Bargains!

Festival of Noantri. Street fair in Trastevere with funfare. Fireworks the last night.

AUGUST: 15 - Ferragosto, Rome on vacation.

SEPTEMBER: Second part of Tevere Expo.

OCTOBER-NOVEMBER: Second antique fair - Via dei Coronari.

Second art fair - Via Margutta.

DECEMBER: 8 - *Piazza di Spagna*. Feast of the Immaculate Conception. The pope, joined by the mayor, holds a religious service at the column of the Virgin.

Piazza Navona. Festival with toys, Christmas decorations and Nativity scene supplies.

24 - Christmas Eve midnight mass. St. Peter's Basilica.

25 - Christmas Day. The pope celebrates Mass.

goods, two banks, Eurail and train information office, newstands, pharmacy, electronics shop, bookstore, toy store just to name a few.

♿ Major train stations have offices dedicated to facilitating travel for the physically challenged. Upon request (24 hrs in advance for Italian trains and 3 working days for international trains), they provide services for wheelchair use, luggage transport and train information. Termini Station: *064881726*; Fiumicino Airport Station: *0665951.*

Transport-for-Rent

Bicycle rentals
Piazza di Spagna.
Piazza del Popolo. **Guy**: *Tel. 3389077449.*
Piazza San Silvestro.
Piazza Augusto Imperatore.
Villa Borghese - Pincio.
Rollerblades and scooters
Villa Borghese - Pincio.
Rental cars
Avis. *Tel. 199100133.*
Hertz. *Tel. 199112211.*
Europcar. *Tel. 800014410.*
Maggiore. *Tel. 848867067.*
Motor scooter rentals

Scooters for Rent. *Via della Purificazione, 84. Tel. 064885485,* scooterrent@hotmile.com
St. Peter's Moto. *Via di Porta Castello, 43. Tel. 066875714.*
Scoot-a-long. *Via Cavour, 302. Tel. 066780206.*

Chauffeur-Driven Cars

Palazzi. Mercedes, stretch limousines and luxury minibuses. Also VIP bodyguard service and planes. *Viale Peruzzi, 46B. Tel. 06870921, fax 0687092222,* www.palazzi.net.
Auto Antiche Ghisu. Somerset Maugham's 1950s Rolls, convertible Cadillacs from the 1960s. *Via Filippo Meda, 183. Tel. 064511357, fax 064506844,* www.ghisu.autonolegio.it.
Airport. Car service to and from airports. *Tel. 063383221,* www.airportconnection.it.
Amadeo Tomasso. Hourly or airport service. *Tel. 3498380023 or 339212033.*
Coop U.A.R.A. Car service with driver; charged by hour. *Via Panisperna, 261. Tel. 066792320,* www.noleggiouara.com.
EUROCAR. *Tel. 3397278624.*
EUROPCAR. *Tel. 80013942,* www.europcar.it.

Hotels

Hostelry and taverns have existed in Rome since time immemorial. The web of consular roads emanating from the ancient capital was interspersed with inns where, while changing horses or mules, you could get a meal and a bed. Medieval hotels had animal names: Albergo la Vacca (cow), l'Orso (bear), Il Gallo (cockerel) and so on. Rome has been noted for its fine hotels since at least 1500 – when the pope's lady friend owned a chain of downtown hostels catering to merchants and wealthy pilgrims. By the 18c the Grand Tour was bringing the first "tourists" – Caesar Ritz and Conrad Hilton did the rest.

Tel. 066991000 is the phone number to reserve any room in any Rome hotel. No fee. Open 8:30 am-10 pm. *Fax 066781469*, e-mail: hr@hotelreservations.it. They claim they can make reservations for hotels, bed-and-breakfasts and apartment rentals anywhere in the world.

B & Bs. These cooperatives book you into private homes or rent short-term flats:
Rome Sweet Home. *Vicolo Due Macelli, 36. Tel. 0669924833, fax 066794074,* www.romesweethome.it, e-mail: romesweethome@tiscalinet.it.
Bed & Breakfast Association of Rome. *Tel./fax 0655302248,* www.b-b.rm.it, e-mail: enquiry@b-b.rm.it.

Rome's official tourist office at *Via Parigi, 11* (open 9 am-7 pm; *tel. 0636004399*), gives information on all hotels and bed-and-breakfasts and lists them online at www.rometurismo.it. Reservations can be made at the hotel reservation offices located in Fiumicino Airport and in Termini railway station (open 7 am-11 pm; *tel. 066991000*) or at the toll-free number *800015772*, as well as online at www.hotel.em.it. Also, check out the individual websites for the hotels listed here (only direct websites are listed), and pick out your favorite room!

Ancient Rome
Colosseum area
Inexpensive

Antica Locanda. Beamed ceilings in some bedrooms, terrace and wine bar. *Via del Boschetto, 84. Tel. 0647881729 or 06484894, fax 064871164, www.antica-locanda.com*, e-mail: info@antica-locanda.com.

Hotel Giardino. For walkers, a good jumping-off place. *Via XXIV Maggio, 51. Tel. 066794584, fax 066795155, www.hotel-giardino-roma.com*, e-mail: info@hotel-giardino-roma.com.

Il Rosario. Pilgrim hotel, but you can go too – the prices are unbeatable. *Via di Sant'Agata dei Goti, 10. Tel. 066792346, fax 0669941106*, e-mail: irodopre@tin.it.

Moderate

Hotel Nerva. Stone's throw from the Roman forums; soundproof high-ceilinged rooms equipped with orthopedic mattresses and satellite TV. *Via Tor de Conti, 3. Tel. 066781835, fax 0669922204, www.hotelnerva.com*, e-mail: info@hotelnerva.com.

Hotel Palatino. Modern business hotel 10 minutes from the forums and Palatine Hill. Opened 1968. *Via Cavour, 213. Tel. 064814927, fax 064740726, www.hotelpalatino.com*, e-mail: info@hotelpalatino.com.

Expensive

Hotel Forum. Ideal for exploring ancient Rome. Terrace restaurant has spectacular views over the forums both night and day. Elegant, small. Reserve. *Via Tor de Conti, 25/30. Tel. 066792446, fax 066786479, www.hotelforumrome.com*, e-mail: info@hotelforum.com.

Mercure Delta Colosseo. Built in 1975, this white cube with darkened glass is right down the street from the Colosseum: the very old and the very new. There are 170 rooms. *Via Labicana, 144. Tel. 06770021, fax 0677250198, www.mercure.com*, e-mail: mercurehotelsroma@accor-hotels.it.

Christian Rome
Aventine area
Inexpensive

Hotel Sourire. Two-star hotel in the Aventine, a residential neighborhood on one of the seven hills of Rome. Good transportation; Circo Massimo Metro stop. *Via delle Terme Deciane, 3. Tel. 065750958, fax 065780514*, e-mail: sourire@tiscalinet.it.

Moderate

Aventino San Anselmo Hotels. Three adjacent and dependable hotels on the Aventine Hill, a quiet, elegant area and home to medieval churches: **Hotel Aventino**, *Via San Domenico, 10. Tel. 065783214, fax 065783604*; **Hotel San Anselmo**, *Piazza San Anselmo, 2. Tel. 065745174 or 065743547, fax 065783604*; **Villa San Pio**, *Via Santa Melania, 19. Tel. 065745231 or 065745232, fax 06574112,* www.aventinohotels.com, e-mail: info@aventinohotels.com.

Hotel Domus Aventina. Within walking distance of Circus Maximus, in one of the most elite areas of Rome. *Via Santa Prisca, 11B. Tel. 065746135, fax 0657300044,* www.domus-aventina.com, e-mail: info@domus-aventina.com.

St. Peter's area

Inexpensive

Hotel Smeraldo. Within walking distance of the Vatican and historical center, this little hotel is also well connected with the bus system. *Vicolo dei Chiodaroli, 9. Tel. 066875929 or 066892121, fax 0668805495,* www.smeraldoroma.com, e-mail: albergosmeraldoroma@tin.it.

Moderate

Bramante. Twenty rooms, just off Borgo Pio, near St. Peter's. *Vicolo delle Palline 24 / 25. Tel. 0668806426, fax 06688133339,* www.hotelbramante.com, e-mail: hotelbramante@libero.it.

Hotel Atlante Garden. A less-smart sister of the better known Atlante Star, also located in the St. Peter's area. *Via Crescenzio, 78. Tel. 066872361, fax 066872315,* www.atlantehotels.com, email: info@atlantehotels.com.

Hotel Atlante Star. A modern 60-room hotel on the edge of the Borgo. Les Étoiles, with its elegant roof-garden terrace, offers a 360-degree view of Rome. *Via Vitelleschi, 34. Tel. 066873233, fax 066872300,* www.atlantehotels.com, e-mail: info@atlantehotels.com.

Hotel Sant'Anna. Comfortable 3-star hotel in Borgo. Air-conditioned. *Borgo Pio, 133. Tel. 0668801602, fax 0668308717,* www.hotelsantanna.com, e-mail: santanna@travel.it.

Expensive

Hotel Columbus. Closest to St. Peter's Basilica, this is a 15c palace with green courtyard and moderately priced restaurant. *Via della Conciliazione, 33. Tel. 066865435, fax 066864874,* www.hotelcolumbus.net, e-mail: columbus@hotelcolumbus.net.

Hotel dei Mellini. Luxury hotel near the Vatican. Suites and junior suites available. *Via Muzio Clementi, 81. Tel. 06324771, fax 0632477801,* www.hotelmellini.com, e-mail: info@hotelmellini.com.

Visconti Palace Hotel. For the businessman; near Castel Sant'Angelo. Not cheap, but it does have four stars. *Via Federico Cesi, 37. Tel. 063684, fax 063200551,* www.viscontipalace.com, e-mail: info@viscontipalace.com.

Trastevere area

Inexpensive

Casa Internazionale delle Donne. This 12-room guest house for women is located in a beautiful defrocked convent (see page 110). Doubles, triples, quadruples, with or without bath – but definitely without men. *Via delle Lungara, 19. Tel. 0668401724, fax 0668401725,* e-mail: orsamaggioreroma@tiscali.net.

Centro Diffusione Spiritualita. Run by nuns, 30 rooms. Curfew at 11 pm and shared bathrooms, but price and location are good. *Via dei Riari, 43 / 44. Tel. 0668806122, fax 0668307975.*

Hotel Cisterna. Small, reasonable, attractive and in the heart of Trastevere. *Via della Cisterna, 7-9. Tel. 065817212, fax 065810091,* www.cisternahotel.it, e-mail: prenotazione@cisternahotel.it.

Hotel Trastevere. Near the outdoor market and Piazza Santa Maria. Spartan but clean. *Via Luciana Manara, 24A. Tel. 065814713, fax 065881016,* www.hoteltrastevere.net, e-mail: info@hoteltrastevere.net.

Suore Dorotee. A small boardinghouse run by the Dorotea nuns. Curfew at 11 pm. *Via del Gianicolo, 4A. Tel. 0668803349, fax 0668803311,* e-mail: casafatima@libero.it.

Villa Lante. Convent run by Sisters of the Sacred Heart. One of Rome's most beautiful gardens. There's a curfew, and you must share a bathroom. *Via San Francesca de Sales, 18. Tel. 0668806032, fax 066893848,* e-mail: villalante@libero.it.

Moderate

Hotel Santa Maria. In a 16c convent next to Piazza Santa Maria in Trastevere; 20 rooms built around a central courtyard; buffet breakfast and wine bar. *Vicolo del Piede, 2. Tel. 065894626, fax 065894815,* www.hotelsantamaria.info, e-mail: info@hotelsantamaria.info.

Trastevere House. Tiny hotel tucked away in the winding streets "across the Tiber." *Vicolo del Buco, 7. Tel./fax 065883774,* www.trasteverehouse.it, e-mail: info@trasteverehouse.it.

Expensive

Grand Hotel del Gianicolo. On top of the Janiculum Hill, with a swimming pool. *Viale delle Mura Gianicolensi, 107. Tel. 0658333405, fax 0658179434,* www.grandhotelgianicolo.it, e-mail: info@ grandhotelgianicolo.it.

Renaissance and Baroque Rome
Campidoglio area
Inexpensive

Casa Kolbe. Named after a Polish priest canonized by Pope John Paul II for courageous acts during WW II; 63 rooms. Just across the street is Palatine Hill. *Via di San Teodoro, 44. Tel. 066794974, fax 0669991550.*

Pantheon area
Inexpensive

Pensione Marcus. All 20 rooms are equipped with TV, air-conditioning and minibars. *Via del Clementino, 94, 2nd floor. Tel. 0668300320 or 066873679, fax 0668300312,* e-mail: solemarco@ hotmail.com.

Moderate

Albergo Portoghesi – Hotel Portoghesi. Three blocks from Piazza Navona. St. Peter's is just across the river. A perfect location without being right in the middle of everything. In business for over 150 years, this early boutique hotel has only 27 rooms. *Via dei Portoghesi, 1. Tel. 066864231, fax 066876976,* www.hotelportoghesiroma.com, e-mail: info@hotelportoghesiroma.com.

Albergo Santa Chiara. A hotel with an aristocratic feeling, elegant and great location. *Via Santa Chiara, 21.*

Tel. 066872979, fax 066873144, www.albergosantachiara. com, e-mail: info@albergosantachiara. com.

Hotel Due Torri. In the old days guests were mainly gentlemen in search of female company. Now it offers a quiet night instead. *Vicolo Leonetto, 23. Tel. 066875765 or 0668806956, fax 066865442,* www.hotelduetorriroma.com, e-mail: hotelduetorri@interfree.it.

Expensive

Colonna Palace Hotel. Less expensive than the hotel across the square, and with attractive personalized room furnishings. On the roof is a Jacuzzi and a charming breakfast area overlooking the *tetti di Roma. Piazza di Montecitorio, 12. Tel. 06675191, fax 066794496,* www.itihotels.it, e-mail: colonnapalace@itihotels.it.

Very expensive

Grand Hotel de la Minerva. No longer Holiday Inn Crowne Plaza, but still just right for those of you who like to feel at home. In the heart of Rome, overlooking the Pantheon. *Piazza della Minerva, 69. Tel. 06695201, fax 066794165,* www.hotel-invest.com, e-mail: minerva@hotel-invest.com.

Hotel Nazionale. Very central, very elegant, very quiet and very pricey. Suites have their own private terraces. *Piazza Montecitorio, 131. Tel. 06695001, fax 066786677,* www.nazionaleroma.it, e-mail: hotel@nazionaleroma.it.

Hotel Sole al Pantheon. In the piazza across from the Pantheon, it dates back to 1467 and claims to be Rome's oldest hotel. The square can get rather noisy and crowded with summer tourists, but the location is fabulous. *Piazza della Rotonda, 63. Tel. 066780441, fax 0669940689,* www.hotelsolealpantheon.com, e-mail: info@hotelsolealpantheon.com.

Piazza Navona area
Inexpensive

Hotel "in Parione." In the heart of the area's meandering medieval streets, this small, relatively inexpensive place offers cozy hospitality, air-conditioning, Internet access and an elevator. *Via dei Chiavari, 32. Tel. 0668802560 or 066892330, fax 066834094,* www.inparione.com, e-mail: info@inparione.com.

Hotel Primavera. Nicely furnished, newly remodeled, and clean. Next to Piazza Navona; 18 rooms with showers; no phones in the rooms. *Piazza San Pantaleo, 3. Tel. 0668803109, fax 06686926S.*

Residenza San Pantaleo. Only five rooms in this boardinghouse next to gorgeous Piazza Navona. Reserve well in advance. *Piazza San Pantaleo, 3. Tel. 0668323 45, fax 066868073,* www.residenzasanpantaleo.com, e-mail: info@residenzasanpantaleo.com.

Suore Fraterna Domus. This bed-and-breakfast is run by the Fraterna Domus order of nuns. Very inexpensive but there is an 11 pm curfew. *Via Monte Brianzo, 62. Tel. 0668802727, fax 066832691,* e-mail: domusrm@tin.it.

Moderate

Hotel Navona. This 21-room hotel in a historic building near Piazza Navona has been run for many years by an Australian family. *Via dei Sediari, 8 (1st floor). Tel. 066864203, fax 0668803802,* www.hotelnavona.com, e-mail: info@hotelnavona.com.

Hotel Teatropace 33. A former cardinal's residence, this 23-room hotel near Piazza Navona offers continental breakfast in bed. *Via del Teatropace, 33. Tel. 066879075, fax 0668192364,* www.hotelteatropace .com, e-mail: info@hotelteatropace.com.

Expensive

Hotel Raphael. The ivy-covered facade makes this one of Rome's most attractive hotels. In the heart of Renaissance and Baroque country, and next to the prime street for antique shopping, Via dei Coronari. The rooms are rather small, but the view from the upper floors makes up for it. *Largo Febo, 2. Tel. 06682831, fax 066878993,* www.raphaelhotel.com, e-mail: info@raphaelhotel.com.

Trevi Fountain area
Moderate

Hotel de Petris. Simple and central, 36 rooms on four floors, with a terrace off the breakfast area. *Via Rasella, 142. Tel. 064819626, fax 064820733,* www.hoteldepetris.com, e-mail: info@hoteldepetris.com.

Hotel Julia. A small new hotel in an old building. One suite has beamed ceilings. *Via Rasella, 29. Tel. 064881637, fax*

064817044, www.hoteljulia.it, e-mail: info@hoteljulia.it.

Expensive

Hotel Fontana di Trevi. A converted 14c monastery overlooking Trevi Fountain. The 25 rooms are filled with antiques, brocades. Breakfast in the roof garden. *Piazza di Trevi, 96. Tel. 066791056 or 066786113, fax 066790024,* www.hotelfontana-trevi.com, e-mail: reservations@hotelfontana-trevi.com.

Via Giulia area
Moderate

Hotel Campo de' Fiori. Around the corner from the famous outdoor flower and vegetable market. There are only 27 small rooms in this once-upon-a-time inn, so reserve well in advance. *Via del Biscione, 6. Tel. 066874886 or 0668806865, fax 066876003,* www.hotelcampodefiori.com, e-mail: info@hotelcampodefiori.com.

Hotel Coronet. Charming. Part of an old palace complex, with 13 rooms, 7 of which overlook the garden. Central but relatively quiet. *Piazza Grazioli, 5. Tel. 066792341 or 066790692, fax 0669922705,* www.hotelcoronet.com, e-mail: info@hotelcoronet.com.

Hotel Rinascimento. There are 19 rooms; ask for room 402, which is a small double room with its own private terrace. *Via del Pellegrino, 122. Tel. 066874813, fax 066833518,* www.hotelrinascimento.com, e-mail: info@hotelrinascimento.com.

Hotel Teatro di Pompeo. A minihotel of 12 rooms near the site of Julius Caesar's assassination. Moderately priced but with all the comforts of a five-star: air-conditioning, minibar and TV. *Largo del Pallaro, 8. Tel. 066872812 or 0668300170, fax 0668805531, www.* hotelteatrodipompeo.it, e-mail: hotel.teatrodipompeo@tiscali.it.

Residenza Farnese. Next to Palazzo Farnese. Large rooms. *Via del Mascherone, 59. Tel. 0668210980, fax 0680321049, www* .residenzafarneserome.com, e-mail: info@residenzafarneseroma.it.

Expensive

Hotel Ponte Sisto. Within walking distance of St. Peter's Basilica. Off Via Giulia. Totally remodeled but still attractive, 103 rooms, 40 nonsmoking. Elevator. *Via dei Pettinari, 64. Tel. 06686310, fax 0668301712,* www.hotelpontesisto.it, e-mail: info@hotelpontesisto.it.

Hotel St. George. Formerly Hotel Cardinal. Moving up-market. In the second half of the 15c, Pope Julius II commissioned the great architect Bramante to design this building as the Palace of the Tribunals, but both died before the building was completed, or perhaps the church ran out of money. Air-conditioning throughout, with balconies on the fifth floor. *Via dei Bresciani, 35 (corner of Via Giulia). Tel. 06686611, fax 0668661230,* www.hotel-invest.com, e-mail: stgeorge@hotel-invest.com.

Tiziano Hotel. Right in the middle of Renaissance and Baroque Rome. The neighborhood has everything you could possibly want: restaurants, sidewalk cafés, pubs, shops and culture! *Corso Vittorio Emanuele, 110. Tel./fax 066865019,* www.tizianohotel.it, e-mail: info@tizianohotel.it.

Shopping and the Grand Tour
Piazza della Repubblica area
Moderate

Hotel Le Cappellette di San Luigi. Converted from a 16c palazzo; high ceilings and an attractive courtyard. Right down the street from Santa Maria Maggiore and Termini railway station. *Via Liberiana, 21. Tel. 0648930495, fax 064814837,* www.lecappellettehotel.com, e-mail: booking@lecappellettehotel.com.

Very expensive

Boscolo Hotel Exedra. Grandiose, impersonal and near the station – but that may be what you want. *Piazza della Repubblica, 47. Tel. 06489381, fax 0648938000,* www.boscolohotels.com, e-mail: reservations@exedra.boscolo.com.

St. Regis Grand Hotel. The original elegant Grand Hotel. Visiting heads of state are often here, just out of the Centro. *Via Vittorio Emanuele Orlando, 3. Tel. 0647091, fax 064747307,* www.stregis.com, e-mail: stregisgrandrome@stregis.com.

Spanish Steps area
Inexpensive

Hotel Panda. Location, location, location. *Via della Croce, 35. Tel. 066780179, fax 0669942151,* www.hotelpanda.it, e-mail: info@hotelpanda.it.

Hotel Parlamento. All 22 rooms have satellite TV and private baths; three have bathtubs. *Via delle Convertite, 5. Tel./fax 0669921000,* www.hotelparlamento.it, e-mail: hotelparlamento@libero.it.

Moderate

Croce di Malta Hotel. Nestled in Rome's shopping area, yet within walking distance of many cultural MUSTS; two birds with one stone. *Via Borgognona, 28. Tel. 066795482, fax 066780675,* www.crocemalta.com, e-mail: ialeo@crocemalta.com.

Hotel Elite. Small hotel literally down the street from Via Veneto. *Via Francesco Crispi, 49. Tel. 0669925250 or 066783083, fax 066791761,* e-mail: hotelelite@libero.it.

Hotel San Carlo. Near Piazza di Spagna. *Via delle Carrozze, 93. Tel. 066784548, fax 0669941197,* www.hotelsancarloroma.com, e-mail: info@hotelsancarloroma.com.

Hotel Siena. Small, newly refurbished. *Via S. Andrea delle Fratte, 33. Tel. 066796121, fax 066787509,* www.hotel-siena.it, e-mail: hotel_siena@flashnet.it.

Residenza Frattina. Cozy; 9 rooms in shopping area. *Via Frattina, 104. Tel. 066783553, fax 066783701,* www.residenzafrattina.it, e-mail: info@residenzafrattina.it.

Expensive

Daniel's Hotel. Rooftop terrace, and shopping too. *Via Frattina, 107. Tel. 0669380203, fax 0669380194,* www.danielshotel.it, e-mail: info@danielshotel.it.

Hotel Carriage. Cozy 24-room hotel in the center of the Golden Mile. Close to bus lines, subway and Spanish Steps. *Via delle Carrozze, 36. Tel. 066990124.* Carriage@hotelcarriage.net.

Hotel Cecil. The rooftop restaurant offers unforgettable views. Located between Via Veneto and Spanish Steps shop. *Via Francesco Crispi, 55. Tel. 066797998 or 066789693, fax 066797996,* www.hotelcecil.it, e-mail: info@hotelcecil.it.

Hotel Condotti. On a side street, near Rome's premium shopping path. Small and recently upgraded. *Via Mario de' Fiori, 37. Tel. 066794661, fax 066790457,* www.hotelcondotti.com, e-mail: info@hotelcondotti.com.

Hotel Gregoriana. A small jewel. Its 19 rooms are cozy and clean. Favorite of top models participating in the fashion show at the Spanish Steps. *Via Gregoriana, 18. Tel. 066794269, fax 066784258.*

Hotel Homs. Five-story, 48-room hotel close to the Spanish Steps has a rooftop terrace. Includes buffet breakfast. *Via della Vite, 71-72. Tel. 066792976, fax 066780482, www.hotelhoms.it, e-mail: info@hotelhoms.it.*

Hotel Madrid. In shopping heaven, you can have breakfast on the roof overlooking the rooftops of Rome. *Via Mario de' Fiori, 93. Tel. 066991510, fax 066791653, www.hotelmadridroma.com, e-mail: info@hotelmadridroma.com.*

Hotel Mozart. Small hotel on a side street near the Spanish Steps. Satellite TV and personalized service. *Via dei Greci, 23B. Tel. 063600191515, fax 063600173535, www.hotelmozart.com, e-mail: info@hotelmozart.com.*

Hotel Piazza di Spagna. A bordello until 50 years ago, this minihotel of 16 rooms is in the middle of the Golden Mile. *Via Mario de Fiori, 61. Tel. 066796412 or 066793061, fax 066790654, www.hotel piazzadispagna.it, e-mail: info@hotelpiazzadispagna.it.*

Hotel Scalinata di Spagna. Coveted pensione over the Spanish Steps. Book ahead, as there are only 16 rooms, two with private terraces. Breakfast on the roof. *Piazza Trinità dei Monti, 17. Tel. 066793006, fax 0669940598, www.hotelscalinata.com, e-mail: info@hotelscalinata.com.*

Very expensive

Grand Hotel Plaza. Established in 1860, this 240-room hotel has an elegant, old-fashioned feel. The bar is popular for drinks before or after dinner. In the Golden Mile. *Via del Corso, 126. Tel. 06674952, fax 0669941575, www.grandhotelplaza.com, e-mail: plaza@grandhotelplaza.com*

Hotel dei Borgognoni. Recently remodeled small hotel ideally located for shoppers. Ask for a room with a terrace above the inner courtyard. *Via del Bufalo, 126. Tel. 0669941505, fax 0669941501, www.hotelborgognoni.it, e-mail: information@hotelborgognoni.it.*

Hotel de la Ville Intercontinental. A favorite with the cognoscenti; near the Spanish Steps. Some rooms are small, but others have terraces with great views. *Via Sistina, 67. Tel. 0667331, fax 066784213, www.rome.intercontinental.com, e-mail: rome@interconti.com.*

Hotel d'Inghilterra. Renovated 17c hotel whose guests have included Mark Twain and Ernest Hemingway. Small rooms. Suite 676 has a giant terrace. *Via Bocca di Leone, 14. Tel. 06699811, fax 0669922243, www.hir.royaldemeure.com, e-mail: reservation.hir@royaldemeure.com.*

Hotel Hassler. Rome's most exclusive and unique hotel; overlooking the Spanish Steps. Roof restaurant has fantastic views and cuisine. Health club. *Piazza Trinità dei Monti, 6. Tel. 06699340, fax 066789991, www.hotelhasslerroma.com, e-mail: booking@hotelhassler.it.*

Palazzo Ruspoli. Palazzo living? Over-the-top suite fit for a queen, or small bedroom with superb terrace view. *Largo Goldoni, 56. Tel./fax 0668808083, www.residenzanapoleone.com, e-mail: info@residenzanapoleone.com.*

Trident area

Inexpensive

Hotel Margutta. Around the corner from pricey Hotel Valadier. Simple hotel of 21 rooms – three on the top floor, each with a private terrace. *Via Laurina, 34. Tel. 063223674, fax 063200395, www.hotelmargutta.it, e-mail: info@hotelmargutta.it*

Moderate

Hotel Forte. Recently remodeled. Twenty rooms with baths/showers. *Via Margutta, 61. Tel. 063200408 or 063207625, fax 063202707, www.hotelforte.com, e-mail: info@hotelforte.com.*

Hotel Locarno. Art nouveau decor with a cozy bar. In the Trident art gallery and shopping area. *Via della Penna, 22. Tel. 063610841, fax 063215249, www.hotellocarno.com, e-mail: info@hotellocarno.com.*

Expensive

Hotel Art. Ancient building with bold modern art and decor; 46 rooms. *Via Margutta, 56. Tel. 0632871, fax 0636003995, www.hotelart.it, e-mail: info@hotelart.it.*

Hotel Manfredi. Once a pensione; 18 rooms with baths/showers, air-conditioning, high prices. On a street of former artists' studios, today all antique stores. *Via Margutta, 61. Tel. 63207676, fax 063207736, www.hotelmanfredi.it,* e-mail: info@hotelmanfredi.it.

Hotel Piranesi. Elegant boutique hotel opposite Hotel de Russie; 32 rooms, some with accommodations for guests with disabilities. *Via del Babuino, 196. Tel. 06328041, fax 063610597,* www.hotelpiranesi.com, e-mail: info@hotelpiranesi.com.

Very expensive

Hotel de Russie. Central, elegant and "in." Courtyard/garden for drinks and dining. *Via del Babuino, 9 (Piazza del Popolo). Tel. 06328881, fax 0632888888,* www.hotelderussie.it, e-mail: reservations@hotelderussie.it.

Hotel Valadier. Between the Spanish Steps and Piazza del Popolo. Small, charming hotel offers all modern conveniences and a fine location; 50 rooms. *Via della Fontanella, 15. Tel. 063611998, fax 063201558, www.hotelvaladier.com,* e-mail: info@hotelvaladier.com.

Via Veneto area

Moderate

Anglo Americano Hotel. Renovated 18c hotel next to Palazzo Barberini; 121 period-style rooms include breakfast. *Via Quattro Fontane, 12. Tel. 06472941, fax 064746428,* www.hotelangloamericano.it, e-mail: info@hotelangloamericano.it.

L'Hotel Cinquantatre. New charming boutique hotel with a small terrace for summer drinks. Room 502 has its own. *Via di San Basilio, 53. Tel. 0642014708, fax 0642014776, www.lhotel53.com, e-mail:* info@lhotel53.com.

Expensive

Hotel Alexandra. High ceilings and close to the American embassy and Villa Borghese, Rome's central park. *Via Veneto, 18. Tel. 064881943, fax 064871804,* www.hotelalexandraroma.com, e-mail: info@hotelalexandraroma.com.

Hotel Eliseo. Ask for a room above the Villa Borghese. Go up to the rooftop restaurant at sunset for a romantic moment. *Via di Porta Pinciana 30*

(Via Veneto). Tel. 064870456 or 064828658, fax 064819629, www.leonardihotels.com, e-mail: eliseo@leonardihotels.com.

Hotel Flora. This hotel dates back to the end of the 19c. Beautifully redecorated, with 176 large rooms, across from the Borghese gardens. *Via Vittorio Veneto, 191. Tel. 06489929, fax 064820359,* www.hotelfloraroma.com, e-mail: info@grandhotelflora.net.

Hotel Imperiale. Right in the middle of Via Veneto, some remember this once being a bordello. Is it really true? In any case, this remains an ideal location for shopping. *Via Veneto, 24. Tel. 064826351, fax 064742583, www.gruppoloan.it, e-mail:* info@hotelimperialeroma.it.

La Residenza. A block from the American embassy, this hotel offers a central location without the confusion. Price includes buffet breakfast. *Via Emilia, 22-24. Tel. 064880789, fax 0648721,* www.hotel-la-residenza.com, e-mail: info@hotel-la-residenza.com.

Nuovo Hotel Quattro Fontane. Up the hill from Piazza Barberini, a businessman's choice for its central location. *Via delle Quattro Fontane, 149 A. Tel. 064884480, fax 064814936, www.gruppotrevi.it,* e-mail: info@gruppotrevi.it.

Very expensive

Aleph. Minimalist design, luxurious dark red, and near Via Veneto. *Via San Basilio, 15. Tel. 06422901, fax 0642290000,* www.boscolohotels.com, e-mail: reservation@aleph.boscolo.com.

Hotel Ambasciatori Palace. Luxurious, exclusive, 140 fine rooms and 8 suites. Sauna to rest your weary bones and dining room if you can't make it to the nearby restaurants. *Via Vittorio Veneto, 62. Tel. 0647493, fax 064743601,* www.ambasciatoripalace.com, e-mail: info@ambasciatoripalace.com.

Hotel Bernini Bristol. Five-star, deluxe, nonglitzy – right in the heart of the city. Great location for buses, subway, films. Visiting officials seem to enjoy staying here. *Piazza Barberini, 23. Tel. 06488931, fax 064824266, www.berninibristol.com,* e-mail: reservationsbb@sinahotels.it.

Hotel Eden. Superb frescoes, chic bar and terrace restaurant. A favorite with today's Hollywoodocracy. *Via Ludovisi, 49. Tel. 06478121, fax 064821584,*

www.hotel-eden.it, e-mail:
reservations@hotel-eden.it.

Hotel Excelsior. *The* favorite of the stars when Via Veneto was *the* place. Pets accepted. *Via Veneto, 125. Tel. 0647081, fax 064826205,* www.westin.com/excelsiorrome, e-mail: excelsiorrome@westin.com.

Regina Hotel Baglioni. Small enough to be intimate but big enough to include all amenities. Unusually helpful employees. *Via Veneto, 72. Tel. 0642111, fax 0642012130,* www.baglionihotels.com, e-mail: regina.roma@baglionihotels.com.

In the Boonies

Cavalieri Hilton. Lamentable outside, but inside vastly comfortable; also a swimming pool, and a terrace for great views. Its La Pergola Restaurant is famed for Rome's most highly praised cuisine. *Via Cadlolo 101. Tel. 0635091, fax 0635092241,* www.cavalieri-hilton.it, e-mail: concierge.rome@hilton.com.

Hilton Airport Hotel. Conference rooms, bar, restaurant, coffee shop, gym. Finally a place to sleep within Fiumicino (Leonardo da Vinci) Airport. *Tel. 0665258, fax 066525625,* www.hilton.com, e-mail: res.romeairport@hilton.com.

Sheraton Golf Hotel. Those who need to sleep far away from the madding crowd, and yet want American comforts, should try this country inn situated off the road to the airport. It also has, of course, a 27-hole golf course and swimming pool. *Viale Parco de' Medici, 167. Tel. 0665288, fax 0665287060, reservations 0665287980,* www.sheraton.com/golfrome, e-mail: info@sheratongolf.it.

Sheraton Roma Hotel. American comforts far from the noisy crowd. En route to the airport. Fine golf course. Spacious. *Viale del Pattinaggio, 100. Tel. 0654531, fax 065940689,* www.sheraton.com/roma, e-mail: res497.sheraton.roma@sheraton.com.

Bed-and-Breakfast Hotels

Family House. Near Termini railway station, 8 rooms with private bathrooms. *Via Bixio, 72. Tel. 067000770, fax 0670497996,* www.family-house.it, e-mail: info@family-house.it.

Also try the central B&B reservations office at *066789222* (9 am-10 pm) or online at www.bbitalia.it or www.b-b.rm.it.

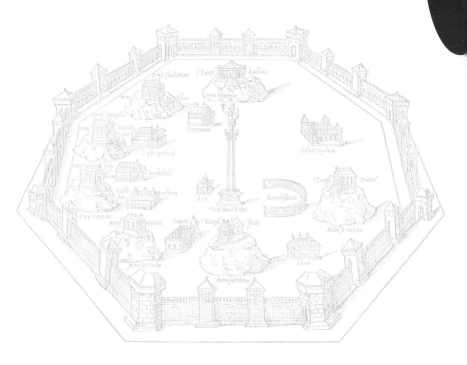

Restaurants

🍴 **Quality of Food**

👔 **Quality of Service**

👁 **Quality of Ambience**

🅃 **Terrace and outside dining**

🅻 **Open late**

Tipping. Though service is included in your bill, you usually round up by the equivalent of $1.00 per person.

Fish and T-bone Prices. Be careful when prices of seafood or *Fiorentina* are listed by the *etto* (100 grams) and not by the portion! It can run your bill up astronomically.

As of December 28, 2004, smoking is prohibited in all restaurants, coffee bars and bars in Italy, with the exception of those establishments that have separate, well-ventilated smoking areas.

Ancient Rome

Colosseum area

Inexpensive

🍴🅃 **Hostaria Isidoro**. No fuss, no worry. If you order "4 assagini," pasta dishes of all sizes and lengths just keep coming. After the fourth one we cried "basta con la pasta," fearing no room for the mousse. Closed Saturday lunch. *Via San Giovanni in Laterano, 61. Tel. 0670493462.*

🅃 **La Taverna**. Funny thing happened on the way to the Forum: an inexpensive mom-and-pop shop. Everything fresh and homemade, served by Tonino and Lucia. *Via Madonna dei Monti, 79. Tel. 064745325.*

Pasqualino al Colosseo. Huge portions. Locals eat here, so you know it's a good deal. Closed Monday. *Via SS Quattro, 66. Tel. 067004576.*

🍴👔🅃 **Valentino**. One of the best places for price/quality ratio. No reservations, so wait to be seated. Luciano will tell you the Roman specials and more. *Gnocchi* (potato dumplings) on Thursday and

tripe on Saturday. Sidewalk dining; down the street from the Forum. Closed Friday. *Via Cavour, 293. Tel. 064881303.*

Moderate

🍴👔👁🅃🅃 **Antica Hostaria da Franco**. Seafood restaurant where the regulars let the waiter order for them: *faccia lei* ("you choose for me"). The house menu has hidden advantages, such as lemon sherbet between courses. Large portions, good fish. Closed Monday. *Via San Giovanni in Laterano, 48. Tel. 067096339.*

🅃 **Cleto**. Great decor of bloodthirsty gladiators dodging around columns. Fettuccine with artichokes, wood-burning oven for pizzas and grilled meats. Dessert: *torta di frutta*, profiteroles. Closed Monday. *Via del Candello 28. Tel. 0669941507.*

👁🅃 **Gli Angeletti**. Attractive eatery in a square. Roman food with a difference. Specializes in meat dishes. *Via dell'Angeletto, 3. Tel. 064743374.*

🍴👔🅃 **Hostaria da Nerone**. Lots of tourists, but this family-run "soup kitchen" (lots of soups) has stayed honest (and delicious). Vast serve-yourself starters, excellent *raviolone* with spinach and ricotta, and more. Closed Sunday. *Via delle Terme di Tito, 96. Tel. 064745207.*

🍴🅃🅻 **La Taverna dei 40**. A cooperative run by young people for young people. Fresh fish Tuesday and Friday, true to Roman tradition. *Via Claudia, 24. Tel. 067000550.*

🍴👔🅃 **Ristorante al Boschetto**. A charming little place specializing in wild porcini mushrooms. Good vegetable-antipasto table and pasta. Baby lamb, veal scallopine and buttered brains. Order one course at a time. Closed Saturday lunch. *Via del Boschetto, 30. Tel. 064744770.*

Expensive

🍴👁🅃 **Da Robertino**. Roberto Pepi continues Goffredo's tradition of fine *cucina*. Seafood salad, foccacia with rosemary (white pizza bread), fettuccine with fresh *funghi porcini*, lamb and green veggies; old-fashioned crème caramel, and mandarin sherbet in its skin. Long pizza menu. House white wine is delicious; red, adequate. Closed Monday. *Via Panisperna, 231, Tel. 064740620.*

Christian Rome

St. Peter's area (Borgo)

Inexpensive

Grotte di Castello. Honest restaurant with decent food. Mamma's in the kitchen. Good house white. Closed Sunday. *Borgo Vittorio, 92. Tel. 066865143.*
Hostaria Cesaretto. Just off Borgo Pio, simple fare at reasonable prices like many near St. Peter's Basilica – catering to pilgrims. Great olive oil and bread. *Vicolo d'Orfeo, 19. Tel. 066879269.*
Il Mozzicone. After your hard day in the museums, this family-run establishment serves home cooking and pizzas. In the summer, dine outdoors next to an ancient fountain. Closed Sunday. *Borgo Pio, 180. Tel. 066861500.*
Passetto di Borgo. Full of priests, so you know the price is right. Baked lasagna, roast lamb and potatoes. Spaghetti *aglio olio* is known as a *cornuto*

("betrayed husband's" dish), since it's quick to prepare. Closed Tuesday. *Borgo Pio, 60-62. Tel. 0668803957.*

Moderate

Alfredo a San Pietro. Offers fresh fish daily and other specials. Closed Friday. *Via Corridori, 60. Tel. 066869554.*
Cesare. Excellent restaurant for the serious business of eating. Vast menu includes beautiful pasta, expensive fish, unusual pizzas from a wood-burning oven. Near Castel Sant'Angelo. Closed Sunday night and Monday. *Via Crescenzio, 15. Tel. 066861227.*
Pierdonati Restaurant. Within Hotel Columbus; a pleasant ambience in the garden. Adequate fare. Closed Thursday. *Via della Conciliazione, 39. Tel. 0668803557.*

Expensive

Da Benito e Gilberto al Falco. No longer looks like a workman's café, but the fish is superb. Closed Sunday and Monday. Reserve. *Via del Falco, 19. Tel. 066867769.*

St. Peter's area (Prati/Vatican Museums)

Inexpensive

Trattoria dei Villini. Everything fresh and delicious. Fish on Tuesdays and Fridays. Great artichokes (seasonal). Pasta, grilled meats. *Via Marcantonio Colonna, 46. Tel. 063216766.*

Moderate

Bella Napoli. Really good fish in all forms. Incredible antipasto, including stuffed squid, raw artichokes, Russian salad and breaded fried zucchini. Try the spaghetti with lobster or *cernia* (white fish) or homemade pasta with newborn fish. Pizza served at night. A bit far from the Vatican but away from the tourists and worth it. Closed Monday. *Via Simone de Saint Bon, 57. Tel. 063751545.*

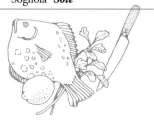 **Ulisse**. Restaurant-pizzeria. Giant portions. Meatball paradise. Slow food: everything is cooked "espresso," meaning when you order it. Fresh fish Tuesday and Friday. *Via Giuseppe Ferrari, 8. Tel. 063217505.*

Expensive

Il Matriciano. Chic movie stars come to get good food, though a bit on the spendy side. Closed Wednesday in winter, Saturday in summer. *Via dei Gracchi, 49. Tel. 063213040.*

Trastevere area

Inexpensive

Al Fontanone. Pizza and Roman fare. Serious restauranteur Pino often excels. Crispy deep-fried artichokes, raw porcini mushroom salad, and fettuccine *al Fontanone* – tuna and porcini: scrumptious. Closed Tuesday. *Piazza Trilussa, 46. Tel. 065817312.*

Casetta di Trastevere. Inside looks like a Roman street with the washing hanging out, and the food is accordingly local, though the management is foreign-friendly. Never closed. *Piazza de' Renzi, 31. Tel. 065800158.*

Da Giovanni. For over 30 years Domenico has served workmen by day and the bourgeoisie at night. It's a small place and fills up quickly, so you might have to wait, but it's worth it. Good Roman fare, low prices. Closed Sunday. *Via della Lungara, 41A. Tel. 066861514.*

Da Ivo Pizzeria. Also pasta and meat dishes. Trastevere's top pizzeria. Closed Tuesday, and Monday lunch. *Via San Francesco a Ripa, 158. Tel. 065817082.*

Da Olindo. Used to be a real *osteria* (you bring the food, they provide the wine) with card playing and dancing. Now a simple student hangout. Portions are big and delicious. Closed Sunday. *Vicolo della Scala, 8. Tel. 065818835.*

Da Vittorio a Trastevere Pizzeria. Come here to try real Neapolitan pizza (heart shaped for kids). Tiny place, low prices, local color. Closed Sunday. *Via San Cosimato, 11A. Tel. 065800353.*

Gli Amici. Organized by the estimable St. Egidio community to support the handicapped – among whom are the

Spigola	*Sea bass*
Orata	*Sea bream*
Dentice	*Snapper*
Merluzzo	*Cod*
Rombo	*Turbot*
Coda di rospo	*Tail of the monk fish*
Sogliola	*Sole*

highly capable staff. Menu changes daily, so you know that the various fish and baby pork are fresh. Dinner only. Closed Sunday. *Piazza Sant'Egidio, 5. Tel. 065806033.*

Il Ponentino Pizzeria. Recruits in uniforms and tourists have found a good deal here. Fresh fish daily and great pizza. Nice terrace away from the hustle and bustle. *Piazza del Drago, 10. Tel. 065880680.*

La Villetta. Charming Trastevere eatery where everything is fresh and delicious. Wood-fired pizza oven. Open daily. *Vicolo del Buco, 2. Tel. 065818949.*

Lucia. A family-run trattoria with genuine Roman fare in a relaxed atmosphere. The sign on the wall says, "If you're in a hurry, go elsewhere." Slow good food. No credit cards. Closed Monday. *Vicolo del Mattonato, 2B. Tel. 065803601.*

Taverna della Scala. Spaghetti as well as pizzas. Unusual fettuccine *al limone* (lemon zest) is excellent, as is the polenta (cornmeal) with rib sauce. Also, a Roman treat not easy to find: breaded lamb chops. Closed Tuesday. *Piazza della Scala, 19. Tel. 065814100.*

Vincenzo alla Lungaretta. Tough to beat price/quality ratio. Spaghetti *alle vongole veraci* (fresh clams), risotto *ai funghi* (with mushrooms), meat and fresh fish, custardy house tiramisu. *Go for it!* *Via della Lungaretta, 17. Tel. 065882876.*

Moderate

Albino il Sardo. Attractive place and fine Sardinian food. Pappardelle with wild boar sauce, giant raviolis and *porchetta* (roast suckling pig), but just a pizza is cheaper. Corvo di Salaparuta (white) and Canonau (red) wine.

Closed Monday. *Via della Luce, 24. Tel. 065800846 or 06589436s.*

Alla Malva. Claudio, an inventive chef, took over this cozily located fish and meat restaurant. Fresh tuna salad, liver Venetian style or grilled, thick chocolate cake, tasty treats. Closed Monday. *Piazza San Giovanni della Malva, 14. Tel. 065816646.*

Antica Trattoria "Da Carlone" (formerly "Da Remo"). Delicious Roman dishes: *pappardelle ai fiori di zucca* (wide noodles with zucchini flowers), spaghetti with *alle noci* (walnut sauce) or *zuppa di funghi porcini e fagioli* (bean with mushroom soup), *coda alla vaccinara* (oxtail). Limited wines: Montepulciano (red) or local white wine. Closed Monday. *Via della Luce, 6. Tel. 065800039.*

What to look for:
- Italian chef (increasingly rare).
- Wood-burning pizza oven – *pizza a legno.*
- Ham cut by hand on the hambone – *prosciutto tagliatto a mano.*
- Big portions.
- Freshly baked country bread – Genzano is best.
- House wine served in carafes – *vino sfuso.*
- Menu that changes daily.

Da Gildo. More than a pizzeria; breezy decor and attractive veggie still-life compositions, and you eat well. Closed Wednesday. *Via della Scala, 31A. Tel. 065800733.*

La Cisterna. Allegedly Rome's oldest. The owner reminisces about Gary Cooper and Rita Hayworth. The lamb with rosemary is delicious. Visit the ancient cistern in the cellar below; aged singers sing in falsetto the same tunes they sang to Audrey Hepburn. Closed Sunday. *Via della Cisterna, 13. Tel. 065812543.*

L'Antico Tevere. Near Porta Portese. Wonderful terrace overlooking the Tiber. Try *strozzapreti messinese* (priest chokers) pasta with squid, tomatoes, olives; or *gnocchi ai frutti di mare* (dumplings with seafood); and pizza as well. Good desserts if you have room. Live music on Tuesday and Friday nights. Closed Sunday. *Via Portuense, 45. Tel. 065816054.*

Miraggio. Red-checked tablecloths give a country tang to this restaurant/pizzeria. Franchises in Fregene, and recently London. The spaghetti *alle vongole* (clams) and the *piccata di limone* (veal with lemon) are delicious. *Panna cotta* (feather-light cream custard) and berries are always in season. *Via della Lungara, 16A. Tel. 066875319.*

Panzanera. Near Porta Portese. Nice family-run restaurant; open on Sunday, if you happen to go to Porta Portese (flea market). Closed Wednesday. *Viale Trastevere, 84. Tel. 065818545.*

Ripa 12. A fish-only restaurant, fresh daily. Exquisite linguini with *calamaretti* (mini-squid), unusual *carpaccio di spigola con rughetta e parmigiano* (raw marinated sea bass with spicy greens and parmesan cheese). Grilled fresh anchovies, *spigola con radicchio* (sea bass with grilled chicory) – creative dishes. Delectable "green" Frascati white wine from Villa Simone. Reserve. *Via San Francesco a Ripa, 12. Tel. 065809093.*

Expensive

Alberto Ciarla. Very elegant and very expensive, but the menu offers noteworthy original dishes based on fish. A complimentary glass of sparkling white wine to start. Reservations required. Closed Sunday. *Piazza San Cosimato, 40. Tel. 065818668.*

Checco er Carattiere. A favorite; everything fresh. Try their potato-tomato smash, pasta with seafood, or fish. Homemade desserts. Just try to find a better meal in a more attractive place! Look for a table in the garden in the summer. Closed Sunday night and Monday. *Via Benedetta, 10. Tel. 065817018.*

Romolo. In this 16c tavern, Raphael courted the model of many of his paintings (La Fornarina). Outdoor dining in a beautiful walled-in garden. *Amburghese alla diavolo* (juicy, flattened cornish hen) and flaming chocolate *tartufo* (truffle) dessert. Closed Monday. *Via di Porta Settimiana, 8. Tel. 065813873 or 065818284.*

IN VINO VERITAS & SNACKS

Ferrara Enoteca in Trastevere. Elegant non-Trasteverino wine and foodery. They also offer courses in wine culture. *Via del Moro, 1A. Tel. 065803769.*

Il Cantiniere. Not just a wine bar. Great salads, cheese fondues and soup. Good bread and great desserts (wild strawberry sherbet). Open 7:20 pm-2 am. Closed Tuesday. *Via di Santa Dorotea, 9. Tel. 065819025.*

Ombre Rosse. You can nibble food here, even pasta dishes. The music insulates you from your neighbor's table. A very mixed crowd – you might be seated next to a Peruvian with ponytail. Ten different types of beer. Open at lunch. *Piazza Sant'Egidio, 12. Tel. 065884155.*

Sabatini. Great location and big prices. Many tourists seem to like dining here, but you have been warned. Terrace in Trastevere's most beautiful piazza. Reserve. Closed Wednesday. *Piazza Santa Maria in Trastevere, 13. Tel. 065812026.*

Spirito di Vino. (See page 124.) This upmarket restaurant serves fine wines and cuisine in an 11c setting. Closed Sunday and lunch. *Via dei Genovesi, 31A. Tel. 065896689.*

Renaissance and Baroque Rome

Pantheon area

Inexpensive

Al Leoncino. A no-frills pizzeria. Wonderful cheapo, good too! Closed Wednesday. *Vicolo del Leoncino, 28. Tel. 066876306.*

Antonio al Pantheon. A jewel, with generous portions, fine house red wine, great fresh bread. Flat pasta with porcini mushrooms (seasonal), various salads with *parmigiano*, *rughetta* (spicy greens), *osso bucco* (braised veal shanks),

fresh fruit salad daily. Closed Sunday. *Via dei Pastini, 12. Tel. 066790798.*

La Nuova Capannina. Tucked behind ritzier restaurants is an inexpensive discovery. Since 1963 Father Ventura and now his sons have been serving decent cooking, with fresh fish a specialty. Son Vittorio says testily, "How can restaurants advertise that they cook better food – and therefore charge double? Any honest restaurant wants to cook the best, but charging won't ensure quality." Closed Monday. *Piazza delle Coppelle, 8. Tel. 0668803921.*

Maccheroni. Paper tablecloths, no fuss, and full of noisy Italians having fun! Usual *maccheroni* (pasta) and the rest of a good meal. (Maybe you'll meet the partner of your dreams!) *Piazza delle Coppelle, 44. Tel. 0668307895.*

Vecchia Locanda. In a historic alley with a low Roman arch, this very small, very attractive restaurant has kept its prices low. Reserve. Closed Sunday. *Vicolo Sinibaldi, 2. Tel. 0668802831.*

Moderate

Armando al Pantheon. Unusual Roman specialties include bulgur wheat balls in gorgonzola sauce, pheasant with porcini mushrooms cooked in dark beer. The fried zucchini flowers are fabulous. *Saltimbocca* (literally, "jump in the mouth") veal with sage and prosciutto. Open early for tourists' lunch (12:15 pm), dinner (7:15 pm). Closed Saturday night and Sunday. *Salita dei Crescenzi, 31. Tel. 0668803034.*

Bacaro. Tiny place with tiny tables. Yuppie heaven. Excellent food but pricey. Closed Sunday. *Via degli Spagnoli, 27. Tel. 066864110.*

Hostaria Piccola Roma. Upstairs lies a hidden world with vaulted rooms. Large antipasto table groaning with goodies. House white excellent from Marino. *Risotto alla gorgonzola*, an entire slice of *pesce spada*. *Via Uffici del Vicario, 36. Tel. 066798606.*

Le Cave di San Ignazio. Pizza plus everything. Sabatino will seat you with others if you're alone. Try a juicy calzone pizza dough stuffed with ham and cheese. Vegetable starters, seafood antipasto and pasta are scrumptious. *Vitello arancio* – veal in orange sauce. Very easy house white is local Frascati. Getting touristy, but in an elegant square. Open daily. *Piazza San Ignazio, 169. Tel. 066797821.*

∎◫⊡ Obika – Mozzarella Bar. Let's face it, we all prefer *primi* (first courses)! Real southern-style buffalo mozzarella and some interesting ways of serving it. For the gourmand: giant (hand-cuddled) buffalo *degustazione* plate. The bar is a little austere, the seating area *carina*. *Via dei Prefetti, 26A.*

∎∎∎◫⊡⊙ Ristorante La Campana. Going back to the 16c, *they* claim to be the oldest restaurant in Rome, and the locals still eat here. Long menu, but look at the chef's recommendations. *Vignarola* soup (artichokes, peas, fava beans, bacon), fried zucchini and flowers, or homemade fettuccine with *ragu* (meat sauce). For seconds: *straccetti con ruggetta* (thin beef slices and raw arugula). A range of desserts. Closed Monday. *Vicolo della Campana, 18. Tel. 066867820.*

∎∎◫⊡⊡ Ristorante Matricianella. Pasta *alle erbe* (herbs) is excellent, as is *polpettine* (meatballs) with arugula and *tartufi* (truffles), but the *tartufo* portion is microscopic. Proud of their wine selection. Closed Sunday. *Via del Leone, 4. Tel. 066832100.*

∎∎∎⊡⊙ Settimio. Close to Parliament. The Mazzonis create an intimate atmosphere with an open kitchen. The raw artichoke salad with thin slices of parmesan cheese and walnuts (seasonal) and the *polenta con cinghiale* (cornmeal with wild boar) are good. If you're lucky there will still be some incredible *sorbetto al pompelmo* (grapefruit sherbet) for dessert. Tuscan wines. Closed Monday. *Via delle Colonnelle, 14. Tel. 066789651.*

Expensive

∎∎∎ Alfredo alla Scrofa. Famous creamy fettuccine Alfredo served with a golden fork and spoon given to them by Douglas Fairbanks Jr. and Mary Pickford. (Mystery of mysteries! There is another Alfredo, *Piazza Augusto Imperatore, 30* – *Tel. 066878734* – claiming to be the original. You choose which one should have the golden fork!). Closed Tuesday. *Via della Scrofa, 104A. Tel. 0668806163.*

∎∎⊙⊡ Fortunato al Pantheon. Caters to ponderous senators and "in" foreigners, like Gore Vidal. This restaurant seems to us to be resting on its laurels, though the service can be charming. A stream of mouthwatering *antipasti* will raise the price, so be sure you want it. Roman artichokes, buffalo mozzarella, spaghetti with *vongole* (clams) and fresh grilled fish

are sure bets. Closed Sunday. *Via del Pantheon, 55. Tel. 066792788.*

⊡ L'Angoletto. The Tudini family has taken over the piazza! Father presides at L'Angoletto, where senators pop 'round after a hard day's vote to sample fresh fish, meats, wonderful pastas and desserts. Pricey. Closed Monday. *Piazza Rondanini, 51. Tel. 066868019.*

⊡ Son opened Le Volte. Same sort of menu as father; pizza added for his younger friends (Moderate). Closed Tuesday. *Piazza Rondanini, 47. Tel. 066877408.*

⊡ Daughter then opened Le Cornacchie (*Inexpensive*), with no fish but a large selection of pasta, meat and dessert. Closed Monday. *Piazza Rondanini, 53. Tel. 0668192096.*

∎∎∎⊡ La Rosetta. Some say this is *the* place to eat fish. Fresh raw shellfish, marinated seafood and fish done in ways you've never dreamed of! These are real professionals. Good but expensive! Closed Sunday and August. *Via della Rosetta, 8. Tel. 066861002.*

∎⊡⊙◫⊡ Myosotis. Refined-pinkie decor, family-run and the menus change daily. Generous portions. Surprising pasta with tomatoes and mushrooms, and *tonnarelli con bottarga* (grated smoked fish eggs). Fish and Scottish Angus beef. For the vegetarian, artichokes with melted *tomino* cheese. Good wine cellar. Closed for lunch. *Vicolo della Vaccarella, 35. Tel. 6865554.*

∎⊡⊙ Osteria dell'Ingegno. Wine bar plus Roman cuisine with a clever twist. Friendly service, attractive relaxed ambi-

Peeled grapes, anyone? At mealtime, imperial Romans enjoyed reclining on a triclinium – a three-sided stone bench surrounding a central table – such as the one shown here.

ence, good food. Sig. Pino, the owner, is behind the bar. We highly recommend the pumpkin ravioli, and the stuffed swordfish. Menus change every month. Closed Sunday. *Piazza di Pietra, 45. Tel. 066780662.*

 **Quinzi e Gabrielli.** Very attractively decorated in a down-to-earth, fishy way. Raw fish starters, *rombo* and tomato, but the prices are high, high, high and the clientele is in, in, in (sometimes). Closed Sunday. *Via delle Coppelle, 5. Tel. 066879389.*

Riccioli Caffè. A buzzy new-comer, where youth gather to sample mixed cocktails at the front bar and discuss worldly matters over the raw fish and large selection of *antipasti* in the two salons. Set-price lunch. Wine bar in back. *Via delle Coppelle, 13. Tel. 0668210313.*

IN VINO VERITAS & SNACKS

Caffè Gotico. An attractive neo-Gothic coffee bar where you can get an Amalfi coast lunch and occasionally in the evening listen to live music. *Via della Stelletta, 7A. Tel. 066873637.*

Le Pain Quotidien. French café. Delicious bread-based lunches and brunches. Delicious *salade composé*. Open until midnight. *Via Tomacelli, 24. Tel. 0668807727.*

Pascucci. Superb, freshly blended fruit shakes to order. *Via di Torre Argentina, 20. Tel. 066864816.*

Ristorante San Eustachio. We recommend the spaghetti with *vongole veraci* (fresh clams) and many other traditional Roman dishes. Excellent fish and meat. Try their famous fried vegetables. Fabulous *semifreddo* (chilled cream) with chocolate sauce. Closed Sunday. *Piazza dei Caprettari, 63. Tel. 066861616.*

Piazza Navona area

Inexpensive

Da Francesco. Pizzeria. At lunch-time it's packed with workers. In the evenings they serve pizza. A fabulous vegetable *antipasti* table. Try the daily special and ask what homemade desserts they have. They still have paper table-cloths! Closed Tuesday. *Piazza del Fico, 29. Tel. 066864009.*

Insalata Ricca. A chain that specializes in salads but serves pasta as well. Good for vegetarians and us! *Largo dei Chiavari, 85-86. Tel. 0668803656.* **Insalata Ricca 2** right across the street. Closed Monday. *Piazza Pasquino, 72. Tel. 0668307881.*

L'Orso 80. Delicate house white (Lanuvio), smooth house red (Montepulciano) wines. Generous antipasto portions. Risotto porcini mushrooms (when fresh) with no cream, a welcome change. Or *risotto pescatore* (seafood risotto), both excellent and abundant. The usual tempting desserts. Wood-fired pizza oven means better-tasting pizza. Closed Monday. *Via dell'Orso, 33. Tel. 066864904.*

Pizzeria La Montecarlo. Very inexpensive for a good pizza. Usually crowded with tourists and students. Also *suppli* (fried rice balls) or *bruschetta* (garlic bread). *Vicolo Savelli, 12. Tel. 066861877.*

Trattoria La Taverna da Giovanni. Inexpensive trattoria over the bridge from Castel Sant'Angelo (Navona side). Closed Monday. *Via Banco di Santo Spirito, 58. Tel. 066864116.*

Moderate

Antica Taverna. Paulo and Michele serve dependable Roman food, sometimes excellent, midday to midnight. If you have to wait, you get a glass of Prosecco and in any case you get a fabulous cake of homemade bread. Open daily. *Via Monte Giordano, 12. Tel. 0668801053.*

Capricci Siciliani. Sicilian, rather elaborate fare in a beautiful vaulted room underneath an ancient palace. Closed Monday. *Via Panico, 83. Tel. 066873666.*

Ciccia Bomba – Pizza & Co. Pizzeria (try zucchini flowers) with sophisticated alternatives. Pastas with clams and *bottarga* (caviar). *Osso bucco* (braised veal shanks) with mushrooms. Peaches in wine (in season). Closed Wednesday. *Via Governo Vecchio, 76. Tel. 0668802108.*

Ristorante ai Banchi Vecchi. If you're feeling the pinch, only order pizza. Foccacia – thin dry pizza either plain or topped with mushrooms, *stracchino* (soft cheese), *proscuitto* or arugula. Heavy starters: *rigatoni alla gorgonzola* (corkscrew pasta with cheese) and *polenta al quattro formaggi* (cornmeal with a sauce of four cheeses). *Panna cotta* (creamy gelatin custard), chocolate cream and other prohibitive things. Closed Sunday. *Via dei Banchi Vecchi, 29-30. Tel. 066832310.*

🍴📷🔆🔅 **Terra di Siena**. Tuscan specialties in this family-run, attractive place. Warm colors make for a cozy atmosphere. Closed Sunday. *Piazza Pasquino, 77-78. Tel. 0668307704.*

Expensive

🍴🍴📷🔆🔅🔆 **Hostaria dell'Orso**. Historic 14c hostelry, where Dante stayed in 1300 for Pope Bonifacio VII's Jubilee (and where a 16c skeleton was found in a walled-up room during a recent renovation!). Now spruced up for the umpteenth time by chef Marchese as luxury restaurant, piano bar and disco. Only in Roma! Closed August, Sunday and lunch. *Via dei Soldati, 25C. Tel. 0668301192.*

🍴🍴🔆🔅🔳🔲 **Il Cantuccio**. Senators can trip across the road to this relaxed, colorful atmosphere. Free nibble food: bread, olives and carrots. "Novella *cucina*" spaghetti with Romano cheese and cherry tomatoes or with *spigola* (white fish) and *rughetta* (spicy greens), or pasta with zucchini flowers and pine nuts. *Corso Rinascimento, 71. Tel. 0668802982.*

🍴🔆 **Il Primoli**. Voguish, pared-down elegance, but plenty of taste treats. Set menus are moderate; à la carte can be pricey. Closed Sunday. *Via dei Soldati, 22. Tel. 0668135277.*

🍴🔆🔅🔲 **Osteria del Gallo**. The exotic breads show creativity, but portions are generous. Salads include *bresaola* (cured beef) with spinach leaves or arugula, shrimp, and fresh goat cheese. Risotto of cress and gorgonzola. Filet steak with artichokes and porcini mushrooms. Desserts: tiramisu and a beautiful *semifreddo con cioccolato* (chilled cream with chocolate sauce). House red and white are smoothly Tuscan. The outdoor area is like a medieval stage set. Closed Sunday. *Vicolo di Montevecchio, 27. Tel. 066873781.*

🍴🔆🔅🔲 **Osteria dell'Antiquario**. Upscale eatery for upwardly mobile youth – both domestic and imported. Risotto of shellfish; grilled sea bass; carrot-based mixed salad; and an unforgettable sherbet of lemon, vodka and champagne. Nice terrace. Closed Sunday. *Piazza di San Simeone, 26-27 (Via Coronari). Tel. 066879694.*

🍴🍴🍴🔆🔅🔆 **Quattro Colonne**. Four magnificent Roman columns make the dining area very elegant. The "in" place for Italian industry giants; refined *cucina* and service. Closed Sunday. *Via della Posta Vecchia, 4. Tel. 06688307152.*

Via Giulia area

Inexpensive

🍴📷🔆 **Giulio**. Venerable Roman *cucina* for 40 years! *Gnocchi fatto in casa* (house dumplings) and genuine *saltimbocca alla Romana* (veal and ham rolls – not for tourists). Tiramisu for desert. Small, calm, well hidden, but worth the detour. *Via della Barchetta, 19. Tel. 0668806466.*

🔳 **Hostaria Farnese**. Between two of the most beautiful piazzas in Rome, this restaurant serves decent grub at great prices. Closed Thursday. *Via Baullari, 109. Tel. 0668801595.*

🔆🔳 **Hostaria Romanesca**. Just a hole in the wall (only eight tables), but the tables outside in the sun are heavenly! Very basic food right on Piazza Campo de' Fiori, in the busy open-air market. Come on Sunday for peace! A haunt of Ben Gazzara. Closed Monday. *Piazza Campo de' Fiori, 40. Tel. 066864024.*

🔳 **Ristorante del Pallaro**. A cheap family affair with a set menu, where dishes keep coming at you. Nice atmosphere. Set into the inner circle of the Theater of Pompeii. Closed Monday. *Largo del Pallaro, 15. Tel. 0668801488.*

🍴🍴 **Santa Anna Ristorante**. Simple and attractive. The *tonarelli* (ribbon pasta) with *astice* (lobster) is good, and the fish in salt a bargain and charged by the portion – not by the gram, whoopee! Closed Sunday. *Via Sant'Anna, 8. Tel. 0668307190.*

Moderate

🍴🍴🍴🍴🍴 **Coccodrillo**. Great location, great terrace, good Roman fare with a crocodile twist. Run by an English ex-journalist. Attractive garden. Closed Wednesday. *Via Giulia, 14. Tel. 0668192650.*

🍴🍴🍴🍴 **Da Luigi**. A reliable standby for good Roman fare. Formulaic menus. In the same square as Polese, they glare at each other and each has its habitués. Spacious terrace for summer eating. *Piazza Sforza Cesarini, 24. Tel. 066865946.*

🍴🍴🍴🍴🍴 **Ditirambo**. Run by a group of young people, this restaurant offers innovative dishes in a very pleasant atmosphere. A real pasta heaven! *Malfatti* (badly made!) *ai fiori di zucca* (with zucchini flowers) with nuts and Romano cheese. *Canestrini al pomodoro* ("little basket" pasta with tomato, ricotta and mint sauce) – incredible! Baby squid and artichoke salad (*insalata di seppioline e carciofi*) is exquisite. Amazing prickly pear sherbet (*fico d'india*). Menu changes every six months. Closed Monday. *Piazza della Cancelleria, 74-75. Tel. 066871626.*

🍴🍴🍴🍴🍴🍴 **Grotte del Teatro di Pompeo**. Built over the ruins of the Theater of Pompeii, where Caesar was murdered. Lino and Antonella offer good-value fish, and the delicious *cucina* includes antipasto, pasta with radicchio or *vongoli veraci* (clams). Wow! Closed Monday. *Via del Biscione, 73. Tel. 0668803686.*

🍴🍴🍴🍴 **Il Drappo**. Sardinian specialties for scrumptious starters, then typical Sardinian pasta *malloreddu* or spaghetti *alla bottarga* (a type of caviar). Roast *porceddu* (suckling pig) is a specialty. A fried cheese-filled crepe (*seadas*) covered with honey and their digestive after-dinner liqueur, Su Mirto. Closed Sunday. *Vicolo del Malpasso, 9. Tel. 066877365.*

🍴🍴🍴🍴🍴🍴 **La Carbonara**. Classic Roman dining: though originally skeptical about the quality of their *cucina*, we are happily surprised by the freshness and

tastiness. The house red wine is remarkable, as are the artichokes, penne alla carbonara and fresh pineapple sherbet. Closed Tuesday. *Campo de' Fiori, 23. Tel. 066864783.*

🍴🍴🍴🍴🍴🍴 **Monserrato**. When an eatery is frequented by locals, you know you're in the right place. Great vegetable starters, seasonal first courses and fish dishes. Has been discovered. Closed Monday. *Via di Monserrato, 96. Tel. 066873386.*

🍴🍴🍴🍴 **Polese**. Not a very extensive menu but it's good! With honest service. *Olive ascolane* (fried meat-stuffed olives) to whet your appetite; pizza with either zucchini flowers and shrimps or salmon or arugula salad and sausage; or *gnocchi alla gorgonzola* (potato dumplings). The baked salmon with green peppercorns and the roast porcini mushrooms (seasonal) are both memorable. Closed Saturday night and Sunday. *Piazza Sforza Cesarini, 40. Tel. 066861709.*

🍴🍴🍴 **Taverna Giulia**. Want a quiet evening? Try regional Ligurian cooking. Start with *fiori di zucca* (fried zucchini flowers) filled with a regional cheese and pine nuts, or *lasagnetta* with abundant pesto. The grilled fish is fresh and delicious. White Greco di tufo is a closing treat. Closed Sunday. *Vicolo dell'Oro, 23. Tel. 066869768.*

Expensive

🍴🍴🍴 **Camponeschi**. One of the most elegant restaurants in the center of Rome, and snooty. For a romantic dinner this is the place – but be prepared to spend some. Terrace has lost some of its charm, as it's all closed in now. *Piazza Farnese, 50. Tel. 066874927*

🍴🍴🍴 **Furore**. Elegant *cucina* from the Amalfi coast. Succulent shellfish and tiny breaded fishcakes, pasta alla carbonara, but with calamari instead of bacon, then any of a dozen fish with light sauces and perhaps stuffed eggplant and peppers. Everything is cooked to your order, so have patience. "Slow food." Dinner only. Closed Sunday. *Vicolo Orbitelli, 13A. Tel. 0668809050.*

🍴🍴🍴🍴🍴🍴🍴 **Hostaria Costanza**. In the ruins of the Theater of Pompeii, this cozy restaurant, run by Paride and Giuseppe, offers unusual dishes. Starters: fresh oysters mozzarella and prosciutto, or tuscan liver pâté and *mascarpone* (creamy cheese). Try the *zuppa di ceci e* *scampi* (chickpea and prawn soup) or spaghetti with *calamaretti* (baby squid) or the ravioli stuffed with artichokes. It's all scrumptious! Finish up with black currants on *panna cotta* (creamy gelatin custard). Closed Sunday. *Piazza del Paradiso, 65. Tel. 066861717.*

🍴🍴🍷🍽 **Pierluigi**. Success has gone to their head (and to their price list) but it's still delicious. Charming terrace on the square. Closed Monday. *Piazza de' Ricci, 144. Tel. 066861302.*

Campidoglio area

Moderate

🍴🍷 **Giggetto al Portico d'Ottavia** (Ghetto). Traditional Roman Jewish cuisine. The difference is the location. As you dine outside you can gaze upon the ancient ruins of the Portico d'Ottavia. Closed Monday. *Via del Portico d'Ottavia, 21A. Tel. 066861105.*

🍷🍽 **La Taverna degli Amici**. In a beautiful piazza often used as a movie set. Typical Roman fare (including tripe and liver) as well as other choices: couscous, spaghetti with mussels, or zucchini flowers and cherry tomatoes. This place has been discovered by tourists. Closed Monday. *Piazza Margana, 36-37. Tel. 0669920637.*

🍴🍽 **Osteria del Campidoglio**. The *antipasti* are original, the food generally Roman. A small but attractive menu. Tuesdays and Fridays traditionally fish. Outdoor dining overlooking the Capitoline. Closed Sunday. *Via dei Fienili, 56. Tel. 066780250.*

Expensive

🍴🍴🍷🍽🍷 **Alvaro al Circo Massimo**. Fish heaven in a jolly tavern. *Alici* (whitebait), shrimp and white fish. The pine-

apple ice cream is perfect, as is the house white wine. Closed Monday. *Via dei Cerchi, 53. Tel. 066786112.*

🍴🍴🍷🍽 **Piperno** (Ghetto). Elegant Roman Jewish restaurant. Great *carciofi alla giudea*, or "Jewish artichokes" – crispy fried outer leaves and tender heart. Fried zucchini flowers, tripe, oxtail and lamb. Reserve. Closed Sunday dinner and Monday. *Via Monte de' Cenci, 9. Tel. 0668806629.*

🍴🍴🍴🍷🍷🍽 **Ristorante Vecchia Roma**. Full of tourists but also full of surprises; wonderful *antipasti*, great pasta and heavenly salads (meals in themselves). Polenta in all of its guises is served in the winter. Nice large terrace. Closed Wednesday. *Piazza Campitelli, 18. Tel. 066864604.*

🍴🍷🍽 **San Teodoro**. Upmarket with considerable style, though service is middling, and tables on the terrace are close together. We recommend *maltagliati* (handmade pasta shreds with cherry tomatoes and aged ricotta). *Via dei Fienili, 49-51. Tel. 066780933.*

🍴🍷 **Sora Lella**. The only restaurant on Tiber Island. Hearty Roman pasta and potato soup; pasta with broccoli in fish broth. Cheese and desserts served with a glass of the appropriate wine. Closed Sunday and August. *Via di Ponte Quattro Capi, 16. Tel. 066861601.*

Shopping and the Grand Tour

Spanish Steps area

Inexpensive

Giggi. Back to basics. Pasta, fresh fish daily, uncomplicated meats and desserts. Handsome steaks, grilled salmon, wild strawberries when in season! Closed Tuesday. *Via Belsiana, 94. Tel. 066791130.*

Hostaria La Scalinata. In the back room are casks of the red and white house wines. *Salade composé*: *Tirolese* – prosciutto, walnuts, gorgonzola, lettuce. Warm and cozy Pompeian red wine. Pizza served during the day. All meats imaginable. *Torta di limone* (lemon tart), tiramisu. Touristy, though. Closed Sunday. *Via Sant'Andrea delle Fratte, 32. Tel. 0669942067.*

Moderate

Ciampini. Two minutes from the Hassler is this panoramic restaurant/bar/ tea room just beyond the top of the Spanish Steps. *Viale Trinità dei Monti, Tel. 06692994287.*

Fiaschetteria Beltramme. Once a hangout for intellectuals. Get here early to get a seat in this neighborhood restaurant. No frills, no decor, just food – right down to business. Closed Sunday and two weeks in August. *Via della Croce, 39. No phone.*

Otello alla Concordia. Walk through the courtyard. Once a meeting place for struggling artists who paid with their work, now a mixed crowd of Romans and foreigners. Daily menus are extensive, plus specials. Ravioli *con ricotta e spinaci* (filled with ricotta and spinach) is excellent. Also good: *cavatelli all'ortolana* – pasta from Puglia with a rich vegetable sauce. Closed Sunday. *Via della Croce, 81. Tel. 066791178.*

Expensive

Babington's Tea Room. Historic, over-priced and uncomfortable, but its location is unbeatable and its Welsh rarebit is delicious. Open 9 am-8 pm. *Piazza di Spagna, 23. Tel. 066786027.*

The Hassler Roof Restaurant. Lobster, caviar and all the luxuries you can dream of. Spectacular view and elegant atmosphere. Roberto Wirth is scrupulous in keeping the standards high. Private parties can be catered on the adjoining roof terrace. Open daily. *Piazza Trinità dei Monti, 6. Tel. 066782651.*

Nino. Florentine food in a traditional restaurant. *Bistecca alla Fiorentina* (T-bone). International movie people seem to favor this establishment close to the Spanish Steps. Closed Sunday. *Via Borgognona, 11. Tel. 066795676.*

Toto alle Carozze. Great dining at high prices (they've gone up, up!). The daily specials are listed on a bulletin board, but have a look at the *antipasti* as well. *Via delle Carrozze, 10. Tel. 06785558.*

IN VINO VERITAS & SNACKS

Café Greco. Stuffed with 19c paintings and engravings, traditional banquettes of red velvet, Venetian floors of marble and even a real live painter transforming not so elegantly dressed patrons into chic clients in his paintings. A historic meeting place for writers, artists and intellectuals. Casanova came here. Expensive but very elegant. Closed Sunday. *Via Candiotti, 86. Tel. 066791700.*

International Wine Academy. Hassler's Roberto Wirth has opened this most exclusive wine-tasting establishment and restaurant for the cognoscente in a 17c palazzetto, a stone's throw from his hotel. Closed Sunday and holidays. *Vicolo del Bottino, 8. Tel. 066990878.*

L'Enoteca Antica. Nice classic winery with charming frescoes. Womb-like. Try three reds: Bardolino, fruity; Great Brunello di Montalcino from Tenute Silvio Nardi, heavy with flavor; lighter Montepulciano. Indulge in your favorite wine while pecking at a little salad, cheese or fried eggs. A bit noisy at peak times. *Via della Croce, 76B. Tel. 066790896.*

Trident / Piazza del Popolo area

Inexpensive

Osteria del Tempo Perso (Tavern of Lost Time). Simple night-owl eatery in a great location. They serve *bruschetta* (crispy garlic bread) while you wait for your order. First courses include *stracciatelli al gorgonzola*, *spaghetti al cartoccio* (with seafood baked in paper). Closed Sunday. *Via dell'Oca, 43. Tel. 063211508.*

Trattoria del Pollarolo. Mom is in the kitchen and her sons and nephews are serving tables. Pizza served in the evening only. Closed Sunday. *Via di Ripetta, 5. Tel. 063610276.*

Moderate

Al Vantaggio. A landmark for almost half a century. Alberto still comes in the morning and prepares the fresh pasta. Or try *straccetti con rughetta*, slivers of lightly cooked beef fillet served with arugula. Desserts too. Open daily. *Via del Vantaggio, 35. Tel. 063236848.*

Café Canova. Opposite Rosati with terrace in the sun. Inside, at lunch, you can eat cafeteria style. *Piazza del Popolo, 16. Tel. 063612231.*

Edy. Small and cozy with jasmine planted on the terrace. *Insalata di polpo con piselli* (octopus with peas), radicchio *al gratin*, fried apple and homemade tiramisu. Their own Velletri wine is good. Closed Sunday. *Vicolo del Babuino, 4. Tel. 0636001738.*

Gusto. Newish, trendy and still growing – wine bar, pizzeria, restaurant and gift shop for gourmets all rolled into one. Thick Neapolitan pizza or Mediterranean dining: macaroni with zucchini, provolone and mint soup; rack of lamb with *rosti* (roast potatoes); sweet fresh fig-and-custard tart with chocolate sauce. Closed Monday. *Piazza Augusto Imperatore, 9. Tel. 063226273.*

Il Gabriello. Down a steep staircase to this colorful restaurant where the owners do the cooking. Tasteful arrangements; unusual combinations. Octopus and potatoes. Closed Sunday. *Via Vittoria, 51. Tel. 066990810.*

Margutta Vegetariano. Attractive remodeling and still strictly vegetarian. Wild rice with asparagus, mushroom burgers, provolone soufflé (though our taste buds cried out for stronger flavors). For dessert the "sex apple" tart, meant to be an aphrodisiac. Good house wine. Piano music on Friday and Saturday night. Open daily. *Via Margutta, 118. Tel. 0632650577.*

Museo Canova-Tadolini. You lunch or sip coffee under giant sculptures by these 19c artists. Delicious food, startling ambience. *Via del Babuino, 150A. Tel. 0632110702.*

Recafé. Flagship of the PizzaRe chain. Ground floor is for Neapolitan pizzas (thicker than Rome's) but also pasta, and so on. Upstairs is a proper restaurant; also a bar with Neapolitan pastries. *Piazza Augusto Imperatore, 36. Tel. 0668134730.*

Ristorante Oplà. A small cozy place away from the madding crowd. Serves both pizza and your traditional Italian food. Closed Wednesday. *Via Angelo Brunetti, 10. Tel. 063219302.*

Rosati. Historic café with a great view, but little sun, now serves proper meals. Traditional. *Piazza del Popolo, 4. Tel. 063225859.*

Settimio all'Arancio. The best of the Arancio chain. (The other two are **Arancio d'Oro**, *Via Monte D'Oro, 17, tel. 066865026*; and **Piccolo Arancio**, *Vicolo Scanderberg, 112, tel. 066786139*. Both of these closed Monday.) "In season" is the operative phrase; so is hand-cut prosciutto *crudo* (raw) and fish priced by the portion and not by weight. *Ravioloni* with ricotta and orange, *farfalle* with zucchini flowers and saffron, rice-filled tomatoes, *mille-feuille* (Genoese pastry) with wild strawberries and excellent (and handsome) waiters. Closed Sunday. *Via dell'Arancio, 50. Tel. 066876119.*

IN VINO VERITAS & SNACKS

Buccone. Superb wine emporium; also serves a light lunch, and dinner on Friday and Saturday. Closed Sunday. *Via di Ripetta, 19. Tel. 063612154.*

Il Brillo Parlante. Snacks, light lunches and dinners. Wine bar upstairs; eatery downstairs. Italian cold cuts, impressive cheese tray. Also get pizzas, grilled meats and vegetables. Closed Sunday lunch. *Via della Fontanella, 12. Tel. 063243334.*

The Verde. Serves and sells green tea plus other teas. *Via Vittoria, 23. Tel. 0632110174.*

Expensive

Casina Valadier. Newly re-opened under the direction of Antonio Sciulo, Italy's first three-star chef. At the Pincio Gardens – a favorite spot for Romans to gloat over their beautiful city. The garden level has a reasonable buffet lunch; the terrace above is fine dining, but the top-level *crociera* is, well, top level. Closed Tuesday. *Villa Borghese, Piazza Bucharest. Tel. 0669922090.*

Dal Bolognese. Once frequented by dolce vita stars, still attracts the entertainment world. Fine cooking from Emilia Romagna. Our favorite: boiled meat with seven sauces; used to be served on a trolley, now on a plate. Great meatballs and mashed potatoes, but save space for exquisite fruits stuffed with sherbets (chestnuts, figs, strawberries and more). Room reserved for cigar smokers. Closed Monday and August. *Piazza del Popolo, 1. Tel. 063611426.*

La Penna d'Oca. Fabulous taste treats, such as *orecchiette* (little ear-shaped pasta) with baby squid, marjoram and fried zucchini flowers. The sea bass, filleted and cooked in a potato pouch, is memorable. Granny Smith sherbet and *tarte tatin* (apple tart) are good for closers. Closed Saturday lunch and Sunday. *Via della Penna, 53. Tel. 063202898.*

Osteria St. Ana. Attractive place very centrally located and great for summer outdoor dining. The pictures on the walls make this place feel like an art gallery. Once a haunt for movie stars and the "in" crowd. Good filet mignon (filetto). Closed Sunday. *Via della Penna, 68. Tel. 063610291.*

Reef. The new "in" place. Five chefs (!) with fish specialties. Excellent antipasto. Minimalist decor with gloomy lighting. Closed Monday lunch. *Piazza Augusto Imperatore, 42. Tel. 0668301430.*

Approximate timetable of *tartufo* and porcini

Tartufo nero di norcia – January, February
Tartufo bianchetto (gray) from Umbria and Marche – February, March
Porcini – May, August, September, November
Ovoli (spectacular scarlet and orange mushrooms) – mid-September
Tartufo bianco di alba – mid-October to end of November

Trevi Fountain area

Inexpensive

Tritone Antica Hosteria. Attractive, family-run trattoria. Polenta with tomato sauce and pork ribs or lamb. Exceptional red currant tart. Red and white wines drawn from barrels. But it has been discovered! And how! Open every day until 11 pm. *Via dei Maroniti, 1. Tel. 066794144.*

Moderate

Colline Emiliane. This rather unpretentious place serves regional cooking from the Northeast (considered by some to be the best food in Italy). Try the tortellini stuffed with pumpkin or their leg of veal with puree (creamy mashed potatoes). To finish, have their egg-noggy mousse (zabaglione). Closed Friday. *Via degli Avignonesi, 22. Tel. 064817538.*

Il Corsaro – Hostaria Romana. The ultimate, but moderately priced, fish place. Seriously fresh, so reserve. Closed Sunday. *Via del Boccaccio, 1. Tel. 064745284.*

Le Lanterne. Tucked into the grand Palazzo Colonna is an upmarket, attractive pizzeria serving everything: soups, luncheon salads, pizzas, pastas, risottos, meat and fresh fish (rest assured that the fish price is by the portion). Strawberries with mille-feuille and crème caramel. Adequate wine list. Closed Sunday. *Via della Pilotta, 21A. Tel. 0669924458.*

Scanderberg. Intimate atmosphere near the Trevi Fountain. The pasta alla carbonara is recommended, but so is tagliolini with fresh whitebait and

IN VINO VERITAS & SNACKS

Bar San Silvestro. In a hurry? Don't need pomp and circumstance? Dishes range from pasta and meat to sandwiches. Delicious fruit salads. Open daily 6 am-2 am. *Piazza San Silvestro, 22.*
Caffè Doria (Trevi area). Tucked under sprawling Palazzo Doria Pamphili is a tearoom with splashing fountain. Elegant and refined. Also private parties. *Via della Gatta, 1A. Tel. 066793805.*

pecorino cheese. Veal with lemon. Typical Roman desserts. Closed Wednesday. *Vicolo Scanderberg, 45. Tel. 066793826.*

Expensive

 **Al Moro**. A favorite with politicians and high-flying tourists, we think it's overpriced, overcrowded and overrated. Arugula, pine nuts, artichoke hearts with Parmesan slivers, thin slices of beef in tomato sauce and *spigola* (sea bass) steamed in *acqua pazza* (crazy water). Unique chestnut and eggnog mousse. Closed Sunday. *Vicolo delle Bollette, 13. Tel. 066783495.*

Via Veneto area

Moderate

Da Tullio. The best T-bone in town! The steak is so large that it feeds two. You are charged only for what you drink from the wine flask on your table. Game pasta dishes, when in season, are delectable! Closed Sunday. *Via San Nicola da Tolentino, 26. Tel. 064874125.*

La Corte dei Leoni. A bit out of the tourist loop, though near Via Veneto, this cozy place is filled with locals. Try the house specialty, spaghetti *alla Corte*. One of the few restaurants in Rome to serve a cheese course. Closed Saturday, and Sunday at lunch. *Via di San Basilio, 70. Tel. 064819005.*

La Lampada. Under new management, less expensive and less pretentious. This is no longer "truffle heaven," but it's heavenly to find honest Italian cuisine at honest prices. Closed Saturday except for two weeks in January; closed Sunday. *Via Quintino Sella, 25. Tel. 064740452.*

La Pentolaccia. Brothers Memmo and Giuseppe have been cooking for years, and it shows! Fabulous warm antipasto of *rughetta* (arugula), raw artichokes (seasonal) and steamed shrimp; and a pasta specialty (which we usually discourage), a tasty *orecchiette* (little ears) in a creamy tomato sauce with spinach and shrimp. The homemade desserts are wonderful. Closed Sunday. *Via Flavia, 38. Tel. 06483477.*

Piccolo Abruzzo. Charming Alessandro has maintained the winning formula of circulating lots of *novella cucina* pasta tasters (e.g., spaghetti with prosciutto and melon) in this intimate setting. Local meat dishes and homemade desserts. Closed for lunch Saturday and Sunday. *Via Sicilia, 237. Tel. 0642820176.*

Ristorante I Tre Moschettieri. In summer don't miss the pasta *fredda* (cold *tonarelli* pasta with tomato, and tuna). The prosciutto is cut by hand *when* you order it (one of our rules for an excellent restaurant). Nothing is oversalted, so relax. Closed Friday night and Saturday. *Via S. Nicola Tolentino, 23. Tel. 064814845.*

Taverna Flavia. Legend: Owner Mimmo prepared Elizabeth Taylor's sandwiches during the filming of *Cleopatra*. She was so satisfied that she offered to help him start a restaurant in Los Angeles. He said no and, instead, she lent him money to open in Rome. International film stars still flock here. Fabulous *antipasti*, good traditional first courses and enormous salads – meals in themselves. Closed for lunch Saturday and Sunday. *Via Flavia, 11. Tel. 064870483.*

Vladimiro e Samir. Marcello left, and his head waiter took over. First shift is Americans who discovered Marcello's in the Access Guide. Romans, who dine later, come later. Price/quality ratio very good. Antipasto and the freshest of vegetables; pasta and meats. The chocolate ice cream is as creamy as mousse. Closed Sunday. *Via Aurora, 37. Tel. 064819467.*

IN VINO VERITAS & SNACKS

Pepys's Bar. Honest prices and decent sandwiches. Small and chaotic. Corner of Piazza Barberini and Via del Tritone. *Via del Tritone, 117.*

Expensive

Edoardo. Edoardo has tried to re-create a dolce vita atmosphere in his restaurant – soft lighting, piano music, elegant furnishings. He also shows his talent as master host, emphasizing the *cucina Abruzzese*. Closed Sunday. *Via Lucullo, 2. Tel. 06486428.*

George's. When in the mood for luxury, come here. Outdoor dining in the courtyard terrace is divine. The renowned cooking school Cordon Bleu operates from here. Want any cooking lessons? Closed Sunday. *Via Marche, 7. Tel. 0642010219.*

Girarrosto Toscano. "The most famous grill in Rome." Good solid Tuscan food. Don't fill up on the *antipasti* if you plan to order a T-bone steak – gigantic. Wash it down with good Chianti. Closed Wednesday. *Via Campania, 29. Tel. 064821899.*

Piazza della Repubblica area
Moderate

Monte Arci (near railway station). Honest Sardinian food. Meat and fish fresh daily at reasonable prices. Wood-burning pizza oven. Closed Sunday. *Via Castelfidardo, 33. Tel. 064941347.*

Ristorante al Giglio. Thirty years of good food next to the opera. Try the raw porcini mushroom (seasonal) salad with slivers of parmesan, or *orechietti* (ear-shaped) pasta with broccoli. Closed Sunday. *Via Torino, 137. Tel. 064881606.*

Trattoria Monti. Specializes in truffles, delicious Jesi white wine out of the barrel, feather-light veggie flans, sautéed anchovies with artichokes, *sformato di zucchin* (zucchini quiche) and guinea fowl in chestnut sauce. Homemade desserts. Closed Monday and Sunday evening. *Via San Vito, 13. Tel. 064466573.*

Expensive

Agata e Romeo. Agata in the kitchen prepares superb dishes while Romeo helps you select wine and food. Inventive *novella cucina*: Salmon rolls stuffed with citrus mousse or fishcake with smoked potatoes, beef strips covered in crispy artichokes. Closed Sunday. *Via Carlo Alberto, 45. Tel. 064466115.*

Out of the Center
Testaccio area
Inexpensive

Da Bucatino. No-nonsense eatery near Testaccio market. *Insalata di frutta di mare* (seafood salad), *alici sott'olio* (anchovies in oil), fettuccine with *funghi* and truffles, *merluzzo alla diavola* (cod with prawn tails in a light wine sauce), crème brûlée *alla catalana*. Open house wine, but also fine bottles. *Simpatico e buono!* Closed Monday. *Via Luca della Robbia, 84-86. Tel. 065746886.*

Picasso. On Friday and Saturday after midnight a DJ replaces the TV, turning this restaurant and bar into a disco. Wood-burning pizza oven. Closed

Monday and July-August. *Via Monte Testaccio, 63. Tel. 065742975.*

Moderate

Luna Piena. Small, noisy, good. Salmon *carpaccio*, fettuccine with *galletto* mushrooms (seasonal). *Semifreddo* (chilled cream) with berries. Closed Monday. *Via Luca della Robbia, 15. Tel. 065750279.*

Expensive

Checchino dal 1887. Opposite the former slaughterhouse, its emphasis is meats and innards. Enormous portions of oxtail, *pagliata* and roast lamb, pot roast with cloves. First courses: fusilli pasta with artichoke sauce and sautéed mortadella (bologna) with broccoli. The two brother-owners are wine connoisseurs with an international cellar. Supercilious service, so not for timorous tourists. Closed Monday and Sunday dinner. *Via Monte Testaccio, 30. Tel. 065743816.*

San Lorenzo area
(newly "in" for eateries)
Inexpensive

Il Maratoneta Pizzeria. This working-class neighborhood offers pizza and things associated – such as *supplì* (rice fritters) and *bruschetta* (the original garlic bread). Closed Sunday. No credit cards. *Via dei Sardi, 20. Tel. 06490027.*

Marcello. Delicious Roman food at reasonable prices. No credit cards. You might have to wait in line, and it can get noisy. Closed Saturday night and Sunday. *Via dei Campani, 12. Tel. 064463311.*

Moderate

Il Dito e la Luna. This part of Rome was bombed by the Allies during WW II. The interior looks like a French bistro. Dishes include *tonnarelli con asparagi e pancetta* (pasta with asparagus and bacon) and typical Roman *cacio e pepe* (Romano cheese and pepper) jazzed up with grated truffles! Hazelnut ice cream, cake and zabaglione. Great wine cellar. Reserve. *Via dei Sabelli, 47-49. Tel. 064940726.*

Beware:
* Places announcing *"Gastronomia"* rarely serve it.
* Fish charged by the *etto* (gram) could double your bill.

Il Pommidoro. Good service and wonderful pasta. The same goes for game, meat, fish and veggies on the grill. Closed Sunday. *Piazza dei Sanniti, 44. Tel. 064452692.*

Uno e Bino. Superb treats in a simple, woody wine bar. Filo pasta stuffed with eggplant; rack of lamb with artichokes or fresh tuna cutlet in breadcrumbs. Historic crème brûlée. But slow service – wadya want? Closed Monday and lunchtime. *Via degli Equi, 58. Tel. 064460702.*

Parioli area
Expensive

Al Ceppo. Refined dining in a cozy atmosphere. Pasta dishes with either porcini, *ovoli* or *finferli* mushrooms; *pugliese* (from Apulia) pasta *orecchiette* (little ears) with duck sauce; pumpkin ravioli, or beans with onions and sea urchins! Closed Monday. *Via Panama, 2A. Tel. 068419696.*

Celestina ai Parioli. King of mozzarella! This upper-class residential area has little to recommend it historically. But culinarily . . . ! They serve 40 kilos of mozzarella a day. Watch the prosciutto/mozzarella *antipasti*, which they bring to your table; it's not a freebie, and if it's touched, you'll be charged per person. *Viale dei Parioli, 184. Tel. 068078242; reservations 068079505.*

Duke's. California bar and restaurant. Decor like a sailing ship. Unusual *cucina*: spaghetti with lobster, *gnochetti* (little dumplings) with asparagus. California ribs and California wine! Closed Saturday. *Viale Parioli, 200. Tel. 0680662455.*

La Scala. Upmarket, but you can order thin, crunchy pizza at dinner (cheaper). Spaghetti with black truffles is a delicacy; spaghetti with *vongole verace* (clams) is their specialty. Fresh fish daily. Try the Sacher chocolate cake or peaches in white wine (in season). Closed Wednesday. *Viale Parioli, 79. Tel. 068083978.*

Via Appia Antica (Appian Way)
Inexpensive

Al Bivio. If you are out near the catacombs off the Appian Way, stop off here. Good selection and quality. Try their chocolate cake. Closed Tuesday. *Via Ardeatina, 225. Tel. 065110013.*

Hostaria da Gianni dei Cacciatori. Genuine home cooking. Great ravioli as big as flying saucers filled with pumpkin and nutmeg, in a cream sauce and covered with nuts. Excellent steaks. Closed Monday. *Via Ardeatina, 402. Tel. 065043276.*

Moderate

Archeologico. Doubled in size and still attractive with its 400-year-old wisteria giving shade. The food is better too. Closed Tuesday. *Via Appia Antica, 139. Tel. 067880499.*

Hostaria all'Eucalipto. Country-style cooking on the grill with a French twist. Steak *au poivre* (pepper steak), escargots. Dinner only. Closed Sunday. *Via Ardeatina, 262. Tel. 065115119.*

Hostaria Antica Roma – Dei Liberti. Massimo fills the classic ruins with Roman *cucina*. Ten minutes from midtown but centuries away in spirit. (See page 67.) Closed Monday. *Via Appia Antica, 87. Tel. 5132888.*

On the River Tiber
Inexpensive

Trattoria Ponte Milvio. Genuine Roman dishes made to order. *Involtini* (rolled, stuffed cutlets). Generous portions. Closed Thursday. *Piazzale Ponte Milvio, 40. Tel. 063333466.*

Moderate

Il Barcone. A barge on the river under the Ponte Duca d'Aosta bridge. Below the Olympic stadium (on the Vatican side of the river) and down the stairs. The pasta and pizza are good; no fish. Closed Sunday. *Via Capoprati. Tel. 0632650543.*

Expensive

Antica Dogana. Right on the riverbank, where it's cool on the very hot days, this upmarket restaurant and grill has replaced beloved low-key landmark Cuccurucu. Grillery galore! *Via Capoprati, 10. Tel. 0637518558.*

Really out of the way
Inexpensive

Antico Falcone (outskirts of Prati area). Historic post house provides a worthy setting for fine food and attentive service. Closed Tuesday. *Via Trionfale, 60. Tel. 0639736404.*

Pomodoro e Basilico – Pomodoro e Mozzarella (EUR area). A minichain of restaurants, they keep prices low by specializing: One is your classic restaurant. *Via della Annunziatella, 5. Tel. 0651603693.* The other serves only pizza. *Via Leonardo da Vinci, 215. Tel. 065430848.* Both closed Monday.

Moderate

Antica Posta (old road to Ostia). Until about 1898 this place was most probably a waiting station for change horses outside Rome. Fresh fish daily. The linguini with crab was a bit too tomatoey and hot for us, but the *cavatelli* pasta with radicchio and *gamberetti* (small shrimp) was abundant! The inside garden makes for cool dining. Closed Monday. *Via Ostiense, 591. Tel. 065911404.*

Il Fungo (EUR area). The famous panoramic restaurant of Rome in EUR. Dine on the 14th floor of this structure known in Rome as Il Fungo (the mushroom). On a clear day you can see the Mediterranean. Closed Saturday lunch and Sunday. *Piazza Pakistan, 1. Tel. 065921980.*

La Nocetta (on the Aurelia Antica). Moderate prices in a country atmosphere. La Nocetta specializes in seafood. Fifteen minutes north of the center, right down the road from a Holiday Inn. Closed Wednesday. *Via Aurelia Antica, 378. Tel. 066623853 or 066623105.*

L'Ortica (near Corso Francia/ Flaminia Vecchia). Nouvelle cuisine carefully prepared and quite delicious. Located in a modern complex. Dinner only. Closed Sunday. *Via Flaminia Vecchia, 573. Tel. 063338709.*

Natalino and Maurizio (Corso Francia/Flaminia area). Still serves the all-time favorite of pasta with vodka sauce; also homemade pasta with eggplant and salted ricotta. Their wood-burning grill offers grilled meat, fish and veggies. Great desserts. Closed Sunday. *Corso Francia, 115. Tel. 063332730.*

Scarpone (Porta San Pancrazio, above Trastevere). On the hill behind the Vatican, you dine in a huge garden with a pergola overhead and pebbles underfoot. Fixed menu as well as à la carte. Reserve because Romans come here when they want to escape the summer heat. Closed Monday. *Via San Pancrazio, 15. Tel. 065814094.*

Expensive

Zodiaco (near Via Triomfale). Below the Cavalieri Hilton Hotel. Elegant dining with a fabulous view over the Eternal city. Seafood antipasto and *tagliolini* pasta with zucchini flowers, shrimp and saffron. Pleasant, unhurried service. Reserve if you want a view. Open daily. *Viale del Parco Mellini, 88-92. Tel. 0635496640.*

BASTA PASTA

Longing for ethnic food? Some suggestions:

Hispanic

Baires. Beefsteaks direct from Argentina with all the South American trimmings are surprisingly savory. *Corso Rinascimento, 1. Tel. 066861293*. Also *Via Cavour, 315. Tel. 0669202164*.

Tapa Loca. If you want paella or just those mouthwatering finger foods that help the drinks go down. *Via Tor Millina, 415. Tel. 066832266*.

Japanese

Good standards since Japanese tourists, hungry for a taste of home, come in droves.

🔲🔲 **Hamasei**. Spartan Japanese, clean lines. Quiet. Special lunch cheapo; dinner prices go way up. Closed Monday. *Via della Mercede, 35-36. Tel. 066792134*.

Hasekura. Sushi, sashimi. But there's only room here for 30. No sushi bar. Closed Sunday. *Via dei Serpenti, 27. Tel. 06483648*.

Chinese

There are literally hundreds of Chinese restaurants around Rome. In fact, the area around Piazza Vittorio is known as Chinatown. Here are a few:

🔲 **Ci Lin**. Tried-and-true: economical but good. Closest cheapo to Piazza Santa Maria in Trastevere. *Via Fonte D'Olio, 6. Tel. 065813930*.

🔲 **Il Giardino del Melograno**. When craving something other than pasta or pizza and longing for some Chinese. *Vicolo dei Chiodaroli, 16-18. Tel. 0668803423*.

🔲 **Jasmine**. Refined and subdued atmosphere. There is a photo of the owner with Chinese martial-arts movie star Jackie Chan, who dined here. Closed Tuesday. *Via Sicilia, 45-47. Tel. 0642884983*.

🔲 **Mandarin**. Elegant, well established, well frequented. Has become slightly Italianized, so do not expect jellyfish. Near Via Veneto. Closed Monday. *Via Emilia, 87. Tel. 064825577*.

🔲🔲🔲 **Ming Yuan**. Favorite Chinese eatery of the Italian-Chinese Club. Open daily. *Via Barberini, 53-57. Tel. 0642011005*.

🔲 **Mongolia Barbecue** (behind Villa Borghese). Inexpensive. *Antipasti* trays for miles. Choose your raw food and take it to the chef, who cooks it for you. Rice cakes and fruit salad for dessert. This is a no-nonsense place, and full to the brim. Noisy at peak eating times. Open daily. *Viale Regina Margherita, 19. Tel. 068547388*.

Vietnamese

Tragically, the other purveyors of this great cuisine have closed.

🔲 **Thien Kim**. Refined Vietnamese cooking in ancient Rome. Especially delicious are *nems* (tiny fried rolls with fresh mint and fish sauce). Closed Sunday. *Via Giulia, 201. Tel. 066861106*.

Indian

🔲 **Maharajah**. An attractive and welcoming place. North Indian cooking, with a vegetarian menu as well. Fixed-price menus for fish. Wine is extra. Open daily. *Via dei Serpenti, 124. Tel. 064747144*.

🔲🔲 **Surya Mahal**. Specialties for the vegetarian. Summer dining outside. Closed Sunday. *Piazza Trilussa, 50. Tel. 065894554*.

Sri Lankan

Lankan Pride. Excellent made-to-order cuisine. Lighter than Indian, partially thanks to the use of lots of coconut. Even curry is different; subtle tastes. *Via del Boschetto, 41. Tel. 064817724*.

Syrian

🔲🔲 **Scian**. High tea and light supper in *1001 Nights* decor. No alcohol. Next door is an Aladin's Cave of bubbly glassware. Open daily 4 pm-2 am. *Via del Pellegrino, 56. Tel. 0668308957*.

Ice Cream Parlors

Italy invented it, so it's everywhere in Rome.

Caffè Maneschi. You'll find 28 varieties of great homemade ice cream here. Just off the Golden Mile. Lunch in the back. *Via del Corso, 66. Tel. 0636001733*.

Giolitti. *Giolitti*, for the Romans, means ice cream. Four locations; this one near the Parliament is the most famous! *Via Uffici del Vicario, 40. Tel. 066991243*.

Montefort. Imagine rose-petal ice cream and almond sherbet. It's here, and it's unimaginably good. Next to the Pantheon. *Via della Rotunda, 22. Tel. 066867720*.

San Crispino. Rolls Royce of ice cream in the Trevi Fountain area. *Via della Panetteria, 42. Tel. 066793924*.

Index

Thanks

Back in the dim past, around Anno Domini 100 and something, a Roman man of letters wrote wearily, "What, yet *another* guide?" saying that *everything* that could be written about Rome *had* been written about Rome. Since that far-off time people haven't stopped writing about Rome. The earliest record we have after the Fall of Rome (AD 478) is of a pilgrim who, around AD 800, walked all the way to Rome from Britain. St. Augustine came in the year 383. The Venerable Bede came circa 700. The earliest printed guide book *Mirabilia und Indulgentiae*, was published in 1475, only a score of years after the invention of printing. In 1574 Vicentio Accolto wrote *Le Cose Maravigliose Dell'Alma Citta di Roma*. In 1703 F. Martinelli wrote *Roma di Nouvo effatament Ricercata nel suo Silo*.

We would like to acclaim all the scholars, friends and authors who have honored Rome, and indirectly helped us with this book: Karl Baedeker, *Rome*; John Murray, *Hand-book: Rome and its Environs* (1872); Georgina Mason, *The Companion Guide to Rome* (1965); Thomas Ashby, *Topographical Dictionary of Ancient Rome* (1929); Prof. Odoardo Anselmi of the Vatican Studio of Mosaics; Prof. Adriano la Regina, former National Superintendent of Roman Antiquities and Amanda Claridge, *Oxford Archaelogical Guides: Rome* (1998), and its illustrator, Sheila Gibson.

Finally, warmest thanks to all those at Getty Publications, and their colleagues, who directly contributed to this project: Dinah Berland, our trusted editor, for her guidance and good humor throughout; Jim Drobka for the handsome cover design and design coordination; Pamela Heath for production coordination; Hespenheide Design for graphic design and typesetting; Nomi Kleinmuntz for copyediting the updated material; Barbara Levy Ratner for Internet research; Karen Stough for her careful proofreading; as well as Mark Greenberg, editor in chief, for his valuable support, and Christopher Hudson, former publisher, without whom this book would not have been possible.